WOLSEY

hARPER ⚜ ɔoRchbooks

*A reference-list of Harper Torchbooks, classified
by subjects, is printed at the end of this volume.*

Thomas Wolsey Cardinal d'yorck autheur du schisme

THOMAS WOLSEY

WOLSEY

Church and State
in Sixteenth-Century England

by

A. F. POLLARD

Introduction to the Torchbook edition by
A. G. DICKENS

HARPER TORCHBOOKS ❦ The Academy Library
Harper & Row, Publishers
New York

WOLSEY

Introduction to the Torchbook edition copyright ©
1966 by A. G. Dickens.

Printed in the United States of America.

This book was originally published in 1929 by Long-
mans, Green and Co. Ltd. of London and New
York with a new edition in 1953.
It is here reprinted by arrangement.

First HARPER TORCHBOOK edition published 1966 by
Harper & Row, Publishers, Incorporated
49 East 33rd Street
New York, N.Y. 10016

CONTENTS

III. LORD CHANCELLOR

IV. PRIME MINISTER

CONTENTS

V. PAPAL LEGATE

VI. THE NEMESIS OF POWER

CONTENTS

CONTENTS

PLATES

THOMAS WOLSEY, *artist unknown*   *Frontispiece*

Drawing, 8 × 7¼ inches. A copy amongst a collection, made about 1560, of similar copies of famous people, now in the Bibliothèque Municipal at Arras. Wolsey appears to be about 40 and is not shown as a Cardinal (elected 1515); the original of this drawing may have been painted by a Flemish artist about the time of Wolsey's visit to Flanders in 1513. It bears a contemporary inscription: *Thomas Vulsey Cardinal dyork* and (in a later hand) *Authour du schisme*.

(A Giraudon photograph.)

HENRY VIII WITH THOMAS WOLSEY, *artist unknown*
                                                        Facing p. 96

This is a detail taken from the large pageant picture of the Field of the Cloth of Gold, June 1520; it was in Charles I's collection, sold by the Commonwealth, recovered at the Restoration, and is now at Hampton Court. The exact date of the painting is not established, but it is certainly an early reconstruction, and the only near-contemporary representation of Henry and Wolsey together (Henry appears older than he was in 1520). The king's head has at some time been cut out, and later replaced. The reproduction is slightly smaller than the actual size.

(Reproduced by gracious permission of H.M. the Queen.)

WILLIAM WARHAM, *by Hans Holbein, dated 1527*   *Facing p. 97*

Painting on panel, 32½ × 26½ inches. Painted during Holbein's first visit to England, it belonged in the early XVII century to the Newton family, then to Thomas Howard, Earl of Arundel, and then to Louis XIV; it is now in the Louvre. A drawing for this is at Windsor Castle; a replica of the painting by Holbein himself is at Lambeth Palace, and a version, probably from his studio, in the National Portrait Gallery.

(Alinari photograph.)

SIR THOMAS MORE, *by Hans Holbein*   *Facing p. 256*

Drawing in coloured chalks, 16 × 12 inches; pricked for transfer for a painting; at Windsor Castle; drawn probably in 1526, it is a study for Holbein's life-size group of the More family at Sir Thomas's house in Chelsea, now lost; a small sketch for the whole composition is in Basle Museum, and a full-size copy, dated 1530, is at Nostell Priory. Later generations of the family had versions concocted from this group, but including also themselves; one such painting is in the National Portrait Gallery. A slightly different portrait of More by Holbein, 1527, is in the Frick collection, New York.

(Reproduced by gracious permission of H.M. the Queen.)

THOMAS CRANMER, *by Gerlach Flicke, 1546, signed*   *Facing p. 257*

Painting on panel, 38½ × 29½ inches; presented to the British Museum in 1776 by J. Mitchell, now in the National Portrait Gallery. On the paper on the table is written: *To the most Reverend fathere in gode and my singulare goode Lorde my Lorde tharchbusshope off Canturbury Hys grace be thes H.*
Inscribed *Anno Etats 57 July 20*, and signed *Gerbarus Flicus Germanus faciebat.* Another version is at Jesus College, Cambridge. Flicke, a German painter, was active in England about 1546 to 1558.

(Reproduced by permission of the Trustees.)

The publishers are indebted to Mr. David Piper for his assistance in compiling these notes.

The illustrations were printed before the death of his late Majesty King George VI, and acknowledgements on them were made accordingly.

INTRODUCTION TO THE TORCHBOOK EDITION

by

A. G. DICKENS

By any criteria Albert Frederick Pollard (1869–1948) must rank high among the historians of the English-speaking world and among the academic statesmen of his day. Both as a scholar and as a planner he had that blend of pertinacity, drive and foresight which carries tasks to completion and builds living monuments. He found exceptional opportunities and he grasped them without a trace of the compromises and hesitations which beset so many scholars. On the other hand, he showed some of the less endearing characteristics of the successful. He sought power and leadership; he often took an autocratic line and seldom proved receptive of opinions which diverged from his own. The quarrels which increasingly surrounded him seemed at times likely to endanger his creations. Like every good historian he sought objectivity and at first sight his books may look much more self-effacing than his career. Nevertheless as we recede from his time and his social-academic background, we detect strong views and period-prejudices. In many respects *Wolsey*, though written only four decades ago, derives from the values of the Victorian world of its author's youth.

Pollard came of a solid Liberal and Wesleyan family living in the Isle of Wight, where his father, an educated chemist and a prominent figure in local affairs, had no less than seven gifted children. Early in life the future historian dropped the Wesleyanism but not the Liberalism. Later on he sometimes attended Anglican churches, but had no strong religious affiliations, a fact which conveyed both advantages and disabilities to a historian of the sixteenth century. The puritanical side of his early background he never shook off as the readers of this book can hardly fail to sense. Disciplined, devoted, energetic, Pollard showed little mercy toward easy-going, self-indulgent or flamboyant habits, wherever they might be found. He did not mellow with age and became a harsh critic of other men's work. He scarcely ever relaxed and his forthcoming qualities were largely applied to issues rather than to human beings. A great talker on history and politics, he was nevertheless fundamentally reserved, and aroused in people admiration rather than affection. His distrust for mystical and philosophical speculation is often apparent; within certain limits he could handle ideas superbly, but his 'no nonsense' outlook did not invariably conduce to the deepest understanding of the age of Renaissance and Reformation.

From his Victorian background he also inherited a deep reverence for the British Constitution, and he was apt to discover evidences of its majestic growth where later historians have found less elevated and progressive forces at work. He could see even in Henry VIII an architect of parliamentary progress and of imperial expansion. He had a host of concepts and characteristics in common with Lord Macaulay, who died only ten years before his birth. He even thought that a career as a Liberal Member of Parliament would be compatible with that of a teacher and academic historian. In 1922 he was to stand as candidate for the University of London in competition with H. G. Wells (Labour), both being defeated by an obscure

Tory. After two further attempts to enter Parliament, Pollard cut his political losses and threw his energies into academic planning and into the present book, the masterpiece of his mature years.

The academic career of A. F. Pollard illustrates a world less well organised for professional scholars than that of our day. At Felsted School and Jesus College Oxford he received good historical and literary instruction, but he found no developed graduate school in history at Oxford or elsewhere. He learned to write admirably, but he did not early in life acquire any great personal interest in discovering, transcribing and editing manuscripts. His whole career hence became subject to a strange paradox. While he did more than any of his British contemporaries to facilitate the 'scientific' investigation of sources, he based almost the whole of his own work upon printed materials. In some sense he maintained links with the pre-professional era of Macaulay; he sought to attain results on a grand scale, and purely by chance circumstances permitted him to do so without much involvement in the most technical and time-consuming aspects of the historian's craft. Nevertheless in Pollard's earlier days scholars without private means often became involved in other forms of academic drudgery. Already engaged in 1891 to the daughter of an Oxford iron-founder, he thought himself fortunate to secure a steady livelihood by accepting the assistant editorship of the *Dictionary of National Biography* under Sir Sidney Lee. With a salary of £200 a year—and a house in Putney given by his wife's family on their marriage—he spent his mornings researching at the British Museum and his afternoons writing up the results at the office of the *D.N.B.* After differences with Lee, he left the project in 1903 and was appointed Professor of Constitutional History at University College in the University of London. But at the time this position was less attractive than it sounded. During the first four years Pollard received merely a proportion of his students' fees; in the first year this amounted to £25.14.6d. (then about $100). Living by journalism, examining, coaching, he can hardly have avoided reflections on the need for university reform in London.

Alongside his work for the *D.N.B.* Pollard began writing his earliest books on Tudor England, which appeared in close succession: *England under Protecter Somerset* in 1900, *Henry VIII* in 1902 and *Cranmer* in 1904. Among these *Henry VIII* was outstanding. It remains the best biography of the King (and has been reprinted in the Torchbook series); it stands most closely related to *Wolsey*, which built upon the foundations provided by its earlier chapters. Though written before Pollard was 33, *Henry VIII* gave a true foretaste of his achievement. It continues to impress by its shrewd judgments of men and events, by fine selection and arrangement, by the quality of its writing: lucid, clean, without frills or obscurities. On the other hand, this book drew heavily upon the labours of others, and despite the excellence of detail the main patterns now seem unduly conservative. It also followed rather too exclusively the printed sources as provided by the *Letters and Papers of Henry VIII*.

This latter remarkable compilation, begun by J. S. Brewer soon after the middle of the nineteenth century, was substantially completed by James Gairdner and R. H. Brodie in 1910, by which time it consisted of about 35 huge volumes, each containing several thousand items. In chronological order it summarises every known letter and state paper relevant to English history from 1509 to 1547, adding at the end of each month a list of items in the Patent Rolls. No other English reign has ever been accorded treatment so handsome, and here lay the unique opportunity grasped by Pollard. This feature of the situation must likewise be borne in mind as we read *Wolsey*. The *Letters and Papers* became Pollard's bible; he knew these volumes wonderfully well and in them he seldom missed an allusion of significance to the topic he was exploring. Yet his very devotion to this vast corpus of record sources made it hard for him to extract full value from the narrative sources like Cavendish's *Life of Wolsey* and Edward Hall's famous chronicle. Even in the cases of very important papers, Pollard would usually accept the imperfect printed summary rather than examine or transcribe the actual document at the Public Record Office or the British Museum. Again, in *Wolsey* as in *Henry VIII*, he sometimes conveys an impression of finality when in fact some enormous mass of unprinted administrative and legal records, entirely outside the purview of the *Letters and Papers*, still requires exploration. Of course, Pollard never imagined he had solved all the major problems, yet today historians are even more conscious of the immensity of the investigations still to be completed. During the last four decades great advances have been made in delineating the social and economic backgrounds. In the somewhat more restricted and frequented fields of central government, the publications of scholars like G. R. Elton of Cambridge and W. C. Richardson of Louisiana afford vivid impressions of tasks relevant to Pollard's work, yet largely untouched in his day.

Even so, the productivity and range of his middle years exceeded that of any contemporary British historian. His *Factors in Modern History* (1907) has clarified the minds of countless young students of sixteenth- and seventeenth-century England. In a volume of the series *The Political History of England* (1910) Pollard surveyed in masterly fashion the reigns of Edward VI, Mary, and Elizabeth; within its terms of reference this remains perhaps the most exemplary of his achievements. In *The Evolution of Parliament* (1920) he boldly entered the late medieval field and (despite his lack of formal training as a medievalist) initiated new lines of thought. He had none of that fear of error which inhibits so many academic historians from embarking on great themes. He also accepted heavy administrative chores without allowing them to become an excuse for academic paralysis. During his productive years he served as Chairman of the London University Board of Studies in History, supervising changes in the undergraduate curriculum and linking it by means of textual studies to the subsequent stage of graduate research. Outside the University his was the main influence behind the foundation and early development of the Historical Association, which (like its American counterpart) furthers the development of the subject at all levels, as well among amateurs as among teachers and professional scholars.

Amid all these schemes Pollard derived great stimulus from his American friends and travels. In 1913 he visited Cornell as Goldwin Smith Lecturer. In 1924-25, as Visiting Professor of Columbia, he made an extensive and successful lecture tour in the eastern states. His letters to his father show how his affirmative mind relished this hectic round of teaching, talking and generous entertainment, then a far less frequent episode in the lives of British scholars than it has become in recent years. On his return he published a book, useful here in its day, called *Factors in American History*. His experiences across the Atlantic also caused him to impress upon his colleagues the inadequacy of funds and facilities for graduate research in England. When the First World War diminished his research seminar at University College, he began his Thursday evening conferences, attended by lovers of history from all parts of the London area. These meetings, at which Pollard presided and did most of the

talking, also attracted many visiting Americans and promoted a mutual stimulus which has ever since marked
historical studies in London. From this rather casual
nucleus the University gradually developed under Pollard's guidance the Institute of Historical Research, with
its library and its facilities for conferences, seminars, and
social intercourse between historians of all nations. As he
would have wished, its annual Anglo-American Conferences have become the highlight of the historian's year
in Britain and they continue to draw an ever-increasing
stream of participants from all countries of the English-
speaking world.

Retiring from his Chair in 1931, Pollard remained
Honorary Director of the Institute for a further eight
years, but he had then gone to live on the south coast, and
maladjustments with his committee in London brought
about his final resignation in an unfortunate atmosphere.
During his long retirement he devoted his failing powers
to the history of Parliament, but *Wolsey* was to remain
his last completed major work. It had grown out of the
Ford Lectures given by its author at Oxford and on its
appearance in 1929 had at once been acclaimed a masterpiece. Since that time its reputation has not substantially
diminished. By any standards *Wolsey* is a great book, the
chief monument to Pollard's historical method and
literary skill. Its virtues will be so clear to any attentive
reader that they need not here be rehearsed. On the other
hand, they should not be allowed to silence all criticism
or to discourage others from entering the field. We now
realise that Pollard could make mistakes and that he left
room for amplification and even for correction.

The book is less a biography than a series of studies
devoted to the Cardinal's various fields of activity. It
affords a splendid analysis of the age of Wolsey, of the
conditions under which the statesman worked, of the issues

involved in his truly marvellous career. Though we learn
much about Wolsey the man, the work seems rather less
successful as an intimate and convincing picture of this
Janus, with his contrasting faces of naïveté and sophisti-
cation. Wolsey himself invited such treatment: despite
his energy and intelligence, he was a great bundle of
privileges, offices and functions, rather than a great human
being. Again, so much of the evidence for his personal
motivation remains second-hand and dubious. Without
making illicit conjectures, it will prove hard to focus the
man very much more clearly than Pollard has done, but
future scholars should at least attempt the feat. To such
scholars Cavendish's life will be more valuable than it
was to Pollard, who here kills this little classic of Tudor
biography with his harsh phrase 'a classic example of
history as it appears to a gentleman-usher.' Re-reading it
in Professor Sylvester's modern edition, the present writer
found himself unable to accept this drumhead sentence.

Readers of Cavendish will notice that the gentleman-
usher was at least perceptive enough to take Thomas
Cromwell as the second significant figure of the last tragic
months. On the contrary, Pollard's generation—with the
notable exception of Paul Van Dyke of Princeton—consistently undervalued Wolsey's chief agent and ultimate
successor in the King's service. Cromwell was in fact no
sordid henchman of Henry VIII but a highly sophisticated
administrator with broadening experience in Italy and
Antwerp, an acknowledged authority on Italian literature,
a student of political philosophy, an enthusiast for biblical
translation, an accomplished drafter of statutes, a great
parliamentarian and an expert in the Common Law.
Under Cromwell's short ministry of 1532–40 there occurred all the great constructive and destructive actions of
this long reign, and if Pollard had attempted a sustained
comparison and contrast between Wolsey and Cromwell,

his insights regarding the former might have been still further deepened. At that juncture of history such ministers needed to be 'universal men' of statecraft, supplying a steady stream of power to all parts of the complex machine. Highly relevant to the present book is the question: why was Cromwell so much more successful than Wolsey in supplying this power? Beyond the obvious differences between their political situations, there loom personality factors easier to sense than to define. Cromwell was indeed such a 'universal man'; Wolsey had the outer semblance without either the steady dynamo or the transmission system whereby to animate men and institutions. In his *Henry VIII* Pollard had conceived of the reign as having two periods, divided by the fall of Wolsey. Most specialists of today would make a separate period of Cromwell's ministry; many would not hesitate to contrast this with the colourful sterility of Wolsey and with the depressing sterility of Henry's last years (1540–47), when the King at last became his own chief minister and expended to little purpose most of the immense resources put by Cromwell into his hands. Naturally enough, those of us who prefer some such scheme would define Wolsey's place in history and his relations with Henry in terms rather different from those of Pollard.

To cite more specific matters, it might be claimed that the largest queries now hang over the chapters on Wolsey's internal administration. Yet most of the current criticisms are themselves somewhat conjectural and depend for full confirmation upon future researches. It may well seem, for example, that Wolsey has far less significance as judge and administrator than Pollard's analysis would suggest. On the evidence as interpreted by Dr. Elton, now our leading authority on these constitutional problems, he looks to be primarily an amasser of titles and credits, at best a hasty improviser rather than an architect of durable solutions. A partial exception seems to appear in his novel subsidy of 1514 (p. 131), an income tax newly assessed upon real data rather than upon the customary figures which had satisfied the flaccid administrators of late medieval England. But Pollard himself shows that Wolsey proceeded to follow this good measure by unpopular exactions of dubious legality. Likewise the notion that Wolsey was a great equitable judge and legal reformer (pp. 69 ff.) would seem based upon a surprisingly narrow platform of positive evidence. And though Pollard tended to perpetuate this impression he well understood that the *Letters and Papers*, together with the few printed Year Books and Law Reports, told him only a part of the story. He knew that further work needed to be done in the little-explored records of the Chancery, the Star Chamber and the Court of Requests. To our own day the Chancery continues a major blind spot in Tudor institutional studies, while no very striking progress has been made in the task of measuring Wolsey's actual influences upon Star Chamber and Requests. But it seems largely agreed that the great expansion in the business of these conciliar courts sprang less from any legal reforms than from the ever-increasing throngs of suitors. The expansion of the commercial world, the rising market in land, new modes of exploiting landed resources, these and other causes have been held to account for the growing litigiousness of a population already amazingly litigious in the previous century. While Wolsey may have taken some part (pp. 77 ff.) in the fashioning of the Star Chamber into a regular court, he neither invented it nor completed its reorganisation. As for the Requests, it can hardly be said to have existed as a clearly distinguishable court until after Wolsey's fall. In his day as in that of Henry VII, there existed several fluctuating committees of councillors hearing the cases of allegedly 'poor' men. Wolsey's personal intervention was occasional; he bears no more than a part-share in the evolution of the Court, which later came into being through a fusion of two hitherto overlapping groups: the special Commissions set up by Wolsey in 1518 and the pre-existent committees of councillors which throughout his ministry continued their independent functions. These problems of a shifting and overlapping conciliar jurisdiction remain in many cases both technically difficult and inadequately documented. While unduly dogmatic attacks on Pollard would seem unwise, it seems at least apparent that—despite his forests of footnotes—the territory still lies wide open to fresh exploration.

Few informed historians would nowadays treat Wolsey's economic and fiscal policies in terms as favourable as Pollard's. Whatever motives may have influenced the Cardinal's thinking on foreign relations, he paid scant regard to the impact of the latter upon the welfare of the English people. Policies involving long estrangement from the rulers of the Netherlands proved exceptionally harmful, since the export of cloth—the one dynamic feature of the English economy—had become so largely concentrated upon the Antwerp market. Actions which choked this funnel to the Continent inevitably gave rise to poverty and unemployment; they sapped the large sectors of the national economy directly and indirectly linked with the trade. Wolsey's foreign policy did in fact exert these effects. Similarly his principles and performance regarding enclosures (pp. 85–86) afford little support to his claims as an economic reformer. He was mistaken insofar as he sought to renew the wholesale prohibition of enclosures designed by the Act of 1489, since enclosure proved far from uniformly harmful. Sometimes it resulted in better arable farming. When aimed at the extension of sheep-runs it could indeed result in rural depopulation, yet it nevertheless created industrial employment. The well-meaning moralists who spoke of 'the sheep eating up the men' were not only exaggerating the actual extent of enclosures but making a one-sided selection from their effects. On the whole it seems fortunate that Wolsey, having collected interesting (though not necessarily impartial) data by his famous commissions of 1518, did not prosecute many offenders or greatly interfere with a process he had not fully analysed.

Concerning Wolsey's management of the national finances a severer judgment than that of Pollard would again seem not unjust. Despite the real promise of reform held out by his subsidy, he failed to evolve any effective plan for raising revenue without quarrelling with the House of Commons. While his foreign policy entailed high expenditure, he lacked the parliamentary touch and deserved his great unpopularity in that quarter. He likewise left to Cromwell the parallel task of reforming ecclesiastical taxation. Had he been less intent on wringing money from wealthy clerics for his own uses (his privilege as legate allowed him infinite opportunities to blackmail all other holders of ecclesiastical jurisdiction) he might have given more thought to rationalising by consent the whole archaic system. He might even have dissolved further effete monasteries for the general good of the Church, as well as for building his own colleges at Oxford and Ipswich. Seldom if ever in the long history of England has a minister incurred so much hatred as the price for so little reform.

In relation to the notorious problems of clerical ignorance and indiscipline, one might well think that a legatine commission lasting so many years gave Wolsey ample time at least to reveal a national plan. Truly, as the experience of both Protestant and Catholic countries was to show throughout the succeeding decades, the task of shifting this immobile mass of custom and complacency never admitted of rapid results. Even if Wolsey had been an English Hildebrand, he might still have died broken-hearted! Yet had Pollard known more than he did about the state of religion in early sixteenth century England, he could hardly have mitigated his adverse verdicts on Wolsey the churchman. The English Church did not entirely lack reforming tendencies. The criticisms of Colet commanded more respect and support among the senior clergy than is often supposed. The Carthusians, the Bridgettines of Syon, the Observants and not a few of the secular clergy and educated laity exemplified in their various ways the influence of the *devotio moderna*, the new piety which for over a century had brought a personal and interior religion within the reach of so many earnest souls throughout Europe. The household of Sir Thomas More was not unique in its intelligent blend of this pietism with classical humanism. The tradition of the great English mystical writers, reinforced by the *Imitation of Christ* and other Continental works, still guided the pens of contemporary devotional writers like William Bonde and Richard Whitford. The new printing presses were still producing little save religious literature. With all these gentle radiances Wolsey had too little in common. Even his patronage of learned humanists brought him such easy prestige that one can hardly avoid questioning its depth and idealism. Certainly Wolsey stood in no position to use the humanists seriously by focussing the full light of their criticism on the darker corners of the Church or by offering the fruits of their biblical scholarship to Church and people.

On the other hand he cannot be classed with the cynics of the Renaissance; he was apparently too naïve to understand how he and many lesser men rationalised their worldliness and selfhood in terms of a religion of 'cheap grace' and observances. This unreflective tradition he appears to have accepted as the norm of Christianity just at the moment when the acuter minds of Europe were questioning it from so many angles. Like so many Catholic statesmen of the century, from Philip II downwards, Wolsey did not understand the resources of Catholicism. He does not however merit the chief blame for all the hoary abuses which he failed to eradicate. He did not plant the noxious trees of ecclesiastical bureaucracy and legalism which bloomed to such sinister perfection during his own career. It was not his fault that the English bishops spent so much of their lives as royal councillors and ambassadors, that civil and canon law formed the staple instruction of higher ecclesiastics, that in general they thought in arid terms of law rather than in creative terms of Christian education.

The responsibilities and opportunities of Wolsey might profitably be reviewed against a somewhat broader background of ecclesiastical and religious history than Pollard here provides. Beside the retrospective glances, we need also to look ahead and to assess Wolsey's links with the English Reformation. Reasonably enough, our author shows that whereas the Cardinal 'rode papal jurisdiction in England to its death' (p. 216), the evidence does not for a moment place him among the authors of the Henrician Schism (p. 340). On the other hand, Wolsey inadvertently helped to hasten the crisis. For many years, it is true, anticlericalism had boiled not far below the surface of English public life. Yet Wolsey's career and behaviour did much to shatter the crust beyond repair, and it was no matter of chance that his fall coincided with the first stages of the parliamentary Reformation. So far as concerns the religious Reformation, Wolsey did not foresee this future development; he did not, like Thomas More, fear lest the heretics, so far trodden down as ants, might soon acquire human stature and in turn oppress the orthodox. Wolsey's relative kindliness toward men charged with heresy reveals not merely his own unfanatical temperament but also that fools' paradise which embraced the Renaissance Papacy and most of its great agents throughout Europe. Yet had Wolsey lived another twenty years and been a model of both discretion and determination, he could hardly have prevented the advent or the successes of Protestantism in England. Pollard, who is here interested in William Tyndale's political thinking rather than in the immense social impact of his biblical translations, never fully understood the English Reformation as a movement at the grass-roots of society. In more recent years we have come increasingly to understand it not merely as an act of State but as a religious movement with an independent dynamic. These developments should be kept in mind as one reads Pollard's wise but somewhat circumscribed assessments of Wolsey the churchman. In some other aspects, the ecclesiastical career of Wolsey will certainly receive amplified treatment by future historians. Dr. Scarisbrick and others have recently thrown light on Anglo-Papal finance and on the true nature of the Praemunire charges springing from Wolsey's abuse of his powers. The administration of Wolsey's innumerable benefices has hitherto received only limited attention, but our gradual exploration of the rich diocesan archives of England—and not solely those of Wolsey's own dioceses —should reveal new data concerning Wolsey's career.

Even a classic like *Wolsey* must not be allowed to create a complacent atmosphere. Historiography either moves forward or dies in its tracks, and Pollard's successors should be concerned to point out opportunities for new discovery and even major revision. If to this rule there should remain a substantial exception, one would most like to see it in the field of Wolsey's foreign policy, where little has happened since Pollard wrote, and that little does not as yet seem to foreshadow radical changes. If here Pollard's spirit should linger untroubled by revisers and iconoclasts, this would seem no more than just, for here if anywhere he displayed the highest professional qualities. When writing his *Henry VIII* Pollard still held the belief that Wolsey sought chiefly to maintain a balance of power between Charles V and Francis I, even though some actions seemed to contravene this principle. Now in *Wolsey* the author reveals how all-important was the personal element in the Cardinal's diplomacy, how his manoeuvres arose from his position as special legate, from his crying need to prevent the domination of the Papacy by a hostile power. Out of this principle the tragedy slowly unfolds with classic balance and stern inevitability. The brilliance with which Pollard compresses the facts into this beautiful mould has naturally excited some suspicion, though it is hard to detect violences or suppressions. But we should perhaps allow more handsomely for mixed motives which comprised a measure of conscious idealism. Garrett Mattingly has shown that even hardened Spanish and Venetian diplomats thought of Wolsey's Treaty of London (October 1518) not as a personal publicity *coup* or as a mask for an Anglo-French alliance, but as a sincere and altruistic attempt to stabilise Europe. This was the statesman's finest hour.

When we have finished criticising the puritanism which tended to alienate Pollard from the exuberant Wolsey—and perhaps from other aspects of the Renaissance world —there remain sober considerations which imply a substantial measure of justice in these verdicts. By any standards Wolsey remains a monstrous phenomenon in the history of Church and State in England. Were we so unrealistic as to exclude ethical and religious judgements, we should part company with Wolsey's own contemporaries, who in their different idiom voiced similar judgements upon the Cardinal. Apart from all their self-centred hatreds, they had after all some ample justifications. Over and above the doomed, the almost absurd politico-ecclesiastical conditions which made possible his career, Wolsey as a man offended the moral and spiritual standards of his own age, and we do that age an injustice if we place such limitless rapacity and arrogance among its norms. And even if we observe in Wolsey's fate the lineaments of a classical tragedy, we cannot summarise its theme in the inflated terms of his own self-deception and self-pity. In S. T. Bindoff's words, he 'paid the penalty not, as he claimed upon his deathbed, of having served his King better than his God, but of having served himself better than his King.' One might take his life as a cautionary tale in the 'falls of princes' tradition, so beloved of sixteenth-century readers. Yet in non-moralising terms one may also see him among the more resplendent animals in the circus of history. Had such men never lived, the grandeur and the fascination of the past would be sadly diminished. In the last resort failure and defeat in the affairs of this sublunary world are the common lot of mankind; while most of us bring little worth watching to the arena, a few like the grazier's son from Ipswich bring a great deal. They sally forth in gorgeous armour and go down spirited and combatant, at once outrageous and outraged, splendidly picturesque even to the end.

King's College, London
March 1966

SUGGESTIONS FOR FURTHER READING

(All these works are published in London, unless otherwise stated)

Bindoff, S. T.,	*Tudor England* (1950)
Cavendish, G.,	*The Life and Death of Cardinal Wolsey*, ed. R. S. Sylvester (Early English Text Soc., 1959)
Clebsch, W. A.,	*England's Earliest Protestants 1520–1535* (New Haven and London, 1964)
Dickens, A. G.,	*The English Reformation* (London; New York, 1964, 1965)
Dietz, F. C.,	*English Government Finance, 1485–1558* (Univ. of Illinois, 1920)
Elton, G. R.,	*The Tudor Revolution in Government* (1953)
Elton, G. R.,	*England under the Tudors* (1955)
Elton, G. R.,	*The Tudor Constitution* (Cambridge, 1960)
Elton, G. R.,	*Henry VIII* (Historical Association Pamphlet G. 51, 1962)
Hexter, J. H.,	*Reappraisals in History* (1961), ch. iii.

Knowles, D.,   *The Religious Orders in England*, vol. iii (Cambridge, 1959)

Mattingly, G.,   *Catherine of Aragon* (1942, 1963)

Mattingly, G.,   *Renaissance Diplomacy* (1955, 1965)

Mozley, J. F.,   *William Tyndale* (1937)

Pollard, A. F.,   *Henry VIII* (1902, 1905, 1913, 1966)

Reid, R. R.,   *The King's Council in the North* (1921)

Richardson, W. C.,   *Tudor Chamber Administration, 1485–1547* (Baton Rouge, 1952)

Rupp, E. G.,   *The English Protestant Tradition* (1947)

Scarisbrick, J. J.,   'The Pardon of the Clergy' in *Cambridge Historical Journal*, xii (1956)

Scarisbrick, J. J.,   'Clerical Taxation in England, 1485–1547' in *Journal of Ecclesiastical History*, xi (1960)

Smith, L. B.,   *Tudor Prelates and Politics* (1953)

Sturge, C.,   *Cuthbert Tunstal* (1938)

Van Dyke, P.,   *Renascence Portraits* (New York, 1905)

Zeeveld, W. G.,   *Foundations of Tudor Policy* (Cambridge, Mass., 1948)

The writer is indebted for particulars on A. F. Pollard to several of his colleagues and to the following printed accounts: V. H. Galbraith in *Proceedings of the British Academy*, xxxv. 257–74; J. E. Neale in *English Historical Review*, lxiv. 198–205; C. H. Williams in *Bulletin of the Institute of Historical Research*, xxii, no. 65.

PREFACE

THIS book originated in an invitation to give the Ford Lectures at Oxford, but three-quarters of it have been written since their delivery in Hilary term, 1928. The subject was determined by my own previous studies and by the obvious need for some valuation of Wolsey's work and career, more recent and less exclusively political than that elaborated more than half a century ago in Brewer's prefaces to the first four volumes of the ' Letters and Papers of Henry VIII.' My own independent examination of the period began with my ' Henry VIII,' originally published in 1902 ; and this study of Wolsey is a companion and complementary volume, embodying the results of research and opinions which have grown during twenty-five years.

I should like to have added a fuller discussion of some of the more important controversial or technical questions involved in Wolsey's career. But lack of time and fear of overloading a study with excursuses and appendices intervened. I hope, however, to deal with some of them in a series of contributions to the ' Bulletin ' of the Institute of Historical Research.

I also wish I could have found some solution of the vexed question of inverted commas, called inelegantly ' quotes ' ; but two or three years ago an attempt to initiate a discussion of the subject in 'The Times Literary Supplement' produced only two replies, the confidence and the simplicity of which indicated complete innocence of the elements of the problem. There appears to be no convention even with regard to single or double 'quotes,' and still less with regard to the dozen or more different degrees of authenticity which they imply or conceal. They may indicate words written by the hand of their author on paper or parchment still preserved, or those words ciphered and deciphered, translated into another language, transformed into modern spelling and phraseology, copied then or later, and badly printed from originals no longer extant ; or spoken words which have also run the gauntlet of misunderstanding from the defective hearing, recollection, or linguistic attainments of the reporter ; and, finally, the document may have been written, dictated, suggested, or merely signed by its putative author. When one quotes 'The Letters and Papers of Henry VIII,' one may be reproducing written or spoken *ipsissima verba* or merely a summary of a third hand report of words which have passed through as many languages and as many fallible processes of dictation, transcription, calendaring, and printing.

All one can do, it appears, is to mark a simple distinction between one's own words and those which are taken from some source indicated in the text or footnotes ; and I have tried to meet what seems to me the most elementary requirement of scholarship, namely to provide the critical reader with the means of checking the evidence on which my statements are based. For this reason I have given specific references in footnotes to the text instead of collecting them at the end of the volume, or compiling a general bibliography which is more useful as an advertisement than as a means of verification. The numeral references to the 'Letters and Papers of Henry VIII' are to the documents contained therein, unless otherwise stated, that being the practice adopted in the indexes to those volumes. The editors of the Spanish, Venetian, and other calendars have, however, varied in their practice; and here the references are, unless otherwise stated, to the pages, that being more convenient where the calendar of a single dispatch not infrequently runs to half a dozen or a dozen pages.

I have thought it unnecessary, in dealing with a half-century in which the unreformed calendar was in general use, to cumber these pages with the double dates between 1 January and 25 March and have treated the year as beginning on the earlier day; for only confusion arises from applying the technical rules for editing documents to the process of writing history. One curiosity may be noted: while the church, the law, and the government began the year with 25 March, popular usage persisted in calling 1 January 'new year's day.' *

More important than this divergence of dating is the discrepancy in monetary values. Half a century ago it was usual to multiply early Tudor figures by 10 or 12 in order to indicate modern equivalents; and this ratio has been commonly retained, even since the war. No general ratio can be more than the roughest average; but to multiply early Tudor figures by something between 15 and 20 would afford a reasonable basis for comparison. The most usual English measure of value was the 'mark,' which was 13s. 4d., i.e. two-thirds of the 240 silver penny weights which make a pound; the Italian *ducat*, the French *écu*, and the Spanish *scudo* were roughly worth an English crown, but varied from 4s. to 5s.; the French 'écu au soleil' was worth about 38 *sous* and the 'écu à la couronne' 35 *sous*; their exchange value in England was fixed by proclamation in 1525 at 4s. 4d. and 4s. respectively, and the ducat at 4s. 6d. The *écu* was then equal to 1.75 *livres* or *francs*, which were therefore worth in England about 2s. 4d., and the *sou* about $1\frac{2}{3}d$.

My thanks are due to my wife for typing my manuscript, reading the proofs, helping with the index, and generally easing the toil of producing research which it is only a pleasure to pursue.

A. F. POLLARD.

24 *January* 1929.

I have inserted in this edition some additional notes and corrections made by my father in his own copy. These will be found in an appendix, their places in the text being marked by an asterisk.

GRAHAM POLLARD.

23 *January* 1952.

CHAPTER I.

WOLSEY'S ADVENT.

THERE is hardly a statesman in English history whose
eminence is so obvious as Wolsey's, and yet whose statesmanship remains so much of an enigma. His name is
familiar in our mouths as household words ; but his
greatness has seldom, if ever, been analysed or defined.
On his common repute there is little need to dwell. In
Shakespeare's 'Henry VIII' he is called ' this bold bad
man ' who charges Cromwell (in vain) to fling away
ambition ; and our familiarity with these phrases is not
greater than it is with the features, purporting to be
Wolsey's, which stare upon us from street hoardings and
in the carriages of metropolitan railways. In the latest
age of commercial publicity Wolsey has achieved that
last indignity of noble mind, a market-value ; and to-day
we are more intimate with wolsey than we are with
brougham carriages, wellington boots, or gladstone bags.
His name has become a symbol, if not a synonym, the
trade-mark, if not the hall-mark, of any kind of excellence
or greatness.

His earliest biographer, George Cavendish,[1] who gives

[1] For Cavendish, see *Dictionary of National Biography*, ix. 346-7. A
garbled edition of his life of Wolsey appeared in 1641 as *The Negotiations
of Thomas Woolsey, the great Cardinal, containing his life and death* ; and
was reprinted in 1667 and 1706 in spite of its gross inaccuracy. In 1809
Dr. Christopher Wordsworth (1774-1846), then chaplain to the archbishop
of Canterbury (Manners-Sutton), printed the earliest modern edition from
two Lambeth MSS. and a third in York cathedral library. S. W. Singer
first used Cavendish's autograph MS. in his two-volume edition (1815 ;
2nd ed. 1827). The references in the text are to John Holmes' edition of
1852. There are earlier accounts of Wolsey in the Venetian state papers
—Giustiniani's ' relazione,' 1519, epitomised in Rawdon Brown's *Four*

I

us the classic example of history as it appears to a gentleman-usher, links his grandeur with the greatness of his
household and laments that he will never see the like
again ;[1] his latest writes of him under the title of
'England's first great war minister.'[2] To one historian he is the founder of England's foreign policy,[3] to
another the author of schism in the church,[4] to a third
a mere victim of Henry VIII,[5] to a fourth the artist
par excellence in politics and ' the greatest political genius
England has ever produced.'[6] A few ecclesiastical sympathisers have dreamed of him as a churchman, who
might have achieved a reformation without tears and
without the embarrassing aid of the secular arm or the
contaminating contact of protestant theology ; might
have dissolved the monasteries without endowing ignoble
families ; have broken the bonds of Rome without imposing a royal supremacy ; and put into the hands of an
independent English church a balance of power between
eastern orthodoxy and western catholicism like that in
which Wolsey is vaguely supposed to have suspended the
unsystematic state of Europe.

Most of these incarnations of greatness manifest the
element of truth in Signor Croce's doctrine that all history
is contemporary history ; and the gloss upon Wolsey's
glory varies from age to age. One need hardly remark

Years at the Court of Henry VIII (1854, ii. 313-15), and in the *Calendar
of Venetian State Papers* (1509-19, pp. 557-63) ; and Falier's ' relazione '
(1531) epitomised in the *Calendar* for 1527-33, pp. 300-1.

[1] Ed. 1852, p. 34, 'And when we shall see any more such subjects,
that shall keepe the like noble house, I am content to be advanced above
him in honour. [But I feare, for my parte, never to see it.] '

[2] By Ernest Law, 1916.

[3] J. S. Brewer, see below, p. 7 ; and cf. Mr. Algernon Cecil on the
third marquis of Salisbury in *D.N.B.* 1901-11, i. 337, ' Like all the great
English foreign ministers from Wolsey downwards, he saw that England's
true function and strength consisted in maintaining the balance of power.'

[4] Sanders, *De Origine ac progressu schismatis Anglicani*, English translation by David Lewis, 1877.

[5] Nicholas Harpsfield (Bémont, *Le premier divorce de Henri VIII*,
1917, p. 9), ' n'a guère vu en lui que la victime de Henry VIII.'

[6] Creighton, *Wolsey* (' Twelve English Statesmen '), pp. 2, 211-13,
217-20.

that the discovery of Wolsey as England's first great war minister dates from the last great war, when the inventor, failing to find an adequate hero in an imperfect present, turned for relief to the vision of a preterpluperfect past. His rôle as an ecclesiastical reformer was similarly illuminated by the limelight of an ecclesiastical controversy at the beginning of the present century ; [1] and his championship of a foreign policy, that was both pacific and spirited, was most learnedly expounded during the régime of Disraeli, as an overture to ' peace with honour.' [2] Wolsey's ' balance of power ' was an earlier impersonation. In the epistle, in which Thomas Rymer dedicated in 1712 the fourteenth volume of his ' Fœdera ' to Queen Anne, he claimed that Henry VIII ' held the balance of power in his hand, and the scale turned according to his direction ' ; and Dr. Richard Fiddes, who published Wolsey's most solid biography in 1724, talks of that ' grand rule ' governing England's policy of ' preserving the balance of power in her hands.' Whether Wolsey's policy was really consistent with that principle is, continues Fiddes with commendable caution, ' a political problem which I shall by no means undertake to resolve.' [3] But the growth of

---

[1] The Rev. Ethelred L. Taunton, *Thomas Wolsey, Legate and Reformer*, 1902.

[2] J. S. Brewer's voluminous prefaces to vols. i.-iv. of the *Letters and Papers* of the reign of Henry VIII appeared between 1862 and 1876 ; the introduction to vol. iv., which deals most fully with Wolsey's foreign policy, is dated Nov. 1875. They were separately published in two volumes, ed. Gairdner, 1884, as a *History of the Reign of Henry VIII*, 1509-1530.

[3] *Life of Cardinal Wolsey*, p. 270. The phrase was a godsend to the Whigs in search of a formula to reconcile the retention of Gibraltar and Minorca with their constitutional objections to the maintenance of standing armies in the time of peace ; and in 1727, after various more specific and less convenient justifications, it was for the first time incorporated in the annual mutiny act, where it remained until 1868. The words ' in her hands ' were, however, left out after ' balance of power ' in order to conceal the meaning of the phrase. For its ambiguities and vogue see my *League of Nations : An Historical Argument*, Oxford, 1918, pp. 18-20, and paper on the ' Balance of Power ' in the Journal of the British (now the Royal) Institute of International Affairs (1923, pp. 51-64). It fell a victim, so far as parliamentary sanction was concerned, to the invectives of John Bright and the strain put upon the phrase when invoked to maintain the integrity of the Ottoman Empire.

Wolsey's repute and of the vogue of the balance of power coincided with, and finally coalesced in, the legend that Wolsey invented that protean phantom.

Wolsey's fame has, indeed, enjoyed a steady appreciation with the lapse of time. During his long administration of eighteen years he received the polite compliments of his colleagues, the adulation of lesser men who had much to gain by his favour, and violent abuse from enemies who escaped by flight abroad or concealment at home the effects of his resentment; and there are few reasonable criticisms that are strictly contemporary on his character and his policy, except in the sheltered correspondence of foreign diplomatists; even that protection was at times inadequate,[1] and the comments vary in tone with the varying relations of friendship or enmity between Wolsey and foreign governments. After his fall none of the numerous factions which combined to bring it about had much to say in his favour. To men of the new learning and the new order he was the protagonist of the conservative cause; to catholics he appeared as its betrayer, as the instigator of the divorce and the author of the schism.

So far as the divorce was concerned, Wolsey himself affirmed and denied his responsibility according to the exigences of the moment.[2] It was affirmed by the emperor Charles V as early as January 1528;[3] and his charge was repeated by cardinal Pole,[4] by Nicholas

Burke had preceded John Bright in vehemently protesting against this use of the doctrine. See below, pp. 118-21.

[1] See below, pp. 315-16.

[2] See Le Grand, *Hist. du Divorce*, iii. 186, 200, 318, 319. According to Cavendish (p. 131) Wolsey denied it before the legatine court and was exculpated by Henry VIII himself.

[3] Le Grand, iii. 46; *L.P.* iv. 3844, cf. 3409. As early as 18 May 1527 Mendoza, Charles' ambassador in London, wrote that Wolsey was planning the divorce ' as a finishing stroke to all his iniquities ' (*Spanish Cal.* 1527-29, p. 193). Catherine of Aragon sent similar information verbally by her servant, Francis Philips, who escaped to Spain in spite of Wolsey's attempts to stop him (*L.P.* iv. pp. 3265, 3278, 3312).

[4] *Apologia ad Cæsarem* (1538), pp. 115-16. Pole, however, only gives this as the general opinion, and himself attributes the origin to Anne Boleyn, who, he says, sent her own ' sacerdotes ' to instil the idea into Henry's mind.

Harpsfield,[1] by Polydore Vergil,[2] and in Roper's life of
Sir Thomas More,[3] and was enshrined, with the additional
gloss that Wolsey was moved by the devil, in the earliest
catholic history of the Reformation.[4] Mary and Philip II,
to whom Harpsfield addressed one of his versions, thought
like their parents, Catherine of Aragon and Charles V;
and Wolsey's memory was thus deprived of the benefit
which accrued through the Marian restoration to the
memory of Sir Thomas More, bishop Fisher, and the
other catholic martyrs of Henry's reign. Cavendish
strove in 1557 [5] to clear his master's reputation of that
slur ; and extracts from his manuscript were published
by Stow in various editions of his 'Annals' during Elizabeth's reign. But it was not until poets and dramatists
began towards the end of the century to deal with
Wolsey's career in an artistic rather than a theological
spirit that men found as much to say in his favour as had
been said by his contemporary, the chronicler Edward
Hall. Churchyard's 'Story of Thomas Wolsey' (1587)
and Storer's 'Life and Death of Thomas Wolsey, Cardinal' (1599), both of them based on Cavendish or on
Stow's extracts,[6] prepared the way for the impartiality of
that dramatic medley, called Shakespeare's 'Henry VIII,'
in which different views of his character are put into the
mouths of different actors by apparently different hands.

The seventeenth century marked a further approach
towards historical perspective. Lord Ellesmere formed a
high opinion of his predecessor's work in chancery, and was
wont to prophesy (with imperfect accuracy) that his own
chaplain, afterwards archbishop and lord-keeper Williams,

---

[1] Harpsfield wrote two divergent accounts of Wolsey (see Bémont,
op. cit. pp. 16-18), and a third which exists only in MS. (Sanders, *op. cit.*
ed. Lewis, pp. li, cxxvii).

[2] *Historia Angl.* ed. 1565, p. 685.   [3] Ed. Singer, p. 30.

[4] Sanders, ed. Lewis, pp. 13, 15, 16 *n.*, 73, 75 *n.*

[5] His autograph MS. states that he began it on 4 Nov. (apparently
in 1557) and finished it on 24 June 1558, including his appended
poems (Singer's *Cavendish*, 1825, i. pp. xvi-xvii; ii. 172). The poem
on Wolsey (*ibid.* ii. 9-18) is a recantation of the encomiums in the
'Life.'

[6] See *D.N.B.* on Churchyard and Storer.

would prove ' another Wolsey.' [1]   Lord Herbert of Cherbury is impartially critical alike of Wolsey and of his detractors.[2]   He is the first to attempt a judicial estimate, but his judgment is somewhat cynical : he thinks that Wolsey was impartial in his administration of justice because he loved nobody, and fell from power because nobody loved him.   More decided symptoms of appreciation appeared at Oxford later in the century.   Evelyn the diarist calls Wolsey ' the magnificent cardinal ' when visiting Leicester where he was buried, and the ' great cardinal ' when he comes to Ipswich where he was born ; and in 1667 he suggested Wolsey as one of the six ' polititians,' whose portraits should adorn the walls of Clarendon House, then just built by the statesman and historian who sat in Wolsey's seat on the woolsack and in Oliver Cromwell's as chancellor of Oxford university.[3]

Oxford contributed largely to this restoration, which also was the work of the tory party : John Aubrey and Anthony Wood spoke well of Wolsey ; Hearne remarks that ' we have very imperfect accounts of the history of that great man,' and regretfully notes the destruction of his diary and two or three volumes of Wolsey's letters by a ' foolish parson,' who only repented his folly on learning that he might have sold them for £50.[4]   He consoles himself with the rumour that Humphry Wanley, Bodley's assistant-librarian, was writing Wolsey's life.   The rumour was greatly exaggerated, but Sir Jonathan Trelawny put up the statue to Wolsey in the gateway of Christ Church in 1719 ; and then in 1724 came Fiddes' monumental volume, the title-page of which calls pointed attention to the fact that the author was chaplain to a prime minister in retirement, the tory earl of Oxford.   Interest in Wolsey spread.   Joseph Grove,[5] who came from the county, but

[1] Sir Simonds D'Ewes, *Autobiography*, ed. J. O. Halliwell [-Phillipps], 1845, i. 204.

[2] *Life and Reign of Henry VIII* (written *c*. 1632-40), ed. 1672, pp. 342-3.

[3] *Diary*, ed. Bray, 9 Aug. 1654, 8 July 1656, 20 Dec. 1668, *n*. The other five were Walsingham, Leicester, Raleigh, Sir T. Smith, and Cardinal Pole—an arbitrary selection not unduly complimentary to Wolsey.

[4] Hearne, *Collectanea* (Oxford Hist. Soc.), ii. 137 ; iv. 412 ; vi. 302, 336.

[5] See *D.N.B.* s.v. ' Grove, Joseph ' (*d*. 1764).

not from the city or university, of Oxford, followed up
Fiddes' folio with four octavo volumes twenty years later;
and John Galt, the Scottish novelist, found fresh material
in the library of Jesus College, Oxford, for a life which,
published in 1812, reached a third edition in 1846.[1] But
the bulk of the evidence for Wolsey's biography was not
available in print until, in the eighteen-sixties and seven-
ties, J. S. Brewer and James Gairdner compressed into
the 8000 pages of the first four volumes of the 'Letters
and Papers of Henry VIII' their summaries of some
20,000 contemporary documents. Even they contain but
fragments of the materials, illustrating Wolsey's activities
as lord chancellor, which still remain in manuscript in the
public record office.[2]

As a result of that progressive revelation Wolsey was
promoted by the late Lord Morley to be one of the
twelve apostles of English statesmanship in his well-known
series; and his place therein is not merely undisputed but
in many ways unique. The series is impartially divided:
there are six sovereigns and half a dozen subjects. Wolsey
is the first subject to penetrate the royal preserve, his
four predecessors being William I, Henry II, Edward I,
and Henry VII. But with Wolsey English kingship
seems to retire into the background of English statesmanship: only two of his successors in that gallery wore a
crown; and one was a woman, Queen Elizabeth, and the
other a Dutchman, William III. Somehow the conditions of English government change about Wolsey's time,
and to some extent they change as a consequence of his
activities. Wolsey, again, is the only cardinal or papal
legate in the series; and not merely that, but the only
churchman, using that word in its older and proper sense
of 'ecclesiastic.' He is also the only lord chancellor and,
if he could be called a lawyer, the only lawyer in the list:
he is, says Maitland, the last lord chancellor to govern

---

[1] Galt in his preface describes these as 'the papers from which Lord
Herbert compiled his *History of Henry VIII*'; but Herbert's main sources
were the MSS. in the royal library to which Charles I gave him access.

[2] See below, pp. 66-9.

England.[1]   Finally, no other legate *a latere* of the pope
since the minority of Henry III could possibly be described, however loosely, as prime minister of England.

Is all this singularity simply accident, or was there
some property in Wolsey's work which accounts for the
sudden effulgence and equally sudden eclipse of ecclesiastical, legal, and legatine eminence in the counsels of the
realm ?   It is not easy for any one with a taste for investigation to avoid getting lost in the maze of records of
Wolsey's activity, or neglecting the general mass in order
to pursue a particular will o' the wisp.   But a philo-
sopher among historians has adjured us to think these
things together ; [2]   and, unless we are captivated by some
such philosophical paradox as Pascal's that, if Cleopatra's
nose had been a little shorter,[3] the face of the earth would
have been different, and apply it to ' the gospel light which
dawned from Bullen's eyes,' we shall not find in a single
cause, or anywhere else a simple explanation, of Wolsey's
singular place in English history.

Any attempt to see the problem in perspective must
needs begin with a revision of some preconceived ideas of
the circumstances and conditions of Wolsey's career.   Of
all the schisms that rend the woven garment of historical
understanding, the worst is that which fixes a deep gulf
between mediæval and modern history.   Not that anything but harm comes from separating ancient from
mediæval history.   But there the sides of the chasm are
the gentle slopes of centuries ; nobody knows exactly
where to draw the line, except for the purposes of lectur-
ing and examination ;   and Byzantium flatly denies its
existence.   The middle ages, however, rolled away for
most of us when the crown rolled off the head of
Richard III at Bosworth field ; and modern history begins
in English text-books with the Tudors.

---

[1] *Collected Papers*, ii. 495.   An exception might, perhaps, be made in
favour of Clarendon ; but Clarendon only wielded a fraction of Wolsey's
power, and from Shaftesbury, Somers, Thurlow, and Brougham downwards, the political activities of lord chancellors have commonly ended
in disappointed ambitions.

[2] Professor Ernest Barker in *History*, vii. 81-2.   [3] *Pensées*, xix. 7.

But the careful student of Henry VII's reign soon finds himself less concerned with the things that began under Henry VII than with the things which did not end with Richard III. Not to mention such personalities as the ghosts and the relatives of the princes in the Tower, there were courts and councils and parliaments, feudal habits and local customs, the church and its vast equipment of wealth and independence of jurisdiction, which were not materially changed by the wars of the roses or by the advent of Henry VII. Few kings were more conservative than the first of the Tudors, and most of the novelty of his reign is the reflected light of a later age. Travel abroad is apt to induce acquiescence in England; and fourteen years of exile had made Henry VII, like Charles II, disinclined for further revolutions when once he had gained the throne. He had, indeed, to pacify the passions and tumult of war, and to repair a shaken fabric of law and order; and he may have invented a rose that was red to match the rose that was white and complete the beauty of Tudor designs.[1] But Henry's was not an original mind, and there is little, if anything, new in his legislation.[2] There is more novelty in his insular concentration and avoidance of foreign adventures, in the constant attention he paid to domestic administration, in the facts that he spent less than he received and was the first (and the last) of English kings to leave a fortune in cash to the crown. There was also a constitutional, as

---

[1] An ingenious critic maintains that, while a white rose was undoubtedly the badge of the Yorkists, the red rose of Lancaster was a Tudor invention designed to give the colour of Skelton's

> The rose both red and white
> In one rose now doth grow

to Hall's 'Union of the two noble and illustre famelies of Lancastre and Yorke,' as his chronicle was entitled. This may, however, be merely a pleasant fiction of the White Rose League; for the true Jacobite is also a Yorkist, though, if the Yorkists had retained the throne, the Stuarts would never have inherited it; and, while Henry VI and the Tudors were troubled by lack of male heirs, the Yorkists were embarrassed by superabundance.

[2] Leadam, *Select Cases in the Star Chamber* (Selden Soc.), vol. i. pp. lxiv, xcv.

well as a financial, significance in Henry's achievement of
this result through his personal control of the king's
chamber, and not through parliamentary control of a
national exchequer ; and it had its effects upon the history
of Wolsey's administration.[1] But Henry VII was lucky
in securing admission to a series from which his son was
excluded, and his reign belongs rather to the middle
ages than to modern history.

Nor did the situation greatly change in 1509, except
that the gay and giddy heir of both the roses succeeded
the grim trustee of the joint estate. The school of
archbishop Morton, which had given place in Henry VII's
later years to his financial experts, Empson and Dudley,
recovered its authority and sent its exacting rivals to the
block—with the result that the revenue from crown-
lands steadily diminished until Wolsey's advent to power.[2]
Regular parliaments were revived, but foreign policy remained the same. Treaties in those days lapsed with a
demise of the crown, unless they were renewed by the
succeeding sovereign. But Henry VIII's council renewed
all those his father had left in force ; and for two years
not a drop of English blood was shed in the wars, in which
Ferdinand of Aragon, the emperor Maximilian, Louis
XII of France, Pope Julius II, and the republics of Venice
and Florence were striving for independence or empires.
In May 1511 fifteen hundred men were sent, as required
by treaty, to aid Margaret of Savoy, the regent of the
Netherlands, against the rebellious duke of Guelders ; and
a similar body of men were taken in the same month by
lord Darcy to help Ferdinand in a crusade against the
Moors. But these were hardly exceptions to the pacific
policy of a council,[3] in which the dominant influence was
that of Richard Foxe—lord privy seal, bishop of Win-

---

[1] See below, pp. 129-31.

[2] See *Letters and Papers of Henry VIII*, ii. 1795.

[3] 'They do not like,' writes Carroz, Ferdinand's ambassador in London,
'to be at enmity or to go to war with any prince whatever' (*Spanish
Cal.* 1509-25 p. 249). The Venetian correspondence contains as many
references to the pacific nature of Henry VIII as to the turbulence of
Wolsey, e.g. R. Brown, i. 237 ; ii. 12, 66.

chester, and founder of Corpus Christi college, Oxford—
who had been, next to Morton, the most trusted of
Henry VII's advisers throughout his reign. He was
supported by his fellow-churchmen, Warham, chancellor
of the realm and of Oxford university and archbishop of
Canterbury, and Ruthal, secretary to the king and bishop
of Durham. What opposition there was may have been
warlike, feudal, anti-clerical, or merely factious. It was
led, apparently, by Thomas Howard, earl of Surrey, who,
pardoned after three years in the Tower for adherence to
Richard III, had rendered yeoman service to Henry VII,
first as ruler of England north of the Trent and then as
lord high treasurer, an office which he and his son held
for half a century. As contrasted with Foxe, who was
devoted solely to the public interest, Surrey was bent on
restoring the family fortunes.[1] His supporters are said
to have been Shrewsbury, the lord steward; Herbert
(afterwards earl of Worcester), the lord chamberlain;
lord Darcy, Sir Edward Poynings, and Sir Harry Marney.
The laymen had a clear majority, and the division of
the council into a clerical peace, and a secular war, party
is too crude to cover the facts : when war came in 1512,
Surrey was its opponent, and the man he denounced as
its author was a priest who as yet held the minor but
promising office of almoner to the king.[2]

The facts of Wolsey's early career are sufficiently
known or easily accessible. I need only refer to one or
two incidents or traditions which seem to throw special
light on his character or career.[3] Born in the latter part

---

[1] Cf. Polydore Vergil, p. 621.

[2] He had been made dean of Lincoln by Henry VII on 2 Feb. 1509;
but the almonership was a surer rung in the ladder of promotion, and
all Henry VIII's almoners after 1509 became bishops at least—Wolsey,
Rawlins, Longland, Stokesley, Edward Lee, Edward Foxe, Rowland Lee,
Nicholas Heath, and Richard Coxe.

[3] See James Gairdner's article in *D.N.B.* lxii. 325-43 (1900). There is
in the *English Hist. Rev.* iii. 458-77 (1888) a long but imaginative and
uncritical article on Wolsey's career down to 1509, which Gairdner does
not mention but Brodie corrects on various points. The principal additions to our knowledge since the *D.N.B.* article are noted by Mr. R. H.
Brodie in his preface to the new edition of vol. i. of the *Letters and Papers*

of 1472 or early in 1473,[1] he was eighteen years older than Henry VIII, who survived him by almost the same period of time. Graduating B.A. from Magdalen college, Oxford,[2] he became more famous as the 'boy-bachelor' than as fellow and bursar of his college. He was ordained priest on the title of his fellowship on 10 March 1498, and was senior bursar in the last year of the fifteenth century; and the traditional account of his leaving that office, if not so becoming as it might have been, is too characteristic to ignore. The future builder of Hampton Court was asked, it is said, to resign because he had spent college funds on the completion of Magdalen tower without the college authority.[3] He was also master of Magdalen college school; among his pupils were the three younger sons of the marquess of Dorset, who invited Wolsey to spend a Christmas with the family and then presented him to the living of Limington near Ilchester in Somerset.

of Henry VIII (1920); but it seems to have escaped comment that in 1506 one Andrew Wolsey was mayor of King's Lynn which the cardinal visited in 1520 * and favoured in its municipal conflict with Bishop Nix of Norwich (Flenley, *Six Town Chronicles*, 1911, pp. 88-90, 189).

[1] See below, p. 276 n. 1. Wolsey describes Ipswich as 'meum natale solum' in writing to Clement VII (Theiner, *Vetera Monumenta*, p. 554 *b*).

[2] Cavendish reports Wolsey as saying, 'past not fifteen yeares of age.' This would leave an unusual interval between his B.A. and the assumed dates of his election as fellow of Magdalen and his M.A. Neither the university nor college registers elucidate the point.

[3] Creighton rejects, but Gairdner accepts, this story. Macray (*Reg. Magdalen*, iii. 19) remarks that 'the account book is unfortunately missing; we are therefore unable to disprove thoroughly the improbable story.' Creighton's chief objection is that the tower was completed ' in the year in which Wolsey became bursar'; but this, while fatal to Fiddes' consideration of 'that noble structure as an early essay of the cardinal's great and enterprising mind' (p. 7), seems hardly conclusive against a charge of anticipating college authority in order to discharge 'the prosaic duty of paying the bills for its erection' (Creighton, p. 19). Worse things have been done by college bursars in more recent times, and it may well have been exaggerated into the charge that Wolsey *aerarium collegii invasit*. When another fellow of Magdalen, Stokesley, afterwards bishop of London, was actually charged with heresy, theft, perjury, adultery, witchcraft, neglect of duties, spending the night at Sandford without leave, and christening a cat (Macray, *Register of Magdalen*, i. 37-60; Bloxam, *Register*, ii. 20-4; *D.N.B.* liv. 403), the recording angel may well have dropped a tear over Wolsey's fiscal indiscretion.

There he gave offence to Sir Amyas Paulet of Hinton St. George, who put him in the stocks, tradition has it for exuberant behaviour after a fair; long afterwards, according to Cavendish, Wolsey, when lord chancellor, took his revenge by confining Paulet for five or six years to the Middle Temple, of which Paulet was treasurer in 1520-1.[1]

These peccadilloes did not interfere with Wolsey's ecclesiastical preferment. In 1501 he obtained a dispensation [2] to hold with Limington two other benefices and be absent from all, became chaplain to archbishop Deane and then to Sir Richard Nanfan, deputy of Calais, who on his death recommended him to Henry VII in 1507.[3] Henry made him his chaplain, employed him on minor diplomatic missions to Scotland and to the Netherlands,[4] and was doubtless impressed by his envoy's expedition and dispatch; but the wonderful story told by Cavendish of his accomplishment of a mission to Flanders and back in three days is inaccurate in various details. Henry's death inflicted a check on Wolsey's career; for Margaret Beaufort, who seems to have exercised much influence during the first three months of her grandson's reign, had apparently no great respect for Wolsey. He was not at once appointed chaplain to Henry VIII, nor royal almoner on Edenham's death in July; and his friend, Darcy, was superseded as vice-chamberlain. It was not until November, on the death of Edenham's successor, Thomas Hobbes, that Henry VIII appointed Wolsey royal almoner and counsellor.[5]

---

[1] J. Hutchinson, *Notable Middle Templars* (1902), p. 185; Hopwood, *Cal. Middle Temple Rec.* (1903) p. 9; *L.P.* ii. 1236.*

[2] Rymer, xii. 783; under this dispensation Wolsey acquired the livings of Redgrave in Suffolk in 1500, Lydd in Kent in 1506, and Great Torrington in Devon in 1510: Limington was valued at £21 and the others at £25, £55, and £58 respectively (Brodie, *op. cit.* p. xii).

[3] The index to the *Cal. of Patent Rolls*, 1495-1509, attributes to Wolsey Nanfan's office as sheriff of Worcester and Cornwall. Nanfan made Wolsey one of his executors.

[4] See Busch, *England under the Tudors*, pp. 225-6, 236-7, and 381-2, and authorities there cited.

[5] Rymer, xiii. 267. He was also dean of Hereford before 4 June 1509, on which date he is described as such (*L.P.* i. new ed. p. 245) in

According to Polydore Vergil, Wolsey's fortunes were pushed by Foxe, who wanted his assistance in counteracting the influence of Surrey ; [1] and the story is confirmed by the earliest private letter of Wolsey's extant.* It is a very significant document.[2] Writing on 30 September 1511 from Windsor in very confidential terms, he tells Foxe how Surrey, meeting with a cool reception at court, had gone home the next day, and proceeds to suggest that with a little help he might be 'utterly excluded' therefrom, 'whereof in my poore juggement no lytyll goode shuld insue.' This was bold language for one, who subscribes himself to Foxe as 'your loving and humble priest,' to use of the lord high treasurer. But in the same letter Wolsey apologises to Foxe himself for having broken his instructions and given independent advice to the king, and expresses fear lest Foxe is displeased with him already, since he has not written 'for this long season.' Grounds for displeasure may be inferred from another incident of a few months earlier, significant both

---

Henry VIII's first pardon roll. Gairdner (*D.N.B.*), following Le Neve (*Fasti*, ed. Hardy, i. 477), says he was dean in 1512 (see Brodie's preface to *L.P.* i. pp. xii-xiv). The appearance, on the same membrane of the same roll, of a pardon to ' Richard, bishop of Hereford, *alias* Richard Mayewe, S.T.P., late almoner of Henry VII, president of Magdalen college, and chancellor of Oxford university,' suggests that not only the deanery of Hereford and appointment as royal almoner, but Wolsey's earlier preferment may have been principally due to the president of his college who was also an active member of Henry VII's council long before he became bishop of Hereford in 1504 (see Leadam, *Court of Requests*, and *Cal. Patent Rolls*, Henry VII, *passim ;* his name occurs in other council MSS in the B.M. besides those printed by Leadam). Like Stokesley, Wolsey appears to have adhered to the side of the absent but influential president against the opposite faction in college. It is possible that Wolsey's recollection of the dispute between Magdalen and Merton over a mill suggested his story to the Venetian ambassador in 1516 about a man who agreed to compromise but insisted on having the mill (*Merton Reg.*, Oxford Hist. Soc. p. 87 ; *Venetian Cal.* 1509-19, No. 738).

[1] *Historia*, p. 632. Foxe, it may be added, had, as bishop of Winchester, been visitor of Magdalen College since 1501.

[2] It is printed *in extenso*, from B.M. Cotton MS. Titus B i. 98, in Fiddes' *Collections*, pp. 8-9, and is calendared in *L.P.* i. new ed. 880, first ed. 3443. Compare also the joint letter of Wolsey and Foxe to the pope (below, p. 168 *n.*).

of Wolsey's character and of the influence he already exercised over the king. The established method of giving legal effect to the king's will had long been as follows : he signed a bill or petition presented to him and handed it to his secretary, who wrote a letter under the king's signet to the lord privy seal, retaining the signed bill as his warrant ; the lord privy seal then wrote under that seal to the lord chancellor as keeper of the great seal, retaining the secretary's letter as his warrant ; and the lord chancellor saw to the issue of the letters patent or close, and his master of the rolls or vice-chancellor to their enrolment on the patent or close roll.[1] On 26 May 1511 Wolsey produced for the chancellor a signed bill which had gone through none of this official routine ; and the chancellor acted without his proper warrant, safeguarding himself by the singular entry on his record that he had expedited the matter because Wolsey had given him the letters by the king's command, *ut asseruit dictus dominus Wulcy*.[2] The man, who had come into conflict with the college authorities at Magdalen and with the justices of the peace in Somerset, was already relying on his favour with the king to short-circuit administrative rules and circumvent his official superiors, Ruthal, Foxe, and Warham.

[1] This procedure was subsequently made statutory by act of parliament, 27 Henry VIII c. 11 ; cf. *L.P.* x. 249 ; 1537 ii. 847 ; 1545 ii. 713 ; and Maxwell-Lyte, *The Great Seal*, 1926, p. 90, *et passim*. The master of the rolls was frequently called the vice-chancellor in Henry VIII's reign, e.g. in *L.P.* ii. 412 ; iii. 2630, 4406, and p. 326.

[2] This passage is not only printed *in extenso* in Brewer's edition of the *L.P.* i. 1685, but in Mr. Brodie's new edition (i. 784 [44]), and in his preface (p. xvi) ; and Mr. Brodie writes to me, ' I cannot recall any other instance of such a note on a warrant of Henry VIII's time. . . . The fact that such a note was made indicates that the case was thought exceptional.' Mr. Brodie also traces Warham's growing jealousy of Wolsey in the archbishop's warning to Darcy against reliance on ' him he writes of ' (*L.P.* i. 725 ; preface, p. xvi), who can hardly be any one else than Wolsey. His influence may perhaps also be seen in the references (one as early as January 1510) to Wolsey as a friend of Venice (*ibid.* p. xii, nos. 322, 1216) ; probably he had made the acquaintance of the Venetian ambassador who lodged in Magdalen in 1496-97 (Macray, *Reg.* i. 29-30 ; *Italian Relation*, Camden Soc. 1847, p. 22).

There is yet another passage of significance in the letter. The pope, Julius II, was reported to be dead or dying: 'yesterday,' writes Wolsey, 'at masse I brake with the kyng in thys matter and shewyd onto hys grace how mych honor and also furtherans of all hys afferys in tyme to kome shuld insue to hym yf that by hys comendacion sume Cardinall myght atteyne to be Pope.' His own time was not yet come; he was only dean of Lincoln, little known even in England outside the court; and the cardinal whom he, in opposition to other members of the council, recommended Henry to favour was Hadrian or Adrian de Castello who had for twenty years represented English interests at Rome.[1] But this earliest letter reveals the drift of Wolsey's thoughts. From the first they turned to Rome as the fulcrum by means of which 'honour and the furtherance of all his affairs in time to come' might ensue to him as well as to his king; and the papal throne was the natural and, indeed, a proper, aim for Wolsey's vast ability and ambition. It is hard to believe that the idea was planted in Wolsey's mature breast by the fostering care of his youthful sovereign and only suffered to grow through Wolsey's devotion to his master's interests.

Regard for his future as well as for Rome led him to throw his influence into the scale for war when Julius II appealed for English aid. On 13 November 1511 Henry signified his adhesion to the holy league, which the pope had formed against Louis XII and the schismatic council at Pisa;[2] and in the preamble to their treaty for joint action, signed four days later, Henry and Ferdinand explained that they had been preparing a crusade against the infidel, when they heard that Julius II was besieged in Bologna by the Most Christian King, and that they were now called by the pope to meet danger to the church in another direction.[3] A month after Wolsey's

[1] See *D.N.B.* i. 146-7, s.v. Adrian de Castello or Corneto. His place in the *D.N.B.* is due to his tenure of two English bishoprics, firstly Hereford and then Bath and Wells; his name is often spelt 'Hadrian.'

[2] *L.P.* i. (new ed.) 939, 945, 969 [40]; *Spanish Cal.* 1509-25, pp. 58-9; *Venetian Cal.* 1509-19 p. 177; Rymer, *Fœdera*, xiii. 305, 311, 323-4.

[3] Edward Howard and the earl of Surrey were successively constituted admirals 'pro succursu papae' and 'pro ecclesiae defensione' (Rymer,

letter to Foxe, Henry VIII 'entered European politics by joining the league.'[1] 'I was dreaming,' wrote Erasmus from London, 'of an age that was really golden and isles that were happy, . . . when that Julian trumpet summoned all the world to arms.'[2]

The peace party in the English government had received a shot between wind and water. Its mainstays had been Foxe and Warham; but how could they resist when the silver trumpet called them not to holy convocations but to war? Henry and Wolsey were at one, but Warham at least held out. There was many a slip between a treaty and its warlike execution: parliament had still to be consulted as to ways and means; and Warham opened it on 4 February 1512 with an address on the text 'justice and peace have kissed' and a reminder that God only permitted war because of the sins of princes and peoples.[3] But a higher authority than the archbishop's was invoked; and on the 20th the pope's appeal was read in an English translation to the lords and communicated to the commons. More mundane and immediate grievances were urged to fan the flame and justify the fact of war: Andrew Barton and other Scots had been making havoc with English shipping by their exercise of the right of search; and war between England's ally, Charles, and the duke of Guelders was hampering English trade with the Netherlands. Parliament granted a tenth

---

Fœdera, xiii. 326, 402). In 1530 Surrey, then duke of Norfolk, declared that it was Ferdinand of Aragon who brought England into the war (*Spanish Cal.* 1529-30 p. 789). Tyndale in 1526 (see below, p. 228) called it 'the pope's quarrel,' and wanted Henry to make the church repay the cost. The war was certainly no fault of Warham's or Foxe's; but one of Palsgrave's charges (see below, pp. 71, 226) is that Wolsey 'began war with France for the defence of the church' (*L.P.* iv. p. 2556). Queen Catherine herself wrote to Wolsey on 26 July 1513 'al the besinesse that the King hath was furst the cause of the churche' (Ellis, 1, i. 80).

[1] Gooch, *Annals of Politics and Culture*, p. 16.
[2] Erasmus, *Epistolae*, ed. Allen, ii. 69.
[3] *Lords' Journals*, i. 10, 12-13. Warham had possibly read the *Encomium Moriae* by Erasmus, whom he had inducted to the living of Aldington in Kent on 22 March, 1511 (Emerton, *Erasmus*, pp. 175, 183-6; cf. P. S. Allen, *Erasmi Epistolae*, i. 501).

and a fifteenth, and the government proceeded with its preparations for a campaign.

The treaty had stipulated that England was not to be required to send forces into Italy; and Ferdinand of Aragon overreached his son-in-law by inducing Henry to attack France from the south-west, and to send 15,000 men under the second marquess of Dorset, the son of Wolsey's patron, to the coast of Guipuscoa. His plea was that he could re-inforce it there for a joint invasion of Guienne, which was to be recovered for England; his plan was to protect his own left flank by means of the English troops while he quietly occupied Spanish Navarre. Having achieved this conquest, he withdrew from the war. Meanwhile, the English troops, sweltering idly under the August sun, drank Spanish wine as though it were English beer, and perished in hundreds like flies in the autumn. Finally they mutinied and sailed home in October in defiance of orders. Officers and men concentrated their resentment on Wolsey: he, they said, was the cause of all this mischief; he was the author of the war, and its ill-success must be attributed to him. The correspondence from Spain is all addressed to Wolsey, and Frenchmen were convinced that the plan of invasion was the work of the English king's new councillors.[1]

Neither Henry nor Wolsey, however, was likely to be moved to anything but anger by the insubordination of English troops or by Ferdinand's desertion. Wolsey's whole career was at stake, and he used every ounce of his immense power of work and driving force to redeem this fiasco by a successful campaign in the following year. The loss of Ferdinand was compensated by the gain of the emperor; and the attack on France was consequently transferred from Guienne to Artois in conjunction with Maximilian, whose daughter, Margaret of Savoy, governed the Netherlands on behalf of his grandson, the future Charles V. The English navy cleared the Channel of French shipping; and Henry, accompanied by Wolsey,

[1] *L.P.* i. (new ed.) 1201, 1247, 1327, 1422; other references in my *Henry VIII*, pp. 56-61.

landed at Calais for a three months' campaign, which
produced the battle of the Spurs and the capture of
Thérouenne and Tournai. A greater victory was simultaneously won by Surrey at Flodden Field : it cost
James IV his life, and left Henry's sister Margaret in
control of the person, if not of the realm, of the infant
James V.

Neither triumph bore much permanent fruit, but the
double event in France and Scotland produced a great
impression in England and abroad. Except in civil war,
Englishmen had won no battle to speak of for nearly
three-quarters of a century ; but men now began to
speak in Europe of 'the overgrown power of England.'[1]
Pope Julius II, however, had given place to the pacific
Leo X in March 1513 ; and Louis XII was old and weary
alike of schism and of war. He submitted to the new pope
in October, and the ostensible ground on which England
had intervened thus disappeared. Henry was satisfied
with the glory he had won, and Wolsey was quick to take
advantage of the turning tide. 'I was the author of the
peace,' he told the Venetian ambassador a few months
later ; and no one else is so likely to have been responsible
for the projects for revenge on Spain and the divorce of
Catherine of Aragon, which were mooted in August 1514
but did not materialise until 1528.[2] The 'perpetual
peace' with France was made during the winter with
the pope's benediction ; and it was cemented, again at
Leo X's suggestion, by marriage.[3] Henry's sister Mary
was released from her contract with Charles, a fiancé
of fourteen, and transferred to Louis XII, a dotard of
fifty-two.[4] The bridegroom surrendered Tournai and

---

[1] Peter Martyr to L. H. Mendoza, Valladolid, 8 March 1514 (*L.P.* i.
new ed. 2707, old ed. 4864).

[2] Rawdon Brown, *Four Years at the Court of Henry VIII*, i. 116, 158 ;
Venetian Cal. ii. 257, 275. On the divorce project of 1514 see *Ven. Cal.* ii.
nos. 479, 482-3, 487, 492, 500 *ad fin.* ; my *Henry VIII*, p. 176 ; and below,
p. 283 *n.* 1.   [3] *L.P.* i. 3132.

[4] That was a considerable age for kings in those times : counting only
natural deaths, Edward IV died at forty-one, Henry VII at fifty-two,
Henry VIII at fifty-five, Edward VI at fifteen, Mary at forty-two, Francis I
at fifty-two, and Charles V at fifty-eight.

increased the annual tribute due to England since the
treaty of Étaples in 1492.[1]

But it was Wolsey who profited most by peace as he
had certainly worked hardest in war. His merits as a
war minister may have been exaggerated, but his activities included all, and more than all, the functions of an
efficient quartermaster-general,[2] and most of those of a
modern chancellor of the exchequer and secretary of state
for foreign affairs. It illustrates the elastic, if not form-
less, character of English government at the time that a
councillor, who controlled no secular department, should
have been able, by the king's favour and the complaisance
of his colleagues, to grasp and convert to the purposes of
war so much of the administrative machine; and it was
another characteristic of the age that a priest should
have been the principal minister of war. Yet, although
cardinals had fought on the field of battle at Ravenna on
Easter day 1512 in a conflict between two rival ecclesiastical councils for the reform of the catholic church,[3] it
was the first time in English history that the dispenser
of the king's alms had organised a war and received such
ample rewards for military success. Wolsey ceased to
be almoner on his promotion to the bishopric of Lincoln
at the beginning of 1514; and his share in the profits
of the treaty with France was the bishopric of Tournai
to be held *in commendam* with that of Lincoln, in spite
of the recent decree of the Lateran council.[4]   But to dis-

---

[1] I.e. fitty thousand 'francorum in coronis auri, unoquoque franco
viginti solidos Turonenses valente': there are many half-yearly receipts
in Rymer's *Fœdera*, e.g. xii. 527, 549, 569, etc.; xiii. 34, 116, 232, 298.

[2] Cf. Wolsey's order to pay for 'certain secret engines' (*L.P.*
i. 2035), and numerous others in the war expenses for 1513 (*ibid.,*
3612-13).

[3] Creighton, *History of the Papacy*, v. 167-72.

[4] *L.P.* i. 3496. He had been appointed dean of York on 19 Feb. 1513;
he was also elected chancellor of Cambridge university in 1514, but made
way for Fisher, bishop of Rochester. According to Hall (p. 567) he was
nominated on 'new year's day' (1 Jan.) although his predecessor did not
die until the 2nd (*D.N.B.* liii. 140 *b*). Erasmus had heard of this promotion on or before the 4th (*Epistolae*, ed. Allen, i. nos. 284, 297; *L.P.*
new ed. i. 2558), and his papal provision is dated Rome, 6 Feb. (Rymer,

pense with the decrees of councils was the highest prerogative of popes.

Before these arrangements were complete, Christopher Bainbridge, the cardinal-archbishop of York and the companion-in-arms of Julius II, died at Rome about 13 July 1514. His last letters to Henry VIII complained that his servants at York were harassed by its archdeacon, Thomas Dalby, who acted for Wolsey in the deanery, and that Silvester de Giglis, who acted for Wolsey in Rome, was a traitor. In a postscript he prayed it might be his fortune to see and to serve Henry where Julius II had wished he should, i.e. as legate *a latere*.[1] The moment the news of Bainbridge's death reached England, Wolsey was, on 5 August, given the temporalities of the archbishopric.[2] A fortnight later he borrowed from English and Italian bankers £2000 of English money and 5704 ducats (about another £1400) of Italian to pay for his pall and the expenses of his promotion.[3] Most of this loan was to be repaid out of his predecessor's estate. Bainbridge's principal executor, Richard Pace (or Pacey),[4] afterwards king's secretary and dean of St. Paul's, demurred to this transaction and expressed to Wolsey the hope that Bainbridge's brothers and kinsfolk would not lose their legacies.

xiii. 392). He was likewise beginning to turn his influence to financial profit, and on 11 June 1513 he received from Lady Margaret Pole, afterwards countess of Salisbury, an annuity of a hundred marks (£66 13s. 4d. = at least £700 in present values) for his counsel and aid (*L.P.* i. p. xvii, no. 1987). The salary for a 'king's counsel' was just being raised from 100 marks to £100. The countess is one of the ladies whose jointures Wolsey 'engrosseth up into his coffer' (W. Roy, *Rede me*, ed. Arber, p. 59).

[1] *L.P.* i. p. xvii, nos. 1653, 3007, 3015; Ellis, ii, i. 232.

[2] The Cardinal de Medici's letter announcing Bainbridge's death is dated Rome, 14 July (Rymer, xiii. 404); Henry's grant of the temporalties, dated 5 August, describes Wolsey as already 'elect' of York (*ibid.* xiii. 412). There cannot have been the barest form of capitular election. Wolsey is referred to as 'postulate of York' in a notarial instrument as early as 30 July (*ibid.* i. 3101).

[3] *L.P.* i. 3166, 3226 [9], 3261, 3497; cf. *ibid.* iv. 5749.

[4] Pacey is the form in which the name still survives, and there is no doubt that Pace was a two-syllable word. Similarly, Sir John Pecche's name survives as Peachey, and Sir John Daunce's is also spelt Dauntsy.

At length he yielded to Wolsey's pressure, trusting that the money would really go to the dilapidations of the see,[1] to Wolsey's satisfaction, and the good of the late archbishop's soul. Any dispute about probate would, of course, be determined in Wolsey's own prerogative court of York.

Wolsey was already pressing for still higher preferment. A month before he was consecrated bishop of Lincoln, he had sent Polydore Vergil to Rome, nominally on the ground that, having been twelve years in England, Polydore wished to visit his old home and kiss the feet of the new pope. His real mission was much more confidential, and is only revealed in the letter he wrote to Wolsey in May, after his arrival in Rome.[2] He had been instructed by Wolsey first to call on that cardinal Hadrian, whom Wolsey had in 1511 recommended as a candidate for the papacy, and to explain to him how completely Wolsey was his friend. Then, if Hadrian showed himself duly grateful, Polydore was to broach the subject of Wolsey's own election to the college of cardinals. Hadrian sounded Leo X, who remarked that, if Wolsey had great influence with Henry, it might be as well to make him a cardinal. Hadrian was to write to Wolsey, when things were well in train, to secure the royal assent. Meanwhile not a word was to be said, and the affair was to be so managed as to appear the spontaneous offer of Leo X ' as,' remarks Vergil to Wolsey, ' your reverend lordship told me it was to be done.'

But Wolsey distrusted men too much to trust to a single agent, and another Italian at Rome with an English see, Silvester de Giglis, bishop of Worcester,[3]

---

[1] Pace's pious hopes were not fulfilled, at least so far as the dilapidations were concerned ; and when, in 1530, Wolsey was driven to his diocese, he was full of lamentations over its ruinous condition (see below, pp. 274, 277).

[2] Aug. Theiner, *Vetera Monumenta Hib. et Scotorum historiam illustr.*, 1864, p. 510 ; *L.P.* i. 2674, 2932.

[3] See *D.N.B.* xxi. 311-12, another Italian admitted to the *D.N.B.* through his English bishopric. Campeggio is a third. A collection of Wolsey's letters to Silvester (1516-20) is printed in Martene and Durand, *Veterum Scriptt. amplissima collectio*, tom. iii. Paris, 1724. The introduction is as hostile to Wolsey as Sanders is.

was already pressing the pope, at Wolsey's own suggestion, to make him legate *a latere* for life.[1] In return, Leo wanted to be given credit, in the text of the marriage contract between Mary and Louis XII, for its original suggestion. If Wolsey could manage this and a few amendments, of which Leo sent a list, in the draft Anglo-French treaty, it would, wrote Silvester in August, bind his holiness to grant the legation, if not for life, at least in prorogation, that is to say, for successive periods of years.[2] Bainbridge's death removed the chief bar to Wolsey's preferment. There was now no archbishop of York, no English cardinal, no rival claimant for the post of legate *a latere*, and no English-born ambassador at the papal court. So, on 12 August, we have the king's letter asking Leo to make Wolsey a cardinal ' with all the honours held by the late cardinal of York.' His merits are such, continues the letter, that the king can do nothing of the least importance without him. The letter[3] was clearly drafted by Wolsey to confirm the pope in his own pre-viously reported opinion that, if Wolsey had sufficient influence with the king, he would be worth, if not worthy of, a cardinal's hat ; Wolsey was styled ' our most secret counsellor.'

Leo, however, was not to be hurried quite so fast. Apart from the bishopric of Lincoln, he had already given Wolsey Tournai and York ; and these, he thought, were sufficient unto the day. Moreover, Wolsey's advocate, the bishop of Worcester, whom Bainbridge had denounced

---

[1] Wolsey's letter to which Silvester is replying, is not known to be extant, but it must have been written before Bainbridge's death ; and Wolsey's opposition to the pope's proposal to make Bainbridge legate *a latere* (see below, pp. 168-9), was obviously due in part to his own desire for the post.

[2] *L.P.* i. 3132.

[3] *Ibid.* i. 3140 ; Theiner, p. 514. Wolsey's ideas of his own influence are indicated in his letter to Sampson, his commissary at Tournai, a French bishop-elect of which was disputing Wolsey's claims : ' ye need not doubt thereof ; the pope would not offend me for one thousand such as the elect is ' (*L.P.* i. 3546).

as a traitor,[1] was now implicated in the alleged poisoning of his accuser; and malice in Rome rumoured that the deed had been done at the instance of some prelate in England, 'being enemye unto my saide late lorde.'[2] Pace, who was ignorant of Silvester's efforts on Wolsey's behalf, was, as executor of Bainbridge, pressing for an investigation of the charge. Silvester was, however, acquitted; and Wolsey promised to pursue his accusers with as ardent a mind as if they were his own, asking Silvester meanwhile to get Leo to sequester Bainbridge's property now in Pace's hands, raise as much money as he could on that security, and send it to Wolsey. Silvester's chief accuser, according to Wolsey, was John Clerk, afterwards bishop of Bath and Wells; he was now on his way to England, but Wolsey advised Silvester that he was quite at liberty 'without breach of the king's laws' to cite him to answer at Rome.[3]

This episode hardly assisted Wolsey's suit for a cardinal's hat; and in November he was instructing Silvester to inquire privately whether Louis XII had really, as he had frequently promised, exerted his influence with the pope on Wolsey's behalf in this respect; though, he remarked, he would much rather obtain the cardinalate through the influence of Henry VIII and of Silvester

---

[1] Ellis, *Original Letters*, 2nd ser. i. 226-32. Cardinals and other great men, he wrote, marvelled that Henry employed ' such an infamed person to be your orator.'

[2] Burbank to Henry VIII, 28 Aug. 1514, in Ellis, 1, i. 104-5; 'whereunto we answerede that our master [Bainbridge] had no suche enemyes in England, ne that prelates of Englande and English borne wer ever disposed unto ony suche actes.' The actual miscreant, a priest, died of self-inflicted wounds, admitting his crime but refusing to ' shew by whoos instance, being so commandid by his confessors ' (*ibid.* p. 107; *L.P.* i. new ed. 3203-4). The ' and English borne ' in Burbank's letter seems deliberately to exclude Silvester de Giglis, bishop of Worcester, from the exculpation of English prelates; and Leo X in 1520 refused to make him a cardinal, despite Wolsey's insistence, telling him that he would not ' incur this infamy ' but would give his reasons openly unless the demand was dropped (*ibid.* i. pp. xix-xx; iii. 1080, 1209). On Burbank see *Erasmi Epistolae*, ed. Allen, iv. 332.

[3] *L.P.* i. 3496-7. Clerk was Bainbridge's chaplain, Pace his secretary, and Burbank his steward.

himself. He had to wait nearly a year for the cardinal's hat, and nearly four for the papal legacy. Before that achievement of ecclesiastical ambition, domestic events had brought into vivid prominence the problems of church and state with which the English cardinal-legate would have to deal. With regard to foreign affairs, we have seen enough to understand the forecast made in 1515 to a Venetian diplomatist by the bishop of Durham, who was also the king's secretary but now ' sang treble to Wolsey's bass.'[1] 'The pope,' said the bishop, in words which have to be borne in mind in reference alike to Wolsey's domestic and foreign policy, ' is now so linked with the king that words cannot exaggerate their mutual good-will; so that, in the affairs of France, the policy of England will be that of Rome.'[2]

The links were of Wolsey's forging. Silvester, cleared from the charge but not from the suspicion of having hastened the end of Bainbridge, was now Henry VIII's representative at Rome, and Ammonius, Wolsey's private, and the king's Latin, secretary, supplanted Polydore Vergil as papal collector and nuncio in England.[3] Papal bouquets in the shape of the golden rose and the sword and cap of maintenance had already descended with papal blessings on Henry VIII: the halo of *fidei defensor* was soon to superscribe his image, and an emperor and a pope [4] to suggest his elevation to the imperial throne; while the papal tiara hovered, in Wolsey's eyes, over his own uplifted brow. The earliest imitative impulse of these exponents of a dawning national self-consciousness was to pour new wine into the old bottles of papacy and empire, and to clothe a nation's growing limbs in the parting garments and shrinking glory of a catholic and a mediæval world.

[1] Rawdon Brown, i. 260.

[2] *Ibid.* i. 115. Wolsey preferred to put it that the policy of Rome would be the policy of England (*ibid.* pp. 112-13, 116; cf. *Venetian Cal.* 1509-19, pp. 254-7, 311), and was already persuaded that he had sufficient influence abroad to prevent any French descent upon Italy.

[3] *Erasmi Epistolae*, ii. 289.   [4] Maximilian and Leo X.

CHAPTER II.

THE PROBLEM OF CHURCH AND STATE.

THE student of Wolsey's career and place in English history is happily not required to plunge into the morass of doctrinal disputation in which the history of the reformation is embogged. Wolsey perhaps indited more state papers, domestic and foreign, than any other English minister; but he left nothing in writing that could be called theology, unless we include the discussions of ecclesiastical law in which he was involved by the divorce. 'As for his learning which was far from exact,' writes Lord Herbert of Cherbury,[1] 'it consisted chiefly in the subtilities of the Thomists, wherewith the king and himself did more often weary than satisfie each other.' He was intelligent enough to see that the patronage of scholars redounded to the credit of the patron as much as to the benefit of learning; but his interest in the 'new learning' was purely political,[2] and there were moments when he, like Charles V, thought that Luther might acquire a political value.[3] This indifference to theology

---

[1] *Life and Raigne of Henry VIII*, p. 343; cf. Polydore Vergil, ed. 1555, p. 634, 'totus erat Thomisticus'; Erasmus, *Epistolae*, ii. 552-3; and W. Roy, *Rede me*, ed. Arber, p. 43.

[2] 'Learning,' of course, here means 'teaching,' and refers to the reformation rather than to the renaissance. Clement VII criticised Wolsey's statutes for his college on the ground that they contained no mention of Greek (*L.P.* iv. 2418). This defect was remedied, and, wrote a legal correspondent, 'the only fault is that there is no place for the lawyers on whom so much depends' (*ibid.* iv. 2565).

[3] Armstrong, *Charles V*, i. 162. When, however, Wolsey threatened Clement VII in 1525 with the loss of England's religious allegiance unless the pope accommodated himself to Wolsey's foreign policy, Giberti replied on behalf of the pope that he could not believe Wolsey was 'so little

could not, however, extend to the constitutional problem of the relations between *regnum* and *sacerdotium*, which had filled the middle ages with strife, and broke out with renewed violence in a novel form in England some years before Luther published his ninety-five theses.

That contest had hitherto been a conflict *in excelsis*—between popes and emperors over the government of the world, between archbishops and kings over their respective provinces and realms, between ecclesiastical and secular courts over the discipline of docile and unprotesting people, between rival authorities, but not between authority and independence. Nor was the protestantism with which Wolsey had to deal a repudiation of catholic doctrine : its novelty consisted in the fact that it was a protest against ecclesiastical jurisdiction by a middle-class laity clamouring, for the first time, for self-determination. The particular provocation arose from the immunity of the clergy from the criminal jurisdiction of the laity and the subjection of the laity to the criminal jurisdiction of the church.[1] The clamour which raised the whole constitutional issue of the reformation, first attained to national importance in the parliament of 1515, the first in which Wolsey sat.[2]

That parliament has passed almost unnoticed in English history. 'In the whole course of its proceedings,' says the old *Parliamentary History*, 'we meet with nothing worth notice, except that tonnage and poundage

cognisant of the greatness of his fortune that he would place himself in peril of losing it' (*L.P.* iv. 1080; cf. *ibid.* 1017, and Ranke, *Die römischen Päpste*, 1889, i. 80-1). There were no papal legates in the Lutheran *weltanschauung*.

[1] Heresy was always the *crimen haereticae pravitatis*, and the ultimate sentence in the ecclesiastical court was a sentence of death by burning, made *ex officio* effective by the Lollard statutes.

[2] 'Sir Thomas Wolcy' was one of the four minor ecclesiastics who were appointed receivers of petitions from England, Ireland, Wales, and Scotland on 4 Feb. 1511-12 (*Lords' Journals*, i. 10); but this hardly involved sitting in parliament. He just missed sitting as bishop of Lincoln in the third session from 23 Jan. to 4 March 1513-14. He was papally provided on 6 Feb., received his temporalties on 4 March, and was consecrated on the 26th (Rymer, xiii. 390-4; Le Neve, ii. 21).

was granted, and a subsidy.' Yet, apart from the fundamental issues raised therein, its records possess considerable matter of interest. It is the first parliament for
which we have any regular record of attendance,[1] the
first in which we can therefore compare the summons to
attend with the actual attendance, and ascertain whether,
for instance, there was on any particular day, or throughout the session as a whole, a clerical or a lay majority in
the lords ; and, with the possible exception of the parliament of 1523, for which we have scanty records, it
was the last parliament in English history in which the
spiritual lords outnumbered their secular colleagues.[2]

The writs had been issued on 23 November 1514, the
elections were held in December, and parliament met on
5 February 1515. Summonses had been sent to twenty-
one bishops,[3] twenty-seven abbots, the prior of Coventry

[1] * This applies only to the lords ; the commons' journals do not begin
until 1547 and have never contained any record of attendance. The
division lists, however, begin to provide some indication in the nineteenth
century. In Harleian MS. 158, f. 135, there is an earlier record of
attendance for 2 and 3 March 1511-12. This record is much fuller than
that in the lords' journals, and raises some curious questions about the
make-up of the latter, which contains no record at all of the formal meeting on 3 March when the lords adjourned on account of convocation.
These Harleian MS. records have not been noted in either edition of *L.P*
vol. i. ; but they are printed *in extenso* in Sir Nicholas Harris Nicolas'
Report on the barony of l'Isle (1829), pp. 418-21.

[2] The same number of spiritual and temporal lords were summoned
to the Reformation parliament which met on 3 Nov. 1529 ; but the
spiritual majority had, as we shall see, been destroyed, not by Henry VIII's
creation of temporal peerages, the number of which remained at forty-
three, but by Wolsey's accumulation of spiritual preferments and by the
number of non-resident foreigners holding English bishoprics (see below,
pp. 173-4).

I avoid the phrase ' spiritual peers,' because it is a meaningless modern
anachronism, not older apparently than the eighteenth century. ' Pieres
espirituelx ' occurs in Keilwey's *Reports*, but means ' fathers in God.'
Cf. ' piers en Dieu ' in *Rot. Parl.* ii. 163*b* [45]. Anstis, who was Garter
king, uses the phrase in 1723 somewhat apologetically, saying there is the
authority of an act of parliament for it (Fiddes, *Collections*, p. 108).

[3] The bishop of Sodor and Man was not usually summoned to English
parliaments. The bishop of St. Asaph also does not occur in the later
official copy of the close roll (the original appears not to be extant) which
is summarised in *L.P.* new ed. i. 3464 ; but his presence is recorded

and the prior of St. John of Jerusalem; but the last, although a prior sat with the temporal lords and had, since Edward IV's reign, been reckoned the premier baron of England. Excluding his ambiguous personality, there were forty-nine spiritual lords, and forty-two laymen, consisting of three dukes, one marquess, ten earls, and twenty-eight barons. But writs of summons are no proof of actual sitting.[1] A full house would have contained ninety-two lords: the highest actual attendance was on 13 February when forty were present, and the smallest was on 17 March when there were eighteen.[2] The average attendance throughout the session was twenty-nine, divided almost equally between spiritual and lay lords, with a slight advantage to the former. On fifteen days the spiritual lords were in a majority and on twelve days the temporalty, and the balance of power frequently seemed to depend on the dual capacity of the prior of St. John's.

The first business of the session was to consider the expiring acts, namely those which had been passed in the previous parliament with the proviso that they were only to last until the next, which by this time was coming to mean, not session as in earlier times, but parliament.[3]

in the lords' journals on a score of days during the first session of 1515. A singular record is that of Wolsey's intermittent presence as 'custos spiritualitatum' of York during the first twelve of the session, after which he appears as archbishop. He had received the temporalities on 5 Aug. 1514 and the papal bulls translating him from Lincoln were dated 15 Sept. and published in York cathedral on 3 Dec. (Le Neve, ed. Hardy, iii. 112-13).

[1] See my *Evolution of Parliament*, 2nd ed. pp. 316-20 and App. 11; and cf. *Cal. Pat. Rolls*, 1494-1509, p. 451, 'exemption [of Lord Stourton] from attending any parliament or council that may be summoned even though a writ, letters, or a mandate should be sent him.'

[2] Four only are recorded as present on Friday, 16 Feb., but that was one of the days on which the lords adjourned on account of convocation; usually no attendances are recorded on those days. Four such adjournments are noted during the first session, two on Fridays and two on Tuesdays; but seven are noted in the second and shorter session of Nov.-Dec., when the controversy over Standish had become acute.

[3] Nevertheless, the clerk of the parliaments in Nov. 1515, after stating that 'hoc presens parliamentum' had been prorogued to 12 Nov., calls the 13th 'secundo die parliamenti' and continues this separate enumeration.

Among these was an act much discussed in the first session (Feb.-March),[1] but not passed until the second session (Nov.-Dec. 1512) of the second parliament of Henry VIII.[2] Lamenting the daily increase of robberies, murders, and felonies, and the immunity criminals enjoyed by reason of their benefit of clergy, it proceeded to deny that benefit to all those clergy who murdered people in their own homes, in hallowed places, or on the king's highway, provided that the criminous clerk was not in holy orders. By holy orders parliament apparently meant the three higher orders of priest, deacon, and sub-deacon. But the majority of criminous clerks were in the four lower orders, and benefit of clergy descended even lower. The physical distinction between clergy and laity was the tonsure; every school-boy, it is said, was tonsured, though no school-girl in those days.[3] Except for this discrimination of sex, the physical distinction agreed with the legal test. If the criminal condemned in the secular courts, which alone had jurisdiction in murder or felony, could read, he could save his neck by reading in court what was called his ' neck-verse,' usually the very appropriate first verse of the 51st Psalm. Having thus established his clerical privilege, he was handed over to his bishop to be kept in the bishop's prison, from which he frequently escaped. If he did not escape surreptitiously, he was after about a year's detention allowed the ancient benefit of compurgation, by which he could be cleared on getting twelve clerical sympathisers to swear to their belief in his innocence. Perjury, it may be remarked, engaged the attention of this same parliament;[4] and clergy of this type were really the half-breeds of later mediæval civilisation. They were laymen except for their privilege and clergy except for their character. Leo X himself de-

---

[1] *Lords' Journals*, 13, 17, and 27 Feb. 1511-12.

[2] 4 Henry VIII, c. 2, *Stat. of the Realm*, iii. 48 ; *Parl. Roll*, 133, no. 11. (In the printed excerpts from the rolls, App. pp. i-xliv, this session is erroneously assigned to 1513.)

[3] Hence no woman could claim benefit of clergy.

[4] In its first session, *Lords' Journals*, 16 Feb. and 6, 20, and 22 March 1511-12.

nounced them as persons who only became clerks in order to escape the criminal law.[1]

This act of 1512 was not only extolled by lawyers as having been the means of bringing large numbers of criminals to justice, but was defended by Dr. John Taylor in an address to convocation, of which he was prolocutor, on 26 June 1514; it was due, he said, to the brawling and dissolute life of the lower clergy.[2] Colet, indeed, had denounced the evils it was intended to correct in the sermon he had preached at the opening of convocation on 6 February 1512.[3] But this happy consensus of opinion broke down before parliament began in February 1515 to consider the renewal of the act. For one thing, Leo X, unknown to the prolocutor of convocation, had on 5 May 1514 declared in the Lateran council that, according to the law of God as well as to the law of man, laymen had no jurisdiction over churchmen.[4] For another, Wolsey's advent had greatly strengthened ecclesiastical influence in the English government; and for a third, popular feeling, in London at any rate, had been inflamed by quarrels between the laity and the ecclesiastical courts over church-dues and jurisdiction.[5] These dissensions culminated over the notorious case of Richard Hunne; it was in many respects unique in English history, and it engaged contro-versial pens from Sir Thomas More, Tyndale, Roy, and Foxe the martyrologist down to lesser church historians

---

[1] Bull of 12 Feb. 1515-16, Rymer's *Fœdera*, xiii. 532-3: 'Sane nuper ad nostrum relatio fidedigna perduxit auditum quod in regno Angliae primam clericalem tonsuram et minores ordines recipiunt, non ut ad superiores sacros ordines ascendant, sed ut excessus et delicta liberius perpetrare et judicis saecularis forum declinare et impunitatem excessuum hujusmodi obtinere valeant . . . ex quo improborum delicta remanent impunita, clericorum status decoloratur, ipsaque justitia non modicum impeditur.'

[2] Keilwey, *Reports*, ed. 1688, f. 180*b*; *L.P.* i. (new ed.)a 3033.

[3] Colet, *Oratio habita*, etc., 4to ed. n.d. (Bodleian Library). It earned him the enmity of his bishop, Fitzjames; 'Londoniensis,' he writes to Erasmus on 20 Oct. 1514, ' non cessat vexare me ' (*Erasmi Epist.*, ed. Allen, ii. 36).

[4] Maitland, *Roman Canon Law*, p. 89.

[5] See Miss E. Jeffries Davis in *Victoria County Hist.*, London, i. 236-8, and *Engl. Hist. Rev.* July 1915, pp. 479-80.

in the succeeding four centuries. The case dominated the parliament of 1515, greatly exercised Wolsey's mind, and provoked the earliest indications of his ecclesiastical policy. It is one in which historical investigation almost rises to the level of detective fiction.

In the early morning of Monday, 4 December 1514, eight days before London chose its members for the parliament of 1515,[1] Hunne was found hanged in the bishop's prison, called the Lollards' tower, in St. Paul's. He was a well-to-do merchant-tailor, noted for his charities; and More, while condemning him as a heretic, commends his 'worldly conversation,'[2] and says he was 'a fair dealer among his neighbours.' His friends believed that his heresy consisted mainly in refusing to pay the mortuary demanded at the burial of his infant son, and then, losing that suit in the ecclesiastical court, in bringing an action for præmunire in the king's bench.[3] The exact chronology of these various legal proceedings has not been ascertained:[4] More maintained that Hunne brought the

[1] The London members were returned on 12 Dec. (A. B. Beaven, *Aldermen*, etc. i. 274).

[2] *Dyaloge concernynge heresyes*, facsimile reprint, 1927, p. 235.

[3] A 'mortuary' was a sort of ecclesiastical heriot, the church claiming the best article belonging to the deceased as a burial fee. Hunne resisted on the ground that his son, being only a few weeks old, had no property in the bearing-sheet which the parson of St. Mary's Spittle, Whitechapel, claimed. See the petition to parliament provoked by Hunne's case (*L.P.* ii. 1315), and protesting against the refusal of the clergy to bury children before receiving the deceased's best jewel, garment, or other best thing; and cf. Lyndwood, *Provinciale*, 1679, pp. 21-2; Tyndale, *Obedience*, p. 237; Saint-German, *Doctor and Student*, ed. 1886, pp. 303-4, 338-9. *

[4] Logic may sometimes supply the defects of historical evidence, and the logical sequence is fairly clear. Hunne resisted the parson's claim, but lost the suit in the ecclesiastical court: his resistance to ecclesiastical claims would be quite enough to provoke the cry, if not a formal charge, of heresy, apart from his sympathy with other victims of ecclesiastical jurisdiction which seems to have been well known; and he may have instituted his further suit in the king's bench under the impression that attack was the best form of defence. His failure in that prosecution probably encouraged the bishop of London's officials to proceed with their counter-charge of heresy; and there is no necessary contradiction between the two aspects of the affair presented by More and Wriothesley. Each party to a dispute is disputing because the other is disputing with him. There are curious points of resemblance between Hunne's case and that

action for præmunire because he was charged with heresy; the popularly accepted view was expressed in the chronicler Wriothesley's words that Hunne 'was made an heretique for suing a præmunire.'[1] In either case, he was in the bishop's prison awaiting his trial for heresy when either he killed himself or was killed by others. The clergy adopted the theory of suicide, the laity that of murder, for which they held that the prisoner's ecclesiastical gaolers were responsible.[2]

The incident brought church and state at once and inevitably into violent conflict. Behind the questions of fact and the matters of detail lay the far-reaching contention of common lawyers that the rival jurisdiction of the church was un-English in its nature and in its derivation. Convocation had protested against this view as fatal to all ecclesiastical jurisdiction in 1447; but the controversy had been smothered by the wars of the roses and the protection accorded by the Yorkists to the church.[3] Hunne may have been the mouthpiece of a party when he revived it by his præmunire suit and thus provoked the anger of the clergy.

Two practical questions had to be decided without delay : firstly, how had Hunne come by his death, and, secondly, should he be given christian burial ? The first was purely a secular matter for the coroner's inquest; the second was entirely for the ecclesiastical court. If the coroner's jury brought in a verdict of *felo de se*, there

of Bartholomew Legate, the last heretic burnt in Smithfield (1612) and between the comments of More and Fuller (*Church History*, 1656, bk. x. pp. 62-4). Legate's ' conversation ' also, says Fuller, was ' very unblameable ; and the poyson of hereticall doctrine is never more dangerous than when served up in clean cups and washed dishes.' Legate, too, ' threatened to sue ' the ecclesiastical court, ' so that his own indiscretion in this kind hastened his execution.'

[1] *Chronicle*, Camden Soc. i. 9 ; cf. W. Roy, *Rede me*, ed. Arber, pp. 104, 169.

[2] Brynklow in his *Complaynt of Roderick Mors*, 1543 (Early English Text Soc., extra series, No. 22) alludes to Hunne's case (p. 13), and alleges another ' murder ' in the lodge of bishop Gardiner's porter, *c.* 1541 ; Foxe (v. 530) says that victim was a priest named Saxy.

[3] See below, pp. 167-8, 248.

would be no ecclesiastical trouble. But the immediate
flight of one of the gaolers to sanctuary and the evidence,
gradually elicited during the course of the coroner's
inquiry, pointed towards a verdict of murder against the
bishop's prison officials ; and their superiors were seized
with panic. They were already in a quandary : if they
gave the corpse christian burial, they would admit that
Hunne was not a heretic and that he had been unjustly
accused and wrongfully kept in prison ; and they were
not inclined to give a man, who had invoked, albeit un-
successfully, the terrible weapon of præmunire, the benefit
of any doubts. They decided to press the charges of
heresy and forestall the result of the coroner's inquest.
On 10 December, the Sunday after Hunne's death, the
preacher at St. Paul's cross read out fresh articles against
him ; on the 16th the corpse was solemnly tried in the
presence of the mayor and aldermen by an ecclesiastical
court,[1] the bishop of London presiding with the assistance

---

[1] Sunday was the regular day for sentencing heretics (*Enc. Brit.* 11th
ed. xiv. 590). Whether this court was technically a provincial convocation
or a London diocesan synod is doubtful. It was held, as Sir T. More says,
' at Poules ' ; but this would be the place in either case. Parliament was
not sitting, but provincial convocations could meet for purely ecclesiastical
business at other times than parliamentary sessions. The bishop of London
was *ex officio* dean of the province of Canterbury ; he claimed to be acting
as Warham's delegate, and the presence of other bishops as assessors points
in the same direction. There was a similar doubt in Legate's case ; ' the
consistory,' says Fuller, ' so replenished for the time being, seemed not so
much a large court as a little convocation ' (*loc. cit.* p. 63). The Lollard
statutes had, indeed, enabled diocesan synods to deal with heresy and had
required the secular magistrate to execute *ex officio* the sentence of the
court (see below, p. 210) ; but those statutes had not prohibited the higher
court of a provincial convocation from exercising its older jurisdiction or
restrained a king like Edward IV from urging ecclesiastics to greater activity
(cf. Scofield, *Edward IV*, ii. 392-8). Its action on this occasion indicates
the unusual importance attached to Hunne's case. The convocation of
Canterbury had sat from 22 June to 1 July 1514 (*L.P.* i. new ed. 3033,
3050), and had then been prorogued to 6 Nov. (*Hereford Reg.*, Mayow,
pp. 199, 205). Mayow appointed his proctors on 16 Oct. Wilkins' phrase
(*Concilia*, iii. 658), ' ad diem 20 Decembris prorogata,' can only mean
prorogued ' on ' or continued to 20 Dec., the day on which Hunne's body
was burnt, though the St. David's register (Cymmrodorion Soc. 1917,
ii. 817) says it was ' continued ' until 23 Dec. (see below, pp. 47, 190 *nn.*).

of three other bishops, including Ruthal the king's secretary; it was condemned and burnt four days later at Smithfield.[1] Hunne's property was thereby forfeit to the crown. The sentence presumed his final persistence in heresy, and professed to be based on the evidence of unnamed witnesses taken by commission. But the final contumacy depended upon whether Hunne was murdered or hanged himself. He was still a prisoner awaiting trial : if he was murdered, there was no proof of final contumacy.[2] That depended upon the assumption that Hunne destroyed himself, a question which the bishop's court had no authority to decide. Nor could witnesses have afforded to admit their presence at Hunne's death by hanging, whether it was suicide or murder. Hunne was a suspected, accused, and imprisoned heretic ; but even by canon law he was not a condemned heretic until six days after his death.

It was doubtless an advantage to get Hunne's case out of the way before the parliament, which had been elected, met. But the coroner's jury was still pursuing its quest with an animus which would not have been lessened by the precipitate action of the ecclesiastical court.[3]   It

---

[1] Sir Thomas More, who was one of the two under-sheriffs of London from 3 Sept. 1510 to 23 July 1518 (when he was made K.C.), tells us that he was present in the bishop's court on this occasion and was convinced of Hunne's heresy by the depositions of witnesses read in court (*Dyaloge*, pp. 235, 239). But these depositions to heresy had, of course, nothing to do with the evidence in the coroner's court, which More ignores. *

[2] ' Nam ante declarationem, si paratus sit corrigi, licet erret, non est dicendus haereticus ' (Lyndwood, *Provinciale*, p. 293 *a*).

[3] Nearly all the difficulties which Gairdner found so puzzling in his account of the case—it occupies the whole of chap. iii. in his *English Church*, 1509-58—arise from his assumption that the proceedings of the coroner's jury were necessarily completed on 5-6 Dec. when it was empanelled and viewed the body. Yet Sir T. Smith, in his chapter ' Of the Coroner ' (*De Republica*, ed. 1906, pp. 91-2 ; see also, C. Gross, *The Coroner*, 1892, and Sir John Jervis, *Office and duties of . . . Coroners*, 6th ed. 1898) remarks that a coroner's jury ' take a day, sometime after xx or xxx daies, more or lesse, as the fact is more evident, or more kept close, to give their evidence ' ; and in 1927-28 there were three cases—the Sevenoaks railway accident, the Epping forest murder, and the Coleford case—in which the coroner's jury took three months or more. The essential date, moreover, which is given in their records, is, like the date

consisted, as More admits, of twenty-four ' right honest men,' several of whose subsequent careers can be traced in the ' Letters and Papers ' and legal proceedings of Henry's reign.   They examined many witnesses, took depositions, and followed out to the minutest detail the statutory duties prescribed for coroners' inquests (4 Edward I, c. 2). But what would happen if they decided that Hunne was not *felo de se*, and found a true bill of murder against the officials of the bishop who had already burnt the body

of acts of parliament, the commencement of the proceedings, because the value of the evidence depends thereon.   It has been held (Chitty, *Justice of the Peace*, ed. Burn, i. 876) that a coroner's jury could not return a verdict as late as seven months after the event ; but there was no statutory limit.   Hunne's case was one of peculiar difficulty, and the detailed account, published about 1537, and incorporated in Hall's *Chronicle* and Foxe's *Acts and Monuments* (iv. 183-98), shows that the coroner's jury was still seeking evidence and taking depositions late in Feb. 1515.   This account appeared as an anonymous tract, because it was illegal to publish the contents of a coroner's report ; and no doubt it was published as good propaganda.   But there is no reason to suppose that it was anything else than what it purported to be, i.e. the coroner's signed report of the proceedings in his court.   The only objections are that Fitzjames's letter seems out of place, that it is addressed to ' Cardinal ' Wolsey, which he did not become until six months later, and that the coroner's name is given in one place as ' William ' instead of Thomas Barnwell.   But the ' cardinal ' only occurs in a headline [Erasmus has also a letter addressed to Wolsey as ' cardinal ' on 30 Aug. 1515, the address being no doubt inserted, as Mr. Allen suggests, in printing, *Epistolae*, ii. 137] ; and the ' William ' is obviously no more than a clerical error or misprint.   The theory of concoction has not been seriously or consistently maintained, and there is no more ground for it than for the similar suggestion with regard to Keilwey's *Reports* (see below, p. 44).   Both corroborate Hall's *Chronicle ;* and since Hall is assumed to have been a ' malicious ' and ' dishonest ' chronicler, anything that corroborates him falls under suspicion (on Hall's professional connexion with a later case before a coroner's jury, see *L.P.* vi. 910). Sir Thomas More's controversial reply to Tyndale, on the other hand, is considered an ' amusing exposure,' although he does not mention any of the evidence in the case (rightly considering himself precluded by the law), is concerned to prove not so much that Hunne hanged himself, as that he was a heretic and that Horsey was guiltless of murder (both of which were probably true).   His amusing exposures are of absurd stories having nothing to do with the real murderers to whom More makes no allusion, although, as he says, he knew the case ' from toppe to toe ' (*Dyaloge*, p. 235).   Like Fitzjames, he is only interested in the clerk, and not in the laymen who were indicted.

and thus destroyed the evidence of crime ?[1]   It was perhaps the only case in English history in which a coroner's
jury has had to deal with such a question ; and this,
combined with the difficulty of obtaining evidence, made
the inquest a prolonged affair.   The most likely criminal,
Charles Joseph the gaoler of Lollard's tower, had ab-
sconded the day after the jury was empanelled, seeking
sanctuary first in Westminster, and then getting away
during the night of 21-22 December to Good Easter, a
secluded village in Essex.[2]   It was not until January that
he was discovered, conveyed to the Tower, and examined
by king's counsel for his purgation.[3]   At first he sought to
establish an alibi to the effect that he had spent the night
of Hunne's death in a house of ill-fame, and his two witnesses were the woman concerned and the keeper of the
house.   This plea was countered by the evidence of half
a dozen witnesses who had seen him making his way from
the Lollard's tower in the twilight of that December
morning.[4]   He then made a confession in which he
accused Dr. Horsey, the bishop's chancellor, and Spalding,
the bell-ringer, as his accomplices.   Apart from Joseph's
charge, there was no direct evidence of Horsey's guilt ;
but he was clearly responsible for the safe-keeping of his
prisoner and for the appointment of Charles Joseph as
his gaoler ; and the coroner's jury returned him, with
Joseph and Spalding, to stand their trial for murder at
the next assizes or in the king's bench.   One of the nine

[1] There was no law to meet the case ; hence its importance.
[2] Hall's 'Good Esture' is corrupted into 'Godsture' in Foxe ;
Gairdner (p. 30) has it rightly 'Good Easter,' but prints his correction
between inverted commas as though it were in his quotation.
[3] For a parallel case of an accused felon gaining sanctuary at Westminster, being removed to the Tower for examination, and then restored
to sanctuary, see *Acts of the Privy Council*, 1556-58, pp. 127-8, 135.   In
neither case should examination by king's counsel be transliterated into
examination before the king's council.
[4] Depositions in Hall, pp. 576-8 ; Foxe, iv. 192-5.   The asterisks,
by which Foxe's text discriminates between the six incriminating depositions and the two pieces of formal or exculpatory evidence, do not occur
in Hall.   The hour specified was about 7.15 a.m. ; on 4 Dec. (14 Dec. in
modern reckoning) the sun rose in London at 8 a.m. precisely.

depositions incorporated in the coroner's report was not shown to the jury until 13 February,[1] and it was probably not until towards the end of that month that the inquest was concluded. Horsey was then arrested and committed to the custody of archbishop Warham.

The ecclesiastical authorities were now in a worse predicament than ever; and Fitzjames, the bishop of London, wrote in great agitation to Wolsey, begging for an audience with him and with the king. He denounced the jury's finding as an untrue quest, asserted that Joseph's accusation had been extorted by 'pain and durance,'[2] and pleaded that London was so maliciously bent in favour of heresy that any twelve men in the city would condemn any clerk though he were as innocent as Abel.[3]

[1] That of Charles Joseph's servant, Julian Littell, who had found refuge in Bethlehem chapel and was examined there. The date is not given by Hall or Foxe, but is in the tract they used (*Engl. Hist. Rev.*, July 1915, p. 379, *n.* 14) and tends to substantiate the accuracy of that account. *

[2] The bishop was not present at Joseph's examination. Four of the coroner's jury, whose names are given 'with many others' who were on oath and were appointed to be present, testified that Joseph's evidence was given 'of his own free will and unconstrained.' Gairdner accepts the bishop's word against the jury; but this involves a charge against the constable of the Tower and the king's counsel who examined Joseph as well as against the coroner's jury. They were only present in the Tower as witnesses, and had no control over Joseph or his treatment.

[3] Hall, Foxe, and all subsequent historians give 'any clerk.' Miss Jeffries Davis (*E.H.R. loc. cit.*) has pointed out that the tract has 'my clerk.' I think, nevertheless, that Fitzjames probably wrote 'any' and that Hall is correcting a very easy misreading or misprint. For Fitzjames has just above called Horsey 'my chancellor'; and why should he reduce him to the lower and vaguer description of 'clerk' and focus upon his head the general hatred of clerical jurisdiction which provoked the petition to parliament against their exactions? The bishop's argument is not that he or his chancellor laboured under a unique and universal opprobrium, but that London citizens were so hostile to their clergy that no jury could be trusted to do justice to a clerk. His letter to Wolsey was not only a plea for Horsey but a protest against the renewal of the act of 1512 depriving the lower clergy of their immunity from lay tribunals. The unpopularity of the clergy, especially in cities, was a common characteristic of the time throughout western Europe (cf. *Cambridge Modern Hist.* ii. 147-8, 159-61). * At Tournai, wrote Sampson (afterwards bishop of Chichester) to Wolsey on 15 Dec. 1514, 'the temporality are much set against the spirituality' (*L.P.* i. 3545).

He besought Wolsey to have the matter examined by impartial counsel in the presence of the parties, and that, Horsey's innocence being thus established, the attorney-general should be instructed to confess the indictment false when the case came up in the king's bench. He made no plea for Horsey's two companions in misfortune ; probably they were not even in lower orders ; and if they were laymen, the bishop's argument based on the anti-clerical bias of juries would not apply. His demand was that the one clerk among the accused should be exempted from trial by jury on the ground that he was a clerk and would certainly be condemned. He would not, of course, be hanged in any case : if convicted in the king's bench, he would claim his benefit of clergy and be handed over to the bishop himself or returned to Warham's custody.[1] Still it would be ignominious for the bishop's chancellor or vicar-general to be noted as a *clericus convictus*. 'Help our infirmities, blessed father,' concluded Fitzjames to Wolsey, ' and we shall be bound to you for ever.'[2]

Wolsey would certainly be a friend in need. Polydore Vergil, writing from London on 3 March to cardinal Hadrian at Rome and referring to Hunne's case,[3] says the people were exclaiming, and would be raging, against the clergy, were not the king appeasing their fury. One concession Henry made to compassion : he signed [4] a bill

---

[1] Blackstone, *Commentaries*, ed. 1772, iv. 368-9.

[2] Hall, p. 579 ; Foxe, iv. 196.

[3] *L.P.* ii. 215, more fully in *E.H.R.* July 1915, p. 481, though the way it is printed there suggests that the words quoted are from bishop Foxe's letters written before 15 Feb. instead of from Polydore Vergil's on 3 March.

[4] Dr. Gairdner (*op. cit.* p. 40) remarks that 'notwithstanding the premature signature,' the lords ' seem to have agreed ' to the bill. But the signature was not premature : the crown had an interest in Hunne's property, and it has always been, and still is, the rule that, before parliament can legislate in such cases, the consent of the crown must be obtained. There were a dozen such ' signed bills ' or provisos introduced in the lords during that session ; and one of them, the duke of Norfolk's, was returned to him *propterea quod regia manu non erat signata*, and was only admitted a week later when he produced it with the king's signature (*Lords' Journals*, i. 26b, 36a, 37a, 38b, 39b, 40a, 41a ; the last of these columns has four

restoring to Hunne's infant children the property forfeited to the crown by the bishop of London's sentence.[1]
The bill passed the commons in March, came up to the
lords on the 28th, and was thrown out at its first reading
on 3 April as an infringement of the laws and liberties
of the church;[2] there were present eleven lords spiritual,
eleven temporal, and the prior of St. John's. A second
bill came up from the commons on 2 April; its title is
misprinted in the 'Lords' Journals,' but even the original
MS. does not make it clear.[3] According to the clerk of
the parliaments, it was a bill concerning an appeal of
homicide on behalf of Hunne's children. By an act of
Henry VII the widow or children could in person or by
proxy still bring an accusation or appeal of murder, within
a year and a day, irrespective of the action of the crown;[4]
but the bishop of London, speaking in the lords presumably on this bill, is alleged to have called it a bill 'to
make the jury that was charged upon the death of Hunne
true men,' and to have declared upon his conscience
that they were 'false perjured caitiffs.'[5] That he used

instances). And 'deliberetur' means 'discharged,' and not 'agreed':
the lords threw out the bill, as the journal states, in spite of Henry's
signature.

[1] It was a very proper provision of the Lollard statute of 1401 that the
ecclesiastical courts should receive no perquisites through the condemnation of heretics. Their property went to the king's almoner, who was
supposed to distribute it in alms (see *L.P.* i. new ed. 3499 [51]), and the
bishops were required to keep the crown informed of its acquisitions
by means of their 'significavits.' These 'significavits' have sometimes
been misinterpreted as if they were always requests for royal writs to
burn the heretics; but royal writs for that purpose had been rendered
superfluous by the Lollard acts (see below, pp. 42, 210-11).

[2] Lyndwood, *Provinciale*, p. 293; 'Sententia . . . super ipsa con-
fiscatione . . . fieri debet per judicem ecclesiasticum et non per judicem
saecularem. . . . Filii vero secundum jura canonica interesse non habent,
neque possunt in talibus bonis succedere.'

[3] *Lords' Journals*, i. 41; see my paper in *Trans. Roy. Hist. Soc.* 1914
(pp. 37-8).

[4] 3 Henry VII, c. 2; Sir T. Smith, *De Rep.*, ed. Alston, pp. 113-15.
Appeals for treason in parliament had been abolished by 1 Henry IV, c. 14
(cf. Vernon-Harcourt, *His Grace the Steward*, p. 369).

[5] Hall, p. 579. The bishop had been not infrequently absent during
the first half of the session, but from 15 March to the prorogation on

opprobrious words of the city is shown by his letter to Wolsey and is confirmed by an extant minute of the court of aldermen, recording the appointment on 17 April of a deputation consisting of the recorder, the common clerk, and four aldermen ' to speke wt the Bisshop of London for certeyn perillous and haynous wordes as ben sur-mysed be hym to be spoken of the hole body of the Citie touchyng heresy specified in a Copy of a letter supposed to be wreton by the seyd Bysshop.'[1]

This second bill got no further than a first reading; and the session ended two days later on 5 April amid a tumult of passion, to which fuel had been added by other episodes than the conflict between the bishop's court and the coroner's court over Hunne's death, and the disagreement between the two houses over the bills arising therefrom. To appreciate the roots of bitterness we have to remember, not only the discontent of the laity with extortion by ecclesiastics in the way of mortuaries, offerings, probate, and other fees,[2] and with a jurisdiction based on no kind

5 April he never missed a sitting. It would appear that he was the heart and soul of the clerical party; for Dean Colet's persecution at the bishop's hands, see *D.N.B.* xi. 325, and above, p. 31 *n.* 3. Fear was at the bottom of this extraordinary outburst. It rested with the court of king's bench to determine Horsey's guilt or innocence; but Fitzjames, besides assert-ing that Hunne had hanged himself, told the lords that, unless they took care, ' I dare not kepe myne awne house, for heretiques.' Against his ' false perjured caitiffs ' must be set More's opinion that they ' found the verdict as themselves thought in their own conscience to be truth ' (*Dyaloge*, p. 238); though he could not agree and thought it more likely that Hunne hanged himself than that he was hanged by Horsey. Here, again, we may agree with More; but what about Charles Joseph, who fled into sanctuary, produced a disgraceful but ineffective alibi, and himself accused Horsey?

[1] *E.H.R.* xxx. 478. The words are presumably ' the woordes,' and the ' copy of a letter ' is ' the copye,' etc., given in Hall, p. 579, who has omitted the polite ' surmysed ' and ' supposed ' of the city's record.

[2] In the Hist. MSS. Comm. report on the MSS. of Wells cathedral (1885), it is noted under 1503 that mortuaries have become more numerous (p. 284). A petition of the inhabitants of London (*L.P.* i. 3602), drafted apparently for this parliament, complains of the ' two pence demanded for the two tapers at mass; exorbitant fees for marriages, burials, month's minds; for burial in the choir; for churchings, for friends prayed for in the bede-roll, for howsel at Easter, for devotions on divers days, for

of consent in heresy, which was more widely interpreted
in the courts of the church than treason was in the courts
of the king,[1] but also the fact that a whole range of safeguards restricted the secular courts in dealing with murder,
without hampering those of the church in dealing with
heresy. For that crime there was no benefit of clergy,
no sanctuary, no *habeas corpus*, no trial by jury. The act
of Henry IV in 1401 had authorised any diocesan synod,
which meant the bishop and (or) his officials,[2] to condemn
heretics without appeal, and had made it part of the
routine duty of sheriffs to carry out the sentence without
recourse to chancery or the king's council for any special
warrant. There are plenty of extant writs for the arrest
of excommunicates during this period, but none for the
burning of heretics, because they were not needed.[3]
There was some doubt about Hunne's heresy and more
about his final contumacy; but there was none about his
anti-clerical action for præmunire,[4] and it seemed that

brotherhoods kept in the church, and for leases of church lands.' The
P.R.O. MS. has disappeared since Brewer calendared it. Even then it
was mutilated, possibly through being 'dashed,' i.e. formally torn in
parliament as a sign of rejection.

[1] There was no legal definition of heresy to correspond with the statutory definitions of treason. When in 1464 a friar was cited by John
(afterwards bishop) Alcock to appear before the archbishop of Canterbury
for preaching that Jesus Christ lived by begging alms, and the friar refused
to obey the citation on the ground that friars were exempt from episcopal
jurisdiction except in heresy, Alcock ' promptly brought an accusation of
heresy against him ' (Scofield, *Edward IV*, ii. 395).

[2] The lower clergy had no part in jurisdiction except as bishop's
officials; and, while they were summoned to grant taxes in provincial
synods, only the parties concerned were invited to share in judicial
proceedings (Dr. Armitage-Robinson in *Church Quarterly Rev.* Oct.
1915, pp. 129-30).

[3] See below, pp 210-11, and Giuseppi, *Guide to the P.R.O.* i. 11, 67,
308.

[4] Sir T. More suggests (*Dyaloge*, p. 239) that Hunne, being ' highe
mynded and sette on the glorie of a victorye, whiche he hoped to have
in the premunyre, wherof he much boasted, as they sayd, among his
familiar frendes, that he trusted to bee spoken of long after hys dayes, and
have his mater in the yeres and termes called Hunne's case ' (i.e. in the
year-books, ' livres des ans ' and ' des termes,' of the lawyers). But, while
Hunne may have commenced his suit with this idea, he would hardly
have hanged himself for the sake of advertisement; and the question at
issue was how he came by his death.

for any offence, which a bishop's court chose to regard
as heresy, men might be burnt without secular restraint.
Leo X had just reiterated the immunity of clerks from
temporal punishment; and an ecclesiastical majority in
the lords seemed to bar the path of remedial legislation.
The preliminaries of the reformation consisted mainly of
two efforts, one to limit clerical immunity for crime, and
the other to repeal the panic legislation against the
Lollards which made the clergy arbiters of laymen's lives.
Resistance to these reforms entailed a revolution.

Leo X probably had not the benefit of clergy act in
mind when he issued his bull of May 1514; but it was
assuredly in the minds of the upper house when it had
met on Monday, 5 February 1515, to consider, among
other things, the renewal of expiring laws. Public attention had been drawn to it by a famous sermon preached
at St. Paul's cross, probably on the preceding Sunday
morning.[1] The preachers were selected by the bishop
of London, whose mind was full of the bane of heresy
and of the benefit of clergy; and he had chosen as preacher
on this occasion Richard Kidderminster, abbot of Winchcombe. Kidderminster was not only present at this parliament, but held proxies for six other abbots as well,
though the only other proxies held by abbots were four
by the abbot of Westminster and one by the abbot of
Reading.[2] He had, moreover, on 4 February 1512, been
appointed one of the English delegates to the Lateran
council; there seems to be no proof that he actually
attended that or any subsequent session, but many years
later Henry VIII commended him to Clement VII as one
who had been to Rome and preached before the pope.[3]
He would in any case be interested in the proceedings of

[1] But possibly not till the following Sunday the 11th: the first
marked attendances in the lords are on Saturday 10 Feb. and the abbot
does not appear till Monday the 12th.

[2] *Lords' Journals*, i. 19-21.

[3] *L.P.* i. (new ed.) 1048, 1067, 1170 [1]; Maitland, *Roman Canon
Law*, pp. 87-9. Henry VIII's reference to the abbot's visit to Rome
(*L.P.* v. p. 154) probably refers to the year he spent there in 1500-1
(see *D.N.B.* s.v. ' Kedermyster ').

the council, and his discourse at St. Paul's was an uncompromising application to current English politics of Leo X's bull and the biblical text ' touch not mine anointed,'[1] which an anonymous supporter attributed to Jesus Christ. The act of 1512 was, he declared, plainly contrary to the law of God and the liberties of holy church ; and all the parties to its passing, both spiritual and temporal, had incurred ecclesiastical censures.[2] He denied the distinc-

[1] 1 Chronicles xvi. 22 ; Psalm cv. 15.

[2] Keilwey, *Reports*, ed. 1688, ff. 180-5. Brewer (*L.P.* ii. 1313) threw doubt upon the value of Keilwey's account on the grounds that he ' lived in Elizabeth's reign,' and that the report does not read like a law report. But, according to the *D.N.B.*, he was born in 1497, and certainly he had risen to be surveyor of the court of wards before the end of Henry VIII's reign (*L.P.* 1546 i. p. 567), and reader at the Inner Temple in 1547. There are many references to him and to his kin in the legal records and in the *L.P.* under a variety of spellings from Calloway to Keylwey. The reports, named after him, were selected—to supply lacunæ in the printed year-books—from his papers and published in 1602 by his friend and neighbour, Sir John Croke (1553-1620), recorder of London, speaker of the house of commons, and justice of the king's bench ; the edition here used was published in 1688 with a testimonial to their value from an imposing list of judges and other lawyers. Brewer does not explain whether his doubts refer to all the cases reported in Keilwey or only to the report of the Standish-Hunne case ; and the unlikeness to law reports apparently refers to nineteenth century reports. Gairdner accepts it for some purposes but not for others, and Maitland with some qualifications due to chronological obscurities which seem to disappear for the most part on closer investigation. The Trinity term, in which Keilwey reports five cases, is, indeed, inaccurately assigned at the beginning of the section to ' 8 Henry VIII,' but each folio is correctly headed ' 7 Henry VIII' ; while the preceding section is ' Pasch. 7 Henry VIII,' and the succeeding one ' Pasch. 7-8 Henry VIII,' the reason for this double date being that in 1516 Easter fell as early as 23 March, and Easter term began before the end (21 April) of 7 Henry VIII. The Standish-Hunne case came up in Easter term (25 April-21 May) or Trinity term, 13-27 June 1515, and was continued in Michaelmas term. Keilwey's report is inaccurate in combining the statement that Kidderminster's sermon was in time of parliament, 7 Henry VIII, with the statement that discussion arose between the charging of the coroner's jury and its verdict ; but they can be reconciled by correcting 7 to 6 Henry VIII, a regnal year which lasted until 22 April. The lawyer is more intent on law than on chronology ; year books and law reports are habitually weak in dates ; and the Keilwey report's account of the abbot's sermon is merely introductory to its report of the legal argument. For the dates of law terms see below, p. 110 *n.* 1.

tion drawn by that act between holy and lesser orders :
all orders, he said, were holy orders, and any clerk in any
order was immune from punishment by lay tribunals for
criminal offences. His doctrine was that it was for the
church and not for parliament or the crown to determine
the limits of criminal and coercive jurisdiction. Thus he
not only raised the fundamental question of the constitutional reformation, namely whether there was or was not
to be any modern sovereignty or modern state, but
also made it a doctrinal issue. The demands for reform
were ascribed to heresy ; and the interposition of the faith
turned criticism of abuses into attacks on the doctrine on
which the defenders based their defence.

The lords agreed with the abbot to the extent of not
renewing the act of 1512. On Saturday 10 February
the ' statute ' was read and dropped ; on that day there
were present sixteen spiritual, thirteen temporal lords,
and the prior of St. John's.[1] The temporal lords and the
commons concentrated their resentment on the abbot's
sermon ; and the king, at the special request of some
knights of the shire and substantial members of the house,
led it appears by Sir Robert Sheffield, speaker of the
offending parliament of 1512, chose from among his
spiritual counsel divers doctors, divines as well as canonists,
to argue the point with the spiritual counsel of the clergy
before the judges and temporal counsel of the king at
Blackfriars. Meanwhile the commons passed a bill to
renew the act which the lords had dropped. We have no
commons' journals till more than thirty years later, but
their bill went up to the lords on Saturday, 10 March.
It was given a first reading on the 12th but got no further ;[2]
and interest shifted to the scene at Blackfriars. There

---

[1] *Lords' Journals*, i. 21. Some of the temporal lords sided with the
spirituality ; Sir Robert Sheffield subsequently complained (*L.P.* ii. 3951),
that variance among the temporal lords during the 1515 parliament
caused their defeat. The division of opinion was roughly the same in
1529—the commons fairly unanimous, the temporal lords divided, and
the spiritual lords united in opposition.

[2] *Lords' Journals*, i. 31*b*, misprints the date *nono*, as it also misprints
the preceding Friday *septimo die*.

Dr. Henry Standish, warden of the mendicant friars of London and afterwards bishop of St. Asaph, who was one of the king's spiritual counsel, defended the act of 1512, quoting the *articuli cleri* of Edward II, a statute which, says bishop Stubbs, ' considered as a concordat between church and state, is not the least important document of the reign.' [1] Its words, indeed, have been put as a motto on the title-page of the most learned attempt to write the constitutional history of the church of England : [2] ' such things,' they run, ' as be thought necessary for the king and the commonwealth ought not to be said to be prejudicial to the liberty of the church.' [3] It was retorted that a papal decree, which all christians were bound to obey under pain of deadly sin, forbade the conventing of criminous clerks before a temporal judge as sin in itself (*peccatum in se*) ; [4] Standish replied that this decree had never been received in England. [5] After further dispute between the divines and the lawyers, the commons approached the bishops with a request that they would require the abbot to renounce his opinions, as publicly as he had pronounced them, at St. Paul's cross, to which they replied that they were bound to maintain those very opinions to the utmost of their power.

The prorogation of parliament and convocation from 5 April till November interrupted this fundamental argu-

[1] *Constitutional History*, ii. 356.

[2] Makower, *Const. Hist. of the Church of England*, Eng. trans. 1895.

[3] 9 Edward II, stat. 1, c. 8 ; *Statutes of the Realm*, i. 171.

[4] Keilwey's reporter was unable to specify this decree, though his 1688 editor refers to William of Newburgh, lib. ii. chap. xvi., and to Lyndwood. Very likely it was Leo X's bull of May 1514. On the other hand, it is Sixtus IV's similar bull of 15 May 1476 (Wilkins, *Concilia*, iii. 609), that we find transcribed into bishop Booth's Hereford register in 1521 (ii. 123).

[5] Standish had perhaps already maintained this doctrine in a sermon he preached before the king in March 1515 (see note of his ' reward ' in *L.P.* ii. 4692). Maitland remarks (*op. cit.* p. 87) that ' about the matter of fact he was in the right, for even in cases of felony our temporal courts had not allowed to the criminous clerk that full measure of immunity which the decretals claimed on his behalf.' But the crucial point was that the clergy denied the competence of temporal courts to receive or not to receive papal decrees, and did not claim it for themselves.

ment. But during the recess Standish maintained in public lectures the position he had defended as king's counsel; and the bishops thought that this publicity gave them a handle against the lecturer which they could not have used against the king's adviser. The archbishop's summons to convocation to re-assemble on 13 November referred to certain matters tending to the grave loss and prejudice of the church universal, which remained to be expedited and determined:[1] Horsey was still in ward and Standish was still at large. Standish was summoned before convocation, and four crucial questions were put to him: (1) can a secular court convent clergy before it? (2) are minor orders holy or not? (3) does a constitution ordained by pope and clergy bind a country whose use is to the contrary? (4) can a temporal ruler restrain a bishop? With Hunne's fate before his eyes Standish appealed to the king for protection. The bishops protested that they were not proceeding against him for

---

[1] Wilkins, *Concilia*, iii. 658, 'in grave damnum et praejudicium ecclesiae universalis . . . remaneant inexpedita et indeterminata.' Wilkins' dates are at first sight puzzling: on 31 May Warham dated his commission to Fitzjames, as dean of the province of Canterbury, to re-summon convocation, and on 26 July Fitzjames summoned it to meet on 13 Nov. the day after the re-assembling of parliament for its second session. Mayow, bishop of Hereford, obtained his licence to be absent on 28 Aug. and appointed his proxies on 1 Nov. (*Register*, i. 216-7). Now Fitzjames, re-capitulating Warham's commission, repeats, on 26 July 1515, its opening reference to 'inchoata nuper sancta synodo provinciali seu convocatione . . . in ecclesia cathedrali sancti Pauli vicesimo secundo Junii ult. praeteriti'; and this has been read as referring to 22 June 1515. But, clearly it refers to 22 June, 1514, when we know from other sources (see above, p. 34 *n.*) that convocation met. The singular feature is that this convocation not only sat in June and November, but voted two-tenths to the king, when there was no session of parliament (Wilkins, *loc. cit.*); however, on 9 April 1516 it met again and voted another two-tenths to the king, when parliament held no session (*L.P.* ii. 1749). Wilkins has nothing about the convocation of Feb.-April, to which the lords' journals record frequent adjournments. I am inclined to doubt the convocation of June 1515 and to divide its alleged proceedings in the Standish case between the spring and autumn convocations coincident with the two sessions of the parliament of 1515. Some of the extraordinary and composite meetings at Blackfriars and Baynard's castle, however, may have coincided with the Trinity term to which Keilwey's report appears to assign them.

anything he had said as king's counsel, but for his lectures long after at St. Paul's and elsewhere ; and in their turn prayed the king's aid in accordance with his coronation oath and in avoidance of the censures of the church. The temporal lords, the judges, and the commons made similar instance to the king to maintain his temporal jurisdiction in accordance with his coronation oath, and to protect Dr. Standish. Henry consulted the dean of his chapel, Dr. Veysey, afterwards bishop of Exeter, who took the same line.

An extraordinary assembly, consisting of the judges, the whole of the king's counsel, and some of the commons, then met at Blackfriars and considered Standish's answers to the charges of convocation. There was a curious discussion about the ' reception ' of papal decrees, in which it was pointed out that celibacy of the clergy was not received by eastern Christians, and that its validity in England was due to its reception there ; but the crucial question by what authority reception took place, if raised, was not reported. Eventually the judges declared that the clergy present at Standish's citation were guilty of præmunire. A fuller assembly of counsel and of both houses of parliament then met at Baynard's castle,[1] where Wolsey—now a cardinal—knelt before Henry and made a partial submission and defence of the clergy. He disclaimed on their behalf all idea of derogating from the prerogative of the crown, but declared that the conventing of clerks before temporal judges seemed to all the clergy contrary to the laws of God and to the liberties of the church, which they were bound by their oaths to maintain. Wherefore he begged the king to be content —to avoid the danger of ecclesiastical censures—that the matter be determined by the pope and his counsel at the court of Rome. Henry retorted that Standish and others had already answered Wolsey on all points. Foxe and Warham supported Wolsey ; chief-justice Fineux remarked that by their own laws the clergy could not determine questions of murder or felony, and asked what was

[1] Sir T. More refers to his presence, presumably at this meeting, at Baynard's castle (*Dyaloge*, p. 235*b*).

the point of committing the clergy to courts where they could not be tried for the crimes with which they were charged. Finally Henry declared that he would maintain the rights of his crown and his temporal jurisdiction as amply as any of his predecessors; the clergy, he said, disobeyed and interpreted their own laws at their pleasure. The discussion apparently ended with a plea from Warham for respite until the clergy could, at their own costs and charges, obtain a solution from Rome.

Meanwhile parliament had met for its second session on Monday, 12 November.[1] On Friday the 16th Warham, as chancellor, directed that bills, passed by the commons but not by the lords during the previous session, should be brought up for a conference on the following Monday between the two houses at their usual place for such purposes, the star chamber. What happened there we do not know, but next day two members, Sir Nicholas Vaux[2] and Sir Thomas Hussey, brought up from the commons a memorandum on these suspended measures including the benefit of clergy bill. On the 22nd the lords gave this memorandum a first reading, and on the 24th committed it to Sir John Ernley, the attorney-general. Frequent adjournments to attend convocation took up most of the rest of the session, and nothing more was heard of the memorandum. The commons grew impatient: they passed the benefit of clergy bill a second time and sent it up on 14 December to the lords who gave it a first reading on the 17th. On the 20th the commons sent up another bill, concerning heresies; it was read, with a note that the lords would consider it further. On the 21st convocation and on the 22nd parliament were dissolved.

Towards the end of its session convocation had been in a chastened frame of mind; and a document in the hand of Wolsey's secretary, Brian Tuke, dated 21 December, contains an apologia for its proceedings.[3] The

---

[1] *Lords' Journals*, i. 43-57.
[2] See *D.N.B.*; he ' shared Buckingham's hatred of Wolsey.'
[3] *L.P.* ii. 1314; its authenticity has, unlike the Keilwey report, not been disputed.

prelates had been alarmed by Henry's attitude and still more, perhaps, by a declaration of the judges—which seems irrelevant unless it referred to the rejection of ecclesiastical reforms by ecclesiastical votes in parliament —to the effect that the king could, if he chose, hold a parliament without summoning bishops or abbots, because they had no place in parliament by virtue of their spiritual character but solely by reason of the temporalities they held of the crown.[1] They admitted that they had convented Standish for heresy and had demanded from him an answer to their test question whether the exemption of clerks from lay jurisdiction was required by the law of God or not ; but they pleaded that a question neither affirmed nor denied,[2] and urged that there should be as much freedom of speech in convocation as in parliament, where ' divers speaketh divers and many things not only against men of the church and against laws of the church, but also sometimes against the king's laws, for the which neither the king nor the prelates of the church have punished them nor yet desireth any punishment for their so speaking.' Therefore they claimed that they might well contend that the act of 1512 was against the law of God. Finally they begged that the king would suffer them to ' keep ' their convocation as his predecessors had done.[3]

The immediate and practical outcome of this contro-

[1] Keilwey, f. 184b. This, of course, was the mediæval constitutional theory, which abbots had, often successfully, urged in order to escape the obligation to attend (see my Evolution of Parliament, pp. 64-5, 75-6, 99, 207-8).

[2] But their question demanded from Standish an answer which would involve him either in heresy or in recantation.

[3] The appearance in L.P. ii. 1131 of a list of peers attending parliament, but containing no abbots or priors suggested (see my Henry VIII, pp. 234-5) the idea of a serious threat to exclude them. But this list is simply a later copy of the lords' journal for the opening day of the second session (12 Nov. ; L.J. i. 43) with the abbots' and priors' names omitted. The names of the temporal peers correspond exactly, but the lords' journal marks as present eleven abbots and the priors of Coventry and of St. John's ; the copy was possibly made after the dissolution of the monasteries. The petition of convocation probably meant that it might be summoned with parliament as heretofore.

versy over high principles was a very mundane compromise. Convocation dropped the proceedings against
Standish and the attorney-general entered what we
should call a *nolle prosequi* against Horsey. But Horsey
had to pay £600 and to seek preferment in the provinces,[1]
while Standish was soon promoted to the bench of bishops.
Pace expressed himself to Wolsey, who had put forward
the claims of a rival candidate, as 'mortified' by this
promotion, but said it could not be helped, for the king
had often praised Standish's doctrine;[2] and, besides the
king's good graces, he enjoyed 'the favour of all the
courtiers for the singular assistance he has rendered
towards subverting the church of England.'[3]   That was
the clerical view of the events of 1515. Dr. John Taylor,
who was both clerk of the parliaments and prolocutor of
convocation—a coincidence which, he somewhat com-
placently remarks, has rarely occurred—noted his impression in identical terms at the end of his record of both
assemblies, reversing only the order in which he named
them : 'in this parliament and convocation there arose
the most dangerous discords between the clergy and the
secular power over the liberties of the church; and the
minister and the fomenter of all the trouble was a certain
friar-minor of the name of Standish.'[4]   Wolsey had indicated his view of the situation by urging on the king

---

[1] About £8000 in modern currency; Simon Fish, *Supplication of
Beggars*, in Foxe, iv. 663-4. Horsey's surrender of his London preferments and compensation elsewhere can be verified from Le Neve's *Fasti*,
ed. Hardy, and Hennessy's *Novum Repertorium ;* he became prebendary
of Chichester and Wells and canon residentiary of Exeter, besides retaining his prebends at Scamlesby (Lincoln) and Tottenham ; he died and
his will was proved in 1543 (Hennessy, p. xvii; Hooker, *Exeter*, ed.
W. J. Harte, pp. 212, 214; *L.P.* 1543 i. 474; Le Neve, i. 185, 266;
ii. 204, 350 ; iii. 322, 350, 395, 440). He was the bishop of London's
chancellor or vicar-general (*L.P.* i. 685 [25]), not chancellor of the diocese
(cf. Le Neve, ii. 360 ; Makower, *Const. Hist.* p. 308).

[2] He was preaching again at court in March 1516 (*L.P.* ii. 4692 ; cf.
Theiner, *Vetera Monumenta*, no. 931).

[3] *Ibid.* ii. 4074, 4083.

[4] *Lords' Journals*, i. 57 ; *L.P.* ii. 1312. Wilkins' *Concilia* has nothing
else about this convocation except the summons to its adjourned meeting
on 13 Nov. (iii. 658).

the prompt dissolution of parliament.[1] He indicated it still more forcibly a year or so later, by finding an opportunity of sending Sir Robert Sheffield to the Tower. There, it appears, he remained like Sir John Eliot until his death,[2] while on parliament was imposed its longest recess till the days of Charles I.[3]

[1] *L.P.* ii. 1223. Wolsey's letter to Henry is, as usual, undated, but he sends to the king for his correction the act of apparel which had a lengthy passage through parliament. Failing to get through in the first session, owing to its ' strictness and circumstance,' it was debated the whole of the second, was referred to three successive committees, read three times on 23 Nov., 10 Dec., and 13 Dec., then received another ' second ' reading on 17 Dec., another ' third ' on 18 Dec., was reported to the commons on the 19th, and read yet a ' fourth ' time on 20 Dec. For Wolsey's administration of it see below, pp. 70-1.

[2] On 17 July 1517, Thomas Allen writes to the earl of Shrewsbury, ' Sir Robert Sheffield is put into the Tower again for the complaint he made to the king of my lord cardinal ' (Lodge, *Illustrations*, i. 32-3). In the record of his repeated examinations before the council (? star chamber) on 6-13 Feb. 1518 (*L.P.* ii. 3951) this charge appears as ' contempt of the king and council,' and Sheffield's second imprisonment is attributed to felony in sheltering servants accused of manslaughter. He and his son Robert were compelled to enter into twenty-nine different recognisances, which were cancelled on 29 Nov. following, Sir Robert being described as deceased (*ibid.* ii. 4616). His successor as steward of the manor of Kyrton had been appointed on 1 Sept., and Sir Robert was certainly dead before 29 Oct. (*ibid.* 4410; *Cal. Inner Temple Records*, i. 43). The burden of debt, in which his son was involved, amounted in 1521 to £8333 6s. 8d., about £100,000 in modern values (*L.P.* iii. p. 427, cf. No. 102 [3] and pp. 1530, 1545). There is no record of Sheffield's release from the Tower, and he was buried in Austin Friars, London, often used for those who died in the Tower. He had been knighted by Henry VII after the battle of Stoke in 1487, was an active member of the Inner Temple, recorder of London till April 1508 (Bernard Andreas, *Annales*, pp. 114-15), and speaker of Henry VIII's second parliament which had two sessions in 1512 and one in the spring of 1514, and for which he was paid the three regular sums of £100 each (*L.P.* ii. 372 and p. 1459; the *D.N.B.* is in error in saying he was speaker in 1510). His grandson became baron Sheffield, and his descendants earls of Mulgrave and dukes of Buckingham and Normanby. For other references see *L.P.* vols. i.-iii. *passim; Cal. Patent Rolls*, Henry VII, vol. ii.; *Spanish Cal.* i. 447; Nicolas, *Testamenta Vet.* pp. 555-6; and below, p. 74.*

[3] This recess, from 21 Dec. 1515 to 15 April 1523, was most nearly approached by the second recess of Wolsey's rule, from 13 Aug. 1523 to 3 Nov. 1529, which was only brought to an end by Wolsey's fall. The next in length was between Henry VII's last parliament of Jan.-Feb.

But Wolsey was too much of a statesman to be content with a purely negative policy in the church. He realised the gravity of the problem of the criminous but unpunished clerk, the strength of the feeling which blind opposition to all reform aroused, and the general confusion which was threatening the mediæval system. He had his remedy, at least for the criminous clerk in minor orders;[1] and throughout the parliament of 1515 he had

1504 and Henry VIII's first, which met on 21 Jan. 1510. The demise of the crown may have lengthened this or shortened it; but in either case, the fact that each of Wolsey's two successive recesses was longer than any other is significant enough.

[1] He also made an attempt, for our knowledge of which we are indebted to Keilwey's *Reports* (ff. 190-2), to deal with the abuse of sanctuary. On 10 and 11 Nov. 1519 Henry VIII himself was brought to sit in the star chamber, along with ' the cardynall, dyvers doctors and canonists, bishops and others' to remedy abuses arising from the sanctuaries at Westminster and St. John's, Clerkenwell, and 'increasing from day to day' (Hall, *Chronicle*, p. 599, mentions that the king sat in the star chamber that month, though he does not report this ecclesiastical discussion, which was probably held in the inner star chamber with only counsel present). There was an interesting argument about the respective authority of popes and kings to create sanctuaries and the validity of charters and of prescription, and some important remarks were made about papal bulls and præmunire (see below, p. 252). On the question of sanctuary Wolsey reported that he and abbot Islip of Westminster had made a form of oath, by which sanctuary-men were to swear that they would commit neither treason nor felony in the sanctuary, nor commit it outside *sub spe redeundi;* but that sanctuary-men continually broke not only sanctuary but this oath, and thus committed perjury. The abbot, however, denied that such an oath could be administered, because it infringed the express words of the privilege granted to men when they took sanctuary, *quod nullus potest diminuere, infringere, nec mutare* their liberties under pain of excommunication. Wolsey appears to have been unable to rebut this argument, although he was now legate *a latere ;* but he did enough to lead his critics to include his reform of ' the abusions of sanctuaries and franchised places' among the things he had ' begun within the realm,' but had either ' not finished or else left as dangerous precedents' (*L.P.* iv. no. 2936, pp. 2558-9, 2562); cf. Polydore Vergil, pp. 656-7, and Skelton, *Works,* ii. 60 :—

> For all privileged places
> He brekes and defaces.
> All places of religion
> He hath them in derisyon.

Sanctuary for treason was not, however, abolished till 1534 (*L.P.* v. 259; vii. 1377; 1538 i. 668).

been secretly pressing the pope for a legatine commission.[1] He thought that the higher his dignity and the greater his powers, the more effective would be his handling of reform. But the legateship was delayed for another three years; and it was with great reluctance that Leo X agreed to Wolsey's demand for the suspension of clerical ordinations in England unless the candidate simultaneously took all orders up to sub-deacon. The prohibition was to last five years; Wolsey had wanted authority not only to make it, but to extend it if no scandal arose, and even to make it perpetual. To this the pope demurred, saying it was much against the laws of the church to grant an elastic faculty of that nature. Nor did he grant it to Wolsey, but himself made the prohibition by a bull of 12 February 1516.[2] This concession to the exceptional need, or exceptional demand, for reform in England met two of the points in Wolsey's policy: some reform was made, and what was more important, it was made by ecclesiastical and not by parliamentary authority.[3] But there was no guarantee for his larger scheme, by which minor orders and with them most of the criminous clerks would have been gradually but permanently abolished, part of the ground for the agitation of 1515 have been removed, and one of the details in the subsequent reformation have been forestalled.[4]

The outlines of Wolsey's ecclesiastical policy were now clear. He wanted as much practical reform of the church as would at least render possible the continuance of ecclesiastical autonomy. He wanted the church to be reformed by itself or rather by himself, but in no event by parlia-

---

[1] *L.P.* ii. 780, 966-8, 1281.

[2] Rymer, *Fœdera*, xiii. 532-3 ; *L.P.* ii. 1532.

[3] Wolsey had made the request to the pope, but cannot have received the answer, before he recommended the dissolution of parliament (see Silvester de Giglis' letters to Ammonius, Nov.-Dec. 1515 (*L.P.* ii. 1105, 1281).

[4] One of the items in Palsgrave's summary of Wolsey's proceedings runs : ' We have begun to send commandment to all ordinaries that they should give the lesser orders and subdeacon all at once ' (*L.P.* iv. p. 2555 ; cf. *ibid.* p. 2558). These minor orders were never formally abolished, but they are not recognised in the ordinal of Edward VI which was re-imposed in 1559 (see R. W. Dixon, *Hist. of the Church of England*, iii. 188-92).

ment. He had little hope, however, that a general reformation of the church universal by the papal curia or
even by a general council would keep pace with the
demand in England. The weary way in which the
Lateran council was even then dragging out the final
stages of its unprogressive existence, was sufficiently conclusive.[1] Wolsey therefore believed in devolution. But
he had little confidence in reform by the convocation of
a province, of which Warham was president and Fitzjames
was dean ; and York—in those days—was content to
wait upon the precedence of Canterbury.[2] For practical
purposes, therefore, devolution meant a papal delegation
to Wolsey himself. A cardinal's hat would prepare the
way for legatine powers, and Wolsey was bent on using
that emblem for all, and more than all, that it was worth.
His means of persuading the pope were a mixture of
threats and cajolery. In July 1515 he wrote to Rome
that he wanted a cardinal's hat mainly to make ' the king
fast to the pope ' therewith. But Henry, he said, ' who
has always been a friend to the pope,' wanted the hat
for Wolsey more than Wolsey wanted it for himself ; and
if Henry forsook the pope, Leo X would ' be in greater
danger on this day two year than ever was pope Julius.'
On 1 August he announced that he, ' no earthly man
helping thereto,' had prevailed upon Henry to consent
to the league with the papacy ' on the red hat being sent.'[3]
Francis I's descent into Italy in July and August [4] gave
point to Wolsey's words, and on 10 September, three
days before Marignano, Leo X was intelligent enough to
give Wolsey his coveted hat.

[1] It sat, with considerable interruptions, from May 1512 to March
1517 and discussed, among greater things, the reform of the calendar
which was not achieved till 1582. Its dissolution was followed on 31 Oct.
by the publication of Luther's xcv theses, and its failure to reform the
church helped to precipitate the ' reformation.'

[2] See below, p. 292.

[3] *L.P.* ii. 647-8, 763, 780. For the league, see Rawdon Brown, i.
114-15 ; Creighton, *Papacy*, v. 236-7 ; Ruthal's remark (above, p. 25)
referred to it ; and in *L.P.* ii. 1280, Wolsey's remark about inducing the
king to undertake ' this law for the church ' (which has long been a
puzzle) should read ' this league for the church.'

[4] See below, p. 111.

It arrived as parliament and convocation were beginning their second session in 1515; and Wolsey arranged an unparalleled display to impress the cantankerous mind of the city of London, and possibly to convey the impression that its public reception implied acquiescence in his authority. The protonotary of the papal court, who brought it, was stopped on his arrival in England in order that he might be more sumptuously arrayed in Wolsey's apparel for the occasion; a bishop and an earl were dispatched to Blackheath to meet it; the mayor and aldermen of London on horseback and the city gilds on foot were turned out to do reverence as it was borne through the city on Thursday, 15 November, to Westminster abbey; and there it reposed upon the high altar until the following Sunday.[1] On that day a ceremony, 'as I have not seen the like,' says Cavendish, 'unlesse it hath bin at the coronation of a mighty prince,' heralded the reign of Shakespeare's 'cardinal-king.' The archbishops of Canterbury, Armagh, and Dublin,[2] eight bishops, and eight abbots assisted in the service. Warham said mass, the bishop of Lincoln[3] read the epistle, and the bishop of Exeter[4] the gospel; and eighteen temporal lords, led by the dukes of Norfolk and Suffolk, conducted the cardinal back to his palace at York place.

The dean of St. Paul's had preached the sermon in

---

[1] *L.P.* ii. 1153; Cavendish, pp. 25-6; Hall, p. 583; Tyndale, *Practice of Prelates*, p. 339. The most circumstantial and authoritative account, however, comes from the ceremonial records in the heralds' office, supplied to Fiddes (*Collections*, pp. 251-3) by John Anstis, Garter king of arms. Wolsey had succeeded Ruthal as registrar of the order on 27 April 1510 (*L.P.* i. 442), and he was subsequently accused by Palsgrave of attempting to make himself its president (*ibid.* iv. pp. 2555, 2560; cf. iv. 3566).

[2] Cavendish remarks (p. 42) that Wolsey 'reigned' a long season. The archbishop of Armagh was Wolsey's friend John Kite, afterwards bishop of Carlisle; and the archbishop of Dublin was William, brother of Sir Richard Rokeby, comptroller of Wolsey's household (see *D.N.B.* for both).

[3] William Atwater, a Magdalen man, who succeeded Wolsey at Lincoln and died in 1521 (*D.N.B.*).

[4] Hugh Oldham (*D.N.B.*).

the abbey, and Colet was not a man to be overawed.[1]
His subject was humility : cardinals came, he reminded
Wolsey, like their master, not to be ministered unto, but
to minister ; 'whosoever,' he quoted, ' shall exalt himself shall be abased, and he that shall humble himself
shall be exalted.' Wolsey's humiliation was only to come
at the hands of others and after ' many summers in a sea
of glory ' ; but his exaltation instantly humbled Warham.
As the archbishop of Canterbury passed down the nave
of Westminster abbey, it was noted that no cross was
borne before him ; and none was ever borne again before
him in Wolsey's presence. Wolsey had two, one as cardinal, one as archbishop, wherever he went : [2] Warham
had not even one in his own province, when it was illum-
ined by Wolsey's superior lustre.

The eclipse included the high court of parliament.
Wolsey had written to Leo on 10 September that it was
necessary for him to have the habit and hat of a cardinal
to wear in the forthcoming session ; [3] and legend had it
that even the benches in the upper house were clothed
in red to reflect the cardinal's glory.[4] A fortnight later
Wolsey urged a dissolution, and parliament met but once
again in the fourteen years of his rule. On the day that

[1] Cf. his convocation sermon, preached on 6 Feb. 1511-12, from the
text ' Be ye not conformed to this world,' which was printed in 1512
and has been frequently reprinted (see above, p. 31 *n*. 3 ; Knight's *Life
of Colet*, 1823, pp. 239, 251 ; Burnet, ed. Pocock, iii. 89-95) ; the old
style date ' 1511 ' was retained until corrected in Seebohm's *Oxford
Reformers*, 1867, p. 156).

[2] See Anstis' disquisition on the etiquette of cardinals, archbishops,
and their crosses, communicated in a letter of 2 Jan. 1723 to Fiddes and
printed by him in his ' Wolsey ' (*Collections*, pp. 108-14 ; cf. W. Roy,
Rede me, ed. Arber, p. 56). Even before he was cardinal, Wolsey had
his cross borne before him in Warham's province (Cavendish, p. 25).

[3] *L.P.* ii. 894. He wanted it for the opening which he said was
to be *in crastino Animarum*, 3 Nov. ; and the same story was told to
Giustiniani (*Venetian Cal.* p. 270). In point of fact parliament had, on
5 April, been adjourned till 12 Nov. and convocation till the 13th (*Lords'
Journals*, i. 42 ; Wilkins, iii. 658). Even so, the hat arrived three days
too late for the opening.

[4] The lords' benches were covered with red say not only in 1529 and
onwards (*L.P.* v. 470 ; vii. 53 ; 1539, ii. 238) but also in Jan. 1514 (*ibid.* i.
2555).

the session ended Warham, who had advised the frequent summons of parliament,[1] surrendered the great seal, and Wolsey became the last cardinal lord chancellor of England.[2] The splendour that was Rome, incarnate in Wolsey's person and effulgent in his robes, had been invoked to pale the ineffectual fires of an insurgent house of commons and to quench the flying sparks of schism in the church.

[1] MS. Parliament roll 132 ; Lords' Journals, i. 10 ; L.P. i. 1046.
[2] The detailed official account of the transference of the great seal is printed from the close roll in Rymer, Fœdera, xiii. 529-30, with the oath Wolsey swore to ' do right to all manner people, poor and rich, after the laws of this realm . . . and purchase the king's profit in all that ye may.' He took this oath on 24 Dec. : the great seal had been transferred to him on the 22nd.

CHAPTER III.

LORD CHANCELLOR.

It has been said to be the mark of a good judge to amplify his jurisdiction. If this be a valid criterion, there can be no doubt that Wolsey was by far the greatest chancellor England ever had; for assuredly no other extended his jurisdiction so much as Wolsey, and not one of his successors has wielded more than a fraction of his authority. But we have to qualify and distinguish. Wolsey was not a lawyer: not only had he never practised in any court, ecclesiastical or lay, but he had not even graduated in canon or civil law at Oxford; and in the ordinary parlance of to-day unless one is a lawyer, one cannot be a judge. Even in the sixteenth century the chancellor was not reckoned among the judges. But others than judges still exercise judicial functions with, we may hope, some judicial capacity. We have our justices of the peace as well as our justices of the high court and our lords justices of the court of appeal; and it would be as great a mistake to assume that the lords justices, who often governed Ireland, and sometimes England, in the eighteenth century, were mainly concerned with judicial business as to think that the Book of Judges is an exclusively legal record. The Norman justiciars were apter at wielding the sword, than weighing the scales, of justice; and, whether or no order is heaven's first law, it was the first concern of a mediæval judge. Our lord-chief-justice is still supreme only in criminal jurisdiction; and we are not yet quite clear whether equity is or is not a part of the law.

In Wolsey's day equity was not so much part of the law as its principal rival; and justice was a bone of

59

contention between the two.[1] The reforms of Henry I and Henry II were a considerable step in the direction of civilisation because they tended to substitute the force of argument for the argument of force. But the substitution of trial by jury for trial by battle was for the most part simply a change in the form of contest. Force gave way to fraud, and as late as the end of the fifteenth century trial by jury was often a contest in perjury, which itself was hardly an offence at common law. But mediæval justice was adopting a humaner guise, partly owing to the renaissance of humaner letters ; and in that transformation the chancellor played a leading part, not as a lawyer but as—in a somewhat later phrase*—the keeper of the king's conscience. He was the king's principal agent for the purpose of mitigating the rigour and the rigidity of the common law, filling the growing gaps which the archaism of that ancient structure exhibited to the needs of a newer age and a subtler civilisation, and welding into a system and into a constitution heterogeneous practices and ideas derived from the law of God and the law of nature, common law and statute, canon law and civil law, the law merchant and the law martial, the custom of the country and the practice on the seas. The chaos, with which this conflict of laws menaced good government during the later middle ages, needed as strong a hand and as firm a treatment as the conflict of arms which came to a head in the wars of the roses. The

[1] See Christopher Saint-German, *Doctor and Student*, chap. xvi., 'What is Equity,' which was first published by Rastell in 1523 (see my article on Saint-German in *D.N.B.* l. 127). For an account of the following literary controversy, see Holdsworth, *Hist. of English Law*, i. 460, v. 266-72. Cf. *ibid.* ii. 595, 'the law of the chancery and the common law were different things,' and iv. p. 282, 'As the sixteenth century advanced [? approached], the chancery developed a definite set of principles, which were, in some cases, directly antagonistic to the principles of common law.' Saint-German's view that property was the law of man, and not of God or reason (*Doctor and Student*, ed. 1668, p. 130), may be compared with More's in the *Utopia*. Saint-German's original dialogues and additions thereto, together with a serjeant-at-law's criticism and Saint-German's rejoinder, are conveniently reprinted in a single volume, ed. Muchall, Cincinnati, 1886.

' new ' monarchy was a response to that need and an impersonation of the modern state : its agent in respect of the conflict of laws was the chancellor ; and the chancellor *par excellence* was Wolsey.

His office had originally little to do with law or justice : that was the business of the justiciar. The chancellor, in bishop Stubbs' apt but modern phrase, was secretary of state for all departments ;[1] and we find his modern counterpart in Metternich and Bismarck, the chancellors of imperial Austria and Germany, though we give their offices the somewhat artificial form of ' chancelleries ' to distinguish their political character from the legal and judicial aspect of our English chancery. The chancellor, then, controlled the issue of all the king's writings whatever their purpose, and his instrument was the great seal,[2] without the impression of which the king's commands lacked their full legal authority : James II thought he could stop a revolution by throwing it into the Thames. But, with the growing work of government and the specialisation of departments, the general control of the king's writs was undermined and sapped by the intervention, between the crown and the chancellor, of more particular and intimate agents of the king's will. Many of them were connected with the king's chamber, retired into the recesses of his court, and almost backed out of it, with his household and with his wardrobe.[3] Behind the chancellor there appears in court a lord controlling a smaller but a privy seal, and behind him a secretary controlling the royal signet. Then the single secretary becomes several ;[4] and, with the absorption of all the estates into the state, the king's secretaries become secretaries of state.

---

[1] Maitland has this phrase (*Lectures on Const. Hist.*, p. 202) with the qualification ' as we now might say ' ; but Stubbs had said it in his *Constitutional History*, ed. 1883, i. 381.*

[2] See Sir H. Maxwell-Lyte's *The Great Seal*, 1926. 'Writs' is too narrow a word ; treaties were included.

[3] See Professor Tout's *Place of Edward II in English History*, 1914, and *Chapters in Mediæval Administrative History*, vols. i. and ii. (1920), iii. and iv. (1928).

[4] See F. M. G. Evans (Mrs. Higham), *The Principal Secretary of State*, 1923.

It is one of the signs of our insularity that, just as our chancellor has mainly to do with domestic matters, so our home secretary remains the first of the principal secretaries of state, while elsewhere precedence is given to foreign affairs.[1]

Wolsey's development, or rather interruption, of this political process belongs to our next chapter: our concern with him here is to show how the chancellor, while retaining formal control, which might be made real, over the general instruments of government, developed a special function in connexion with law and justice. This came to him by gradual, though not specific, delegation from the council.[2] The expansion of the king's council into the king's parliaments, effected mainly by Edward I, had led to the fusion of individual into common petitions for redress and to the remedy of grievances by what are now called public acts of parliament.[3] But the mass of individual petitions, which flowed into the parliaments of the fourteenth century, was too vast and too various to be dealt with by the judicial skill, or in the time, at the disposal of a representative assembly; and long before the century ended, parliament had got into the habit of referring petitions, which were not matters of common interest, to the council to decide. This gave a parliamentary sanction to the jurisdiction of the council, and its decisions were often entered on the rolls of parliament, although they were not reached until long after parliament had dispersed; and in time the petitioners learnt to avoid the circumlocution of an address to parliament and sent their bills direct to the council. But the council itself, when busy at all in the fifteenth century, was often busy with other matters; and, while it retained an undisputed control over all complaints addressed to it, it in turn began to refer them more and more to individual

[1] In the United States of America the secretary for foreign affairs was and remains the only American secretary of state (my *Factors in American History*, 1925, p. 108 and n. 2).

[2] W. P. Baildon, *Select Cases in Chancery*, 1364-1471 (Selden Soc.), p. xlv.

[3] See my *Evolution of Parliament*, pp. 118-20.

members, chiefly to the chancellor who was still in theory at least the head of the king's secretariat.[1]

Now, quite inevitably, the great majority of these complaints referred to grievances for which the common-law courts provided no remedy, because their subject-matter did not come within the precise and stereotyped limits and formalism of the common law, and because, owing to their doctrine that the evasion of legal duties is not itself illegal, they were unable to enforce specific performance;[2] and it was left for chancery to devise new and more expeditious remedies for new wrongs. For then, as always, the growth of civilisation and education was accompanied by the growing pains of growing mis-demeanours, torts, and crimes. The more people learnt to read and write, the greater their means of forgery; the more general the use of trial by jury, the greater the scope for perjury; the more men met and talked, the greater the mass of libel and slander. The more they traded with one another, the more frequent and complex the cases of commercial fraud; and the more they went down to the sea in ships, the better it was for pirates. The more men borrowed, the greater the bulk of bank-ruptcy; the more they lent, the louder the outcry of usury; the more common the trust and the use, the more frequent the misfeasance and abuse. Men's wits, as James I remarked, 'increase so much by civilitie.'[3]

All this provided the council with fresh food for thought and jurisdiction. It dealt with it in different

[1] *Evolution of Parliament*, pp. 128-30; *Eng. Hist. Rev.* Oct. 1922, pp. 532, 539.

[2] Carey's *Reports in Chancery*, 1650, pp. 3-5, 10-11, 15-20, 23, 42, 50, 59, 64, 80; Saint-German, *Doctor and Student*, *passim*; Maitland, *Lectures*, pp. 225-6; Holdsworth, *Hist. Eng. Law*, i. 456-8; iv. 418-20, 446-7; v. 287-98. Nor could they deal with unincorporate bodies (*ibid.* v. 280). It was, however, claimed in James I's chancery decree, 18 July 1616, that ' the chancery doth supply the law, and not crosse it ' (Carey, *Reports*, p. 116, *recte* 132), a claim inconsistent with chancery's frequent injunctions unless ' the law ' means something wider than the common law. Cf. Saint-German, *Doctor and Student*, ed. 1668, pp. 52, 60.

[3] *Political Works*, ed. McIlwain, p. 312.

ways. Questions relating to life and, what was considered more important,[1] to property were matters for common law and were left to those courts; but actions tending but not extending to crime, such as riots, tumultuous assemblies, the maintenance of law-breakers, and the keeping of retainers who had no predisposition to peace, were taken by the council. Its usual chamber for all purposes in the fifteenth century was the star chamber; but during the Yorkist period we find references to an inner star chamber in which an inner ring of the council discussed its more confidential business: the outer star chamber, or court as it was afterwards called, was that in which the council exercised its public jurisdiction. Before the end of the century this outer star chamber was known as the chancellor's court; and here he always presided when present, although he had no such pre-eminence at the council-board in the inner room. These semi-criminal matters, dealt with in the star chamber, were such as the lords of the council could normally understand. But trusts and uses, commercial contracts, slander and libel, required more expert knowledge, a finer discrimination, and a humaner sense of justice.[2] With these cases most of the council abstained from interference; and in 1474 we find the chancellor sitting, or at least signing a decree, alone.[3] Chancery had become a court; and it was pre-eminently the court of the king's conscience with the chancellor as its only judge.

But the earliest instance we know of an appeal to the chancellor on the ground of 'reason and conscience,' which dates from about 1442, arises not only out of the

[1] Even in the American constitutional debates of 1789 Gouverneur Morris remarked, ' Life and liberty were generally said to be of more value than property. An accurate view of the matter would, nevertheless, prove that property was the main object of society ' (C. A. Beard, *The Supreme Court and the Constitution*, pp. 81, 92).

[2] Similarly, in 1603 lord chancellor Egerton reserved for chancery even a case about the possession of land ' to be discerned by books and deeds, of which the court was better able to judge than a jury of ploughmen ' (Carey, *Reports*, p. 23). Only the common-law courts were hampered by juries.

[3] Baildon, *Select Cases in Chancery* (Selden Soc.), p. xx.

defects of the common law but also out of those of the
spiritual courts.[1] The complainant's case is that he is
entitled to the benefit of a nuncupatory will, and that
he cannot have remedy against the executors ' in this
behalf by the law of holy church nor by the common law
of the land.' He therefore begs the chancellor for a
writ ' in the honour of God and on account of righteousness' summoning them to appear before him ' in the
king's chancery which is the court of conscience.' This
recourse to chancery in the name of conscience was facilitated by the fact that the chancellor was generally a
bishop and almost invariably a churchman.[2] Still, chancery was a king's court and not a court of the church;
and we cannot fathom that subtle and pervasive process,
by which the *regnum* conveyed to itself so much of the
jurisdiction, power, and wealth of the *sacerdotium* in the
sixteenth century, unless we take account of the conscience
with which episcopal chancellors invested and endowed
the king in chancery. If the state acquired a conscience,
there was no knowing what might not happen to the
church. Educated by the church and moved by its conscience, the state might even develop a religion of its own.

The part which Wolsey played in developing this
conscience of the king in chancery cannot at present be
ascertained with any exactitude. It depends upon no
less indefinite estimates of the work of his predecessors in
the fifteenth century. Archbishop Morton may have
done a good deal; but that would be rather an inference

[1] Baildon, *Select Cases in Chancery* (Selden Soc.), p. 121.
[2] Most of the lay holders of the great seal in the middle ages were
temporary caretakers, but Sir Robert Parving was chancellor for nearly
two years (1341-43), and Sir Robert Thorpe for fifteen months (1371-72).
Thorpe had been appointed in consequence of a petition from the commons
for lay chancellors, and his successor, Sir John Knyvet, held the office for
four years and a half (1372-77). Michael de la Pole held it from March
1383 till Oct. 1386, Thomas Beaufort for two years (1410-12), and
Richard Neville, earl of Salisbury, for nearly a year (1454-55). No other
layman was chancellor until the appointment of Sir T. More in Oct.
1529. English government under the Lancastrians and Yorkists was
far more ecclesiastically-minded than it had been under the first three
Edwards and Richard II.

from his general position in the counsels of Henry VII
than from any specific tradition or record of judicial
activity. He died in 1500 and his immediate successors
were transitory phantoms. Warham, who became a
fixture for thirteen years, had the stability of a conservative rather than the driving force of a legal reformer ;
he was overshadowed by Foxe in politics and seems to
have shown but little initiative in his own department
of chancery. That Wolsey's work in chancery was far
greater than any of these is not a mere inference from his
known capacity in other fields, but is proved by the
constant reference to it in contemporary sources, public
and private correspondence, chronicles, the accusations
of his enemies,[1] and the testimony of his friends. But
these sources are lacking in precision, and Wolsey himself
was much more occupied in doing things than in keeping
records of what he did or even formulating principles or
rules of practice. It is, however, a fair inference from
what we know, that extensions of jurisdiction, for which
we only find recorded rules under Wriothesley, Nicholas
Bacon, or even Ellesmere, owed their origin to the un-
rivalled impetus of Wolsey.

The difficulty about precision is not the absence of
records but the vastness of their bulk which has prevented even their surface from being more than scratched.
The published volumes of orders in chancery, acts of
chancery, reports, and select cases in chancery contain
practically nothing for the period of Wolsey's administration :[2] even the MS. reports of the masters in chancery

[1] Especially the charges of Lord Darcy and John Palsgrave, printed
with some fulness in *L.P.* iv. pp. 2548-62.

[2] G. W. Sanders' *Orders in Chancery*, 2 vols. 1845-46, contain practically nothing before the middle of the sixteenth century, partly because
the editor was concerned only with the law and relegates, for instance, to
an appendix Wolsey's detailed order regulating the household of the 14th
earl of Oxford, on the ground that its ' motives were of a private or
political nature ' and it ' did not therefore properly come into the body
of this work.'   Cecil Monro's *Acta Cancellariae* (2 parts, 1847) is similarly
limited ; and the earliest published *Reports in Chancery* are Sir George
Carey's (1650), which were collected, the title-page tells us, ' out of the
labours ' of the famous antiquary, William Lambarde, ' in anno 1601.'

do not begin till 1544.[1] On the other hand, the unpublished proceedings in chancery, beginning with a trickle in the fourteenth century, swell to over a hundred thousand documents by the time of Philip and Mary. The mere list of cases down to 1529, published by the P.R.O., fills five folio volumes, of which Wolsey's fourteen years as chancellor occupy one. But these documents generally contain no indication whatever of date, for

Lambarde died on 29 Aug. that year, and Carey has made certain additions of a later date (e.g. pp. 32-3) apart from the chancery decree of 1616, added by Carey's anonymous editor. Lambarde's notes extended apparently from Philip and Mary to 22 Elizabeth; but there are valuable references to cases going back to the fifteenth century. The title-page has 'Sir George Cary, one of the masters of requests,' but he is more familiar as Sir George Carew (see *D.N.B.* ix. 50); he died in 1612. Baildon's *Select Cases* (Selden Soc.) only come down to 1471.

[1] Giuseppi, *Guide to the Public Records*, 1923, i. 55. This date may be connected with Wriothesley's delegation on 17 Oct. 1544 of the hearing of cases in chancery to Sir Robert Southwell, master of the rolls, and three masters in chancery (*L.P.* 1544 ii. 527 [24]; there are three copies of this commission in the B.M., *ibid.* No. 447). Their reports are continuous from that date until the abolition of masters in chancery in 1852. Wolsey had made a similar delegation in 1529 (see below, pp. 88-9). His immediate and common-law successors, More and Audley, did not apparently venture to imitate him; but Wriothesley was a civilian rather than a common-lawyer, and ultimately lost the chancellorship owing to common-law opposition. The entry books of decrees and orders in chancery begin in the same year, 1544 (Giuseppi, i. 52). On the other hand, the decree rolls and their original docquets begin in 1534 when Thomas Cromwell became both the king's principal secretary and master of the rolls; and his recording habit, unlike Wolsey's, was inveterate and invincible.

The bills, petitions, and proceedings in chancery, as distinct from reports, orders, and decrees, go back to the fourteenth century; and the list of them (down to 1529) fills five volumes (each about 600 pages) in the P.R.O. Lists and Indexes xii., xvi., xx., xxix., and xxviii. Vol. i. extends from Richard II to 1467, vol. ii. 1467-85, vol. iii. 1485-1500, vol. iv. 1500-15, vol. v. 1515-29.

Apart from the proceedings in chancery are those now listed under 'court of requests,' though the earliest use Leadam could find of that phrase dates from 1529, and it did not become common until the middle of the century. Hall has no special name for the court, and it is not mentioned in Sir T. Smith's *De Republica* until the edition of 1589. Sir Julius Cæsar, himself a master of requests, writes in 1598 of its records being 'nowe disposed in xvii great volumes in folio' (Leadam, *C.R.*

lawyers are professionally as indifferent to chronology as historians are to points of law. It may sometimes be roughly inferred from the name of a chancellor, the identification of parties to the suit, and so forth : but no exact chronological order is possible ; and until that has been ascertained, we cannot know precisely where Wolsey's work begins and ends, nor apportion the credit or the responsibility for the development of chancery practice with regard to such things as trusts, wills, uses, perjury, forgery, libel, and the mass of detail or principle which came to constitute equity in England. In default of more precise information, which will not be available for many years, we have to rely on occasional cases in year-books rapidly petering out and law reports barely begun,[1]

p. xxiv). For its extant books of orders and decrees, see *ibid*. p. lii, and Giuseppi, *op. cit*. i. 270-1. Its proceedings for this period are listed in P.R.O. Lists and Indexes, xxi. (1906). Leadam has edited a volume of ' Select Cases ' for the Selden Soc. (1898), and there is a good deal of information among Cæsar's papers in B.M. Lansdowne MSS.

The early star chamber proceedings have been listed in P.R.O. Lists and Indexes, xiii. (1901). Its decrees and orders disappeared about the end of the seventeenth century. Two volumes of ' Select Cases ' have been edited by Leadam for the Selden Soc. (1904, 1911). The controversial literature on the subject, 1597-1641, is enormous, cf. bibliography in Scofield, *Star Chamber*, 1900, pp. iii-xxii. In addition to these materials there is a good deal of information scattered about, sometimes under misleading descriptions and often unindexed, throughout the printed *Letters and Papers* of Henry VIII.

[1] The reasons for the ' cessation ' of year-books in 1535 have been discussed by Maitland (e.g. in *English Law and the Renaissance*, pp. 78-82) and others for thirty years without any satisfactory solution to the question. The evidence for the fact itself is doubtful. We have, indeed, in print no year-books after 1535, but that may be due only to accident in the windfalls of MSS. which came into the hands of Richard Tottel, who monopolised their publication. He has none for the first eleven years of Henry VIII ; for only one year has he books for all four terms, and that is for 1535, which does not suggest a steady dwindling : his books for that one year fill sixty folio pages, more than all his material for the twelve preceding years. Maitland's ' dramatic appropriateness ' of the cessation ' at the moment when the Henrician Terror is at its height ' (*op. cit*. p. 77) is hardly consistent with the fulness of Tottel's books for that year and their absence for 1509-19 and 1527-33. Besides the four for 1535, the terms represented in Tottel are two each for 1520, 1521, 1523, and 1527, three for 1534, and one each for 1522 and 1526. The change,

on the more frequent but still fragmentary notices in the correspondence of the time, on the chroniclers, of whom none is of much value excepting Edward Hall, and on the many specific charges, brought against him in parliament and in the king's bench, or elaborated in the private studies of Wolsey's contemporary critics. These last have been idly dismissed as trivial or untrue; and this is unfortunate, not so much because confirmation for all of them can be found elsewhere, as because they undesignedly illustrate the extent and greatness of Wolsey's work as lord chancellor. Ignored by his later biographers, it impressed his contemporaries more favourably than the foreign policy which has in recent times been considered his principal title to fame.

It falls into three principal categories of administration, criminal or semi-criminal[1] jurisdiction, and civil jurisdiction. With regard to the first, we have to remember that chancery was still the chief administrative department of government, and Wolsey discharged duties

moreover, is not from legal publicity to silence, but from year-books to law reports; and it was probably due to increasing judicial activity and consequent growth of specialisation. The royal supremacy indirectly brought within the sphere of laymen a great deal of ecclesiastical and semi-ecclesiastical jurisdiction, which had hitherto not been 'reported' at all; and, while year-books had sought to deal with all of interest to the law student in a single series, law reports tend to specialise in particular courts (see Holdsworth's table, v. 358-63). The process would probably be clearer if the printed reports were more than a haphazard fraction of the reports that were written. As it is, only Keilwey, Broke, and Dyer's *Reports* contain much (and that is little) about Wolsey's period; and they, of course, deal almost exclusively with the common law which was not Wolsey's principal concern.

[1] 'Crime' had not in the sixteenth century acquired its modern specialised meaning, and was used of all sorts of minor offences. Even Blackstone writes of 'crimes and mis-demenors; which, properly speaking, are mere synonymous terms' (*Commentaries,* ed. 1773, iv. 5). One of the difficulties of the legal historian is that he feels constrained to use a modern terminology of periods to which it does not apply. As late as 1891 Gladstone had to point out that 'crime' meant different things in England and in Ireland, and that what was crime in one country was not in another; see *N.E.D.* Sin may be the law of nature, but crime is the creation of the state—and church which had its *crimen haereticae pravitatis.*

now assigned to the home secretary as well as others now discharged by the attorney-general and the public prosecutor. He was also the chief of the executive committee of the king's council, consisting of the chancellor, treasurer, and lord privy seal (the president of the council was added after Wolsey's fall), who, with some assessors, were charged with most of the council's administrative, as distinct from its advisory, functions, such as regulating prices, drafting proclamations, and maintaining law and order.[1] Under Wolsey this triumvirate became a dictatorship :[2] his colleagues were the old duke of Norfolk as treasurer, and bishop Ruthal, who succeeded Foxe as lord privy seal in 1516. Norfolk, content with having more than restored the fortunes of the Howards after their disaster at Bosworth, interfered very little, while Ruthal, as we have heard, sang treble to Wolsey's bass.[3]

The vigour and the minuteness of detail with which Wolsey exercised these powers, is exemplified in his regulation of the nation's apparel and diet : all classes were rigorously restricted to the garments and food suitable to the station in life to which it had pleased Providence to call them. Ostentation and gluttony were, indeed, among the vices of the age ; but the moral effect of Wolsey's measures was somewhat marred by the fact that, while burgesses were restricted to their appropriate

[1] They also, before Wolsey's time, drafted star chamber decrees, which were then submitted to, or at least subscribed by, other councillors (cf. Leadam, *Select Cases in the Star Chamber*, vol. ii. p. x).

[2] After charging Wolsey with taking the great seal from Warham, and the privy seal from Foxe, Palsgrave (*L.P.* iv. p. 2560) says, ' we found means to order the signet at our pleasure.' This was achieved, firstly by appointing his own secretaries—Ammonius, Vannes, Pace, Tuke, Gardiner —as secretaries to the king, and then, if they secured too much influence, keeping them continually employed in embassies abroad.

[3] Norfolk was succeeded in 1524 by his son, who already had grievances against Wolsey and gradually began to take a more independent line. When Ruthal died in 1523 he was succeeded by Sir Henry, lord Marney, in February ; but he died on 24 May following, and Tunstal became lord privy seal. He was Wolsey's vice-chancellor or master of the rolls, and Tyndale unfairly represents him as Wolsey's puppet ; but in 1527 he is mentioned as one of Wolsey's opponents in council (see below, p. 221). Still Tunstal had a habit of accommodating himself to circumstances.

homespun, the clergy were encouraged—for the first time, said Wolsey's critics [1]—to appear publicly in silk and velvet ; and, while three dishes a meal was the limit imposed on ordinary gentlemen and six on lords of parliament, lord mayors, or knights of the garter, nine was the number the cardinal fixed in the same proclamation for himself.[2]   He carried his cardinal's benefit with him to festive boards which he honoured with his presence : the number of dishes allowed, the proclamation concludes, is determined by the rank of the most distinguished guest.

These were the social amenities of Wolsey's administration.   With regard to his enforcement of law and order, John Palsgrave,[3] author of the first French grammar in English and tutor to Henry VIII's sister Mary and to his son, the duke of Richmond, puts an imaginary confession into Wolsey's mouth in these expressive terms : 'We have Towered, Fleeted, and put to the walls at Calais a great number of the noblemen of England, and many of them for light causes. . . . We have hanged, pressed, and banished more men since we were in authority than have suffered death by way of justice in all Christendom beside.' [4]   But this was the talk of the opposition on the eve of Wolsey's fall and of the general election in 1529.   When the duke of Buckingham could plead in 1521 that it was consistent neither with his dignity nor with his safety to travel from one country house to another with a bodyguard of less than three or four hundred armed men,[5] it seems clear that Henry VII's enactments against

---

[1] Palsgrave in *L.P.* iv. p. 2558. Cf. Hall, *Chron.* p. 583. Polydore Vergil (p. 633) charges Wolsey himself with being the first priest to wear *vestitum exteriorem sericum ;* cf. R. Hall's *Life of Fisher* (E.E.T.S. p. 34) and Sir T. More, *English Works*, p. 892. The 1515 'act of apparel,' which got passed with such difficulty on account of its 'strictness and circumstances' (see above, p. 52 *n.* 1), was undoubtedly Wolsey's work.

[2] Steele, *Proclamations*, i. No. 75.

[3] See *D.N.B.*, *Erasmi Epistolae*, ii. 412, 420, iii, 20, 46, 111, and below, pp. 91, 95, 226.

[4] *L.P.* iv. p. 2561 ; cf. Skelton, *Works*, ii. 40. The Tower was the prison for treason and other state offences ; the Fleet was used mainly by the star chamber. The Counter in Wood Street was the city prison for disorderly persons of both sexes.*

[5] *Ibid.* iii. 1070.

retainers had put legal aspirations on the statute-book rather than ensured their effective execution; and there was a case for Wolsey's vigorous administration of the law.

This was the principal use he made of the star chamber, of the fame of which he was the creator. We need not here repeat what is written elsewhere [1] with regard to the legend of Henry VII's modest act of 1487, nor retail the process of interpolation on the rolls of parliament and misconstruction of the statute, which produced in the later sixteenth and early seventeenth centuries the fiction that the star chamber, abolished by the Long parliament, had been the special creation of an act of parliament in 1487. The 'courte at Westminster commonly called the Starre chamber'—to quote an act of Elizabeth [2]— was the king's original council which had, for a century before 1487, sat at Westminster under the lord chancellor for the enforcing of law and order: it never sat anywhere else nor in vacation, and was always a public court sharply distinguished from the private counsellors of the king who went with him wherever he went, sat indifferently in both vacation and term, and dealt with policy rather than with law. In that private council, which was later on formulated into the privy council, the chancellor had, as he has to-day, no official pre-eminence, and its president is some one else. The star chamber, on the other hand, was his peculiar sphere; in addition to his emoluments as chancellor, he received a special £50 a quarter for sitting there; [3] and it was in this public court at Westminster that Wolsey impressed himself upon the public mind. To him more than to anyone else was due the fact that the suitor to that court saw, in the words of Sir Thomas Smith, 'as it were the majesty of the whole realm before him'; [4] that Coke could describe it as 'the most honourable court (our parliament excepted) that is in the Christian world'; and its seventeenth-century historian, William Hudson, could say 'it is well called *schola reipublicae.*' [5]

---

[1] *Eng. Hist. Rev.*, July and Oct. 1922 and Jan. 1923.

[2] 5 Elizabeth, c. 9.   [3] See below, p. 324 *n*. 4.

[4] *De Republica Anglorum*, ed. 1906, p. 116.

[5] Coke, *Fourth Institute*, ed. 1797, p. 65; Hudson, *Star Chamber* in Hargrave's *Collectanea Juridica*, 1792, ii. 22.

In that public school of the commonwealth, Wolsey taught what he called, in August, 1517, the ' new law of the star chamber.'[1] He meant a new dispensation of his own, new as distinct from the letter of the old testament of the common law, and instinct with the spirit of the new justice ; new also in the vigour with which it was to be administered. The last parliament of Henry VII had complained, notwithstanding the act of 1487, that, so far as punishment for giving liveries and keeping retainers went, little or nothing had been or was being done.[2] Wolsey's tone is very different : ' and for your realm,' he tells Henry VIII in his letter of August 1517, ' our Lord be thanked, it was never in such peace nor tranquillity ; for all this summer I have had neither of riot, felony, nor forcible entry, but that your laws be in every place indifferently ministered without leaning of any manner.' He wrote in similar terms to de Giglis at Rome six months later : ' the kingdom was never in greater harmony and repose, *tanti enim justitiam et aequitatem facio, absit jactantiae crimen*'.[3]

[1] *L.P.* ii. App. 38. Wolsey's phraseology in this letter varies somewhat. He first says : ' I trust the next term to learn them law of the star chamber,' i.e. to teach them law by means of, or in, the star chamber. But he continues : ' They be both learned in the temporal law, and I doubt not good example shall ensue to see them learn the new law of the star chamber.' The fact that one of these pupils was Thomas Piggott (*d.* 1520), justice of assize and king's serjeant-at-law (created 9 May 1513, *L.P.* i. 1948 [44]), and the other was Sir Andrew Windsor, keeper of the king's great wardrobe, indicates at once the nature of Wolsey's task and the high spirit in which he undertook it. Their offence was a fray between their servants ' for the seisin of a ward, whereto they both pretend titles ; in the which one man was slain ' ; and it shows how ' murder ' came into the star chamber. It did not necessarily mean anything worse than justifiable homicide : Hall (*Chron.* p. 771), in describing the siege of Vienna, speaks of the Turks losing over 80,000 men ' by murder, sickness, and cold.'

This letter of Wolsey's, which is undated, has been assigned to August 1518 ; its other contents, and particularly its references to the negotiations for the retrocession of Tournai, however, show that its date must be 1517 (see Giustiniani's dispatches in Brown, ii. 93, 99, 135, 137 ; and *Venetian Cal.* ii. nos. 913, 920, 987, 992).

[2] 19 Henry VII, c. 14 ; *Statutes of the Realm*, ii. 658.

[3] Martene and Durand, *Veterum Scriptorum . . . amplissima collectio*, 1724, iii. 1281 ; *L.P.* ii. 3973.

Wolsey sometimes protests too much. His encomium on the orderliness of the kingdom and the harmony of the council was intended to refute a rumour, which had reached his Roman correspondent, of a plot in England to drive him from power; it was a belated reflection of baronial discontent with Wolsey's enforcement of the statutes against retainers and enclosures, which was genuine enough; and the 'harmony' in the council was being illustrated by the imprisonment of some members, the expulsion of others, and the retirement of more. A bill attacking the king and council had been nailed on St. Paul's door; a correspondent of the lord steward (Shrewsbury) told him of 'great snarling at court' and referred mysteriously to things that were not to be written;[1] Sir Robert Sheffield was sent to the Tower on a charge of having said that, if the temporal lords had only been of one mind in the last parliament, they might have made Wolsey's body as red as his cardinal's hat;[2] and vulgar folk were being prosecuted for spreading reports that Wolsey had threatened to burn all common beggars in a barn, that Henry had refused without Warham's consent, and that Warham would only consent if Wolsey were put in the barn and burnt as well.[3] As for law and order, an agent in Durham wrote in June 1518, that six hundred complaints of spoils and robberies had been presented at sessions of the peace in the bishopric since the beginning of the reign, and that he expected as many more at the next assizes.[4] In the Welsh marches there were still worse reports,[5] and even in the peaceful atmosphere of Oxford university the vice-chancellor wrote on 16 April 1517 to Wolsey lamenting that one John Haynes had armed four turbulent Benedictines and three secular priests to murder one of the proctors.[6]

Yet, in spite of the heavy discount which has always

---

[1] Lodge, *Illustrations of British History*, i. 9, 13, 16, 22-3, 27-30. No. xii. in Lodge's documents should come between nos. ix. and x.; *L.P.* ii. 1832, 1836, 1861, 1959, 2018, 3487.

[2] See above, p. 52 *n.* 2.   [3] *L.P.* ii. 3852.

[4] *Ibid.* ii. p. 1321; cf. R. R. Reid, *Council in the North*, pp. 93-4.

[5] *L.P.* iii. App. 28.   [6] Fiddes, *Collections*, p. 36.

to be made from Wolsey's appreciation of his own services, there is substantial truth in his claim. Foxe, who was critical of Wolsey's foreign policy, and More, who was commenting adversely upon his autocracy in the council, agree in emphatic testimony to his early administration of law and order.[1] A somewhat less impartial critic, Nicholas West, the bishop of Ely, writes some two years later to Wolsey of 'the honourable renown and great fame of your grace in administration of indifferent justice, and keeping this noble realm in such good order, tranquillity, and peace as never was seen within the memory of man.'[2] The most convincing testimony because of its critical discrimination, is that of Hall: 'This yere'—he is writing of 1516, Wolsey's first year as chancellor [3]—' by the Cardinal were all men called to accompt that had the occupying of the kinges money in the warres or els where, not to euery mans contentacion; for some were found in arrerages, and some saued them selfes by pollecy and brybory and waxed ryche, and some innocents were punished. And for a truthe he so punished periurye with open punyshment and open papers werynge, that in his tyme it was less used.[4] He punyshed also lordes, knyghtes, and men of all sortes for ryottes, beryng,[5] and mayntenaunce in their countryes that the pooremen lyued quyetly, so that no man durst beare for feare of imprisonment, but he himselfe and his seruants were well punished therefor. The poore people perceaued that he punished the ryche, then they complayned without number, and brought many an honest man to trouble and vexacion. And when the Cardynall at the last had perceaued their untrue surmises and fayned complaintes for the most parte, he then waxed wery of herynge their causes.'

[1] L.P. ii. 1552, 1814.   [2] Ibid. iii. App. 21.
[3] Chronicle, ed. Ellis, 1811, p. 585.
[4] In 1528 Warham wrote of his clergy, ' now they valueth ther goods to the vttermoost for fear of perjurie ' (Ellis, iii, ii. 32).
[5] ' Bearing ' here seems to mean oppression or ' bearing down,' as against maintenance or ' bearing up.' Cf. Cavendish, Wolsey, p. 212, and the stock-exchange use of ' bear.' It is, however, often used as though it were identical with ' maintenance.'

Hall here touches upon the chief evils which Wolsey attempted to remedy by means of the star chamber, and each of his points could be illustrated at length from the 'Letters and Papers' of the reign. Perjury was an offence of which a common-law court took no cognisance unless it was committed in that particular court;[1] and with riot, oppression, and maintenance the common law had notoriously failed to cope. Henry VII is said to have fined the earl of Oxford £10,000 for keeping forbidden retainers; but it is not until Wolsey's chancellorship that we have any record of such vigorous execution of the law as began in 1516. In May of that year the earl of Northumberland was examined before the king in the star chamber and sent to the Fleet; the marquis of Dorset, the earl of Surrey, and lord Abergavenny were put out of the council chamber, and with lord Hastings, Sir Edward Guilford, Sir Richard Sacheverell and others were indicted in the king's bench and also called before the star chamber for keeping retainers.[2] Sir William Bulmer was sent to the Tower for preferring to serve the duke of Buckingham rather than the king, and the lord steward himself was warned to be on his guard.[3] An inquest of sheriffs was then begun, and Sir John Savage, who still held that office by feudal tenure in

[1] Cf. Holdsworth, *Hist. Eng. Law*, iii. 400; iv. 515-16; *L.P.* ii. 2579; iii. 763; iv. pp. 2557, 2562; Keilwey, *Reports*, f. 192; Carey's *Reports*, p. 63; Furnivall's *Ballads from MSS.* i. 163; and Skelton, *Works*, ii. 23, 61 :—

> All periuris he wolde oppresse ;
> And yet this gracelesse elfe,
> He is periured himselfe.

[2] Lodge, *Illustrations*, i. 13, 16, 23, 27-8; 'I heard,' writes T. Allen, 'my Lord Cardinal command them to bring in every man's name which was with them in their livery at the said time' [of Queen Margaret of Scotland's visit].

[3] *L.P.* ii. 2733; iii. p. 492. 'We have begun,' says Palsgrave (*ibid.* iv. p. 2557) 'to put in execution the penalty of the statute of retainer by the punishing of Sir Wm. Bulmer.' Hall (p. 599) says that besides Bulmer, proceedings were taken in the star chamber in Nov. 1519 against lord Ogle, lord [Edmund] Howard, Sir Matthew Browne, and John Scott of Camberwell. For Ogle's case see Leadam, *Star Chamber*, i. p. xix; Howard was the father of Henry VIII's fifth queen.

Worcestershire, was deprived after criminal proceedings.[1]
A list of fines levied in the star chamber in 1517-18 bears
testimony to the financial profits of Wolsey's vigour.[2]

But these offences relate only to one aspect of his
activity in the star chamber. Debarred from the use of
force, criminous laymen betook themselves to fraud, and
Wolsey pursued them in their flight from open to under-
hand illegality. The star chamber opened its doors and
stretched out its arms to comprehend forgery as well as
perjury, libel, and slander, and punished contempt in
whatever court it was committed.[3] It extended in other
directions by increasing its interference with municipal
finance and its regulation of prices and control of trade,
particularly trade in food-supplies, possibly on the ground
that scarcity led to disorder and was therefore one of
those conditions tending to crime, which called for the
preventive jurisdiction of the council in the star chamber.[4]
Enclosures, too, often led to riots and thus came into

[1] *L.P.* ii. 2579, 2684; Keilwey, *Reports*, ff. 192, 194-6. Wolsey may
have had something to do with the passing of the act of 1512 'against
the abuses of sheriffs' (3 Henry VIII, c. 12), under which these proceedings were apparently taken. Savage was succeeded as sheriff by Sir
W. Compton, who was given the office for life (*D.N.B.* xi. 453; P.R.O.
List of Sheriffs, 1898). In 1515 Wolsey took the unusual step of striking
out all the three names submitted for pricking for Northumberland and
substituted a candidate of his own (*L.P.* ii. 1120).

[2] *Ibid.* ii. App. 60.

[3] Leadam, *Select Cases in the Star Chamber*, vol. ii. pp. xxxiii-xxxiv.
Many instances will be found in the P.R.O. List (xiii.) of Star Chamber
proceedings. There is a catalogue of star chamber punishments for forgery, beginning in 1538, in B.M. Lansd. MS. 6, f. 33, and see Holdsworth, ii. 166; iv. 501. Palsgrave and Hall animadvert upon Wolsey's
frequent uses of the pillory as a punishment for these offences. Perjury,
when committed in chancery, was punished there; but when committed
in other courts was punished in the star chamber (C. Monro, *Acta Cancellariae*, 1847, p. 413). 'In the mediæval law of the lay courts,' says
Maitland (*Constit. Hist.* p. 508), 'we find no such headings as slander
and libel; these matters are dealt with as sins by the tribunals of the
church' (cf. Leadam, *Star Chamber*, i. p. xxix). But the ecclesiastical
courts could not give damages, and for other reasons the star chamber
gradually assumed a growing jurisdiction over defamation, slander, and
libel (Holdsworth, v. 205-10). The jurisdiction was patent enough in
Elizabeth's reign; I think there are a number of cases under Wolsey.

[4] *Ibid.* ii. pp. xxi-xxx, xliv, ci-cxii.

Wolsey's court. We cannot predicate absolute originality on Wolsey's part for any of these developments, but there is ample evidence of the multiplied activities of the star chamber under the stimulus he provided. One bundle is all that survives of its proceedings under Henry VII : there are sixteen bound volumes and eighteen bundles for the reign of Henry VIII ; and Wolsey's extension of the buildings, called the star chamber, in 1517 is evidence which points in the same direction : part of the funds were provided by fines which Wolsey, unconscious of his doom, levied for breaches of the statute of præmunire.[1] Everything, in fact, goes to show that Sir Thomas Smith was as right in ignoring the act of 1487 in his account of the star chamber as he was in the dominating part he ascribes to Wolsey. 'This court,' he says,[2] 'began long before, but tooke great augmentation and authoritie at that time that Cardinal Wolsey, Archbishop of York, was Chauncellor of Englande, who of some was thought to have first devised the Court, because that he after some intermission by negligence of time, augmented the authoritie of it, which was at that time marvellous necessary to doe, to represse the insolencie of the noble men and gentlemen of the north partes of Englande, who being farre from the king and the seat of justice made almost as it were an ordinarie warre among themselves, and made their force their Lawe, banding themselves with their tenaunts and servaunts to doe or revenge injurie one against another as they listed.'

This anti-feudal policy has been liberally coloured by a recent historian, who remarks[3] that ' the new policy of relying on the people against the aristocracy was the creation of Wolsey ; and the first eminent example of it was the fall of the most tyrannical magnate of his day, Edward Stafford, duke of Buckingham. To the support

---

[1] *L.P.* ii. 3741, p. 1476 ; see below, p. 194 *n.*

[2] *De Republica*, ed. Alston, p. 117.

[3] Leadam, *Select Cases in the Court of Requests*, Selden Soc. 1898 p. lv. Cf. the same writer in *Trans. Roy. Hist. Soc.* 1892, p. 189 ; *Law Quarterly Rev.*, 1893, p. 394 ; *Domesday of Inclosures*, 1897, i. 6-14 ; and *Star Chamber Cases*, ii. (1911) pp. lix-lxxvi.

of this policy the Court of Requests and the Star Chamber were alike invoked.' The anti-feudal is clearer than the popular motive : Pace, the new secretary, was discoursing in 1517 on the effect of illiteracy in excluding noblemen and gentlemen from employment in the state, and demonstrating how much better was learning than noble blood blended with ignorance of letters.[1] But Wolsey was certainly then at the height of his favour in public opinion. The Venetian ambassador, Giustiniani, who had had many diplomatic rubs with Wolsey during his four years in London, reported to the signory on his return that the cardinal had the reputation of being extremely just, that he favoured the people exceedingly, especially the poor, hearing their suits in person, seeking to dispatch them promptly, and requiring counsel to plead their causes without fee.[2]

---

[1] *L.P.* ii. 3765. Cf. Skelton on Wolsey's contempt for the nobility in ' Why come ye nat to courte ? ' (*Works*, ii. 36) :

> For all their noble blode
> He pluckes the hode,
> And shakes them by the eare,
> And brynges them in such feare ;
> He baytethe them lyke a bere,
> Lyke an oxe or a bull :
> Theyr wyttes, he saith, are dull ;
> He sayth they have no brayne
> Theyr astate to mayntayne ;
> And maketh them to bow theyr kne
> Before his maieste.

[2] Rawdon Brown, ii. 314 ; *Venetian Cal.* 1509-19, p. 560. The provision of legal assistance *gratis* for poor suitors was no novelty in Wolsey's time. It had received statutory sanction as early as 1423 (Leadam, *Star Chamber*, ii. pp. xxxiv, 319), and by 11 Henry VII, c. 12 (see my *Henry VII*, ii. 176-7 ; *Statutes of the Realm*, ii. 578) the chancellor and judges were, at their discretion, to see that the poor got their writs for nothing and also their counsel and attorneys. But everything depended upon the ' discretion ' in determining who was poor and deserving. In 1588 Sir C. Hatton, who like Wolsey, ' laboured to make good by equity and justice what he wanted in knowledge of the law ' (Camden), excluded from this benefit in chancery suitors who had 40s. a year in land or otherwise, and referred the poorer suitors to the court of requests ; this limit was raised in 1596 to £10 a year (Sanders, *Orders in Chancery*, 1845-46, i. 10, 61, 69 ; *Egerton Papers*, Camden Soc. pp. 125-6 ; Holdsworth, iv. 538).

Wolsey was at his best in the star chamber, despite
the browbeating of which Skelton complains;[1] and
there he did his most permanent work in building up the
unity of the state by convincing the greatest and most
refractory of feudal lords that in the government of England there could be only one will at one time, however
complex, imperfect, and even unjust might be the processes by which that will was formulated and expressed.
He gloried in that work and in the manifestation of his
authority. The young king himself was brought into
the star chamber on various occasions at the beginning of
Wolsey's presidency to grace his chancellor's court and
to advertise his power;[2] indeed, throughout his administration Wolsey was better provided with counsel in the
star chamber than was Henry at his court, and Henry
sometimes complained of the scanty attendance on him.[3]
The first outward and visible sign of his fall was his
desertion in the star chamber by the bevy of king's
counsel who were wont to attend him there.[4]

The star chamber was, however, only one of the main
spheres of Wolsey's energy as lord chancellor. We have
still to deal with the court of requests, the court of
chancery itself, and other indeterminate jurisdictions
which he exercised, or with which he interfered, either
as chancellor or as the mouthpiece of an otherwise in-
articulate council. These are often as difficult to differen-
tiate as it was, during the later stages of the great war, to

[1] See below, p. 314 n. 3.

[2] Cf. Lodge, *Illustr.* i. 13 : ' The morrow after Ascension day [1516]
... the king's grace sat in the star chamber '; Hall, p. 599 : ' The kyng
came from Lambith to Westminster hall and so to the starre chamber
... for diuerse riottes.' He also sat in the star chamber on 2 May 1516,
when judgment was given on the franchises of Newcastle-on-Tyne (Leadam,
Star Chamber, ii. pp. xi-xii), and on 10 and 11 Nov. 1519 (see above,
p. 53 n. 1).

[3] In May 1518 Henry had only Buckingham, Suffolk, Lovell, and
Marney with him at Woodstock when Wolsey requested Suffolk's attendance on him in London Henry objected that he had only these four
(*L.P.* ii. 4054, 4060, 4124, 4355). Cavendish (p. 41) remarks that Henry's
court was ' but slenderly furnished ' in Wolsey's absence.

[4] See below, p. 242.

determine the precise functions of the cabinet or the prime minister, and for a similar reason. The emergence of a dominating and pervading personality at a period of crisis and confusion further disturbed the routine of administration and the conservative habit of acquiescence; and Wolsey's combination of offices and multiplication of functions enabled him to deal out justice at discretion. For instance, on 29 June 1521, the earl of Arundel complains to Wolsey that his bailiff has been brought by one of the cardinal's servants before the court of chancery, the star chamber, and the court of common pleas on the same charge at the same time, and himself suggests a fourth method of procedure, namely, that Wolsey should commission some of his own counsel to try the case.[1] In 1527 a petitioner prays that his adversary may 'be restrained from proceeding until the 'murder' be inquired into before the court of chancery.'[2] We have seen how cases of homicide might come, in connexion with riots, into the star chamber; enclosure complaints might be heard there, in the court of requests, or at common law; and, indeed, the jurisdiction of the council and its derivative courts grew very largely out of a duplication of jurisdiction based on a distinction not of law but of persons.

For the mediæval England of laymen and clerks was merging into the modern England of rich and poor whom Disraeli called two nations, and a new economic cleavage was overriding the old juridical division of the legal system into courts christian and the courts of the king; and, the common law of the land being mostly the land law of the lords,[3] it was left to the new monarchy with its civil law, its jurisprudence, and its prerogative courts

---

[1] *L.P.* iii. 1374.

[2] *Ibid.* iv. 3212(1); cf. *ibid.* 3741, 3862. For other proceedings in chancery, see *ibid.* iii. 2441, 2557 (in which Cromwell is involved), 2587, 3681, 3692; iv. 5511, 6005.

[3] 'If we are to learn anything about the constitution it is necessary first and foremost that we should learn a good deal about the land law. ... Indeed, our whole constitutional law seems at times to be but an appendix to the law of real property ' (Maitland, *Lectures*, p. 538).

to redress the balance in the interests of the poor and to
accelerate the halting process by which the law for the
gentry slowly broadened down into the law for all.[1] Even
the duke of Suffolk appeals to Wolsey on behalf of a
servant on the ground that the poor man ' is not able to
sue against lord Dacre or abide the long process of the
law.'[2] The legal system was in a state of liquidation,
and Wolsey's spirit brooded over the waters, seeking
foundations for patriarchal and paternal justice. There
were few fixed categories to impede the scope of his wayward conscience, and he was not inclined to rule out from
the chancellor's jurisdiction any chance of doing what he
thought was right. He believed of himself, as Tyndale
believed of the king, that he received unto himself damnation if he lent his authority to the execution of judgments his conscience condemned ;[3] and poverty was a
plea on which the venue could be changed to chancery
in almost any case. Common pleas might be removed
from the cognisance of the common bench into the star
chamber, court of requests, or chancery on the ground
that the plaintiff was too poor or weak and the defendant
was too rich or strong for justice to be had at common
law ; and it has even been maintained that the whole
domestic case for the new monarchy grew out of the
incompetence of the common law to administer common
justice to the common man.[4]

The particular resort for ' poor men's complaints '

[1] Pollock and Maitland, ii. 436 ; Holdsworth, iii. 510 ; v. 34. It
was really these prerogative courts which brought serfs within the scope
and protection of national law. Apart from criminal pleas which the king
claimed for his bench, villeins had been left in the middle ages to the local
justice of manorial courts, and their legal emancipation was due to the
equity of chancery and not to the common law of the land. Pleas of
bondmen are the most characteristic cases in the court of requests ; its
members, too, were men of common sense rather than common lawyers,
and it was not till after Wolsey's time that its personnel became specialised
(Leadam, *Court of Requests*, pp. xvi, 42, 54).

[2] *L.P.* iii. 608.   [3] See below, p. 359.

[4] Added to this confusion was the fact that each court, including the
high court of parliament itself, was a liberty and claimed a general jurisdiction over its own members and their exemption from the jurisdiction
of other courts (cf. Carey, *Reports in Chancery*, pp. 68, 72, 96, 102).

ultimately, however, became the court of requests, and Wolsey's connexion with its evolution is of considerable interest and obscurity. We first hear of a special clerk of the council being detailed to deal with these requests under the Yorkists.[1] Then, about 1494, certain members of the council began to specialise in this class of business, of whom the chief was the lord privy seal, the chancellor having, it was thought, enough to do elsewhere; and Foxe's long tenure of that office from 1487 to 1516 established a seemingly permanent association of the lord privy seal with this court:[2] its instrument was the privy seal under which its writs went out. But its separate identity has certainly been ante-dated; its members were councillors who also sat frequently, if not as often, in the star chamber,[3] and the cases with which they were concerned might also be taken there.[4] At any rate, when Foxe surrendered the privy seal in May 1516, if not before, the distinction disappeared, and his successor, Ruthal, had little to do with the court.[5] Wolsey invaded or rather re-absorbed it for the moment into the star

[1] See *Eng. Hist. Rev.* July 1922, pp. 344-5; Davies, *York Records,* p. 289.

[2] In 1506 the 'six clerks' of chancery seem to have had a special concern with 'poor men's causes'; the archdeacon of Wells writes: 'The vi. clerks of the said chauncerye be so besyd in the king's causes that they can attend no pore men yet' (*Wells Cathedral MSS.,* Hist. MSS. Comm. p. 147). On the 'six clerks' see Giuseppi, *Guide,* i. 47.

[3] See the lists in B.M. Lansdowne MSS. 1, 83, 125, and 160, Harleian MSS. 297 and 305, Hargrave MS. 216, and Addit. MS. 4521. Some are printed in Leadam's *Court of Requests,* pp. cii-cx. Leadam (*ibid.* p. xi) says its members 'were furnished from the star chamber,' but this is not true of all.

[4] Its 'earliest suits are almost indistinguishable from those of the star chamber, except that the form of process sought is generally described as a writ of privy seal, and not a writ of *subpoena*' (P.R.O. Lists and Indexes, no. xxi, *Court of Requests,* vol. i. preface, p. iii). The 'poor men's causes' which Wolsey delegated to the court of requests in 1518 were already 'depending in the star chamber.'

[5] His name seldom appears in the above-mentioned lists. There are no extant orders and decrees, and apparently no cases for the first seven years of Henry's reign (Leadam, *op. cit.* p. lii). Wolsey's appearance in chancery clearly marked an epoch.

chamber, and himself, as Hall and the Venetian ambassador tell us, took infinite pains to administer speedy, free, and effective justice in poor men's causes. But his popular sympathies lost their illusion when he found that the poor were sometimes too plausible ; and, growing weary of his self-appointed task after a year or two,[1] he transferred the poor men's suits ' dependyng in the sterred chambre,' to four committees of counsel, one of which sat in the white hall,[2] another at the Rolls in the afternoon, a third in the treasurer's chamber near the star chamber, while a fourth met under the guidance of Stokesley, the king's almoner, a man, says Hall, who had more learning than discretion to be a judge.[3] These courts, continues Hall, were greatly haunted for a time, but at last people found increasing delays and few conclusions : even when their suits were ended, no one was bound at law by the result, and so they resorted again to the common law. Two courts, including Stokesley's, had disappeared before Wolsey's fall, leaving only those

---

[1] *L.P.* iii. 571, printed *in extenso* in Leadam, *Court of Requests*, pp. lxxxi-lxxxii. The order is undated ; Brewer places it at the end of 1519, Leadam (*op. cit.* p. xiii) prefers ' either 1516 or 1517.' But this is inconsistent with Leadam's identification (p. lxxxii) of the dean of St Paul's —one of the commissioners—with Pace, who did not succeed Colet as dean until 25 Oct. 1519. Probably Colet is meant, and this would explain Erasmus' statement, made in a letter written after Pace's visit to him at Brussels in May 1519 (*L.P.* iii. 251, 345 ; *Erasmi Epistolae*, ed. Allen, iii. 602), that Colet ' is of the council.' I have found no other reference to Colet being of Henry's counsel. According to Giustiniani (*L.P.* ii. 3885) Pace had ' the third place in the secret council ' in Jan. 1518 ; and as the king's busiest secretary he is out of place among the ' counsel ' to whom Wolsey delegated these ' poor men's causes.' The most probable date of the order is 1518 when Wolsey's appointment as legate *a latere* may have had something to do with his weariness of poor men's causes. Hall, in dealing with the general question under 1516, legitimately anticipates chronology, but implies that the delegation was some time later, when Wolsey had wearied of hearing the poor men's suits (p. 585).

[2] In *L.P.* iii. p. 129, is reference to a suit ' in the white hall before the dean of the chapel,' who then was Veysey, afterwards bishop of Exeter (*ibid.* no. 366).

[3] Erasmus (*Epistolae*, iii. 357), praises him as well skilled in three tongues and says he was royal chaplain in July 1518.

at the Rolls and in the white hall;[1] and they, too, merged into the latter which became the permanent seat and the usual name of the court of requests.[2]

Nevertheless, Wolsey's temporary association with poor men's causes provoked, or at least was followed by, one great effort at popular justice. On 28 May 1517 he appointed his famous commission to inquire into, and report to chancery upon, all enclosures of land made since 1485. A second commission was appointed in 1518 and on 12 July in that year he issued a decree ordering the destruction of all enclosures that had been returned as contrary to the statutes. Portions of the commissioners' reports fill two stout volumes of the publications of the Royal Historical Society, and their interpretation and even their arithmetic has been disputed among economic historians ever since. There is no less doubt about the effectiveness of Wolsey's executive decree. A considerable number of proceedings were taken by the crown in 1518, and some of Wolsey's friends felt the blow. Foxe was among the first: he admitted enclosing, pleaded ignorance of the law, and offered to pay whatever fine Wolsey might impose.[3] But of any persistent execution there is very little evidence. Wolsey revived his policy in 1526 in an effort to recover his lost popularity; he issued a third proclamation against enclosures on 14 July in that year and a number of offenders were subpœnaed to appear in chancery in November.[4] A fourth decree was issued

---

[1] This is an inference from the facts that Palsgrave in 1529 only mentions these two (*L.P.* iv. pp. 2557, 2562) and that no trace has been found of the others.

[2] For the local courts of requests at the Guildhall, Southwark, Westminster, Bristol, and Gloucester, see Leadam, pp. liii-liv. *

[3] *L.P.* ii. 4540; Leadam, *Domesday of Inclosures*, i. 57. An unexpected transcript of the questionnaire of the Hereford commission, with the answers, is printed in Booth's episcopal register (Canterbury and York Soc.) ii. 61-4; and interesting references to Wolsey's commission and to judges assembled ' in chancery ' on the question occur in Keilwey, ff. 197-8.

[4] Steele, *Proclamations*, i. nos. 103, 106-7, 111, 115; *L.P.* iv. 2650, 2660; cf. bishop Longland's letter to Wolsey on 30 Sept. 1528 (*L.P.* iv. 4796): after remarking that ' there was never thing done in England more for the commonweal than to redress these enormous decays of towns and making of enclosures,' he goes on, ' for if your Grace did, at the eyes,

on 15 February 1528, and in 1529 the sheriff of North-amptonshire actually destroyed some enclosures on a writ to that effect from chancery.[1] The enclosers, encouraged by Wolsey's declining power, declared that his action was illegal; and Sir Thomas More, on succeeding Wolsey as chancellor, reversed his policy and committed some of the leading opponents of the enclosures to the Fleet.[2]

Wolsey's policy had, in fact, been of doubtful legality, if law meant the common law. With considerable diffi-culty the parliament of 1515 had been induced to pass an act directing the restoration to tillage of land en-closed since 1485; but it had refused, or at least had omitted, to authorise any means for carrying out the act.[3] Wolsey on his own authority had attempted to supply the defect, thus reviving, it is said, 'the coercive jurisdiction of the council against which, during the fifteenth century, the house of commons had incessantly struggled.'[4] The same failure attended every other at-

---

see as I have now seen, your heart would mourn to see the towns, villages, hamlets, manor places, in ruin and decay, the people gone, the plough laid down, the living of many honest husbandmen in one man's hand, the breed of mannery by this means suppressed, few people there stirring, the commons in many places taken away from the poor people, whereby they are compelled to forsake their houses, and so wearied out that they wot not where to live, and so maketh their lamentation.' Cf. Sir E. Guilford to Wolsey on 24 June 1528 (*ibid*. iv. 4414). W. Roy (*Rede me*, pp. 99-100) characteristically lays the chief blame on the abbeys:

> Pouer cilly shepperds they gett
> Whome into their farmes they sett
> Lyvynge on mylke, whyg, and whey.

[1] Leadam, *Star Chamber*, ii. pp. lxx-lxxi. A similar order was given to the sheriff of Kent on 15 Feb. 1529 (*L.P.* iv. 5297). Pynson's payment for printing the proclamation is recorded, *ibid*. v. p. 311.

[2] Leadam, *Star Chamber*, ii. pp. lxxv-lxxvi.

[3] 7 Henry VIII, c. 1; *Lords' Journals*, i. 26a, 29b, 30a and b, 31a, 32a, 33a, 34a, 35b, 41b. The bill was read five times and twice committed to different committees in the lords before it was sent down to the commons. It re-appeared and is said to have been read a third time on 5 April (*ibid*. p. 42b). Even so, it was to expire at Christmas; and a new bill was intro-duced to prolong it in the autumn session on 23 Nov. (*ibid*. pp. 46b, 47b). On 3 Dec. *jam de novo reformata*, it was read a first and a second time, and on the 4th a third and passed (*ibid*. p. 50).

[4] Leadam, *op. cit*. ii. p. lxxi.

tempt to stop the enclosure movement throughout the century.[1] Wolsey exercised, in 1518 at least, far greater authority than any other of the social reformers or reactionaries ; and possibly he might have achieved better success had he really bent his energies to the task. But in the month in which he issued his first enclosure decree, he received a higher commission as legate *a latere* from Leo X, and set about the more exacting reformation of the church. The delegation of poor men's causes to sub-committees of the council, the delay and dwindling of their business, and the halting execution of Wolsey's decrees against enclosures were due, in part at least, to the fact that Wolsey's mind had turned to other matters.

Enclosures, however, were but one item in the business of the court of requests, and any suit in which a poor man was involved might come before it. Its early proceedings include testamentary,[2] matrimonial,[3] and maritime [4] causes, which seem to belong to the ecclesiastical or admiralty courts ; occasional cases of burglary and assault,[5] with which the common law usually dealt ; and trusts and uses, which commonly went to chancery.[6] 'The court of requests, like the star chamber, was simply one form of the activity of the council.' [7] So, indeed, was the court of chancery, except that its jurisdiction was exercised not by a committee of counsel but by one great counsellor, the chancellor, and his subordinate masters in chancery ; and in Wolsey's time the venue seems to have been decided by him and not by the council. The delegation of poor men's causes was decreed by him, and he retained in chancery whatever cases he thought fit. 'It is fairly clear that Wolsey made use of his position as the chief minister of the state to increase the jurisdiction of his court, and to settle it finally as a court of equity, quite distinct from the Council or the Star

---

[1] See R. H. Tawney, *The Agrarian Problem in the Sixteenth Century*, 1912.

[2] *P.R.O. Lists and Indexes*, no. xxi (1906), vol. i. pp. 57, 70, 110.

[3] *Ibid.* pp. 45, 73.　　　　[4] *Ibid.* pp. 88, 90, 93, 114.

[5] *Ibid.* pp. 94-5, 100.　　　[6] *Ibid.* pp. 68, 98.

[7] *Ibid.* preface, p. iii.

Chamber.'[1] Its proceedings are more voluminous if not
more multifarious than those of either the star chamber
or the court of requests ; but the business which, as
Maitland says,[2] 'made the fortune of chancery' was its
jurisdiction in trusts and uses. That had been developing for at least a century and a half, and the vast
and still undigested mass of material prohibits any more
precise conclusion than that Wolsey exerted a dominant
influence in the promotion of this jurisdiction which,
in the reaction against chancery after his fall, was transferred to common law.[3]

Despite Wolsey's unbounded activity, driving force,
and power of work, it was impossible for him to administer
in person the vast mass of the jurisdiction he had absorbed
or created ; and he was driven, more by necessity than
by inclination, to delegate the detail, reserving to himself
the supervision. Defying the opinion of common lawyers,
which became constitutional dogma in the mouth of Sir
Edward Coke, that the crown could not erect a court of
equity by royal commission,[4] Wolsey issued commissions
in all directions. Many of these commissions were temporary appointments of particular persons to deal with
individual cases, and were only of general importance by
reason of their cumulative effect in reducing recourse to
the regular courts of common law. Others were comprehensive delegations to hear causes in chancery like those
which, twenty years later, precipitated the fall of his

---

[1] Holdsworth, *Hist. of Eng. Law*, v. 219. This is, I think, highly probable, but one could wish that the evidence were more specific. Wolsey's
predecessors, particularly Morton, may have done more than we know ;
and, in view of the reaction against chancery after Wolsey's fall (see
below, pp. 346-7), something might be said for the postponement of the
' final ' settlement.

[2] Holdsworth, i. 454. I have not traced those particular words, but
in his brilliant essay on ' Trust and Corporation ' (*Collected Papers*, iii.
335) Maitland writes : ' If the Court of Chancery saved the Trust, the
Trust saved the Court of Chancery ' ; cf. his essay on ' The Unincorporate Body ' (*ibid.* iii. 275-84), and his *Lectures on Const. Hist.*
(pp. 224-6). W. Roy (*op. cit.* p. 87) denounces ' uses ' as the means by
which the friars, dedicate to poverty, acquired wealth.

[3] Holdsworth, i. 454-5 ; iv. 449-80 ; v. 304-6.

[4] Leadam, *Court of Requests*, p. xvi ; Coke, *Fourth Instit.*, 1797, p. 96 *f.*

successor, lord chancellor Wriothesley.[1]   Others, again,
like a commission in 1517 to determine cases of piracy
'without any form or process or recourse to common law'
prepared the way for the permanent delegation of this
growing sphere of the council's jurisdiction to separate
courts of admiralty.[2]   For the admiral was only converted
into a seaman by Henry VIII : throughout Henry VII's
reign the vice-admiral had been the clerk of the council,[3]
and even in 1519 he was a chancery lawyer,[4] recognising
as his chief, sometimes the lord high admiral and sometimes cardinal Wolsey.

This delegation to special admiralty courts is dated
'after 1524'; [5] and, if so, coincides with a wider development of the same policy expressed in the establishment in
1525 of the princess Mary's council in the marches of
Wales and the duke of Richmond's council in the North.
'In the time of Cardinal Wolsey,' writes William Hudson
in his 'Treatise on the Star Chamber,'[6] 'who entertained
all suits and of all kinds, when the court was overlayed,
he sent, at a clap, all causes arising within the marches to
those courts ; all within the duke of Richmond's limitts
he remitted to his council . . . . some to the duchy ; some
to his commissioners of oyer and terminer ; and those
within the county palatine of Chester to the marches of

---

[1] Wolsey only issued this on 11 June 1529 on the eve of his fall (Rymer,
xiv. 299 ; L.P. iv. 5666).

[2] L.P. ii. 3520 ; iii. 375 ; iv. 5770.

[3] Robert Rydon. See Eng. Hist. Rev., July 1922, pp. 345-7, and
references there given.   Rydon died in 1509 and one of the most singular
errors in the L.P. is the assignment to 6 June 1531 (v. 286) of a letter
to him about the star chamber from Warham, who had ceased to be
chancellor in 1515.

[4] Christopher Middylton, L.P. iii. 272 ; cf. Leadam, Court of Requests,
p. cxviii n. 113.   But Sir Henry Sherborne, who appears as vice-admiral
in July 1523 (ibid. iii. 3160), was a seaman who took an active part in
naval operations under the lord high admiral against Scotland (ibid.
nos. 2960, 3071, 3116, 3139).   The famous Coligny, admiral of France,
was no more a seaman than the thirteenth earl of Oxford ; even to-day
we only expect seamanship of 'sea' lords of the admiralty.

[5] R. G. Marsden, Select Cases in the Admiralty, Selden Soc., pp. lvi-
lvii.

[6] In Collectanea Juridica, 1792, ii. 116 ; cf. R. R. Reid, Council in the
North, p. 107 n. 65

Wales.' 'Than,' writes Sir Thomas Elyot to Cromwell, 'was there newly delegate from the sterre chamber all maters of the North partes and Wales as ye know; those few that remayned were for the more parte the complaynts of beggars.'[1] The process was carried further in 1528 : 'my lord legate,' runs a council minute of 13 February in that year,[2] 'openly yn the sterre chambre declaryd what order was taken touching [[3]] causes dependyng as well yn thys cort as yn all oder the kynges cortes to be herd and determyned by the justices of assises yn their circute and oder to theim associate, and yn case anye of the parties be obstinate to certifie to my legate. And such maters as can not be determyned yn their circute the said justices and oder to determyn it if they can at their owne houses.'

The council of the north illustrates some interesting points in Wolsey's domestic policy.[4] All Tudors were nervous of feudal influence, especially in the north, and entrusted its government whenever possible to ecclesiastics; archbishops of York nd bishops of Durham were presidents under both the Henries. Wolsey felt all and more than all of this Tudor jealousy; but before 1525 he had debarred himself from their expedient by securing for himself a simultaneous tenure of the great seal, the archbishopric of York, and the bishopric of Durham. He satisfied Henry and himself by appointing as president Henry's natural son, then eight years old, and giving the boy a council consisting almost exclusively of Wolsey's own servants.[5] At the head of it as chancellor was the

[1] Ellis, *Original Letters*, 1, ii. 115.

[2] *Bulletin Inst. Hist. Research*, v. 26. It is calendared, with other council proceedings, in *L.P.* iv. 3926, under the misleading heading 'indictments in Kent.'

[3] The word is almost illegible; *L.P.* gives 'minite'; cf. Wolsey's use of 'demynute,' *ibid*. iii. 1713 (1), and iv. 6555, and *N.E.D.* s.v. 'diminute.'

[4] On 14 August 1523 Surrey had reported from Newcastle, 'the judges think that it is ten times more necessary to have a council here than in the marches of Wales ' (*L.P.* iii. 3240).

[5] Rachel R. Reid, *The King's Council in the North*, 1921, pp. 101-4. It is curious that Wolsey did not include John Kite, who had been arch-

dean of York, with two archdeacons of the diocese as his principal coadjutors. Delegation was to be stripped of its inconveniences by the faithfulness of its repetition, and the president in the north was a close copy of the monarch in the south—a figurehead moved by ecclesiastical hands. Henry VIII, however, was a better screen than the duke of Richmond, who was still being subjected to what the tutor of James VI subsequently described as ' dorsal discipline ' ; [1] and secular insurgence against ecclesiastical domination declared itself against the copy at York before it was made manifest against the original at Westminster. Some months before Wolsey's overthrow Darcy and Palsgrave were inditing their secret charges against the cardinal.[2] Darcy was wholly of the north and Palsgrave had been a member of the council at York ; [3] and More's attack on Wolsey when parliament met on 3 November encouraged a more formal petition from Darcy denouncing the rule of spiritual men ' not meet to govern us nor other temporal men within any shire or country within this your realm.' Nor, he suggested, was it consistent with canon law, civil law, or ' the laudable custom of this your realm that any spiritual men should sit upon murders, felonies, and other divers causes ' necessarily entrusted to the council of the north [4]; and further, he remarked, ' as great clerks do report, there is no manner of state within this your realm that hath more need of reformation nor to be put under good government than the spiritual men, which we do remit to the noble approved wisdom

---

bishop of Armagh and was now bishop of Carlisle ; he was one of Wolsey's particular friends (see *D.N.B.*) but his gifts seem to have been diplomatic rather than administrative.

[1] *L.P.* iv. 3135 ; his ribald attendants taught him to say to his reverend tutor, Dr. Richard Croke, ' *si tu me verberes, ego te verberabo* ' ; cf. Palsgrave's letters to the boy's father and mother and Sir T. More (*ibid.* iv. 5806-7).

[2] See below, pp. 226-8.   [3] R. R. Reid, *op. cit.* p. 104.

[4] Cf. Skelton, ii. 62 :

> Nor no law canonicall
> Shall let the preest pontificall
> To sit *in causa sanguinis.*

of your grace and the lords of your council.'[1] 'The North,' says Dr. Reid, ' was catholic, but it was as anti-clerical as the South.'[2]

The chief defect in these delegations was that the conciliar and common law courts at Westminster retained not merely an appellate but a concurrent and original jurisdiction; and a litigant, cast in the provinces, could re-commence the whole case again in the capital : [3] even the partial relief which Wolsey obtained was always being neutralised by the insistence of his supervision and his inveterate tendency to amplify his jurisdiction. He put forward an apparently novel claim that the chancellor's jurisdiction extended to the king's dominions overseas, and one of the signs of Henry's growing independence was an interesting passage of arms in which he convinced Wolsey that his patronage did not stretch to Calais.[4] He had taken the great seal more than once with him to Calais and once at least beyond the king's dominions to Bruges. On that occasion he also took with him Tunstal, master of the rolls; and Henry had to ask that the latter might return, bringing the great seal with him, in order that Michaelmas term might be kept to the satisfaction of his subjects and the replenishing of his revenue.[5] In July 1527, on his mission to France, Wolsey was accused of having taken with him ' all the seals of the realm so

[1] R. R. Reid, *op. cit.* pp. 110-12. Her reference in notes 79 and 81, to *L.P.* x. 186 (38), should be to *L.P.* 1537 ii. 186 (38). Darcy's complaint is placed in *L.P.* under 1537 because it was seized among his papers in that year, but it dates from 1529. His exordium refers to petitioners being encouraged by the king's words and also by ' your chancellor and speaker of your high court of parliament,' which can only refer to More's speech on opening parliament on 3 Nov. 1529 (see below, p. 256).

[2] Mary's council in the marches of Wales had a bishop, Veysey of Exeter, as its president and an ecclesiastic, James Denton, as chancellor (he had been chancellor to Mary, ex-queen of France) ; but the lay element, which included the future speaker and lord-chancellor Audley and the future earl of Bedford, was far stronger than in the north (see list in Madden, *Privy Purse Expenses of the Princess Mary,* p. xxxix).

[3] For instances see *L.P.* iv. 1872, 1887, 2201.

[4] *Ibid.* iv. 3304.

[5] *Ibid.* iii. 1650, 1675, 1680, 1762.

that none act could pass from the king until Wolsey came home again.'[1]

Wolsey not only clung to the great seal as though it were his personal property, but disregarded the limitations which custom and regulation had placed upon its unfettered use. The main distinction was between writs *de cursu* or 'of course,' to which he could affix it *ex officio* without any special warrant from the council, and others which required such authorisation.[2] But this distinction had been almost obliterated by Wolsey's monopoly of the counsel given to the king; and control of the council, combined with that of the great seal, made him absolute master of the jurisdictions which derived therefrom, including the star chamber, courts of requests, chancery, and admiralty. When, for instance, his officers were indicted in an oyer and terminer at York for taking a shilling in the pound for probate of wills, he removed the indictments by *certiorari* into chancery and rebuked the judge, Sir Anthony Fitzherbert.[3] To this comprehensive authority which had rarely, if ever, been exercised before Wolsey added another which in itself gives him a unique position in English history. As legate *a latere* of three successive popes, and by virtue of the increasing powers which he extorted from their growing

[1] *L.P.* iv. p. 2560. He had taken it to Calais, where Taylor, now master of the rolls, kept it while Wolsey went on to Amiens (Cavendish, pp. 83-4). In Sept. Taylor was commanded by the king 'straitly, without any delay' to seal and deliver certain letters patent. But, writes the master to Wolsey, 'remembering your commandment that I should advertise you before I sealed any other thing than common writs, and that [John] Croke, who should make the said writs, is with you, I have sent him the warrant. I desire to know your pleasure, when I receive the said letters patents, whether I shall seal them or not '—in spite of the king's strait commands (*ibid.* iv. 3410).

[2] There is an interesting account of the clerk of the hanaper for fifteen months at the beginning of Henry's reign in *L.P.* i. (new ed.) 579; it deals with 12,740 'original' writs, and 16,592 'judicial' writs at 6d. each, besides various kinds of charters, etc. A valuable study on 'The administrative work of the lord chancellor in the early seventeenth century' was written by Miss Jean Wilson for her Ph.D. degree in the university of London in 1927 (Institute of Historical Research).

[3] Herbert, *Henry VIII*, p. 299; *L.P.* iv. pp. 2551, 2554, 2713.

necessities, he controlled the whole system of ecclesiastical jurisdiction in both the provinces of Canterbury and York; and this combination of secular and ecclesiastical jurisdiction in the same hand facilitated a conveyance which profoundly affected the whole of English legal and constitutional history.

Maitland has referred to the time when chancery began to 'steal' from the ecclesiastical courts,[1] and there is hardly an item in their jurisdiction of which Wolsey did not convey samples at least into chancery. But 'stealing' is an opprobrious word: conveyance the wise call it. Was Wolsey, as papal legate, likely to restrain himself as chancellor from dealing, in chancery or in the star chamber, with testaments and legacies, forgery and libel, perjury and slander, the pulpit, the printing press, and even heresy? Could he distinguish clearly between conscience in his legatine court and conscience in a court of equity, or even between the faith or trust of the chancery lawyer and that of the canonist and the theologian? Would he, as chancellor, restrain the usurpations of his equity or 'absolute' jurisdiction upon the ordinary or common law side of chancery? In his chancery and star chamber proceedings we meet with cases of all kinds even including heresy;[2] and it is hardly an exaggeration to say that any case, save those preserved for the common law by certain laws of the king, could be taken in any court which Wolsey called his own. The chancellor never defined his sphere of legitimate aspiration; he trespassed and caused others to trespass wherever conscience found a loophole in the ruinous walls of mediæval common law.

That the conveyance of jurisdiction was into chancery, and not out of it into the ecclesiastical courts, was due to those laws of the king, commonly called the præmunire statutes[3]; and even with those the cardinal came into

---

[1] *English Law and the Renaissance*, p. 86.

[2] *P.R.O. Lists and Indexes*, xiii. 14.

[3] Coke, of course, subsequently contended that conveyance into chancery, the admiralty courts, and, indeed, anywhere out of the common-law courts was præmunire (3rd *Institute*, chapter 54).

conflict at last.   So long as the conveyance was confined to
the various courts, which derived their practice and their
principles from the Roman civil or Roman canon law
and their authority from the council or from Wolsey as
papal legate, there was comparative acquiescence because
there was no clear ground on which to base resistance.
But the common law was, in Maitland's now familiar
phrase, tough law ; and its exponents on the bench were
not unprepared to resist the attack which Wolsey had in
mind.   He did a good deal in detail by means of injunctions staying the execution of what the judges called law
in the interests of what Wolsey called equity.[1]   The
common law certainly needed reform ; and on 16 November 1528 Richard Rich, himself a common lawyer and
afterwards lord chancellor, wrote to Wolsey referring to
the 'abuses daily used' and offering to suggest remedies,
knowing, he said, Wolsey's great zeal for the reform of the
common law and his inability to attend to it because he
was too busy.[2]   But that he had 'begun to reform the
abusions of the temporal law' is repeatedly stated in
Palsgrave's articles, though it is not quite clear whether
the gravamen of that charge lies in his only having begun
reform or in having begun it at all.[3]

Like the reformation of the church, the reform of the
common law had to wait for a day which for Wolsey
never came.   But had it dawned on him, it is easy to see
the shape his reform would have taken.   It would have
borne a strong resemblance to that 'reception' of the
Roman law which Reginald Pole, afterwards himself a
cardinal, was but little later urging.   The civil law of the
Romans was, he remarked, 'now the commyn law almost
of al chrystyan natyons' ; and all the reform that was

[1] *L.P.* iv. p. 2552 : 'Item, injunctions . . . ,' and *ibid.* p. 2557 :
'We have begun to take up all the great matters in suit in England, to
determine between the parties after our discretion' (cf. p. 2562).

[2] *Ibid.* iv. 4937.

[3] 'Every of these enterprises,' writes Palsgrave, 'were great, and the
least of them to our commonwealth much expedient, especially the
executing of our laws made in our own day, but that they have been
begun and brought to no good end' (*ibid.* iv. p. 2562).

needed was to receive that civil law as the common law of England.[1] Wolsey stated his own ideals in words he addressed to Mr. Justice Shelley after his fall:[2] 'I counsaile you and all other judges and learned men of his [the king's] counsaile to put no more into his heade than lawe tnat may stande with conscience; for when ye tell him this is the lawe, it were well done ye should tell him also that although *this* be the lawe, yet *this* is conscience; for lawe without conscience is not mete to be given to a king by his counsell to be ministered by him ne by any of his ministers: for every counsellor to a king ought to have a respect to conscience before the rigour of the lawe. . . . The kinge ought for his royall dignity and prerogative to mitigate the rigour of the lawe, where conscience hath the more force; and therefore in his princely place he hath constituted a chauncellor to order for him the same. And therefore the courte of the chauncery hath been commonly called the courte of conscience; because it hath jurisdiction to command the lawe in every case to desist from the execution of the rigour of the same, whereas conscience hath most effect.'

Admirable sentiments! But, retorted the common-law critic of Saint-German, 'in what uncertainty shall the king's subjects be when they shall be put from the law of the realm, and be compelled to be ordered by the discretion and conscience of one man.' For 'divers men, divers conscience,' and the chancellor 'regarding no law, but trusting to his own wit and wisdom giveth judgement as it pleaseth himself.' As for the question whether 'law will stand with conscience,' 'the law of the realm is a sufficient rule to order you and your conscience'.[3]

So also complained the common lawyers, who accused lord chancellor Wriothesley in 1547 of doing what Wolsey had done on a larger scale, 'These commen

[1] *Starkey's England* (Early English Text Soc.), pp. 192-4.
[2] Cavendish, pp. 188-9.
[3] Saint-German, *Doctor and Student*, ed. Muchall, pp. 346-9. The identity of Wolsey's and his critic's phraseology tends to substantiate Cavendish's report of Wolsey's words.

HENRY VIII WITH THOMAS WOLSEY

(Reproduced by gracious permission of H.M. the King)

WILLIAM WARHAM

Lawes of this realme, partly by injunctions aswel before verdictes, jugementes, and execucions as after, and partly by writtes of *sub pena* issuing owte of the Kinges courte of chauncery, hath not been only stayed of their directe course, but also many times altrid and violated by reason of decrees made in the saide Courte of chauncery, moste grounded upon the lawe civile and apon matter depending in the conscience and discrecion of the hearers thereof, who, being civilians and nat lerned in the comen lawes, setting aside the saide commen lawes, determine the waighty causes of this realme according either to the saide Lawe Civile or to their owne conscience; which Lawe Civile is to the subjectes of this realme unknowne, and they nat bounden ne inheritable to the same lawe, and which Jugementes and Decrees grownded apon conscience ar nat grownded ne made apon any rule certaine or lawe written.' [1]

Selden digested the substance of these complaints into his aphorism about equity accommodating itself to the conscience of him that is chancellor and being as erratic a standard of law as the measure of a chancellor's foot.[2] *Hoc volo, sic jubeo*, quotes Giustiniani as Wolsey's characteristic attitude;[3] ' his own opinion was his law ' echoes Catherine of Aragon in Shakespeare's ' Henry VIII.' Bacon adopted Wolsey's words with regard to the chancellor's conscience, qualifying them with the condition that he must be a good man;[4] and Wolsey held as firmly as Bacon that equity stood to common law in the relation

[1] *Acts of the Privy Council*, 1547-50, pp. 49-58; my *England under Protector Somerset*, 1900, pp. 31-2. Wriothesley's commission of 1547 was only a repetition of one he had made out on 17 Oct. 1544 soon after succeeding Audley as lord-chancellor; see my life of Wriothesley in *D.N.B.*; Rymer, xv. 58; and *L.P.* 1544 ii. 447, 527 [24]. His offence in 1547 was that he acted without warrant from the council; the judges, to whom the question was referred, would not, like Coke, have ventured to declare such a commission illegal if so authorised.

[2] Holdsworth, *Hist. Eng. Law*, i. 467-9.

[3] *Venetian Cal.* 1509-19 p. 500; cf. Skelton, *Works*, i. 274, 278, ii. 16-17, 36-37, 39, 60, and below, p. 370.

[4] *Works*, ed. Spedding, vi. 85. Cf. James I's speech in the star chamber, 1616 (*Political Works*, ed. M'Ilwain, p. 334).

of the absolute to the ordinary power of a king.[1] He may even have inoculated his royal pupil with a conscience, superior to the canon law of marriage, and prepared the way for the reformation. *Ubi spiritus Dei, ibi libertas*, quoted Henry VIII to the Lutheran princes of Germany in 1534; 'though the law of every man's private conscience be but a private court, yet it is the highest and supreme court for judgement or justice.'[2] We must not say that Wolsey was the only begetter of that particular conscience, still less of the private judgement of protestant theology, or of the 'higher law' of anarchist morality. Yet 'divers men, divers conscience'; and we do not see very deep into the cross-currents of the turbulent stream of Tudor history if we discern no connexion between Wolsey's conscience of the chancellor and Henry's reformation of the church.

[1] This idea had been expressed by the chancellor, bishop Stillington, in 1468 (Holdsworth, ii. 596; cf. Giuseppi, *Guide to P.R.O.* i. 46).

[2] Henry's instructions to Paget sent to the princes of Germany, Jan. 1534, in *L.P.* vii. p. 58; Burnet, *Reformation*, ed. Pocock, vi. 94.

CHAPTER IV.

PRIME MINISTER.

It requires some apology or at least some explanation to justify the application to Wolsey of the familiar phrase 'prime minister.' Henry VIII, it is true, asks him in the pages of Shakespeare 'have I not made you the prime man of the state?' and there could be no doubt or ambiguity about the answer. But the very familiarity of the modern title involves confusion when it is applied to Tudor times.[1] Wolsey's position was in many respects greater than that of a prime minister to-day; in some it was less; in few did it coincide. He had no cabinet to safeguard or control him; he hardly had colleagues whom he need consult; and he was not responsible to parliament. The house of commons indeed on one occasion refused to grant more than part of the supply he demanded, but he proceeded to obtain it by other means; and no thought of parliament entered his head in connexion with his foreign policy, dissolution of monasteries, or the multifarious legal and other reforms he had in mind. From the day that he received the great seal parliament met but once during his fourteen years of power.

But independence in politics commonly involves a lack of organised support. Wolsey's independence of colleagues meant that they were not bound to him. They were not really colleagues at all:[2] they were bound

---

[1] The phrase occurs in Polydore Vergil's *Historia*, 1555, p. 621; but it is applied to Sir William Compton, and *primus minister in regis cubiculo* is simply the Latin for 'chief gentleman of the bedchamber.'

[2] At the trial of Secretary Davison in the star-chamber in 1587 Sir Walter Mildmay, chancellor of the exchequer, said: 'No prince's

by their several oaths to the king to keep secret his counsel but reveal the crimes of each other ; and it was counsel who concerted Wolsey's fall, indicted him in the king's bench, and produced accusations against him in parliament. They, like Wolsey, ministered to the king but not to one another. There was thus no cabinet to sustain the cardinal ; and support from the lords and the house of commons he always disdained. He lacked the indispensable basis of a modern prime minister's power, the confidence of colleagues, themselves relying upon the confidence of parliament and ultimately of the country. Wolsey could dispense with these modern necessities, but he could not dispense with the confidence of his sovereign, and his dependence on Henry VIII was absolute. How far the king himself was dependent upon any sort of public opinion is a question which almost defies analysis. Foreign ambassadors at his court were apt to point—sometimes in scorn, sometimes in hope—to the English as a peculiar people given to revolution and violent methods of dealing with crowned heads,[1] and

counsellors are farther made privy to any thing than it pleaseth the prince ; and often-times what is imparted to one that is concealed from another with great cause ' (Nicolas, *Life of Davison*, pp. 339-40 ; for his authorities see *ibid*. p. 302).

[1] Charles V's ambassador, Eustace Chapuys, in Nov. 1530 remarked to Henry VIII that ' he would find it no easy matter to control his people, naturally prone to revolution ' (*Spanish Cal.* 1529-30, p. 801) ; and later on he frequently referred to the ease with which Richard III had been removed (see my *Henry VIII*, pp. 304-6). Wolsey was quite nervous enough on the subject, and warned Henry VIII in 1518 against ' great personages ' resorting to court, meaning apparently Buckingham and Suffolk (*L.P.* ii. 4057) : Buckingham was sent to the scaffold on the eve of Henry's second war with France, just as De la Pole had been in 1513 after being kept in the Tower seven years. The university of Paris somewhat maladroitly and inaccurately congratulated Henry's sister Mary on her marriage in 1514 to the king of a country where, since the days of Clovis, kings had been privileged never to be killed in battle, slain by their own people, or chased out of their own country (*L.P.* i. 3478). In 1528 Charles V's chancellor, Gattinara, declared that Henry would be driven out of his realm by his own subjects (*ibid*. iv. 4909 ; cf. nos. 5177, 5501). Charles V's agent at Rome in Nov. 1530 said the English ' mutiny for any occasion or for none, and often lay their hands upon their kings ' (*L.P.* iv. 6739).

to argue that there was no real difficulty in treating Henry VIII like Edward II, Richard II, Henry VI, and Richard III, or at least in rebelling against him with as much success as against Stephen, John, Henry III, and Edward IV. From one project at any rate, the war against Charles V in 1528, Wolsey had to desist not so much because Henry VIII disapproved as because the English people, by the unanimous witness of contemporaries, would have none of it.

Wolsey, however, had good reason to think that, so long as he enjoyed the confidence of the king, he could dispense with other support ; and Henry seemed to place an unbounded and almost exclusive reliance upon the cardinal's political genius. The fascination Wolsey exerted over his mind was attributed by the discontented to witchcraft ; [1] and more sober critics lamented that the king was compromising the royal dignity by the abandon with which he surrendered the affairs of state to the control of the cardinal. ' Have they not in Englonde a kinge ? ' is Roy's indignant question from Strassburg.[2]

[1] Cf. ' An impeachment of Wolsey ' (Furnivall, *Ballads from MSS.* i. 357) :

> Symond Magus assendyd alsoo
> By arte Magike ; down came he tho'.

Skelton threatens Wolsey in a similar way (*Works*, ii. 48) and writes (*ibid.* ii. 47) :

> It is a wonders case :
> That the kynges grace
> Is toward him so mynded,
> And so far blynded,
> That he can not perceyue
> How he doth hym disceyue,
> I dought lest by sorsery,
> Or such other loselry,
> As wychecraft or charmyng ;
> For he is the kynges derling.

And again : ' He caryeth a kyng in his sleve, yf all the worlde fayle ' (*ibid.* ii. 21). Skelton wrote a lost drama, entitled *The Nigramansir* (Dyce, ii. 355) which probably dealt with Wolsey. Cf. Shakespeare, *Henry VIII*, III, ii. 18-19 : ' He hath a witchcraft over the king in's tongue.' See below, p. 225 *n.* 1.

[2] *Rede me*, ed. Arber, p. 49.

To do with the king, complained Giustiniani, is to do nothing; 'the cardinal, for authority, may in point of fact be styled *ipse rex*.' Wolsey, remarked Sir Thomas More in 1518, settled affairs by himself and then consulted the council, so that even the king hardly knew in what state they were; no one in the realm, complained Foxe, dares attempt aught in opposition to Wolsey's interests.[1]

The king, who was only twenty-three years of age when Wolsey became his chancellor, was still absorbed in the pageantry of monarchy and a passion for athletics; he spared, wrote the unsympathetic Pace, no pains to convert the sport of hunting into a martyrdom.[2] When he turned to more serious things his first interests were in a singular combination of theology and the navy; and the Defender of the Faith earned a less ambiguous title to fame in the defence of the realm. Apart from these affairs, which Wolsey thought innocent diversions for a king, and an occasional difference of opinion over the appointment of a bishop or the rights of the crown, the cardinal had a free hand. He made Henry go hither and thither, remarked Leo X, just as he liked, and the king signed state papers without knowing their contents.[3]

---

[1] Rawdon Brown, i. 115, 155; ii. 216; *L.P.* ii. 3558, 4438; *Venetian Cal.* 1509-19, pp. 412, 457, 476. In Jan. 1516 Giustiniani describes Wolsey as *rex et autor omnium* (Brown, i. 160; cf. Erasmus, *Epist.* ii. 69).

[2] *L.P.* iii. 950; cf. *ibid.* 1160.

[3] *Spanish Cal.* 1509-25, pp. 306-7. On 22 Feb. 1523 Wolsey, by the hand of his secretary, makes Henry describe him not only as 'consiliarius noster intimus et primarius,' but 'nobis perinde ac uterinus frater percarus' (Theiner, no. 939; not in *L.P.*). Some of the phrases in this 'royal' letter to Clement VII are identical with phrases in Wolsey's own, sent at the same time (*ibid.* no. 942). This is not so inartistic as it seems: Wolsey wanted popes to think that Henry wrote as well as did what their legate wished. He told Ghinucci, Leo X's nuncio to England in May 1520, that ' he could do or undo whatever he liked, and conclude or not conclude an alliance between Henry VIII, Charles V, and Francis I.' Manuel, the emperor's ambassador at Rome, thought ' the cardinal would do well to be more careful in the words he uses when he speaks of what he can do,' and reported that ' the statesmen in Rome are persuaded that the cardinal will do what is most lucrative for himself

'This cardinal,' reported Giustiniani in 1519 after four years in England, ' is the person who rules both the king and the entire kingdom.' 'When,' he continues, ' he first arrived in England, Wolsey used to say to him ' His Majesty will do so and so '; subsequently, by degrees he went on forgetting himself and commenced saying ' we shall do so and so '; at present he has reached such a pitch that he says ' I shall do so and so.' '[1]   But Wolsey's

as, for his own private interests, he has already, on a former occasion, induced his master to undertake a war, which was by no means profitable to the king.' Skelton (*Works*, ii. 47) wonders

> How suche a hoddypoule
> So boldely dare controule,
> And so malapertly withstande
> The kynges owne hande,
> And settys nat by it a myte ;
> He sayth the kynge doth wryte
> And writeth he wottith nat what ;
> And yet for all that
> The kynge his clemency
> Despensyth with his demensy.

Referring to Buckingham's arrest, Manuel remarks, ' it is generally believed that the violent manner in which the cardinal governs England will produce great inconvenience in the country ' (*Spanish Cal.* ii. 350).

[1] Rawdon Brown, ii. 314 ; *Venetian Cal.* 1509-19, p. 560.   Giustiniani found by experience that it was better to make his proposals to Wolsey than to Henry VIII, ' lest he should resent the precedence conceded to the king ' (R. Brown, ii. 269 ; *Venetian Cal.* p. 521).   Shakespeare's charge against Wolsey of writing 'Ego et rex meus' (*Henry VIII*, III, ii. 315) is also to be found in the lords' impeachment of Wolsey in 1529 and in the Venetian Calendar (iii. p. 43 ; but cf. my *Henry VIII*, p. 110).   See also Skelton's

> Why come ye nat to court ?
> To whyche court ?
> To the kynges courte,
> Or to Hampton Court ?
> Nay, to the kynges court :
> The Kynges courte
> Shulde have the excellence ;
> But Hampton Court
> Hath the preemynence.
>
> —(*Works*, ed. Dyce, ii. 39.)

Cf. *ibid.* ii. 7 :

    ' ' Bo ho ' doth bark well, but ' Hough ho,' he rulyth the ring.'

qualities accounted for his eminence. 'He is,' continues the Venetian, 'very handsome, learned, extremely eloquent, and indefatigable. He alone transacts the same business as that which occupies all the magistracies, offices, and councils of Venice, both civil and criminal; and all state affairs likewise are managed by him, let their nature be what it may. . . . He is in very great repute—seven times more so than if he were pope.'

Even that reputation and Henry VIII's favour do not quite explain the position Wolsey achieved; for, unlike the modern prime minister, he had not chosen his colleagues. Feudal influence was doubtless dying, but it clung tenaciously to office; and, while the great offices of state were not exactly hereditary, they were commonly held for life and reserved for nobles with great estates. The first two Tudors had only three lord high treasurers, two of them dukes of Norfolk, throughout sixty years of their rule. The earls of Shrewsbury and of Worcester retained their offices as lord steward and lord chamberlain until they died respectively in 1538 and 1526. Others like Poynings, Lovell, Wyatt, Marney, and the two Guilfords, who had been in office under Henry VII, remained there till they died, all of them more than ten, and some of them more than twenty years after 1509. Nor did the tenure of the more clerical offices, usually held by bishops, lack an element of permanence and security: of the three successive archbishops of Canterbury whom Henry VII appointed chancellor, two died in office [1] and the third survived the king.[2] Foxe, after being secretary, was lord privy seal for twenty-nine years; [3] Oliver King, who succeeded him as secretary, remained in office till his death, and was succeeded in 1503 by Ruthal, who re-

and ii. 45 :

> And he wyll play checke mate
> With ryall maieste
> Counte him selfe as good as he.

[1] Morton and Deane.   [2] Warham.

[3] 1489-1516; he was appointed on 24 Feb. 1487 (*Cal. Patent Rolls*, 1485-94, pp. 171, 174; Campbell, *Materials*, ii. 158; the *D.N.B.* does not give the date).

tained the signet until Wolsey gave him the privy seal in 1516. The first of the Tudors established a record of fidelity to ministers which was only surpassed by the astonishing steadfastness of the last, who retained all her principal ministers till their death, Burghley for forty, Leicester for more than thirty, and Walsingham for over twenty years. The fickleness of Tudor princes compares favourably with the fidelity of peoples; and Wolsey never had the power, which a general election puts into the hands of a new prime minister, of forming a new administration.

His relation to the council is even more ambiguous, and the early Tudor council still defies historical definition. One misconception can, however, be removed: the council was not an administrative, but an advisory body; even our modern cabinet is an executive body, not because it is a committee of the privy council, but a group of heads of administrative departments united by a subtle and complex commission. In Wolsey's time there was no distinction, in form or in meaning, between the words counsel and council:[1] the king's council consisted of king's counsel,[2] of whom there were

---

[1] E.g. the annuity to Wolsey, mentioned above (p. 21 n.), was 'pro bono concilio.'

[2] The queen also had her council consisting of similar counsel; cf. L.P. iii. p. 256, where Charles V's ambassador in London tells how Catherine tried to prevent Henry's interview with Francis I at the Field of Cloth of Gold: 'Some days ago the queen assembled her council to confer about this interview, and while she was holding it the king arrived. On his asking what was going on, the queen told him why she had called them, and finally they said that she had made such representations, and showed such reasons, against the voyage, as one would not have supposed she would have dared to do, or even to imagine. On this account she is held in greater esteem by the king and his council than ever she was.' Ferdinand of Aragon and his ambassadors in London had always impressed it upon Catherine that her first duty was to Spain, but sometimes, to her credit, found her recalcitrant (Spanish Cal. 1509-25, pp. 248-9). The princess Mary, the duke of Richmond, and the marquis of Exeter also had councils, expanded into the councils of the North, of Wales and its marches, and of the West. So had the dukes of Suffolk and Buckingham, with their chancellors, treasurers, and other counterparts of the king's ministers; while the king, of course, had—as he still has—a separate council for the duchy of Lancaster, with its chancellor, etc.

more than a hundred, retained by the king at a fee of £100 a year—unless they held more lucrative posts— some of them learned in various kinds of law to give him legal advice, some of them expert in finance, diplomacy, languages, or arms.[1] Out of this body of counsel were formed from time to time more particular and concrete groups to sit in counsel at the star chamber, in the court of requests, or with the king wherever he might be, or to be permanently located in Dublin, at Calais, at York as king's counsel in the north or at Ludlow as the king's counsel in the marches of Wales. Out of the numerous counsel not detailed for extra-mural service kings were in the habit—one can scarcely call it more—of selecting from time to time a few for more private and regular consultation on what were beginning to be called matters of state, i.e. affecting the king's estate. In time these consultations grew into an institution called the king's private or privy council, and the king's secretary developed into the secretary of state. But the persons thus consulted were not necessarily the heads of executive departments, who were frequently absent from court by choice or by constraint, and were thus excluded from participation in the king's deliberations and decisions. We have seen Wolsey suggesting that even the lord high treasurer might be permanently excluded ; a man's favour or influence was gauged by whether he came to court or not, and Skelton's ' Why come ye nat to court ? ' is a mordant satire on Wolsey's exclusive propensities.

Whether or not these heads of departments came to

[1] For instance, a list of the king's council who were to accompany him to the Field of Cloth of Gold, after giving the names of forty-one peers and prelates, refers summarily to ' all knights and others of the king's council '—excluding, of course, the council left in England (*L.P.* iii. 703). A provisional list, that is being compiled for Henry's reign, already includes over two hundred ' counsel.' The problem has been obscured by the inveterate habit of interpolating ' privy ' before ' council ' wherever it occurs in Tudor times : occasionally in *L.P.* ' privy council ' is a misreading or misprint for ' prince's council ' (e.g. iii. 1076, 2103). For the ' prince's council chamber ' see *Rotuli Parliamentorum*, Suppl. pp. xix*b*, xcvi*a*, xcviii*a*, ciii*a* ; *L.P.* xvii. 362 [7] ; 1543, i. 100 [24] ; 1546, i. 149 [21].

court, their departments had to carry out the king's orders; and security of tenure in Tudor times meant that the tenants of office were civil servants rather than confidential advisers. The policy or the principle of these orders was determined in private consultation with the king, if he cared to attend, and without him if his advisers dared to take the responsibility; and they were formulated as orders by the chancellor, treasurer, and lord privy seal whose action was authorised by various acts of parliament.[1] A fourth had been added to the group during Henry VII's reign in the person of the president of the council; but he in Henry's later years was the notorious Edmund Dudley, and when his rivals at Henry VIII's accession sent him to the Tower they let his office lapse.[2] Wolsey had no desire to elevate a rival in 1516, and the office was not revived till after his fall. He became chancellor himself, obtained the privy seal for his faithful henchman, Ruthal, and secured the acquiescence of the aged treasurer, Norfolk, and the frequent absence of his more pushing son.[3] To succeed Ruthal, Pace was promoted from being Wolsey's to be the king's secretary; and he ingratiated himself so successfully in Henry's favour that Wolsey after 1518 kept him almost continuously employed abroad until 1527, when he was committed to the Tower for criticising the chancellor and his change of policy.[4]

[1] See above, p. 70.

[2] *English Hist. Review*, July 1922, pp. 352-5.

[3] Ruthal's salary of £1 a day as lord privy seal dated from 18 May (Rymer, xiii. 553). Surrey had been ' put out of the council ' with other lords in May 1516, the month in which Foxe surrendered the privy seal (see above, p. 83); and in April, 1520, he was sent as lord-deputy to Ireland (*L.P.* iii. 669-70), at Wolsey's instigation, it was believed, to get him out of the way (Polydore Vergil, p. 659; Hall, p. 601); during his absence, his father-in-law, Buckingham, was brought to the scaffold in May 1521.

[4] See below, pp. 255 n. 1, 316. Pace was a strong advocate of an imperial rather than a French alliance (cf. *Spanish Cal.* 1509-25, pp. 482, 553, 566, 571-2, 698). His imperial colleague during Pace's mission to Venice in 1523 remarks that Pace received no letters from his government, and complains of this negligence (*ibid.* p. 530). In his absence his secretarial duties were temporarily discharged by Sampson, Sir Thomas More,

That policy could be changed without a change of
personnel is made clear by the transition from peace to
war in 1512-13; and that administration could be made
to fall into line was shown by Wolsey's action, when only
almoner, as minister for war in organising the French
campaign.[1] His correspondence during 1513 and 1514
proves beyond a doubt that he was in full control of
English diplomacy and war before he held any office that
was not purely ecclesiastical; and he is charged by Hall
with interfering so constantly in the departmental affairs
of chancery that Warham was driven to resign.[2] Foxe
followed four months later in May 1516; and Suffolk's
impulsive marriage with Henry's sister Mary, whom he
had been sent to bring back from France after the death
of Louis XII, had already enabled Wolsey to get rid of
another rival. In 1513 Suffolk and Wolsey had been
described as the two obstinate men who governed everything at Henry's court, and in another letter the duke
was called, like Foxe, 'a second king.'[3] His marriage
into the royal family may have angered other nobles,
and Wolsey was not averse from fanning the flame.[4] But

Brian Tuke, and others. Dr. William Knight was appointed to succeed
him as 'principal secretary' in 1526, and was himself replaced by Gardiner
in July 1529. Gardiner had, like his predecessors, been Wolsey's secretary
before becoming the king's; but he certainly did nothing to break Wolsey's
fall (see below, pp. 234-5, 239-40).

[1] See above, p. 20.

[2] *Chronicle*, p. 583. Palsgrave (*L.P.* iv. p. 2560) says Wolsey 'took
away from my lord of Canterbury the chancellorship'; and even Cavendish (p. 27) says Wolsey found means with the king to have Warham
'dismissed.' * Polydore Vergil says (p. 645) that Warham surrendered
the great seal *sponte sua*, but (p. 646) that he and Foxe retired from
court in disgust, as did Norfolk and Suffolk. In July 1515, when Leo X
sent a joint letter to Wolsey and Foxe, Wolsey requested the pope to
use no other services than his own (*L.P.* ii. 647, 700). Giustiniani remarked at the same time that Wolsey 'really seems to have the management of the whole of this kingdom' (Rawdon Brown, i. 110, 129, 139).

[3] *L.P.* i. (new ed.) 2141, 2171.

[4] He did his best to impress upon Suffolk, while still in France, the
danger which threatened him on his return to England, and he had sent
two friars to Mary herself to warn her. But, as she reminded Henry, she
had only consented to marry Louis XII for political reasons and on condition that, if she survived him, she should be allowed to choose a second

Henry himself manifested no resentment : three months after Suffolk's return, Giustiniani found him at court acting ' with authority scarcely inferior to that of the king himself ' ;[1] and after Wolsey's fall Henry made Suffolk president of his council. But Suffolk was too friendly towards France to abet Wolsey's change of policy in 1515 ; and either through Wolsey's influence or because the duke was attached to country life and his beautiful bride, he kept or was kept for the time away from court.

Shrewsbury also held aloof ; and one after another Henry VII's old counsellors like Sir Thomas Lovell and Sir Edward Poynings dropped out of active politics. The retirement of Warham and Foxe has been represented as entirely voluntary ; but it was only voluntary in the sense that they preferred their episcopal duties to super-session in the government by a protégé of whose foreign policy, at least, they thoroughly disapproved, and whose trespasses into their own departments they were unable to control. Giustiniani described these ministerial changes as ' of extreme importance.'[2] But he had for months been insisting, in his dispatches, on the ' supreme authority ' of Wolsey ; and the importance consisted in the substitution of an open for a concealed control of the machinery of government, and in the removal of any checks which the elder statesmen might have imposed on Wolsey's wayward genius.

Foxe's friendly and parting advice to Wolsey, after an

husband herself ; and according to Polydore Vergil, Brandon had been created duke of Suffolk in 1513 in order to pave the way for his marriage. He had been Henry's boon companion for many years, and their life-long friendship only terminated with Suffolk's death thirty years later. The one shadow on that friendship was cast by Wolsey himself ; and his subsequent claim, reported by Cavendish, to have saved Suffolk from the scaffold in 1515, is, if it was ever made, one of Wolsey's boldest inventions (see below, p. 234 n. 4).

[1] Rawdon Brown, i. 119. Brown in a note (p. 123) refers these words to Wolsey instead of Suffolk, although Giustiniani congratulates ' him ' on his marriage to Mary ; but he does not repeat this interpretation thirteen years later in his *Venetian Cal.* ii. 258.

[2] Rawdon Brown, i. 252 ; *Venetian Cal.* 1509-19, p. 310.

encomium on his early reform of law and order, was ' and,
good my lord, when the term is done, keep the council
with the king wherever he be.' [1]   The advice was significant of much.   The anarchy which culminated in the
wars of the roses had been the outcome of Henry VI's
inability to keep together in counsel a band of magnates
bent on feudal independence; and Foxe probably feared,
either a recurrence of disorder if Henry, careless it seemed
of public affairs, were left to himself for vacations which
lasted eight months of the year, or too much adventure
abroad if he were left with Wolsey as sole counsellor.   The
latter was the greater danger : there was no lack of gover-
nance under Wolsey, but the lack of counsel with the
king was a matter of which Henry himself made complaint,
while others complained that he had no counsel but
Wolsey.[2]   Even the household reform contemplated in
the Eltham ordinances of 1526[3] only provided the king
with a regular attendance of two or four councillors;
and nothing was more conspicuous during Wolsey's later
administration than the contrast between the impressive
attendance at the chancellor's court of star chamber
and the scanty attendance on the king *ubicunque fuerit*.[4]

[1] *L.P.* ii. 1814.   The council was still primarily the council in the
star chamber and only sat in term time, which amounted to no more
than fifteen weeks a year ; see Sir T. Smith, *De Republica*, ed. 1906, p. 69 ;
Nicolas, *Chronology of History*, p. 385 ; Leadam, *Star Chamber*, ii. 321.
Even these terms were not infrequently abbreviated because of the plague
or other reasons (cf. *L.P.* 1545, ii. 424), and occasionally, as when Wolsey
was at Calais and Bruges in the autumn of 1521, not held at all.   Yet
such notes of council proceedings as have been collected for Wolsey's
régime relate almost entirely to legal matters, suggesting counsel in the
star chamber; and during the insurrections of April-May 1525 Norfolk
and Suffolk urge that ' they never saw the time so needful for the king
to call his council to determine what should be done ' (*L.P.* iv. 1329).

[2] *L.P.* ii. 4355 ; iv. pp. 2555, 2560.

[3] On these see *Eng. Hist. Rev.*, July 1922, pp. 358-9.   Their importance has probably been exaggerated : as documents they provide a good
deal of information on the royal household ; but it does not appear that
they were ever enforced, or exercised the remotest influence on the development of the council or anything else.   Wolsey had been reforming
the king's household ever since 1516 (cf. Lodge, *Illustr.* i. 22 ; *L.P.* iii.
576 [19]).

[4] See above, pp. 72, 80 *n*. 3.

Foxe's advice, we may add, indicates also that the key
to the problem of the distinction between the king's
mediæval council and the incipient privy council of Tudor
times is the distinction between a council, which met
only at Westminster during term, and a council which
met all the year round and sat with the king wherever
he might be. While Wolsey made the fortunes of the
Tudor star chamber, the irruption of his dominant personality into the king's entourage interrupted the growth
of the privy council and reduced it for the time to political
and constitutional insignificance.

The foreign adventure which Foxe probably had in
mind when he wrote was already under weigh ; and few
of the council were in the secret.[1] The edifice of peace
which Wolsey had erected upon the victories in France
and at Flodden Field, was dissolved like the baseless fabric
of a vision by the death, on 1 January 1515, of Louis
XII and the succession of Francis I, who was even younger
and more adventurous than Henry VIII. He signalised
his accession, not by three years of peace, but by plunging
at once into the vortex of Italian war. To claims on
Milan he added more shadowy claims on Naples ; and
his reign was one long protest against French exclusion
from Italy which had been imposed by Wolsey's peace on
the senile Louis XII. Within nine months of his advent
to the throne Francis had crossed the Alps and won the
battle of Marignano (13 September) which shattered the
military prestige of the Swiss and subjected Italy, as far
south as the frontiers of the kingdom of Naples, to French
domination. Marignano was a far more resounding blow
than all the English victories of 1513, and there seemed no
way of counteracting its effects. Ferdinand of Aragon
was too old for fresh adventures. Leo X was bent on
peace and pleasure ; Maximilian's credit was exhausted ;
and the Flemish council of his grandson Charles succumbed
to the fascination of French success. They thought
ignominious peace a better method of guarding against
French designs on the Netherlands than a war without

[1] See below, p. 113 n.

dependable allies. 'The pope is French,' wrote Dr.
William Knight to Wolsey, 'and everything else from
Rome to Calais.' [1]

That Rome should remain under the shadow of the
wing of a rival seemed fatal to the hopes which Wolsey
consistently founded on his influence with the papacy; and
he was bent on putting a spoke in the wheel of Francis I's
triumphal car. Direct and open war was impossible
without Spain, the pope, or the Netherlands to help.
Nor was Wolsey himself much concerned about French
frontiers in the Pyrenees or in Artois: it was in Italy
that he dreaded the extension of French control because
of its effect on Rome. Personal interest and fidelity to
the papacy coincided: if the pope were not independent
of greater powers, he would not be amenable to persuasion
coming from England. From first to last, the keystone
in Wolsey's conception of the balance of power was the
duchy of Milan, because on its possession depended the
independence of Rome; and Wolsey's riposte to Marignano was an attempt to wrest from the victor those particular spoils of his victory. An English expeditionary
force was out of the question, and the only alternative
agent was the emperor Maximilian. Milan was a fief of
the empire; the native claimants to the duchy were the
Sforzas who were generally supported by Italian sentiment, and by non-Italian princes when they wished to
rescue the duchy from the hands of a secular rival:
Sforza himself found it more difficult to rescue the prey
from its saviours. Wolsey's plan was to bribe Maximilian
and the Swiss to renew the contest against Francis I and
his Venetian allies; and Pace was selected for the difficult
task of conveying a vast English subsidy to the Swiss
troops without letting it slip into the impecunious hands
of the emperor who was to command the expedition.
Sforza was to be restored, and he undertook to pay Wolsey
ten thousand ducats a year from the date of his restoration.[2]

---

[1] *L.P.* ii. 2930.

[2] Rymer, xiii. 525-6; *L.P.* ii. 1053, 1066; Wolsey was accused of
making the king spend money on the expedition for his own profit (*ibid.*
ii. 1931). The 'profit' was more probably Wolsey's cardinalate than
Sforza's bribe.

Pace set out in October 1515 and reached Zurich in time to prevent an agreement between Francis I and the Swiss; and the winter was spent in preparing for Maximilian's descent from the Alps in the spring. Parliament had not been consulted, and Henry's counsel were mostly averse from the scheme. Not only Warham and Foxe, but younger men like Tunstal and More deplored the adventure.[1] Indeed, it was this divergence on foreign policy which produced, according to Giustiniani, the change of ministry. The scheme was Wolsey's 'own work' and to it alone, according to the papal chamberlain Paris de Grassis, he owed his creation as cardinal by Leo X.[2] It has been vaunted as the first occasion on which the arm of England was stretched out to so distant a sphere of influence; but whatever its value as a precedent, its immediate consequences were unfortunate. Maximilian's

---

[1] Rawdon Brown, i. 307-9, 319, 326; ii. 9; *Venetian Cal.* 1509-19, nos. 791-2, 798, 801, 811, 823; *L.P.* ii. 2183, 2270. Giustiniani describes More as 'the most linked with me in friendship of any in this kingdom' (ii. 162; cf. *ibid.* 165, 215-16) and More reciprocated his sentiments (More to Erasmus, *Epistolae*, ii. 339; cf. *ibid.* 514-17, 549, 577, 594-7). Brewer attributed Foxe's absence to 'no better authority than Polydore Vergil' (*L.P.* ii. preface, p. cliv), and he has been generally followed. But, apart from Giustiniani's repeated statements, e.g. that Foxe 'has hitherto been absent from hence, not having chosen to interfere in these impassioned resolves' (18 Nov. 1516), T. Allen writes to Shrewsbury on 8 June 1516 (misdated 1517 in Lodge's *Illustr.* i. 29), 'my lord of Winchester comes not here.' The councillors whom Giustiniani names as being present on 18 Oct. were Wolsey, Ruthal, bishop Nix of Norwich, Norfolk, Lovell, and Marney; in April he had said that the truth of the war preparations was 'known only to the king and four members of the privy council, who keep everything most secret' (Brown, ii. 218). Giustiniani writes on 28 Jan. 1517, 'the bishop of Winchester even declines my visits, because he is suspected of thwarting the interests of the emperor' (*ibid.* ii. 28). Wolsey's attitude is indicated by the fact that in order to secure the ruin of 'that poisonous fellow'—*veneficum hominem*—cardinal Hadrian, he sent to Silvester an extract from a letter written by Hadrian's agent, Chieregati, to Warham and Foxe, which Wolsey had seized (Martene and Durand, cols. 1281-2).

[2] *L.P.* ii. 664; Rawdon Brown, ii. 12; Creighton, *Hist. of the Papacy*, v. 315: 'Et hoc unum est, quod hic archiepiscopus, qui etiam mediator extitit quod rex Angliae capiat arma contra Gallos, ex nunc fiat cardinalis.'

campaign was a complete fiasco. After advancing within
nine miles of Milan in March 1516 he withdrew into the
mountains without striking a blow, leaving north Italy
under the undisputed sway of France and Venice. The
pope had already made his peace with France at Bologna in
Dec. 1515 ; Ferdinand of Aragon had died in January, leaving his dominions to his grandson Charles ; and Charles, to
protect Naples as well as the Netherlands, made an ignominious peace with Francis at Noyon in July. Wolsey
still hoped that money might induce Maximilian to break
it ; and another English subsidy was forthcoming, as vain
as that for the reconquest of Milan. Maximilian came
down to the Netherlands in January 1517 ; and there he
was persuaded by 75,000 French crowns, instead of breaking, to join in the peace of Noyon. 'Mon fils,' he had
said to Charles, ' vous allez tromper les Français ; et moi,
je vais tromper les Anglais. '[1]

There was no more war to be made just yet, and
Wolsey bethought himself of the victories of peace. It
is one of the most striking tributes to his versatility and
diplomacy that he should have secured so much of the
credit, at the time and in the eyes of posterity, for the
pacification of 1518. Leo X had sent Chieregati to
negotiate it in April 1516, when Wolsey was 'leading
the dance' of war. The credit was doubtless the cardinal's due ; 'he being quieted,' wrote Giustiniani,
'the whole turmoil would cease.'[2] The old counsellors,
who had opposed Wolsey's adventures and had been dis-
placed, were as sincere as they were profuse in their con-
gratulations : 'it is the best deed,' wrote Foxe, 'that ever
was done in England ; and, next to the king, the praise of
it is due to you.'[3] English diplomatists—Tunstal, West,
Knight, and More—seem to have been unanimous in
urging Wolsey to abandon active resentment with Maximilian, Charles, and Francis, assuring him that the treaty
of Noyon contained in itself the seeds of its own dissolution, that patience and peace would serve England
better than passion and war, and that time would soon

[1] *L.P.* ii. 2930.   [2] Rawdon Brown, i. 212, 319-20.
                    [3] *L.P.* ii. 4540.

make both Francis and Charles competitors for England's
alliance.   For Charles had promised to Francis more
than he could perform : he had undertaken to restore
Spanish Navarre, which Spain would never permit, and
to marry the French king's infant daughter, for whom
neither Charles nor his subjects would be content to
wait.[1]

For the moment Wolsey grasped and expressed what
was really the mind of Europe, however diverse the paths
which led to peace.   France had been confirmed in its
position in north Italy ; Venice had recovered most of
what it had been robbed by the league of Cambrai ;
increasing years and an apoplectic stroke had given a
pious turn to Maximilian's aspirations : he was dreaming
of exchanging the imperial crown for the papal tiara, of
recovering the holy sepulchre, and of ultimate canonisa-
tion.[2]   Leo X wanted a crusade against the Turk, or at
least financial contributions which, failing a crusade, might
perhaps be spent on building St. Peter's ; [3] Charles needed
peace to establish himself in his turbulent Spanish kingdoms, which he had never yet seen and to whose language
and thoughts he was alien ; and all men's minds were
turned to an approaching election in which national rivalry
gave an unprecedented importance to a contest for the
imperial crown.

The hush before the storm was turned by Wolsey to
good account.   London was made the scene of the negotiations for general peace ; and thither Leo X dispatched
Campeggio as his legate, alike for the treaty and for the
collection of funds for the proposed crusade.   He was
stopped at Calais : it was not the English custom, wrote
Wolsey, to admit any ' foreign ' cardinal as legate *a latere*
to England until it was clear that he brought no papal

---

[1] See the report by the bishop of Badajos to cardinal Ximenes on
Charles' situation, *Spanish Cal.* 1509-25, pp. 281-3.

[2] *L.P.* ii. 1398, 1878, 1902, 1923, 2218, 2911, 4257.

[3] For a criticism of Leo X's reputation as builder of St. Peter's, see
Camb. Mod. Hist. ii. 12 ; and for Erasmus' outburst on the pretence of a
Turkish crusade, see his *Epistolae* iii. 241, ' qui tumultus si procedant,
tolerabilius fuerit Turcarum imperium quam horum christianorum ferre.'

bulls that might be prejudicial to the English crown. The king thought Campeggio's mission innocent enough but Wolsey wanted more than innocence. Campeggio was kept at Calais and the business of Europe in suspense until Wolsey's personal requirements were satisfied. He had been kept waiting himself four years for his own appointment as papal legate ; it was now the turn of Leo X. Campeggio should not enter England and Leo should wait for his crusading grants and his share in the treaty of peace until his envoy brought Wolsey his bulls. These were granted on 17 May, but Wolsey wanted more; interest always accrued on his demands when satisfaction was delayed. He had fallen out with his old allies and agents, cardinal Hadrian and Polydore Vergil : Polydore's letters to Hadrian criticising Wolsey, had been opened in England, and he was sent to the Tower where, in spite of papal remonstrance, he was kept in prison a year. Hadrian was not only implicated in an alleged plot to poison Leo, but had opposed in consistory Wolsey's elevation to the cardinalate.[2]

The pope was more forgiving than Wolsey ; and Campeggio's admission to England was further delayed until he could bring with him Hadrian's deprivation from his bishopric of Bath and Wells. The administration of that see had been in the hands of Foxe as bishop of Winchester, but Wolsey wanted the bishopric himself as compensation for the loss of Tournai, and received it on 26 Aug. 1518. Francis was demanding the rendition of that city as part of the treaty of peace, but was willing to pay Wolsey 12,000 livres a year for the surrender of his rights.[3] His control of Tournai had, owing to popular

[1] 'Exterum quempiam cardinalem legatione fungentem,' Martene and Durand, col. 1284 ; *L.P.* ii. 4034, 4055, 4073.

[2] *L.P.* ii. 967. On the belief in poison at Rome, see Creighton, *Papacy*, v. 301-4 ; and for Wolsey's demands from the pope see *Venetian Cal.* 1509-19, p. 451.

[3] Rymer, xiii. 610, 624 ; *L.P.* ii. 4354 ; the payment to Wolsey of 6000 livres half yearly on 1 Nov. and 1 May is recorded in the French archives from 1 Nov. 1519 to 1 May 1521 ; it dated from 31 July 1518. This was in addition to a yearly pension of 2800 livres which Wolsey had been receiving since 1515 (*Spanish Cal.* 1509-25, pp. 284, 286, 289

opposition, the pope's revocation of his letters of administration at the instance of Francis I,[1] and the existence
of a rival French bishop, never been effective. He had
given Erasmus a prebend there which Erasmus described
as δῶρον ἄδωρον; even Wolsey's commissary, he wrote,
was excommunicate in Tournai—such was the respect
they paid to the cardinal.[2] Three years earlier, lord
Mountjoy, the English governor, had suggested the advisability of an exchange, and Wolsey himself may well have
considered his pension and the bishopric of Bath and
Wells an adequate compensation. But his main object
in pursuing Hadrian was to show that, while he might
not be able to expel the French from Milan, his arm was
long enough to drive his enemies from the papal curia at
Rome.

These details being settled to Wolsey's satisfaction, the
general peace was concluded amid festivities which participants thought exceeded in luxury and ostentation
anything recorded in Roman or oriental history.[3] Behind the general pacification lay a particular and more
intimate understanding with France confirmed by another
marriage of Wolsey's contriving. This time it was
Henry's infant daughter Mary who was to be wedded to
the equally juvenile dauphin, a prospect as remote as
Charles's wedding with the dauphin's sister. 'Fancy,'
Wolsey had exclaimed on the former proposal to Gius-
iniani, 'how advantageous this must prove for the
catholic king [Charles], having to wait fifteen years for
a wife!'[4] A more immediate symbol of friendship was
to be a personal interview between Henry and Francis in

93, 295-6, 300, 325, 345). There were pensions to nine other English
councillors as well: the earl of Worcester had 1700 livres; Norfolk,
Suffolk, and Shrewsbury 875 each; bishop Foxe 525, Sir W. Compton
50, Lovel 175, and Meautis and Clarenceux king-at-arms 87 each.
Wolsey had already extorted a pension of 3000 livres from Charles
on 8 June 1517, and it was increased to 7000 on 29 March 1520 (Rymer,
iii. 591-2, 714; see below, p. 324 n. 2).

[1] *L.P.* ii. 2886.
[2] *Ibid.* ii. 701, 905; Erasmus, *Epist.* ed. P. S. Allen, ii. 149-50.
[3] Rawdon Brown, ii. 225-6; *Venetian Cal.* 1509-19, pp. 462-3.
[4] Brown, i. 256.

1519; but the preparations were interrupted by the news of Maximilian's death in January and the ensuing contest for the empire. The seven electors might, to enhance the price of their votes, pretend that the field was open ; but the only possible alternative to Charles was the elector of Saxony whom Leo X and all the rivals of the Habsburg would have preferred. There was not, in that age of youthful vigorous nationalism, the remotest chance of German votes being given to any but a German candidate; and Habsburgs had been emperors continuously since 1438 and intermittently for two centuries and a half. Charles V was elected unanimously amid popular acclamation on 28 June,[1] and the stage was thus set for that rivalry of three princes, Henry, aged twenty-eight, Francis, twenty-six, and Charles, nineteen, which dominated Europe far beyond the span of Wolsey's life.

His foreign policy, generally accounted his masterpiece in politics, has been variously explained on contradictory principles which are all of them inconsistent with serious and stubborn facts. The favourite interpretation is that of the ' balance of power ' ; and that is comparatively plausible, because it involves no constant adherence to any particular alliance, but requires frequent modification or reversals to suit the fluctuating scales.[2] The next theory, that Wolsey was the consistent friend of France is difficult to reconcile with the war of 1513, the Milan adventure of 1516, or that into which Wolsey was presently to plunge. It has been said that war with France

---

[1] *L.P.* iii. 339. Pace's voluminous correspondence with Wolsey one of the best sources for the history of the election. There is a good deal in the Venetian Calendar, but nothing in the Spanish because Bergenroth, its editor, was unaware of the existence of Charles V's corre- spondence at Vienna (see Pascual de Gayangos' preface to vol. iii. of the *Spanish Cal.*, where he expresses his indebtedness to Froude for his know- ledge of the Vienna documents : selections had, in fact, been published in 1850 by William Bradford in his *Correspondence of Charles V* (1850) by Karl Lanz in *Monumenta Habsburgica*, II, i. (1857), and by Le Glay in his *Negociations diplomatiques* (vol. ii. Paris, 1845). See also W. Busch *Drei Jähre englischer Vermittlungspolitik*, 1518-21 (Bonn, 1884), and *Cardinal Wolsey und die englisch-kaiserliche Allianz*, 1522-5 (Bonn, 1886)

[2] See above, p. 3 *n*. 3

was no part of his policy; he might, indeed, have liked to get the French out of Milan without a war, but that he wished to get them out is certain. The representation of him as England's first great war minister seems to cancel the theory that he was always bent on peace; and the most convenient, though hardly the most convincing, interpretation is that his successes were due to his own consummate ability and his failures to the bungling interference of the king.[1] But this again is not consistent with Wolsey's own correspondence, the testimony of his colleagues and of foreign ambassadors, and the evidence of contemporary letter-writers and chroniclers. Wolsey undoubtedly had a foreign policy of his own and exceptional opportunities for its pursuit: few English ministers have enjoyed so great a liberty of action or so long a period in which to carry out their schemes.

The 'balance of power' is a later phrase that has not been traced to Wolsey or even to his age; but the idea probably dates back to the prehistoric age when three children first indulged in the simple game of see-saw. As a political principle it was certainly known to the Medes and Persians, the Greeks, and the Romans; and its modern vogue is due to the acute eruption of national rivalry which accompanied the decline of the mediæval conception of catholic unity in the christian world. Fiddes, however, was wise in his refusal to attempt a solution of the problem whether Wolsey's policy was really consistent

---

[1] Creighton, *Wolsey*, p. 106. Wolsey had, of course, to secure Henry's general concurrence, and the king cannot escape his responsibility. But the policy was Wolsey's conception, not Henry's; and when Wolsey fell, the policy was changed. Stubbs pointed out that 'there was very little real war' in Henry's reign (*Seventeen Lectures*, 1887, p. 279); and all of it outside Great Britain, except the Boulogne expedition in 1544, occurred in Wolsey's administration. Henry's own attitude was summed up in his words to Giustiniani in 1516: 'I content myself with my own; I only wish to command my own subjects; but on the other hand I do not choose any one to have it in his power to command me' (Rawdon Brown, 237). His subjects agreed with him in this attitude (cf. *L.P.* iii. 1669; vii. p. 706; *Spanish Cal.* ii. 249; Hall, *Chron.* pp. 724, 744, 747). Two lay lords, however, grumbled, when Venice acquired Cyprus in 1516, that 'it ought to belong to our king' (Brown, i. 204).

with the theory of balance current in the early eighteenth century; and, if more recent historians have been more confident in their attribution, it is partly because the phrase has become still more elastic and may bear almost any interpretation. The words 'in our hands,' which gave to the preservation of the balance of power some definite meaning, may have been dropped to conciliate the inert occupants of the scales to be balanced for England's benefit; and we have not yet answered the simple but crucial question whether by the balance of power we mean a simple or a multiple equilibrium.[1] Castlereagh had a clear and sensible conception: to him the European system was a multiple balance of five or six independent states in which, if any one—like France under Napoleon— grew too powerful, the other four or five combined to outweigh it. But this multiple balance changed in the century after Waterloo into a simple balance between two vast agglomerations of power in the 'triple alliance' and the 'triple entente': there was no one outside to hold the balance. A consequent race for armaments ensued between the two more or less equally balanced forces; and still people talked of preserving the balance of power as if the problem remained as stereotyped as the phrase.

Now, a similar change took place during Wolsey's administration, owing partly to Francis I's conquest of Milan but more to Charles V coming into four distinct inheritances from his four grandparents—Aragon and Castile, the Habsburg dominions and Burgundy—to which was added the imperial crown with its claims to suzerainty over other lands. The multiple balance existing before was thus changed into a simple balance between Habsburg and Valois, with the odds in favour of Charles V; and it would seem that England's policy, if the preservation of the balance of power was her object, was to side with France; or, if there were any doubt of the preponderance, to wait and see which way the balance was turning rather than plunge at once into the weightier scale. Assuredly, a victory for France was not so certain, and

[1] Still less the question how far the scope of the balance is to extend, to sea as well as to land power, to Africa and America as well as to Europe.

would not be so swift and dangerous, as to require immediate intervention on behalf of Charles V; and it might be argued that Wolsey was less concerned about the balance of power than anxious to share the spoils with the probable victor. 'The victory,' wrote Pace from Windsor on 27 June 1521 to the papal nuncio in England, 'we think, for many reasons, will be with the emperor';[1] and when the duke of Bourbon revolted against Francis I in 1523 and rendered French prospects almost desperate, Wolsey, instead of redressing the balance, seemed more eager than ever to press the advantage, even to the dismemberment of France. It is doubtful, however, whether the balance of power entered into his calculations at all. A European system hardly yet existed; and it certainly did not lend itself readily to so abstract, academic, and mathematical an arrangement as a balance. Governments and peoples were moved by considerations that were sometimes more sentimental and sometimes more practical, but nearly always more immediate. The fact that Catherine of Aragon was queen was not without its influence on English foreign relations;[2] and still more potent were the commercial links which kept England and the Netherlands at peace, however their rulers might disagree.

A much simpler and straighter thread runs throughout Wolsey's foreign policy than the 'balance of power.' We have seen from his earliest extant letter how his thoughts turned towards Rome, and have noted the forecast made by his henchman Ruthal in 1516 that England's policy towards France would be that of the papal curia;[3] and after his fall in 1529 Wolsey remarked to Norfolk that in his papal legacy 'stode all my high honour.'[4] It is all to Wolsey's credit that he should have regarded that position as incompatible with any other policy than that of the closest understanding with the papacy from which it was derived; and every change in his attitude towards other European powers coincided with a change in the

[1] *L.P.* iii. 1370.   [2] See above, p. 105 *n* 2.
[3] Above, pp. 16, 25.
[4] Cavendish, *Wolsey*, p. 186. See below, p. 165 *n*. 1.

policy of the papal curia. So long as Wolsey influenced England's conduct, Henry VIII remained the favourite son of the Roman church. The summons of Julius II, supported by Wolsey, had brought England from peace into war against Louis XII and his schismatic council.[1] The pacific Leo X was responsible for the peace of 1514 and the marriage of Mary to the French king; and Wolsey owed his creation as cardinal to Leo's expectations from the Milan adventure.[2] When Leo made his peace with Francis, Wolsey followed suit, and maintained that attitude until, for reasons which are even now by no means clear, the pope signalised the last year of his life by abetting Charles V in his natural ambition to drive the French from Milan and convincing the English government that it had 'no other choice but to conclude an alliance with the emperor.'[3]

This fidelity to papal policy provides the most plausible grounds for Wolsey's association with the doctrine of the balance of power. For, if any potentate felt the need of some such doctrine, it was the ruler of the papal states, placed as they were between the upper mill-stone of the French in Milan and the nether mill-stone of the Spaniards in Naples. But it is by no means certain that papal policy was mainly actuated by this mundane principle. It is possible that Leo X resented the concordat, extorted by Francis I in 1516, by which the pope was deprived of all influence over ecclesiastical preferments in France: he had not concealed his alarm at Marignano and the military eclipse of his natural allies the Swiss; as a Medici he feared French influence in Florence and longed for the recovery of Parma and Piacenza; and as an Italian he wanted Italians and not the French to rule in Milan. Charles V

---

[1] Sir T. More in *Erasmi Epistolae*, iv. 221, 294; and Erasmus to Leo X (*ibid.* ii. 83), 'te autore deposuit arma . . . . . Julii instinctu suscepit arma.'

[2] See above, p. 113 *n.* 2. The distinction was emphasised by the fact that Wolsey was created 'sole' cardinal on this occasion, a very unusual event. Wolsey had asked for this 'sole' creation in 1514 (*L.P.* i. 3496).

[3] Juan Manuel to Charles V, 19 Oct. 1520 (*Spanish Cal.* 1509-25, p. 322).

held out all these inducements, and also implied a threat : if the empire fell foul of the papacy, Charles V might find in Luther a far more effective ally than France had discovered in Savonarola. Family, national, and papal considerations counselled a papal-imperial alliance : it was dated on 8 May 1521, the day on which Luther was out-lawed at the Diet of Worms ; [1] and Charles V afterwards alleged that it was Leo's cousin and counsellor, Giulio de Medici, the future Clement VII, who inveigled him into war.[2] But Medici motives had more to do with Machiavelli's doctrine of the danger of neutrality to a weak state than with English ideas of the balance of power. The English ambassador at Rome remonstrated with Leo on his precipitancy in siding with the emperor, but ' with-out effect. They are all so bent on ' down with the French-men, whom they think weak and the emperor strong.' [3]

War between Francis I and Charles V had natural if not rational foundations. They have been explained by Pascal : '' ce chien est à moi ' disent ces pauvres enfants ; ' c'est là ma place au soleil ' : voilà le com-mencement et l'image de l'usurpation de toute la terre.' [4] France had despoiled Charles of much of the Burgundian inheritance he claimed and was in military occupation of the imperial fief of Milan. Charles, on the other hand, was detaining Spanish Navarre which he had pro-mised to restore ; was refusing to carry out other promises he had made at the treaty of Noyon ; and by the mere facts of his fortunate inheritances had almost completed the encirclement of France. On his side, Charles V was impelled by the need of establishing com-munications between the vast dominions now first united under one sceptre in Germany and Italy, the Nether-lands and Spain. There were two alternative routes : the first through the straits of Dover, and the second

[1] Creighton, *Papacy*, vi. 184 *n.* ; *Camb. Mod. Hist.* ii. 141 ; Ranke, *Die Römischen Päpste*, ed. 1889, i. 56.

[2] *Spanish Cal.* 1509-25, pp. 699-700 ; cf. *ibid.* pp. 322, 325, 343, 354, 356. Charles V's accusation was justified : ' He is consulted,' wrote bishop Clerk of Giulio de Medici from Rome on 9 July 1521, ' by the pope in all things ' (*L.P.* iii. 1402).

[3] *Ibid.*   [4] *Pensées*, xxiv. 34.

from Barcelona to Genoa and thence through Milan to the Tyrol. France might threaten both : her threat in the English Channel could be parried by an English alliance ; and for this reason Charles, in spite of all provocation, maintained his friendship with Henry VIII and married his son to Henry's daughter.[1] There was no such shield for the other route : Francis I, especially with the help of his Turkish ally, could threaten Charles's Mediterranean communications ; and he barred them on land by his occupation of Milan. The Italian states were the Balkans of that age : their internecine strife invited intervention from powerful neighbours with cross-purposes in mind ; and offered to France an escape from encirclement by Charles, and to Charles a means of closing the gap in his communications. Control of the duchy of Milan and of its sea-gate at Genoa was the main objective of Charles's Italian policy ; and its achievement secured for Spain two and a half centuries of predominance in Italian politics and in the papal curia.

Wolsey contributed to this end, not because he believed in a balance of power and mistook Charles for the lighter and Francis for the heavier weight, but because he consistently followed a papal policy and was led by personal interests in the same direction.[2] Henry VIII was not made *fidei defensor* for nothing, and Wolsey extorted a good deal more than a title from Leo X and his successors ; an ampler commission than he had yet received as papal legate preceded, in April 1521, his adhesion to the latest phase of papal policy.[3] In the following

[1] Henry used this argument to Charles in 1521 : ' If the marriage between Mary and the dauphin go on,' he pointed out, ' and he [the dauphin] become king of France and, in her right, of England, the navies of England and France will shut him [Charles V] out of the seas ' (*L.P.* iii. p. 425).

[2] See below, pp. 161-4. The pope, writes Manuel to Charles V on 3 Nov. 1520, has ordered his nuncio in England to tell Wolsey to use his influence to bring about an intimate friendship between the holy see, the emperor, and Henry (*Spanish Cal.* 1509-25, p. 325).

[3] See below, pp. 180-1. The bulls, while dated 1 April, were not dispatched until 29 June (*L.P.* iii. 1403) ; Clerk describes them as containing ' faculties the like of which have not been seen in England for many years.'

month of May, in which Leo X made his treaty with
Charles and Luther was banned by the empire, Henry
VIII presented his book against Luther to the pope;
Wolsey, with the papal nuncio and the imperial ambassador at his feet, presided over a sermon by Fisher at
St. Paul's cross and a holocaust of Luther's works; and
the future Clement VII was given the bishopric of Worcester. Throughout the late summer and early autumn
Wolsey was at Calais and at Bruges playing the part of
arbiter between the rivals; but it was all what Skelton
calls 'a webbe of lylse wulse' intended to distract
Francis and extort higher bids from Charles.[1] Early
in July Leo X had dilated to Wolsey on the 'presumption and insolency' with which he had lately been
treated by the French, denounced Francis I as untrust-
worthy, undertook to 'spend his blood' in driving the
Frenchmen out of Italy, refused to have anything to do
with the conference at Calais, and said Henry would do
better to assist in restraining Francis than in making peace
between him and Charles.[2] Wolsey concluded a secret
treaty with Charles at Bruges on 25 August, but continued
to pretend friendship with Francis until 24 November,
when he threw off the mask.* Five days earlier the papal-
imperial troops had overrun the duchy of Milan, and
Wolsey rushed to the rescue of the conqueror.

The motives of his policy puzzled his contemporaries.
We have it on Sir Thomas More's authority that, when
the question of peace or war was discussed in council and
'some thought it wisdom to sit still and leave Charles
and Francis alone,' Wolsey often repeated a certain fable
of a country where the rain turned all whom it wetted
into fools, and wise men sheltered themselves in caves,
thinking afterwards to rule the fools; but the fools insisted on ruling themselves; and this fable, continues
More, 'has helped the king and the realm to spend many

---

[1] *Works*, ed. Dyce, ii. 30 (= linsey-woolsey, see *N.E.D.*). 'The
treating of truce,' Clerk told the pope, 'was only a color to deceive
the French king' (*L.P.* iii. 1574).
[2] *L.P.* iii. 1402; cf. *ibid.* 1430, 1895.

a fair penny.'[1] It also helped Wolsey to his fall; for his intervention in the war did not prevent Charles and Francis from making an independent peace in 1529, which finally discredited Wolsey's foreign policy.

Both French and imperial critics had expected that England would hold aloof and make her profit out of the loss the combatants inflicted on one another; even the pope, wrote Manuel on 6 February 1521, suspects the good faith of the king, and in a much higher degree, of the cardinal of England.[2] But neither Leo X nor Sir Thomas More was aware of the special inducement which turned the scale in favour of intervention. The French, wrote Charles V's ambassador in London on 7 April 1520, 'have promised, what we might have done much better, to make Wolsey pope.' The emperor took the hint and Wolsey accepted the bait; Charles undertook at Bruges to do his best to secure Wolsey's election as pope,[3] whenever a vacancy occurred. It came with unexpected rapidity: Leo X died on 2 December 1521, 'rejoicing more' at the recovery of Milan 'than at his election,'[4] and Wolsey, to the scandal of the Spanish bishop who represented Charles V at Henry's court, offered to subsidize a Spanish expedition to overawe the papal conclave.[5]

Five weeks later the emperor's old tutor was elected on 9 January 1522, taking the title of Adrian VI; and

[1] Sir T. More, *Englysh Workes*, ed. 1557, p. 1433; Roper, *Life of More*, ed. Singer, p. 133; *L.P.* vii. 1113.

[2] *Ibid.* iii. 2026; *Spanish Cal.* 1509-25, pp. 330, 338, 343, 346, 348-9, 354, 357-80.

[3] *L.P.* iii. 768, 1868, 1876-7, 1880, 1884, 1904-7. 'Vous direz,' wrote Charles to his ambassador in England on 14 Dec. 1521, on hearing of Leo's death, ' de par nous a Mons. le Legat comme nous avons toujours en notre bonne souvenance son avancement et exaltation, et le tenons racors de propos que luy avons tenuz à Bruges touchant la papalité . . . et nous y employerons très voluntier sans y riens espargner ' (Bradford, *Correspondence of Charles V*, 1850, p. 22). The French were reported to have repeated their promise at the time of the Field of Cloth of Gold (*Spanish Cal.* ii. 310). Charles also undertook to pay Wolsey's French pensions (Rymer, xiii. 769).

[4] *L.P.* iii. 1795; *Spanish Cal.* ii. 381-2.

[5] *L.P.* iii. 1892; Bradford, *Correspondence of Charles V*, pp. 26-7.

Charles apologised to Wolsey, declaring that his ambassador at Rome had received no instructions to advocate any other claim than Wolsey's : he had nevertheless proposed Adrian's name on the day that the conclave opened. The brevity of Adrian's pontificate provided another electoral opportunity in October 1523. This time Charles V did write letters in Wolsey's favour, dispatched them to his ambassador at Rome, and sent copies to Wolsey to prove his fidelity to his promise. But this did not exhaust the resources of Charles V's diplomacy. He also took the simple precaution of detaining the bearer of his letters to Rome at Barcelona until the election was over.[1] Once more the successful candidate was the emperor's nominee. It was not Wolsey, but that Giulio de Medici who had been the real author of the papal-imperial alliance of 1521 ; and he took the title of Clement VII. Charles's perfidy was really a compliment to Wolsey ; the emperor could not conceive of the English cardinal proving a pliant instrument of imperial policy.

It was now clear to Wolsey that he would never become pope by the favour of Charles V, and the imperial alliance lost its glamour ; even his pensions from Spanish bishoprics were not being paid.[2] The war, too, was accumulating costs which Wolsey had not counted, and public finance was provoking problems which he had hitherto ignored. They have been equally ignored by historians who have based on little evidence the most comprehensive but casual guesses at truth ; and Tudor

[1] L.P. iii. 3569, 3647 ; Spanish Cal. ii. 587, 590, 597. For Wolsey's efforts to secure his own election see L.P. iii. 3377, 3389, 3399, 3439, 3464, 3514, 3547, 3587-8, 3592-4. He not only wrote letters in his own recommendation for Henry to sign, but one to the emperor which he begged Henry to copy out in his own hand, 'putting therunto your secret sign and mark between your grace and the said emperor.' The comforting assurances Wolsey received from his agents at Rome during the progress of the election were not reflected in the ballot : he did not get a single vote. On his unpopularity at Rome see Spanish Cal. ii. 307, 309. Wolsey himself told Henry VIII that the cardinals were 'principally bent' on electing him (L.P. iii. 3609).

[2] Ibid. 3032, 3244, 3591 ; iv. 233, 261.

finance is, in spite of some good preliminary work, a mystery which still awaits elucidation. The reason is not lack of material, but its superabundance and the confusion into which it has been brought by successive changes in administrative categories. Dominated, for instance, by the familiar conceptions with which the historian inevitably starts, he thinks of public finance as depending exclusively on parliamentary supplies and as administered by the treasury or the exchequer ; and it is some time before he discovers that the key to financial history before 1688 is not to be found in parliamentary grants or in the records of the lord treasurer or of the chancellor of the exchequer. The general cause of this confusion has been laid bare by recent research in mediæval administrative history.[1] As parliament began to envelop the royal court and establish control over its older departments and outworks, the chancery and the exchequer, the king, so to speak, retired further within his palace, and constructed interior defences behind which his household, chamber, and wardrobe developed an administrative system immune from parliamentary attacks. In other words, side by side with a public finance dependent on parliamentary grants, there grew up an increasing amount of private royal finance, independent of that control, administered by household officials, and not accounted for in the exchequer. The survival to our own day of a chancellor of the duchy of Lancaster reminds us that the Lancastrians and their successors maintained that duchy as a distinct estate from the crown ; and the wars of the roses brought many other great estates into the hands of the Tudors, who carefully kept the ensuing revenues out of the hands of the exchequer and in the hands of the king's chamber.

The sums dealt with in the king's chamber came to include not only revenues from lands but loans to the king and fines for all sorts of offences, and largely exceeded in

---

[1] See Professor Tout's *Place of Edward II in English History*, 1914, preface, p. vi, and *Chapters in the Mediæval Administrative History*, vols. i. and ii. (1920) ; iii. and iv. (1928).

time those which were accounted for in the exchequer ; [1] and the effect was to liberate the greater part of the king's revenue from the stereotyped control of the exchequer and place it more readily at the disposal of the king or his favourite minister. Wolsey was popularly accused of this innovation. 'We have begun,' John Palsgrave makes him say, ' to break the order of the exchequer, without whose authority sometime there was no manner treasure delivered to be dispent for preparation of war, and by sending of our signet or commandment to the Tower for any manner sums we would ; and whereas the exchequer was wont, after war finished, to make process against all such as were charged with any sums of the king's treasure to call them to their account, we neither have nor can give account thereof, save only that there came out of the Tower, employed by our disposition, 1,300,000*l*.' [2]   In point of fact the change was one of Henry VII's achievements ; but during the reaction of the first three years of Henry VIII the exchequer recovered a good deal of its authority.[3]   Wolsey's advent to power made a change in this as in other matters : an act of

---

[1] In 1529 (*L.P.* iv. App. 250), John Hyde, clerk of the pipe or ' engrosser of the great roll of the exchequer ' (*ibid.* iii. 529 [27]) complains that ' the great accountants now account before the king's general surveyors instead of in the exchequer ' ; and ' the surveyors' court is the chamber ' (*ibid.* 1545, ii. 769 and *n.*, ' the treasurer of the chamber was *ex officio* treasurer of the court of general surveyors ' ; cf. *ibid.* ii. 910 [60] and 1546, i. 149 [21], where the locality of the new building to replace the old ' prince's chamber,' is described). A summary note of their sources of revenue is in *ibid.* v. 397. For Sir H. Wyatt's accounts for the loan of 1522, see *ibid.* iv. 214 ; he was treasurer of the chamber.

[2] *Ibid.* iv. p. 2557. Accounts were in fact carefully kept ; but no one controlled Wolsey's warrants for expenditure, and the treasurer of the chamber was accountable not to the exchequer but only to the king or such person as he should appoint (*Rot. Parl.* Suppl. p. c*a*).

[3] See Professor A. P. Newton in *Eng. Hist. Rev.* 1917, pp. 348-72, continued in *Tudor Studies*, ed. R. W. Seton-Watson, 1924, pp. 231-56. Palsgrave seems to have realised his error. He continues his charge : ' We have begun to reform the abusions used in the processes made out of the exchequer [and to establish surveyors of the king's revenues, and much of his prerogatives which fore-time were accustomed to be accounted in the exchequer].' But the words between square brackets have been struck through in the MS.

1512 sanctioned the practice of Henry VII; and Wolsey obtained a free hand to dispose, with Henry's connivance, of the greater part of the revenues of the crown.[1]

[1] The import of this act, passed in the second session of the second parliament of Henry VIII (12 Nov.-20 Dec. 1512) is obscured by its title 'pro Roberto Suthwell, milite' (*Rot. Parl.* Suppl. pp. xviii-xxiii). It begins by reciting how Henry VII's receivers 'did accompt, by his commandment by mouth afore' Sir Reginald Bray, Sir Robert Southwell, and others whom Henry appointed 'as well for the more speedy payment of his revenues to be had, and for the accompts of the same more speedily to be taken, than . . . after the course of his exchequer, as for the greater ease and less charge of the foresaid accomptants.' After his death and the attainder of Empson and Dudley, the exchequer refused to recognise this practice, and Henry's agents remained in 1512 'yet chargeable to accompt and to make their payments in the said exchequer . . . continually vexed and troubled . . . and also there to be compelled to make new payments for the same in the king's receipt of the said exchequer, as if they never had accompted nor made payments . . . against all right reason and good conscience.' The act proceeds to legalise accounting in the king's chamber 'in manner and form above said' before Southwell and Bartholomew Westby, his special commissioners; to declare that they shall henceforth be called 'general surveyors'; that John Heron 'be from henceforth treasurer of the king's chamber,' and be accountable to 'no other than the king in his chamber, and not in the said exchequer.'

The act was 'to endure and be effectual unto the next parliament,' which met on 5 Feb. 1515 (the second parliament had a third session from 23 Jan.-4 March 1513-14, but no act dealing with the matter was passed in that year; see list in *L.P.* new ed. i. 2590). The bill to renew the expiring act had a curious passage: it was introduced in the lords by the attorney-general and read first on 7 March; it was read a second time and committed to the attorney-general to be 'reformed,' on 15 March; on the 17th it was 'tradita cuidam Astley famulo et nuntio, ut asserebat, Johannis Ernley, attornat. regis, per mandatum eiusdem attornat.' On the 22nd it was read a third time and 'reddita Johanni Ernley'; on the 23rd a bill 'annectenda billae concernenti generales receptores' was received in the lords, read a first time, and sent with the original bill to the commons. No more is said of it until the autumn session when on 16 Nov. a 'billa concernens generales regis receptores, prius per dominos et communes assentita, lecta est.' No more is heard of either bill; but two acts appear on the parliament roll, one as 6 Henry VIII, c. 24, and the other as 7 Henry VIII, c. 7, these dates implying that one was passed in the first, and the other in the second, session of 1515. This act was to come into force on 1 Jan. 1516 and to continue until the dissolution of the next parliament (1523), which passed yet another continuing act extending the privileges and powers of the king's chamber (*Rot. Parl.* Suppl. pp. xcv-cv; *Lords' Journals*, i. 29, 33-4, 36-7, 45; *Statutes of the Realm*, iii. 219-30).

The financial results of Wolsey's emancipation from the control of the exchequer are summed up in somewhat unexpected terms by the only student who has hitherto made a special study of this aspect of the subject.[1] 'The increases in expenditure,' we are told, 'made by Henry VIII were comparatively small, and in no way show undue luxury or extravagance on the part of the king or the court;' and 'it seems that the crown resources . . . would have been sufficient for many years to meet the needs of government, had no extraordinary drains been made upon them.' For the first three years of the reign, the annual expenditure of the treasurer of the chamber did not exceed £65,000. But the war policy adopted in 1512 produced a significant change. In that year expenditure rose from £64,000 to nearly £270,000, and in 1513 to nearly £700,000. To meet this phenomenal increase [2] Wolsey obtained from parliament in 1513 an unsuccessful poll-tax, and in 1514—in addition to a mediæval tenth and fifteenth—a novel subsidy of 1s. in the £ on income from land and wages, and a capital levy of 1s. in the £ on the value of goods. This subsidy produced £90,000, three times the yield of a tenth and a fifteenth; and it remained the regular form of tax for more than a century.[3] Wolsey supplemented these resources in 1515 by a rigorous inquisition into war-profiteering and a resumption of crown lands.[4] Never-

---

[1] F. C. Dietz, *English Government Finance*, 1485-1558 (1921), pp. 90-101.

[2] It was even more rapid, proportionally, than the increase in English budgets during the war of 1914-18 ; see my article on the political history of England, 1911-26, in the *Encyclopædia Britannica*, supplementary vols. (1926). Professor Dietz had not, I think, seen Palsgrave's charges, and it is rather remarkable that his £270,000 for 1512, £700,000 for 1513, and £155,000 for 1514 (excluding the issues of the exchequer) should come so nearly to Palsgrave's total of £1,300,000 (above, p. 129) and Tyndale's £1,400,000 (below, p. 228).

[3] Dr. James Tait's admirably lucid introduction to *Taxation in Salford Hundred*, 1524-1802 (Chetham Soc. 1924, pp. xx-xxvi) contains the clearest exposition that I know of the development and nature of the Tudor subsidy.

[4] *L.P.* ii. 1435, 1455, 1595, 1795 ; Hall, p. 585 (above, p. 75). Palsgrave's charge that Wolsey rendered no account did not imply that he

theless, the treasure left by Henry VII had been largely depleted, and financial prudence as well as papal precept had counselled the peace of London in 1518.

But papal precept, combined with papal example, outweighed financial prudence in 1521 ; and war was resumed without any apparent thought of how its expenses were to be met. Parliament was not consulted nor asked for any supplies. Henry VIII had suggested its summons, to deal with Buckingham's case and other matters in 1521,[1] but none met until 1523. Yet for the sake of war in Europe, he was in 1521 compelled by lack of money to leave Scotland to the French faction and Ireland to stew in its native juice. By 1522 there was no money in the king's coffers to pay for the war with France : £20,000 were borrowed of London in June and £352,231 were raised by forced loans within the next twelve months.[2] But this met less than half the cost of one year's war, and a parliament was inevitable : on 15 April 1523 it met for the first time since 1515, and for the first and only time in Tudor history to meet the whole cost of a war.

For the loan of 1522 Wolsey had made a rigorous assessment which raised the productivity of 1s. in the £ from the £90,000 of 1514 to £200,000 ;[3] and he now

demanded no account from others. There was also an inquiry why the subsidies in certain shires were worse in 1515-16 than in 1513-14 (*L.P.* vii. p. 344 [xviii]).

[1] *L.P.* iii. 1204 : ' et pro ea re et Hibernicis convocabit . . . parliamentum.'

[2] Dietz, *loc. cit.* The loan was to be a quarter of each man's possessions and was to be paid in five yearly instalments ; a certain amount was obtained by ' the anticipation ' (*L.P.* iii. 1050). The individual assessments on the spiritualty for the loan are given in *L.P.* iii. 2483. They range from Wolsey's £4000 downwards : several abbots are assessed, like the archbishop of Canterbury, at £1000, but Abingdon at £1333 6s. 8d. On its method of assessment, see bishop West to Wolsey, *ibid.* iii. 2615 ; cf. 2485-8 and other references s.v. ' Loan ' in the index to *L.P.* iii. An adverse opinion on its legality was given by Mr. Justice Pollard ; but Sir Robert Wingfield, writing to Wolsey on 17 July 1522, says he has shown the king ' what dexterity your grace used to defeat the said opinion ' (*L.P.* iii. 2393).

[3] Tait, *loc. cit.* Hall (p. 642) says this loan was only demanded from the rich.

demanded £800,000 to be raised by a tax of 4s. in the £ on land and goods. The commons offered half that amount, the payment to be spread over two years, 1s. in the £ in 1523, and the other in 1524. A curious conflict arose between the knights of the shires and the burgesses, who voted separately ; and Sir Thomas More, as speaker, took strategic advantage of it to secure a third shilling in the £ both on land and goods.[1] Wolsey, in the most gracious of his letters, wrote highly to Henry VIII of More's services in the matter, and on account of them and of the length of the session obtained for him a £100 ' reward ' in addition to the £100 which was the speaker's regular fee.[2] But the session had been a stormy one : Wolsey had tried to browbeat the house of commons, and in spite of More's skill in conciliation,[3] it was not until 13 August that a parliament, opened on 15 April, could be induced to grant a part of Wolsey's demands. His tax on goods was a capital levy, not an income-tax ; ' goods ' were extended to include coin as well as plate ; and an attempt was made to tax wages. The vote of the commons to spread the payment over a period of years was overridden by Wolsey after the dissolution by what he called an ' anticipation,' a term, says Hall, that was new

---

[1] Hall (*Chron.* pp. 652, 655-7) gives the fullest and best account of this parliament. The formal business and acts are recorded on the parliament roll (*Rot. Parl.* Suppl. pp. lxxv-cxlix), but there are no journals extant. A contemporary letter to the earl of Surrey, giving an account of the tax debate, is printed in Ellis, *Original Letters*, 1, i. 220-3, and summarised in *L.P.* iii. 3024. The well-known and very able speech, usually attributed to Cromwell, is printed *in extenso* in R. B. Merriman's *Life and Letters of Cromwell*, 1902, i. 30-44, and summarised in *L.P.* iii. 2958. Cromwell's undoubted letter on the subject is printed in Merriman, i. 313-14, and summarised in *L.P.* iii. 3249. The complicated details of the subsidy voted are on pp. lxxvii-xc of the *Rot. Parl.* The commissioners are given in *L.P.* iii. 3282, 3504.

[2] *State Papers*, i. 124.

[3] Roper's story (*More*, pp. 19-20) about Wolsey's displeasure is either fictitious or much exaggerated ; cf. More's acknowledgements (*L.P.* iii. 3270, 3291, 3363). For the cardinal's browbeating of John Bridgeman, a very independent Exeter M.P., see W. J. Harte, *Gleanings from . . . John Hooker* (Exeter, 1925 ?) p. 34.

to the commonalty ;[1] and commissions were issued to collect the whole subsidy at once. The clergy were as discontented as the commons, and Wolsey treated convocation worse than parliament. It granted a half-year's income from benefices to be levied in five annual instalments ; but inasmuch as the abbey of St. Albans was alleged to be in debt, Wolsey was left as legate to decide how much he as abbot should pay.[2]

The difficulty of collecting the general parliamentary taxes was not eased by the fact that Wolsey's commissioners were still extorting the loan of 1522 under privy seals.[3] There had been no enthusiasm for Wolsey's wars at any time ; and the only unofficial speech that remains from the parliament of 1523 is a remarkable attack, attributed to Cromwell, on Wolsey's neglect of the British Isles and fondness for continental war. Apart from the participation in Julius II's holy league, no parliamentary sanction had been sought for these European adventures. People acquiesced so long as they were not compelled to pay. But when Henry VII's treasure had been exhausted and parliament was confronted in 1523 with a bill for the whole of the costs, the nation began to display a stubborn preference for peace. Still, the country was law-abiding and patriotic ; and when in October, while Suffolk was leading an army on Paris and Surrey another on the Scottish borders, Wolsey sent out commissions to demand the whole parliamentary subsidy in ' anticipation ' of the statutory dates, it was paid ' out of hand without delay.'[4]

---

[1] *Chronicle*, p. 672 ; the term is used of the loan of 1522 in *L.P.* iii. p. 1050.

[2] Wilkins, *Concilia*, iii. 699 ; *L.P.* iii. 3239. See below, pp. 190-1. If the benefice was worth less than £8 a year, it paid one-third instead of a half. The record of the collection of the 1526 instalment in Lincoln diocese has been edited for the Oxford Historical Society (1909) by the Rev. H. E. Salter, who points out that the assessment was made on Wolsey's new valuation of benefices, and not, as Brewer thought, on the old ' taxatio ' of 1291 (pp. iv-vi).

[3] *L.P.* iii. 3476, 3491, 3519, 3584-5 ; iv. 214 (Wyatt's account).

[4] Hall, p. 672. The dates fixed by parliament had been : 11 Nov. for the assessment, 13 Jan. 1524 for certification into the exchequer, and 9 Feb. for payment. Hall is referring primarily to London ; in Wilt-

Peace, however, was growing not merely a national but a European necessity. While the emperor and 'catholic king' of Spain, the 'most christian king' of France, and the English 'defender of the faith' were exposing the discord of christendom, the Turks were battering its defences. The fall of Belgrade on 29 August 1521 was followed by the surrender of Rhodes on 28 December 1522. If the Turks came to Italy, wrote Wolsey's master of the rolls from Rome, they would find it defenceless [1]; and pope Adrian set himself to make peace among christian princes. Legates were appointed to various courts for the purpose, but not to England. 'There is already a papal legate in England,' said Wolsey's agent to the pope; and Wolsey, wrote Campeggio, 'is expected to turn Henry's mind to peace.' [2] But, while that legate was reproaching Charles V for having kept none of his promises, he was deaf to the pope's appeal and blind to the Moslem peril.[3] He would give no aid to Ferdinand in Hungary and declared that the only Turk he knew was Francis I. Francis himself would not listen to a truce unless Milan were restored; and, as a justification

shire it was found necessary on 27 Feb. to send the commissioners 'a memorial for their direction in consequence of the misinterpretation and misapplication of the act' and instructions to apologise for 'the said defaults' (L.P. iv. 122). From Yorkshire Lord Clifford reported on 28 May that 'all the commons in Craven and other places were well-disposed, giving in their bills, till they heard of the misbehaviour of the commons of Richmondshire, when they would proceed no further, nor indent with the commissioners, who can therefore make no return into the exchequer' (ibid. 377-8). Confusion arises from the fact that moneys paid in 'anticipation' of the subsidy are also called loans (ibid iii. 3650, 3683-8) and were paid into the chamber, not into the exchequer. For the singular conspiracy at Coventry to seize the collected subsidy and occupy Kenilworth castle, see Hall, p. 673; R. Hill's Chron. (E.E.T.S. 1907) p. 159; L.P. iv. 105, 1568.

[1] Ibid. iii. 2841. He had described Rhodes as 'the key of christendom,' and declared that 'if that island were taken, the pope could not stay in Rome' (Hannibal to Wolsey, Rome, 13 Jan. 1523, L.P. iii. 2771; cf. ibid. 2849 where Adrian describes Rhodes and Belgrade as 'the outworks of Christendom,' and depicts the ease with which the Turk could conquer Hungary, Sicily, and Italy).

[2] Ibid. iii. 2863, 2871-3.   [3] Ibid. iii. 2881, 2891, 3093.

for his demand for unprecedented taxation in England, Wolsey had promised parliament ' such a war in France as hath not been seen.' The duke of Bourbon had revolted against Francis I, Venice had joined the allies,[1] and Suffolk was sent in the autumn to harry France nearly up to the gates of Paris : never hereafter, wrote Wolsey to Henry on 3 November 1523, would there be a better chance of enforcing his title to the French crown.[2]

But the ground was crumbling beneath his feet. On 17 October he had written to Henry apologising for having to call upon him for money, but the armies of Surrey, Bourbon, and Suffolk had required twice as much as he and the king had estimated : he could find no money for Suffolk's troops in November unless Henry could spare ten thousand pounds which should be repaid as soon as possible ; he had pressed so hard to levy taxes that nothing more could be done.[3] It was perhaps more ominous for Wolsey that the king than that his people should be called upon to pay ; and, in spite of his assurance that nothing could be done, he issued on 2 November further commissions for the payment ' by anticipation ' of the subsidy voted by parliament.[4] The commissions were prefaced by a glowing account of how Suffolk had taken Ancre and Braye, crossed the Somme, and was ' on his way to Paris,' while Bourbon, ' one of the greatest princes in France and now the declared enemy of the French king,' was also ' in pursuit of the said king with ten thousand Almains in the pay of England.' This fancy sketch soon faded into greyer hues. Montdidier was the furthest point in Suffolk's advance ; he received neither pay for his troops

---

[1] L.P. iii. 3145 ; Spanish Cal. ii. 444 ; Hall, p. 655.

[2] State Papers, i. 143. Suffolk's was, wrote Wolsey, the largest army that had ' passed out of this realm for a hundred years ' (L.P. iii. 3207, 3248, 3271, 3281, 3505).

[3] State Papers, i. 144 ; L.P. iii. 3433.

[4] Ibid. iii. 3504 ; Egerton Papers (Camden Soc.), pp. 4-7. London is not mentioned in these commissions, and presumably they only apply to the rest of the country the pressure which, according to Hall, was put upon the city in October, though Hall says they were sent ' in October through the realm.'

nor reinforcements. Charles V's Burgundians were no better provided and retired within their frontiers, leaving Suffolk with no choice but to follow suit. Bourbon, instead of pursuing his king, fled to the emperor for protection. The campaign ended in mutual recriminations between the two allies; and stalemate in the war led them to explore the paths of secret and separate approach to peace, each accusing the other of the treachery common to both.

On the top of this military disappointment came on 6 December the news of Wolsey's second failure in the papal election. He had promised his supporters to be in Rome within three months if he were successful; and in spite of his professions to Henry VIII that he 'would rather continue to serve him than be ten popes,'[1] he was not a man to take lightly the defeat of his highest ambition. He rightly ascribed it to the intervention of Charles V and never forgave the emperor; thenceforth there was enmity between the two until Wolsey fell. The new pope, Clement VII, encouraged Wolsey's detachment from the imperial cause and disappointed the hopes Charles entertained of his devotion; 'he is so called upon for peace,' wrote Clerk, 'and is so expected to promote it, that he cannot openly show himself against France for a season. . . . There is as much craft and policy in him as in any man.'[2] His Medicean and Machiavellian principle was to begin treating with a foe as soon as he had contracted with a friend;[3] and he has better claims than Wolsey to whatever credit attaches to the invention of the doctrine of the balance of power. *Judas non dormit*, was bishop Clerk's comprehensive comment; and within a year of his election Clement concluded a secret treaty with France. Wolsey, as usual, took his cue from Rome, and a few weeks after the receipt of Clerk's information a skilful French agent[4] was secretly

[1] *L.P.* iii. 3372, 3389, 3609.   [2] *Ibid.* iii. 3594; cf. *ibid.* 3651.
[3] Ranke, *Die römischen Päpste*, i. 55, a counsel attributed to Leo X by Antonio Suriano in his Roman 'relazione,' 1533.
[4] *L.P.* iv. 271-4, 662, 678, 680; Gilbert Jacqueton, *La politique extérieure de Louise de Savoie*, 1892, pp. 46-97. Giovanni Giovacchino

in London negotiating with the cardinal. England took no part in the operations of 1524, and peace with France would have followed but for the thunderclap of Pavia on Charles V's twenty-fifth birthday, 24 February 1525. The French army was almost annihilated and Francis I himself was taken prisoner to Spain. Clement VII and Wolsey had done their best to ruin the French by siding with Charles in 1521, and had then withdrawn from the struggle just in time to deprive themselves of all claim to gratitude from the victor and all share in the spoils of victory. For the rest of their lives they were both paying forfeit for their imprudence.

Wolsey's first idea, so far from redressing the balance of power, was to call on Charles to complete the ruin of France by deposing the Valois dynasty and restoring to Henry VIII the provinces conquered by Edward III and Henry V ;[1] and he sent the lord privy seal (Tunstal) and

di Passano, afterwards sieur de Vaux and known in England as John Jochim (see below, pp. 269-71 ; Cavendish, pp. 64-66 ; and Hall, pp. 691, 693, 697, 704, 711 *). On 20 Oct. Charles V demanded the dismissal of this French envoy, who had arrived in London on 22 June 1524 (Jacqueton, p. 50), in accordance with the treaty of Windsor, on the ground of the injury his long stay did to their common affairs. He had heard that Francis I expected to get what he wanted from Wolsey, and that he had only been encouraged to concentrate against the imperialists in Provence by assurance that the English would make no attack in Picardy (ibid. iv. 752). Clement VII had the same information (ibid. 883). On 16 Jan. 1525 Wolsey, while denouncing Clement VII's agreement with Francis I, said the pope 'is not to credit any sinister reports that may be spread by reason of the French king's mother's servant being in England' (ibid. p. 446). On 12 Feb. he wrote to Henry congratulating him that, in case the imperialists got the worst of it in Italy, his affairs were 'in more assured and substantial train, by such communications as be set forth with France apart, than others in outward places would suppose' (ibid. no. 1078). For Wolsey's other falsehoods about John Jochim's mission see his letter to Dr. Sampson on 13 Feb. 1525 (ibid. no. 1083). Wolsey had made things worse by imprisoning Charles V's ambassador in London for having detected this intrigue and described it to Charles with some unfavourable comments on Wolsey in dispatches, which the cardinal had intercepted and opened (Spanish Cal. 1525-6, pp. 13-16, 42, 50, 64, 112 ; L.P iv. 1083, 1154, 1190, 1213, 1237, 1247-8, 1380).

[1] Ibid. iv. 1212, 1301 ; he even wanted to exclude 'all French-born kings of France' (ibid. p. 572).

the chancellor of the duchy of Lancaster (Sir Richard Wingfield) [1] to join the dean of the chapel royal (Sampson) in the embassy at Madrid, and press the emperor to make the joint invasion which 'Providence had postponed' in 1524. Charles was as alive to the folly of such a policy as he was dead to an appeal from Wolsey to the sanctity of treaties. 'The negotiations with Joachim,' wrote Tunstal from Toledo to Wolsey in cipher, 'are perfectly known here'; and he thought the French ambassadors, coming to treat for their sovereign's release, would bring all the letters with them to try and separate Henry and Charles.[2] The emperor wanted also an explanation of the reports de Praet sent him that Wolsey had talked of Charles aspiring to universal monarchy and being prevented by Henry with Wolsey's advice and aid; had called him a liar, his aunt Margaret a ribald, his brother Ferdinand a child, and Bourbon a traitor; and had said that Henry 'had other things to do with his money than to spend it for the pleasure of four such personages.' Wolsey, said Charles, must either have meant these things, or have spoken 'to threat him,' or 'in a fume and haste, the which he most believed, by other times that he had known him in like passions.'[3] Charles was now bent on marrying the wealthy Isabella of Portugal in lieu of waiting for Mary of England and depending on hypothetical English supplies. Only after this rebuff did Wolsey finally turn to the French alliance and balance of power; and he did so, not because he loved France or the balance, but because he loved Charles V less than either.

[1] Not to be confused with his brother, Sir Robert Wingfield, who was simultaneously sent on a similar errand to the regent of the Netherlands. According to Roper, Wolsey 'for the revengement of his displeasure, counselled the king to send' More 'ambassador to Spain,' and More prudently declined on the ground of health (*Life of More*, pp. 20-1). Wingfield died at Toledo on 22 July 1525, and More succeeded him as chancellor of the duchy; Tunstal and Sampson also fell seriously ill (*ibid.* iv. 1555).

[2] *L.P.* iv. 1378-80; cf. Sampson's 'three reasons why the emperor feels less bound to Wolsey' (*ibid.* iv. 1190).

[3] Ellis, *Original Letters*, III, ii. 14; *L.P.* iv. 1379.

Clement VII had already refused any truck with Wolsey's proposals for renewing the war on France, in spite of Wolsey's threats that his refusal would irritate English and Germans ' who are ready,' he said, ' to take any occasion against the holy see.'[1] It was the continuance of wars, replied the pope, that subverted the faith : he spoke of the ruin of Germany, distracted by schism and peasants' revolts, and concluded that ' if the wars continued, we should see a new world shortly.' Circumstances were too strong for Clement VII : he wanted peace with France, but he also wanted Italy freed from the incubus of imperial troops ; and his peace with France was to prepare a crusade of Italian princes, France, and England for that purpose. Only, wrote Giberti, the papal datary, ' let there be given to the king of England and to the cardinal of York all the glory and the incense which they covet ; for if you gain him this once, you gain him for ever.'[2] It was, however, neither love of glory nor Roman incense that constrained Wolsey to peace. Their reception by Charles convinced Henry's ambassadors that, if France was to be invaded in 1525, he must invade it alone. If the English wish for war, Charles had written on 26 March, he leaves to them the responsibility for it ; and the attitude of Henry's subjects forbade any invasion at all.[3]

Five days before Wolsey sent ambassadors to revive the emperor's martial spirit, he set to work to raise supplies from the English people. The news of Pavia had reached England on 9 March, and on the 21st Wolsey was commissioned to ' treat with ' the city of London, while other commissioners were appointed throughout the country to collect money for a fresh campaign. The king, it was announced, intended to go in person, and stress was laid on the defeat and captivity of Francis I and on the need of turning the victory of the allies to the best account.[4] The second instalment of the parliamentary subsidy was still being paid,[5] when the duke of Norfolk was selected

---

[1] *L.P.* iv. 1336.   [2] *Ibid.* iv. 1467, 1492-3.
[3] *Ibid.* iv. 1213, 1378 (p. 615).   [4] *Ibid.* iv. 1199, 1200.
[5] *Ibid.* iv. 331, 417, 522, 638, 969-70, 1134, 1299, 1321, 1327.

to begin the experiment of collecting an unauthorised, forced, and additional loan, based on the assessment of their property which Wolsey had induced people to make in 1522 under a pledge that no one should see their assessments but himself and the king. Norfolk reached Norwich on Wednesday 29 March, appointed 'discreet persons to declare to the people the great overthrow of the French king,' ordered bonfires to be lit in accordance with Wolsey's instructions in every town on the following Sunday to celebrate the event, and began 'after dinner' to practise with the most likely subscribers to the loan. Even then they could or would not provide ready money, though they offered smaller sums in plate. Norfolk thought their offers should be accepted : the plate could be coined into dandiprats which 'would be good enough for the army to spend in France'; but there would be great difficulty in raising money generally throughout the shire.[1]

His forebodings were justified. Warham began in Kent the day after Norfolk. He reported [2] that it would be hard to raise the money, especially as the parliamentary grants were now payable, and proceeded to retail for Wolsey's secret ear what men were saying : they spoke 'cursedly . . . rekonyng themselues, their childrene, and wyfes as desperats, and not greately caring what they doo or what become of thayme';[3] saying they would never

---

[1] Norfolk to Wolsey, 1 April 1525, Ellis, III, i. 376-81 ; L.P. iv. 1235, 1261. Cf. his letter to Wolsey on April 10 (L.P. iv. App. 36) : 'The commissioners sent to the duke two hundred persons whom they could not induce to the grant, and he has so treated them that not one has refused . . . they have shed many salt tears for doubt how to find money.' According to Tyndale (Practice of Prelates, Parker Soc. p. 306) Henry VII coined 'dandiprats' for his army to spend in France in 1492, thereby saving a quarter of his expenses.

[2] To Wolsey, 5 April, Ellis, III, i. 369-75 ; L.P. iv. 1243. Cf. Hall, p. 696 : 'The poore cursed, the riche repugned, the light wittes railed, but in conclusion, all the people cursed the cardinal and his coadherents as subversor of the lawes and libertie of Englande.' See also Warham's letter to Wolsey on 21 April (L.P. iv. App. 39).

[3] Cf. Roy, Rede me, p. 50,

> That poure commens with their wyves
> In maner are weary of their lyves.

have rest from payments so long as Wolsey lived; that other commissioners than Warham would not, for fear of the people, press their demands; that the last loan had not been repaid as promised out of the parliamentary subsidy, nor would this; that if the king did win France, it would only impoverish England, for it would cost more to keep than to win; that they had more cause to weep than to make bonfires over the French king's captivity;[1] and that after all these wars and expenditure Henry VIII 'hath not one foot of land more in Fraunce than his most noble father hadd, which lakked no riches or wisdom to wyne the kingdome of Fraunce if he hadd thought it expedient.'

The duke of Suffolk found that county apparently more amenable, the laity merely complaining that, while they were expected to make bonfires, the clergy offered no thanksgivings in their churches. But he wanted to know what authority the commissioners had in case anyone refused to pay 'the sum he has granted.'[2] That word 'grant' was the crux of the situation. The demand had been variously described as a loan, a subsidy, and a 'voluntary aid.' A subsidy, at any rate, was a parliamentary tax, a loan was supposed to be repaid, and 'aids' were feudal customs which centuries of constitutional struggle had restricted to specific persons and specific occasions. But Wolsey, in a letter to Norfolk on 11 April, translated 'voluntary aid' into 'amicable grant,' by which designation the attempted extortion has ever since been known. It was perhaps the most violent financial exaction in English history: the amicable grant was a capital levy of one-sixth on the goods of the laity and one-third on those of the clergy, and a similar tax on incomes from lands, benefices, salaries, and wages; and these rates were fixed not, of course, by parliament, nor even in any commission from the king, but in the secret instructions which Wolsey sent the commissioners

[1] Cf. J. L. Vives to Henry VIII from Oxford, 12 March (*L.P.* iv. 1177), saying that the misfortunes of France excited compassion everywhere and exhorting him 'not to pluck out one of the eyes of all Europe.'
[2] *Ibid.* iv. 1260.

after their appointment.[1]   It was, in fact, a systematic
extension to people with less than £20 capital and to
wage-earners, of the 'benevolences' which had been
extracted from wealthier folk, largely by the personal
blandishments of Edward IV, and had been forbidden
by parliament under Richard III.[2]

Warham found the clergy even more recalcitrant than
the laity.[3]   The religious were particularly sore because
of Wolsey's monastic dissolutions ; and the archbishop
took the opportunity of suggesting the postponement of
the dissolutions until the business of the grant was finished:
' it hath been thought good policy in times past not to
broach too many matters of displeasure at once.' [4]   Three
days later he emphasised to Sir T. Boleyn his warnings of
general resistance : ' I have been in this shire twentie
yeres and above, and as yet I have not seen men but wold
be conformable to reason, and wold be enduced to good
ordre, tyll this tyme ' ; [5]   it was hopeless, he wrote, to
proceed with the men from £20 downwards while their

[1] Cf. Norfolk's references to ' the rates expressed in the instructions,'
which he distinguishes from the ' letters ' and the ' commissions,' and
Warham's to ' the streictness of the instructions ' (Ellis, III, i. 370,
376-7).   The instructions to Warham are calendared in *L.P.* iv. App. 34 ;
and the archbishop is there told that if any of the persons, whose names
are inclosed, are not taxed at one-third, he must assess them at that
figure himself.

[2] Scofield, *Edward IV*, 1923, ii. 104-6, 304-5, 385-6.   For the assessment of wage-earners, see Tait, *op. cit.* p. xxvi.

[3] Cf. Hall, p. 696 : ' They saied that the cardinall and all the doers
thereof were enemies to the kyng and to the commonwealthe.   This
infamie was spoken in preachynges and euerywhere ; ' and Skelton, ed.
Dyce, i. 356-8, where ' us ' is Wolsey :

> At Powles crosse or els where,
> Openly at Westmynstere,
> At Saynt Mary Spyttell,
> They set not by us a whystell :
> At the Austen fryers
> They count us for lyers :
> At Saynt Thomas of Akers
> They carpe us lyke crakers,
> Howe we wyll rule all at wyll
> Without good reason or skyll

[4] *L.P.* iv. 1263.   [5] Ellis, III, i. 365-6.

richer neighbours stood out. The clergy, he wrote the same day to Wolsey, acknowledged their obligation to pay taxes voted in convocation ; but Wolsey's demand for a third of their goods would prevent them from supporting their fathers and mothers or dispensing hospitality to the poor.[1] Bishop West wrote in much the same strain on 19 April from Ely ; he 'feared trouble unless the matter be soberly and politicly handled.'[2]

Wolsey's handling of the city of London, for which he was sole commissioner, was neither sober nor politic. He sent for the mayor, aldermen, and 'divers hedde comminers,' told them the king was 'compelled of verie force to entre into a new war,' basing his case on a most unveracious account of his dealings with France, on its being brought to 'such penury and wretchedness that in many yeres it will not be recouered,' on the defeat and capture of Francis, and on the poet's saying—which, he said, the king remembered—that 'it is more mastery to use victory gotten, than to get it.' He had told his ambassadors in Spain that 'all the shires were willing to contribute ' ;[3] and he now told the city fathers that the church had given a third of its lands, and the temporal lords a sixth, besides offering ' to jeopard their bodies in pain and travaill.' 'What,' he asked, 'should they give which abide at home ? Forsooth, I think that halfe your substance were too little.' Not, he said, that the king was asking so much—only a sixth from those with £50 and upwards, and a shilling in the pound from those with less than £20 ; 'and resist not, nor ruffill not in this case, for it may fortune to cost some their heddes.' For the next fortnight he sent every day for a certain number of commoners, some of whom answered him with such words that they were sent to prison.[4]

During that fortnight the south-eastern shires were in an uproar. 'Many have been put in hope,' wrote Norfolk on 30 April, ' to pay nothing by rumors that those of London nor the other shires will consent to the first rates ' ; Norwich, he said, would not have offered

---

[1] Fiddes, *Collections*, pp. 29-31 ; cf. Hall, p. 696.
[2] *L.P.* iv. 1272.   [3] *Ibid.* 1249.   [4] Hall, pp. 694-6.

a sixth of what it had if the news from London had
come first, and commissioners were refusing to act on
their commissions. In Kent the demands for taxes had
rendered cattle and corn unsaleable in the markets, and
no good had been done by reports that London had secured
a remission.[1] ' The commons,' says a summary of letters
written early in May, some of which are now lost,[2] ' will
not grant anything by letters missive, but only by act of
parliament. . . . In some places the people arose up in
arms against the commissioners ; in others, those who
condescended to the grant were threatened by their
neighbours ; and some recalled their grant.' Lavenham
in Suffolk was a principal centre of disturbance, though
the dukes of Norfolk and Suffolk feared ' insurrection in
other shires more than this,' and warned the king that ' if
this business spreads, he should look to lords Stafford and
Abergavenny,' the son and son-in-law of Buckingham.[3]
In Essex its earl and lord Fitzwalter wrote of an unlawful
assembly of a thousand persons, declared that ' there is
great danger of more insurrections,' and suspended their
further proceedings till they had fresh instructions. On
the 11th the two dukes declared that not only Suffolk
and Essex, but the town and scholars of Cambridge had
all combined, to the number of twenty thousand, ' while
other countries are looking out for a stir that they may
do the same.' [4]   Bishop Longland of Lincoln feared for

---

[1] *L.P.* iv. 1295 ; Warham to Wolsey, *ibid.* 1305-6 ; cf. 1311.

[2] *Ibid.* iv. 1318.

[3] *Ibid.* iv. 1319. Lavenham was pronounced ' Lainham ' (cf.
Daventry = Daintry), and Skelton's lines (*Works*, ed. Dyce, ii. 55) on
' Good Sprynge of Lanam ' refer to John Spring of Lavenham (Dyce,
ii. 369, wrongly identifies it with Langham in Essex), a wealthy clothier
who acted as intermediary between the dukes and the insurgents, with
Thomas Jermyn or Germain (Hall, p. 700 ; *L.P.* iv. 1343 ; *Ancaster
MSS.* pp. 489-99). Several of the dukes' letters are dated from Lavenham.
Skelton's lines are to show how
> My lordis grace wyll brynge
> Downe this hye Sprynge.

[4] *L.P.* iv. 1321, 1323 ; *Hist. MSS. Comm.* 3rd Rep. p. 202 *a*. The
King's Lynn chronicler makes the precise but unconvincing statement
that ' 40,004 men ' rose in Suffolk (Flenley, *Six Town Chronicles*, p. 195).

that county ; in Huntingdonshire the commissioners were
forcibly prevented from sitting. Berkshire refused to pay
more than half Wolsey's demands and lord Lisle, who
wrote out their offer, was threatened by the cardinal with
the loss of his head and his lands ; and in the diocese of
Salisbury, while the abbots and priors would consent to
a part, the secular clergy would give nothing.[1] Enough
was known of the peasants' revolt then raging in Germany
to make authorities nervous, though there was little in
common between that uprising and England's dislike of a
capital levy ; and there was substance in the reports which
Louise of Savoy published throughout France before the
end of May that the English had mutinied and had too
much to do at home to think of invading their neighbour.[2]
Wolsey himself slowly admitted the truth and reluctantly
conveyed to the ambassadors in Spain the painful impression that ' the king's coffers are not furnished for a
continuance of war, and his subjects cannot help him.'[3]

His conversion from revenge to pity on France and
to legality in England was a partial and painful process.
The clamour had been too loud not to reach the king's
ears ; Henry declared that he had never heard of the rates
imposed in Wolsey's instructions and sent out letters that
he would demand no fixed sums, but only such as his
subjects would willingly grant. On 26 April Wolsey
announced that concession to London as due to his intercession with the king, whose letters were read in common
council on the 28th ; and on 8 May Wolsey sent again
for the mayor and aldermen to hear what they had done
in response. Their doings had not been wise : each
alderman had assembled his ward and proposed a benevolence, which the wards refused. Wolsey was equally
irate : ' you have no such commission,' he said, ' I am
your commissioner ; I will examine you one by one

---

[1] *L.P.* iv. 1330, 1345 ; Hall, pp. 696, 699, 701.

[2] *L.P.* iv. 1364, 1401, 1464.

[3] *Ibid.* iv. 1488. On 19 May he announced to the city that the king
was now considering ' the great fall of the French king, which is yet a
prisoner ' and his daily suits to Henry for peace ; but Wolsey still trusted
that all Henry's ' right and title shall be to him delivered ' (Hall, p. 701).

myself, and then I shall know the good will you bear to
our prince.' A councillor reminded him of the act of
Richard III : that king, retorted Wolsey, ' was a usurper
and murderer of his own nephews' ; the councillor replied that nevertheless it was an act of parliament, made
by the consent of the whole realm. This constitutional
interjection alarmed the mayor more than Wolsey ; for
the city council itself had made a ' statute ' for the aldermen's wards to grant a benevolence, though by 19 Henry
VII, c. 7 municipal legislation required the chancellor's
consent. The mayor asked that the city statute might
be revoked. Wolsey, of course, agreed ; ' but,' he said,
' now I will entre into the kynges commission : you
Maior, and you Master Aldermen, what will you geve ? '
It might cost him his life, said the mayor, to make any
offer ; but the common council had no option but to
repeal their statute on the following day and to trust,
without much confidence, in the mayor's assurance that
they would be gently treated when they went to Wolsey
with their benevolence.[1]

Wolsey was still (11 May) urging on Norfolk and
Suffolk that severe measures should be used, since the
rebels in those shires had not submitted until an armed
force was sent against them.[2] The rising had, indeed,
attained alarming proportions in East Anglia : the gentry
broke down the bridges to prevent unlawful assemblies,
but refused further help to the dukes. ' Poverty,' said
the insurgents' ringleader, ' was their captain, for he and
his cousin Necessity, had brought them to this doing.'
'The commons,' wrote the two dukes to Wolsey, ' lay
all the blame on him, and say that, if any insurrection
follow, the quarrel shall be only against him.' Wolsey
replied that he did not stand alone in that matter, and
Henry summoned a great council to inquire into the
responsibility for the ' straitness of the demand for a
sixth of every man's substance.'[3] Wolsey alleged the
judges' opinion that he might lawfully demand any sum

---

[1] Hall, pp. 698-9.   [2] L.P. iv. 1324.
[3] Hall, p. 700 ; L.P. iv. 1318.

by commission and the prelates' opinion that the demand
agreed with God's law, for Joseph had taken a fifth from
the Egyptians.   Insurrection was then a novel experience
in Henry's reign, and the king, says Hall, was 'sorely
moved': he declared he would have no more of this
trouble but pardon all who, whether secretly or openly,
had refused the demand.   He was as good as his word;
only a few ringleaders were on 29-30 May brought before
the bar of the star chamber and severely reprimanded.
But the orders, in which Wolsey expressed the king's will,
contained inconsistent assertions that the cardinal had
never assented to the demand for a sixth, that he had
followed therein the whole council's advice, and that the
release from the grant was due to his humble request.
They also contained an instruction to pray for the cardinal's soul; but the people, says Hall, preferred to say
'God save the king.'

Wolsey was now, writes Giberti, ' I do not say inclined
to, but ardent with desire for, arrangement with France '
and peace was concluded on 30 August.[1]   It affected but
little the terms which Charles V extorted from his royal
captive at the treaty of Madrid five months later.[2]   For
Francis I's release from the exorbitant English demand
for their old possessions in France left him with more to
meet Charles' terms; and Wolsey's inability to interven
by force of arms reduced to slender proportions the pressure he could apply to the emperor.   England, indeed,
gained nothing save peace without honour; but Wolsey
found his consolations.   The queen-regent of France
made him the secret present of 100,000 crowns she had
promised if he made peace; and the instalments of
this raised his French pension from twelve thousand to
twenty-five thousand crowns a year, while Louise also
promised Wolsey that he should be ' conductor and gover-

----

[1] *L.P.* iv. 1474.   For the treaty of The Moor or More (Wolsey's
palace between Rickmansworth and Northwood) see *ibid.* iv. 1600 and
Rymer, xiv. 48.   Wolsey invited Warham to stay at his palace for the
signing, but Warham preferred to lodge with ' his old host, the vicar of
Rickmansworth ' (*ibid.* iv. 1591).

[2] 14 Jan. 1526, *ibid.* iv. 1891.

or of all enterprises.'[1] Tunstal had from Toledo viewed he negotiations with alarm : he wrote to Wolsey on 10 August that he might do ' the greatest service he ever id ' by not forestalling the emperor, who had waited for England : if he made a separate peace with France, ' he would undoubtedly lose the emperor for ever, and God knows what danger may ensue by combining the emperor with France. . . . Whatever the French say, they hate Wolsey as much or more than the king and consider them both as the cause of their calamity ; which, indeed, they say openly.'[2] But to forestall Charles V was Wolsey's chief desire ; and the pope, wrote Giberti on 19 September, ' regards the agreement with France as a great counterpoise to restrain the French from precipitating an agreement with the emperor.' As soon as the treaty of Madrid was signed and Francis I recovered his liberty (7 March 1526), Wolsey wrote to the queen-mother and regent of France urging her not ' to observe in any part the dishonourable and unreasonable treaty violently extorted from her son, as he is not bound by it either in honour or in conscience.' Clement VII absolved him from his oath, and ' all Italy rejoiced at this striking illustration of Machiavelli's chapter ' How far princes should keep faith.' '[3]

---

[1] The first instalment was to be paid to Wolsey in Nov. ; but he agreed with the French that no one else should receive anything until the following May (*ibid.* iv. 1617). He was also simultaneously demanding from Charles and Francis pensions in lieu of Tournai (*ibid.* iv. 2493). In the French accounts (*ibid.* iv. 3619) Wolsey's total is said to be ' for his pension and other causes not here declared.' That Louise's present was secret is proved by Wolsey's agonised request in Oct. 1529 that she would not reveal it to Henry (see below, p. 257). Wolsey had at the beginning of the negotiations represented himself as inclined to peace, but Henry as bent on the conquest of the French crown (Wolsey to Sampson, *State Papers*, vi. 306 ; Jacqueton, *op. cit.* pp. 50, 144-7) and the 100,000 crowns were to be his reward for overcoming the obstacle he alleged. Wolsey ordered daily prayers to be said for Louise in his college at Oxford (*L.P.* iv. p. 1407).

[2] *Ibid.* iv. 1555, 1557.

[3] *Ibid.* iv. 1648, 2032, 2036 ; Armstrong, *Charles V*, i. 164. At the same time Wolsey sent ambassadors to Francis I with detailed instructions as to means of exasperating him against the emperor and encouraging

The pope's 'holy league' for the defence of Italy
proclaimed on 19 January 1525, had been shattered a
Pavia. It was now reconstructed at Cognac on 22 May
1526; and on 19 June Sanga, the papal secretary, referred
to Henry's 'intention to declare war on Spain.' Sanga
himself was sent to England to press on Henry the caus
of the pope and Italian independence, and Morett
followed suit on behalf of France.[1] 'These men,' wrot
Clerk from Paris to Wolsey on 14 October, 'must need
fall to you; and doubtless, whatever it shall cost them
they will have you in this league. . . . Your grace may
handle them with the posie, *cui haereo vincit*, but ou
Lord for all that keep us *ab adherendo* so long as may
be his pleasure.'[2] Italy, indeed, was not an attractive
or even a possible force to which to adhere, for it ha
hardly a vestige of cohesion itself. Pescara's Spanish
blood prevailed over the Italian traditions of himself and
his wife Vittoria Colonna. He betrayed his tempte
Morone, and seized for Charles the Lombard towns
Milan capitulated on 25 July 1526; and in Septembe
Italian and Spanish troops, let loose by a cardinal, Pompe
Colonna, occupied Rome, rifled St. Peter's, and sacke
the sacred palace, while Clement himself fled to the castl
of St. Angelo.[3] He sent insistent appeals to Wolsey an
Henry for help and Giberti claimed that the pope ha
only entered the league at Henry's persuasion; was i
for nothing that the king had been styled its protector ?
Wolsey could only reply, as he wrote to More, by ' s
couching and qualifying the letters of consolation to th
pope that they will give satisfaction to his holiness with
out binding the king to anything that might redoun
to his charge.'[5] The English government had ' fanne
the Italian flame, but declined to burn its fingers.'[6]

him with hopes of allies; but they were not to say anything ' that migh
sound against the emperor ' until assured of the warlike disposition of th
French (*L.P.* iv. 2039).   [1] *Ibid.* iv. 2261, 2369, 2477-9.
[2] *Ibid.* iv. 2561; cf. 2481.   [3] Armstrong, *Charles V*, i. 163-
    [4] *L.P.* iv. 2267, 2274, 2477-80, 2490, 2506, 2511-16; but cf. p. 1263.
[5] *Ibid.* iv. 2535, 2541.
    [6] Armstrong, *op. cit.* i. 165; Henry, however, sent the pope 30,00
crowns (*L.P.* iv. 2558, 2870).

The lesson of 1525 and the amicable grant had not
yet been forgotten, and something else had been learnt.
'Happy be we,' wrote Clerk to Wolsey, ' who, through
your grace's policy, have not been drawn into the Italian
league which, through their negligence is come to nothing.
. . For they reckon the pope is ruined and the French
are slack and have little care for their own interests and
none for those of christendom.' [1]   After his year's captivity Francis had arrears of pleasure to make up : ' what
were Milan and Cremona in comparison with the beast
of the forest and the beauty of the court ? ' [2]   Wolsey
put more trust in the queen-mother, Louise of Savoy.
But he found it a sisyphean task to bring France, after
Pavia, up to the pitch of a declaration of war on the
emperor and a fresh adventure in Italy ; and he could
only by slow degrees loosen the bonds, in which Francis
was bound by the treaty of Madrid and by the presence
of his two eldest sons as hostages in Spain. The lever
on which he mainly relied was matrimonial ; and he hoped
to break the engagement of Francis I to Charles V's sister
Eleanor, and to effect his ' closer conjunction with the
king of England.' [3]   This closer conjunction was to consist, in the first place, in Francis I's marriage to Henry's
daughter, and ultimately of Henry's own marriage to
Renée the daughter of Louis XII.   But Francis was
pledged already and Henry was still married ; and to
which ' divorce ' Clerk referred, when he wrote on 13
September 1526, that there would be great difficulty at
Rome *circa istud benedictum divortium*, is obscure. [4]

Another and greater raid on Rome in 1527 assisted
Wolsey's schemes.   In December 1526 Francis I was informed that Henry desired ' perpetual peace ' with France, [5]
of which it was Wolsey's chief boast that he was the author ;
and in March 1527 there arrived in London the bishop

---

[1] *L.P.* iv. 2544.   [2] Armstrong, *Charles V*, i. 164.
[3] *L.P.* iv. 2198.
[4] *Ibid.* iv. 2482.   Brewer thought it referred to Catherine of Aragon's ;
more recent opinion refers it to breaking Eleanor's engagement ; but, for
reasons too long to state here, I think that Brewer was right.
[5] *L.P.* iv. 2726, 2728.

of Tarbes' noted embassy, of which a minute and vivid
account kept by its secretary survives.[1] It resulted in
the treaties of Westminster, signed on 30 April, which
were treaties for war on Charles and ' perpetual peace '
with France. The war was to be declared as soon as
Charles refused the allies' demands for the liberation of
Francis' sons and the payment of Henry's debts ; if it
were not carried on, the treaty was to be void ; Mary
was to marry Francis himself or his second son, and a
month after that point was settled, the treaty of perpetual
peace should be ratified.[2] Wolsey proposed to go to
France to clinch these matters in May and arrange for
the war which was to begin on 15 July.[3] But before he
set out he took the initial steps in Henry's proceedings
for a divorce from the emperor's aunt, and Charles V's
troops had taken and pillaged Rome.

That unparalleled scene of sacrilege was not the emperor's design but the deed of his starving and mutinous,
Spanish and Lutheran, troops. Still, Charles had intended his army to put pressure on Clement VII, and
ever since the pope's tergiversation in 1524 the emperor
had borne him no goodwill. Three weeks before Pavia
he had sworn ' revenge on those who may have wronged
me, and most specially on that villain pope. Some day
or other, perhaps, Luther may become a man of worth.' [4]
On 17 September 1526 he had replied to the league of
Cognac and to a papal brief detailing his own enormities,
with his famous ' Apologia,' which was printed in Spain,
Germany, and the Netherlands, covered the whole field
of papal offences since 1518, and seemed to portend a
revival of the palmiest days of Guelf and Ghibelline war-
fare.[5] The sack of Rome ranged him in public opinion
on the side of Luther against the pope. Protestants

---

[1] B.M. *Add. MS.* 12192, ff. 43 *et seqq.*, calendared in *L.P.* iv. pp
1397-1415.

[2] Dumont, *Corps univ. dipl.* IV, i. 476 ; *L.P.* iv. 3080.

[3] *Ibid.* p. 1410 ; cf. nos. 3143-5.

[4] Armstrong, *Charles V*, i. 162, 172-3.

[5] B.M. *Add. MS.* 2103, ff. 12 *et seqq.* ; Goldast, *Constitutiones Imperiales*
i. 479.   Cf. Charles V's remarks to Ghinucci and Lee, *L.P.* iv. 3051.

aw therein the fall of Babylon foretold by Daniel the
prophet; and Charles' own representatives at Rome
sked for instructions 'whether the holy see is to be
etained or not.'[1]   The great Napoleon once remarked
hat Charles V could have conquered Europe, had he
hosen to side with Luther.   That is more than doubtful:
s between Italy and the pope on the one hand and
_utheran Germany on the other, the emperor had no
hoice.   He had preferred the Mediterranean to the
3altic and the north when he sailed for Spain in 1517;
nd his whole life was a process of transformation from
Burgundian unto a Spaniard.   But he could not hold
taly without bringing the pope into line; and that
neant a fight to a finish with Wolsey and his ambitions.

For the moment he seemed to have played into
Wolsey's hands.   There was fierce opposition in England
o the cardinal's new anti-imperial policy.   Norfolk had
igh words with him in the king's presence; many of
he council had urged Henry to break off the French
egotiations in April; and his ambassadors in Spain
vrote strongly against the war, urging the old amity of
England, Burgundy, and Castile, the injury that its breach
vould do to trade and to the whole of christendom, the
onsideration shown by the emperor in releasing Francis
t Henry's request on such easy terms, and his readiness
o make further concessions.[2] 'The whole country,' wrote
le Praet's successor, Mendoza, from London in May, 'is
oused against the cardinal . . . he is universally hated.'[3]
3ut the sack of Rome threw all these things into the shade:
'this,' wrote Wolsey to Henry on 2 June, 'must stir
he hearts of all christian princes.'[4]   Charles' agents at
Rome thought it might stir them to set up churches of
heir own independent of Rome; but nothing was further
rom Wolsey's mind.   He did not aim at a papacy
ermanently restricted to England and controlled by
Henry VIII; and his immediate objects, as he journeyed

[1] Il sacco di Roma, ed. Milanesi, pp. 499, 517.
[2] L.P. iv. pp. 1400, 1411, nos. 2828, 3152, 3374, 3513.
[3] Spanish Cal. 1527-29, pp. 192-3, 207-9, 275.
[4] L.P. iv. 3147.

to France in July with the title of the king's lieutenant, the powers of a plenipotentiary, and the pomp of a viceroy, were to secure the ratification of the treaties of April,[1] arrange for the prosecution of the war, and get himself made vicar-general of the pope for the term of Clement VII's imprisonment and subjection to Charles V. The papacy was not less essential to him than it was to Charles.

He wrote to Henry, and perhaps he believed, that the pope would be removed to Spain, 'where he will probably be poisoned and the see apostolic established in Spain for ever';[2] and he proposed a conclave of independent cardinals at Avignon and even a general council. Avignon had a sound that boded ill for the unity of the church, and Clement VII would never consent to summon a general council. Fears were expressed that the papacy was about to undergo another Babylonish captivity and that Wolsey was perpending another schism.[3] He hoped to avoid that appearance by a formal commission from the captive pope, and he drafted not only that but eight articles for the government of the church in case Charles refused to liberate Clement; and he even selected sub-delegates to himself as vicar-general.[4]

[1] *L.P.* iv. 3186; *Erasmi Epist.* vii. 112-13, 26 July 1527. Cavendish devotes thirty pages to an admiring account of Wolsey's display during this mission (pp. 75-104). The treaties were confirmed by Francis I at Amiens on 18 Aug., *L.P.* iv. 3342, 3353, 3356-7.

[2] *State Papers*, i. 267; *L.P.* iv. 3400; cf. 3247, 3263, 3311, 3340, 3365.

[3] *Ibid.* iv. 3350. Francis was said to have offered Wolsey 'the *papalité* of Fraunce *vel patriachatum*, for the Frenchemen wolde no more obey the churche of Rome' (Lee to Wolsey, 14 July 1527, Ellis, III, ii. 98); it was also said that he might have the legacy of lower Germany, if he desired it (*ibid.*). 'It is rumoured,' wrote Ghinucci on 22 July, 'that your reverence is going into France to separate the church of England and of France from the Roman, not merely during the captivity of the pope and to effect his liberation, but for a perpetual division (*L.P.* iv. 3291). Salviati said much the same; see his letters to Guicciardini in Ehses, *Römische Dok*, pp. 249-52. He much preferred that the pope should owe his liberation to Charles V's friendship than to Francis I's arms.

[4] Pocock, *Records of the Reformation*, i. 19; *L.P.* iv. 3401; *Spanish Cal.* 1527-29, p. 437. Salviati was his nominee for Italy, and the arch

An incidental advantage, as he pointed out to Henry, of a
' general faculty for me *omnia faciendi et exequendi durante
captivitate summi pontificis*,' would be that he could
determine the divorce of Catherine of Aragon by papal
authority, ' without informing the pope of your purpose.'
Charles, however, had already heard of that project and
demanded from Clement a revocation of Wolsey's legatine
powers.[1] He was now convinced that the pope was
worth more than Luther : only by papal authority could
he defeat what he regarded as Wolsey's last effort to ruin
the Habsburg cause in England. But, while the pope
might well be the emperor's chaplain, he must not be his
obvious captive. The prisoner of the Vatican was allowed
to escape before the end of the year to Orvieto,[2] the
Italian cardinals shied at Avignon, and Wolsey's conclave
was reduced to Compiègne for its *mise en scène*, with
himself, one Italian, and three French cardinals, for its
constitution.

Wolsey returned at the end of September, rejoicing
at the ' ruinous ' state of the emperor's affairs,[3] and full
of zeal for his own part as redeemer of Charles V's captive.
It befitted a legate and possible successor of the pope. He
ordered a three days' fast every week for Clement's liberation ; and when a special French embassy came in October
to bring Henry the order of St. Michael [4] and receive
his ratification of the treaty of Amiens, Wolsey staged
a dramatic performance at Greenwich on Sunday, 10
November, in the preparations for which men had been
kept working night and day since 12 October.[5] St. Peter

bishop of Mainz for Germany. Salviati is very frank and also accurate
in his account of Wolsey's designs : writing from Compiègne on 10 Sept.
to Baldasarre Castiglione, papal nuncio in Spain, he says Wolsey has concluded ' la pace perpetua . . . con questo pretexto di liberare N. Signore,
farà entrare nella guerra d'Italia, et forse di Fiandra gagliardamente il
suo re, pensa d'esser legato in Inghilterre et Francia et come dire Ponti-
fice ' (Ehses, p. 248).

[1] *L.P.* iv. 3312, p. 1502.
[2] See his agreement with Charles V, 26 Nov., in Le Grand, iii. 48-57.
[3] Wolsey to Henry VIII, 5 Sept. 1527 ; *L.P.* iv. 3400 ; *Chron. of
Calais*, p. 40.
[4] Francis I was simultaneously given the Garter.
[5] See Gibson's accounts for the revels, *L.P.* iv. 3563-4.

appeared on the stage to commission the legate to restore to the pope his liberty and to the church her independence; and then came the two sons of Francis I to complain of Charles V's refusal to let them go and to claim the cardinal's intercession, 'who wrought so . . . that he brought the emperor to a peace and caused the two young princes to be deliuered.'[1] Peace had been the text of Wolsey's star chamber address on the first day of Michaelmas term to the lords spiritual and temporal of the king's council, the mayor and aldermen of London, the judges, and all the justices of the peace then at Westminster. 'I have knit,' he said, 'the realmes of England and Fraunce in suche a perfite knot that it shall neuer fayle . . . this is a peace *in secula seculorum* ; and he held up the golden bull, with which it was sealed, to signify the golden age of revenues to accrue from France and the absence of taxes to pay for wars against it.[2]

He did not mention his pensions from France nor the expense of the war he was preparing against the emperor. Merchants had already been warned to restrict their mart to Calais and export no goods to Charles' dominions, to which, says Hall, they would in no wise assent.[3] The harvest of 1527 was poor, and Wolsey had no grounds for thinking he would get any consent in England to his war on Charles V. But things were going badly for Charles in Italy ; they went worse, as Wolsey predicted, when Doria deserted the emperor and conveyed Genoa and the command of the sea to the side of Francis I ; and he was bent on bringing England in on

[1] Hall, pp. 734-5 ; *Spanish Cal.* 1527-29, p. 458. Mendoza's account of this performance reached Charles at Burgos in December (*L.P.* iv. 3518 ; this letter is misdated and misplaced under 26 Oct., although its first sentence reports the arrival of Bayard on '9 December.' It should be dated 26 Dec.). More vulgar pageants had greeted Wolsey's arrival at Boulogne on 22 July—three Spaniards and three Germans violating a nun, who is rescued by a cardinal, who also pulls down an emperor and raises a pope lying at his feet (Hall, p. 729).

[2] *Ibid.* pp. 732, 736; Cavendish, pp. 105-6 ; *State Papers*, i. 275-6 ; Rymer, xiv. 227 ; *Encyc. Brit.*, 11th ed. viii. 303. According to Cavendish Wolsey averred that ' both territories ' would seem ' but one monarchy.'

[3] Hall, p. 724 ; cf. *L.P.* iv. 3262.

what he believed was the winning side : all would be well if he won. He had prepared the diplomatic as well as the military measures during his three months in France, and from Amiens and Compiègne he had sent to Spain instructions to the English ambassadors, Edward Lee, the king's almoner, and Ghinucci, bishop of Worcester, without their contents being known to Henry or to the council he left to advise the king in England while he was himself in France.[1] The French envoys in Spain were to make the declaration of war on Charles, and their English colleagues were instructed to co-operate with them without knowing what they were going to do.

They, in point of fact, spent fifteen days in trying to dissuade the French from the intimation of war ; and it was only when the Frenchmen threatened to act alone, though with Wolsey's secret support, that Lee and Ghinucci consented to join in the declaration. Even then, they wrote, they would have refused, but ' feared to do so because Wolsey had expressly warned them against causing the French any suspicion,' let alone a rupture. When news of their opposition reached London du Bellay, the French ambassador, pressed Henry to send Lee ' a new declaration of his will that he might no longer mistake it.' Henry replied that fresh offers of peace had come from Charles, which should be considered first ; but Wolsey ' enlarged upon the almoner's fault, saying frequently that, unless he could show a good excuse, his life would answer for it.' [2] Ambassadors have seldom been placed in a worse quandary ; but Lee received some satisfaction when, three years later, he was given the archbishopric of York in succes-

[1] *L.P.* iv. 3327, 3343, 3411-12. In July Henry was entertaining a group very unfriendly to Wolsey, comprising Norfolk, Suffolk, the marquis of Exeter, the earls of Oxford, Essex, and Rutland, and viscounts Fitzwalter and Rochford (*ibid.* iv. 3318). A conspiracy against Wolsey was reported in October when Pace was sent to the Tower (*ibid.* iv. 3509; *Sp. Cal.*, pp. 440-4), and a bill had been posted in London in April attacking him (Hall, p. 721). The Spanish dispatches for these months contain many evidences of Wolsey's unpopularity in London (see below, p. 221).

[2] See their dispatch of 21 Jan. 1528, *L.P.* iv. 3826 ; *Ambassades de du Bellay*, ed. 1905, pp. 130-6, and *L.P.* iv. App. 123, 147.

sion to Wolsey. Wolsey had practically made his own declaration of war. On Sunday, 5 January 1528, he had arranged a demonstration at St. Paul's, where, with the imperial ambassador on his right hand and the French on his left, he listened to a preconcerted oration on the shameful injuries inflicted on the pope by 'the men of war belonging to the emperor.' A day or so later he was proposing the emperor's deposition to du Bellay, who 'did not wish to deprive him of the honor of suggesting it.' Wolsey was at that moment congratulating the pope on the recovery of his liberty, and knew that the most plausible reason for war no longer existed: Clement himself kept the peace.[1]

War was declared jointly by the French and English on Charles at Burgos on 22 January and Mendoza, the Spanish ambassador, was arrested in London on 10 February. In his reply to the intimation [2] the emperor alleged that Wolsey had asked him, in letters written by himself and in others obtained from Henry VIII, to employ the imperial forces in Italy to make him pope, and that on his refusal had threatened to make him repent even though it ruined England.[3] How far the emperor's charges should be discounted by the English herald's suggestion to Wolsey that they emanated from Charles's chancellor, Gattinara, who himself hoped for the papacy by similar means, is open to question; [4] but the English

[1] *L.P.* iv. 3764, 3767, 3770-1, 3783; Fiddes, *Collections*, pp. 179-80; du Bellay, *Ambassades*, pp. 88, 92-3; *Venetian Cal.* 1527-33, pp. 114-16. Wolsey had known since 20 Dec. of the pope's liberation (du Bellay, p. 70).

[2] Printed in full in Le Grand, *Hist. du Divorce*, iii. 27-48, and in Léonard, *Traités de Paix*, ii. 329 *et seqq.*; summarised in *L.P.* iv. 3844.

[3] 'Encoires que le royaume d'Angleterre se deust perdre' (Le Grand, i. 46); 'yea, though it should cost the whole realm of England' is the translation of Tyndale (*Practice of Prelates*, p. 322), who had seen the emperor's 'little book in print, both in Spanish and also in Dutch.'

[4] *L.P.* iv. 3940; Wolsey has noted this passage in the herald's dispatch. He accused Thomas Benolt, who was Clarenceux herald (see *D.N.B.*), of acting without Henry's sanction, which was true, and threatened him with execution at Calais on his return. Benolt received a friendly warning, crossed from Boulogne to Rye, and showed the king three letters he had received from Wolsey, charging him to make the

people had no doubt that the challenge to Charles was Wolsey's work, and that the war would be their undoing. Half the population, it was said in 1533, depended for subsistence upon intercourse with the Netherlands; and the disturbance of trade caused by the declaration threw thousands out of work. Vainly did Wolsey attribute the unemployment to the presence of Hanseatic merchants and apprentices in London.[1] ' He is doing,' wrote *son grand mignon*, as du Bellay termed himself, ' all he can to find this war good, but cannot make it so. . . . People were crying out ' murder,' and some would like to see everything go wrong, that they might say ' see what the legate has done.' . . . You may be sure he is playing a terrible game, for I believe he is the only Englishman who wishes a war with Flanders.'[2] Sedition broke out again throughout East Anglia and in Wiltshire: an insurrection in Somerset prevented the holding of the assizes; and the justices of the peace, who reported it on 3 April, gloomily remarked, ' it is expected that other parts will rise.' In Kent, where men threatened, if they got hold of Wolsey, to send him to sea in a boat with holes bored in it, there were a considerable number of executions on the avowed principle of *obsta principiis*.[3]

So serious was the position that the Spanish war had to be abandoned. An arrangement was made in March that commercial intercourse with the Netherlands should continue despite it; and on 15 June a truce was concluded so far as the Netherlands were concerned.[4] It was not to extend to Italy, where Wolsey relied on his allies to reestablish his influence over the pope and thus achieve the divorce of Catherine of Aragon. There they enjoyed some transient gleams of success. The French

---

declaration of war. Henry, says Hall (p. 745), mistrusted Wolsey ever after. The charge made against him by Norfolk and others that the Spanish war was Wolsey's unauthorised work, was amply justified.

[1] *L.P.* vi. 1528; iv. 5177, cf. 3915, 3926, 4012, 4040, 4058, 4085; Hall, pp. 745-8; *Spanish Cal.* 1527-29, pp. 862, 878, 887.

[2] Le Grand, iii. 81; *L.P.* iv. 3930; cf. *ibid.* 3889; Du Bellay, p. 350.

[3] *L.P.* iv. 4043-4, 4129, 4141, 4145, 4276, 4296, 4300, 4310, 4331.

[4] *Ibid.* iv. 5260.

commander Lautrec had marched through Italy and by
the end of April had shut up the Spaniards in Naples,
while Charles's fleet was destroyed by the Genoese under
Doria in the gulf of Salerno. The combined squadrons
of Genoa, Venice, and France commanded the western
Mediterranean and intercepted communications with
Spain : Italy seemed to be at the disposal of the Holy
League ; and Campeggio was dispatched to England to
hear, and with a secret commission to pronounce, the
divorce of Catherine. 'If Lautrec advances,' wrote
Casale to Wolsey on 22 December 1527, when first commissioned to demand the divorce, 'the pope will do all
you want ; but if not, he will do nothing.'[1]

The opportunity of centuries was frittered away in
three months. Lautrec alienated the Neapolitan nobles
who had joined him, and Francis himself drove Doria
back into Charles's arms. The command of the sea was
lost, Naples was relieved, Lautrec died of malaria, and the
whole French army capitulated in September. Francis
made one more effort in the spring of 1529 ; but his
forces were cut to pieces at Landriano on 21 June before
they could deploy on the plains of Lombardy. The pope
had a settled conviction at last : 'I have quite made up
my mind,' he said to the archbishop of Capua, 'to become
an imperialist and live and die as such.'[2] Eight days
after the battle of Landriano the treaty of Barcelona was
signed. It was a family compact between the Habsburgs
and the Medici : Clement VII's nephew was to marry
the emperor's illegitimate daughter, Margaret of Parma,
the future regent of the Netherlands ; Medici rule was
to be re-established in Florence ; Zapolya, Ferdinand's
rival as king of Hungary, was to be excommunicated ;
and Wolsey's and Campeggio's commission to try Henry's
suit for a divorce from Catherine of Aragon was revoked.[3]

The treaty of Barcelona was followed by that of Cambrai, the 'ladies' peace,' as it was called because it was

---

[1] *L.P.* iv. 3682 ; cf. *ibid.* 3751, 3758.
[2] *Spanish Cal.* 1529-30, p. 73.
[3] *Ibid.* nos. 117, 161 ; *L.P.* iv. 5705, 5767, 5779.

negotiated between Margaret of Savoy and her sister-in-law Louise, one the aunt of Charles V and the other the mother of Francis I. There was no alternative for France but acquiescence in the imperial-papal compact. Italy and, with it, the papacy were to be subject to Spanish and not to French predominance; and the pope, as Wolsey had so often feared, was to become the chaplain of another monarch than Henry VIII. Wolsey had been as powerless to prevent that fatal consummation as he was to prevent the peace between Francis and Charles. When he first got wind of the negotiations, he staked his head to Henry that the rumour was ' an invention of the enemy ' : [1] he could not believe in a pacification in which his was not the master hand. The price of his head was not exacted; but he paid forfeit with his power, not for the failure of his foreign policy alone, but for other reasons with which we have still to deal and for which there was less excuse. For there was at least an element of principle and consistency in his foreign policy, disastrous though it proved.

From the time of his creation as papal legate, he protested in February 1525, he had always considered it a crime of *lèse-majesté* to speak disrespectfully of the pope.[2] ' The king,' he wrote, ' has hitherto relied entirely on my constant assurance that his holiness will not be moved from his constancy either by fear or adversity, even though he should be compelled to flee from Rome.' [3] The strongest argument, he averred on 6 December 1527, that he could think of to induce Clement VII to grant Henry's requests was ' the friendship with which I have inspired the king towards his holiness—a friendship which will be permanent, unless some occasion should be offered for alienating the king's mind, in which event it will never be in my power to serve his holiness.' [4] His remarks about Clement being made chaplain to Francis I or Charles V

---

[1] *L.P.* iv. 5231. Art. 9 of Wolsey's impeachment charged him with a habit of saying ' I will lay my head that no such thing will happen ' (see below, pp. 223, 260-1).

[2] *Spanish Cal.* 1525-26, p. 64.

[3] *L.P.* iv. 1017.   [4] *Ibid.* iv. 3644.

were charges against those monarchs and not reflections
on this pope; and it is to Wolsey's credit, as a cardinal and
a legate *a latere*, that he should consistently have adapted
his policy to that of the sovereign pontiff from whom he
derived the dignities and the powers he valued most.
The grounds of criticism lie in the incompatibility between
that allegiance and the position of chief minister to an
English king; in the fidelity with which Wolsey copied
the Machiavellian principles and practices of Medicean
popes; and in his efforts to serve the temporal interests
of the papacy and to extract advantage for his king, his
country, and himself out of the Anglo-papal union. We
have seen from his earliest extant letter [1] how his thoughts
turned to Rome as the pivot of his policy; how England
embarked on war at the invitation of Julius II, made peace
at the behest of Leo X, attempted by the Milan expedition
to relieve the papacy of the embarrassment of France,
renewed the war in the footsteps of Leo X in 1521, began
to withdraw with Clement VII in 1524, endeavoured to
rescue the holy see from the clutches of Charles V, and
suffered with the pope from their common eclipse at
Barcelona and Cambrai.

But what was England doing in this convulsion which
centred in Italy and pivoted on Rome? The control of
Italy was the essential bone of contention between Francis I
and Charles V. 'The French king,' wrote the master
of the rolls in 1523, 'esteems Milan more than Nor-
mandy, Picardy, or Brittany, for which he is not to be
blamed; for if once he were lord of Italy, he would set
little by any prince.' [2] Italy, echoes du Bellay in May
1529, 'is the principal pillar of prosperity or ruin on
either side.' [3] Wolsey's fatal immersion began with the
Milan expedition in 1516, which led to the resignation of Foxe, if not of Warham as well, and was opposed
by most of the council; and he sometimes pursued
this Italian will o' the wisp without consulting the king.
One of the charges against him in 1529 was that he

[1] Above, p. 16.
[2] Dr. Thomas Hannibal to Wolsey, *L.P.* iii. 2771.
[3] *Ibid.* iv. 5601.

concluded a league with the duke of Ferrara without informing Henry VIII ; and he instructed his ambassador at Rome to inform the pope that, ' although he had not mentioned the matter to the king,' Henry was willing to enter a league with France and the papacy for the defence of Italy.[1] It might gratify chauvinistic minds that England's arm should appear to stretch as far as Rome ; but neither her army nor her fleet was available at that distance, and Wolsey had to depend for personal success on his diplomacy, on English gold, and on the forces of friends whom he could neither trust nor control. His subsidies to his allies wasted the savings of Henry VII, and taxation provoked conflicts with parliament and a popular discontent which reached a climax when the Italian vortex involved a quarrel with Charles V. For the emperor resented Wolsey's opposition in Italy far more than he did the divorce of his aunt by Henry VIII ; and when, after Wolsey's fall, Henry abjured Italian adventures, he was able—despite the divorce and the breach with Rome— to keep the peace with Charles and even enjoy his alliance throughout the rest of his reign. The basis of that understanding was that Henry abandoned Italy and the papacy to Charles, while Charles left Henry a free hand within the British Isles. The emperor had tacitly accepted the application of the doctrine *cujus regio ejus religio* to international relations long before he was constrained, at the peace of Augsburg in 1555, to acquiesce in its application to the princes of his empire.

There was thus an intimate connexion between papal jurisdiction and English foreign policy ; and the repudiation of Rome was a natural consequence of the abandonment of Italy to imperial domination.[2] To Wolsey, on

---

[1] *L.P.* iv. 5314. Wolsey himself admitted in Feb. 1528 that Henry ' had never approved of the affair of Ferrara ' (du Bellay, *Ambassades*, p. 153 ; *L.P.* iv. App. 149), and that what had been done, had been done without commission, though he put the blame on his subordinate Casale. The treaty had guaranteed the duke Modena and Reggio, which he had wrested from the papacy, and Clement VII naturally repudiated the arrangement on his release (*Ambassades de du Bellay*, p. 100, *n.*).

[2] ' Therefore, the establishment of the Spanish dominion over Italy was quickly followed by the rejection of papal supremacy in favour of the

the other hand, the Roman nexus was essential; and his
foreign policy has been deprived of consistency and almost
of meaning by attempts to convert the most papally-
minded of English statesmen into a nationalist of the type
of Henry VIII or queen Elizabeth. Was he not papal
legate to an extent no Englishman had been before, and
did he not rely on Rome for powers which he alone had
extorted? His unique dependence on Rome as legate
a latere bound England and bound himself to a papal
foreign policy. He made war on France in 1522-23 because ' if Milan is taken, Naples and Sicily will go, and
the pope will be under French control'; and he plunged
into war with the emperor in 1528 to save Clement VII
from Charles V. In 1523 he thought Clement VII might
' become no better than the French king's chaplain,' in
1526 ' no better than that of Charles V' :[1] he would
have to become Henry VIII's to meet the needs of
a papal legate who was also English prime minister.
Wolsey was driven thereto by that necessity arising from
that incompatible union; and the Anglo-papal firm, of
which he strove to be the managing director, broke up
when he failed to make England the predominant partner.
The crucial consideration in his foreign policy was not the
balance of power but the fact that he was special envoy
for life from the papal curia to the court of Henry VIII.
The pope, he lamented on 24 June 1529, ' has refused all
the concessions which, relying on him, I had promised
the king . . . and that will be my ruin.'

English state. . . . England broke with the papacy on these, and not on
strictly religious grounds ' (Acton, *Lectures on Mod. Hist.* p. 141).

[1] *L.P.* iii. pp. 1166, 1516; iv. pp. 444, 446; *State Papers*, vii. 189.

CHAPTER V.

PAPAL LEGATE.

'FOR my legacy,' said Wolsey, after his fall, to Norfolk, 'is gone, wherein stode all my high honour.' 'A strawe,' retorted Norfolk, 'for your legacy. I never esteemed your honnor the higher for that. But I esteemed your honnor for that ye were archbishop of Yorke and a cardinal, whose estate and honnor surmounteth any duke within this realme; and even so will I honnor you and acknowledge the same in doing you reverence and honnor accordingly.'[1] Norfolk was here expressing at once the respect which conservatives felt for the mediæval catholic church and the prejudice they entertained against the intruding autocracy involved in the legatine powers which Wolsey had acquired. These were unique in themselves, and they were further unique in being combined with the equally unprecedented authority he exercised as a minister of state. But their significance has been obscured by the ambiguity of the term papal legate and the infinite variety of legatine commissions. The word itself, like the secular ambassador, merely implies a delegated or representative authority, without defining its nature, scope, or duration. The papal legate might be *natus* or *a latere*,[2]

---

[1] Cavendish, p. 186. Cf. Campeggio to the papal secretary Sanga, 28 Oct. 1528, 'all his grandeur is connected with the authority of the Apostolic See' (*L.P.* iv. 4881), and de Praet to Charles V (Sept. 1527), 'his legatine powers . . . are the strongest part of his armour' (*Spanish Cal.* 1527-29, p. 274).

[2] *De latere* seems to have been more usual in Wolsey's day and was Englished as 'legate of the side.' Skelton connects it 'with tytles of all pride' (*Works* ii. 439; *N.E.D.* under 'legate' and 'side'). Wolsey's own description of his legateship was 'apostolicae sedis non solum natus, sed etiam per universum Angliae regnum et alia loca illi adjacentia de latere legatus' (Fiddes, *Collections*, p. 228).

ordinary or extraordinary; he might be a native or a foreigner, a resident or a visitor; he might have general powers or a special commission. He might be the diplomatic representative of the pope at a secular sovereign's court or the executive agent of papal sovereignty in the ecclesiastical government of the kingdom to which he was sent. With the growth of papal states and of secular diplomatic relations, and with the decline of papal sovereignty in other states, the custom developed in the sixteenth century of calling the pope's diplomatic representatives nuncios instead of legates; and, whereas the legate exercised papal jurisdiction, the nuncio merely negotiated with a secular sovereign.[1] But in earlier times the difference was one of status rather than of function and is unimportant compared with the fundamental distinction, concealed behind the common name of legate but expressed in the qualifications of *natus* or *a latere*.

The *legatus natus* was a resident agent of papal jurisdiction; he was, at least in the later middle ages, commonly a native of the country in which he resided, a subject of its secular ruler, and therefore not a proper diplomatic representative of another sovereign. His position was sufficiently ambiguous without that complication. From the twelfth century onwards archbishops of Canterbury and York took their palls from Rome as a symbol of their authority and of the source from which it was derived; and while there was constant friction between the two spheres of ecclesi-

---

[1] This distinction was made clear in practice during Wolsey's time. While he was exercising the pope's jurisdiction in England as legate *a latere*, various papal nuncios were sent to England, e.g. Ghinucci, Melchior Lang, Nicholas Schomberg (archb. of Capua), Gambara, Giberti, Sanga, Casale (*L.P.* iii. 994, 1222, 2509; iv. 1995; Theiner, pp. 540-2, 554, 566). It was made still clearer in 1530 when the pope sent the baron del Borgo as nuncio to England to ask for aid against the Turk (*Spanish Cal.* 1529-30, p. 719). Dr. Gairdner fails to notice it in writing (*D.N.B.* xxvi. 84*a*, s.v. 'Henry VIII'), 'It seemed strange to punish [the bishops for acquiescing in Wolsey's legatine jurisdiction] when the king himself had sent for another legate from Rome on his own special business.' The baron was a layman who could exercise no ecclesiastical jurisdiction; his functions were purely diplomatic and he was always called 'nuncio,' not 'legate' (see below p. 289).

astical and secular commission, one deriving from the pope and the other from the crown, there was little objection to the ecclesiastical derivation from Rome until, in the fifteenth century the common lawyers began to use nationalist sentiment to extend their own jurisdiction, and to argue that the rival ecclesiastical authority deriving from Rome was *ipso facto* 'foreign' to England and incompatible with Richard II's statute of præmunire. Convocation protested strongly against this interpretation in 1447, and on 2 November 1462 Edward IV, who appears to have been the most papally-minded of English kings with the exception of Henry III, granted a remarkable 'charter of liberties' to the church, in which he dispensed, for himself and his heirs, with the statute of Richard II and asserted the fullest immunity of the clergy from secular jurisdiction.[1] The catholic view, which had been stated by Grosseteste, was finally expressed by Warham in 1532 when, almost on his death-bed, he drafted a speech to be delivered in parliament, in which he declared that he was but the commissary of the pope, that bishops were really appointed in the papal consistory at Rome, and thence derived their jurisdiction.[2]

But neither Warham nor any other English *legatus natus* ever denied that he was a subject of the English king; and none of the trouble provoked by Wolsey's legacy arose out of the fact that, when he was made archbishop of York, he became *legatus natus* of the pope. It was not a legacy

[1] Wilkins, *Concilia*, iii. 555-6, 582; Rymer, xi. 493-5; Stubbs, *Const. Hist.* iii. 204 and 342 n. 2; and *Seventeen Lectures*, p. 364; *Eccles. Courts Comm. Report*, i. 27; Maitland, *Roman Canon Law*, pp. 116, 119; Scofield, *Edward IV*, ii. 390-2. This charter of Edward IV was thought worth transcribing into Booth's Hereford episcopal register in 1521, along with Sixtus IV's bull of 15 May 1476 prohibiting the conventing of clerks before temporal judges (Booth, *Episcopal Reg.*, Cant. and York Soc. ii. 119-24; cf. Wilkins, iii. 609; Stubbs, *Const. Hist.* iii. 204). Stubbs seems to understate the effect of Edward IV's 'charter' in describing it merely as 'letters patent which guaranteed the confirmation of ecclesiastical privilege.'

[2] *L.P.* v. 1247; cf. *ibid.* iv. 5235, where objection is raised to a clause which Wolsey wanted in the bull authorising him to 'erect abbeys into cathedrals,' on the ground that it 'will detract from the honor of the see of Rome if bishops are created except at Rome, or receive their investiture from any one but the pope.'

he would share with Warham which had excited his
ambition, when, while still only bishop of Lincoln, he was
pressing Leo X to make him *legatus a latere* for life. A
precedent for his claim had been provided exactly a century
before by cardinal Beaufort, who resembled Wolsey in being
cardinal, chancellor, papal legate *a latere*, and a candidate
for the papacy, as well as in his vast accumulation of wealth,
passion for magnificence, and unpopularity with the citizens
of London and with his colleagues on the council. He had
been chosen in 1418 by Martin V, after his election as pope
at the council of Constance, to be the pope's agent in his
efforts to re-establish papal authority in England by securing
the repeal of the statutes of provisors and præmunire. But
Henry V, moved perhaps by archbishop Chichele's protest,
refused to allow Beaufort to accept the papal offers ; and
Humphrey, duke of Gloucester, adopted a similar attitude
during the minority of Henry VI. When Beaufort in
1426 accepted the cardinalate and legatine commission, the
papal letters were seized at Dover and in 1431 the king's
council issued a writ of præmunire against him. * He was ex-
onerated in parliament, but his effective action as legate
a latere was confined to his crusade against the Hussites.

Gloucester also declared that Beaufort's cardinalate was
incompatible with membership of the king's council ; but
the council agreed to his presence, except when questions
affecting the papacy were concerned ; he had resigned the
great seal in 1426 before he accepted his papal appointments.
Archbishops Kemp and Morton, however, both of them
held the great seal while they were cardinals ; but no one
before Wolsey combined either the chancellorship or an
archbishopric with a commission as legate *a latere*. When
Leo X proposed to make Bainbridge legate *a latere* in
1514, Wolsey himself protested.[1] His grounds were

---

[1] *L.P.* i. (new ed.) 2611. He associated Foxe with him in the protest,
but the asseveration, that ' we twain *qui non solum in hac sanctissima
causa, verum in omnibus aliis sumus semper unius animi*,' betrays Wolsey's
hand. The chief objection alleged is that Bainbridge, having been so
long Henry's ambassador with the pope, could not be the pope's legate
a latere to Henry ' without suspicion ; nor is the king willing to admit a
legate into England or Calais.' The cases were to alter the circumstances

personal ; the valid objection was that to combine the two kinds of legateship would make one English primate supreme over the other ; and it was not till Warham and Foxe had left the government that Wolsey succeeded in obtaining ecclesiastical as well as political supremacy.

The implications in Wolsey's position as legate *a latere* were so anomalous that, quite apart from the unparalleled extensions of legatine power he secured, they were almost bound to provoke a constitutional breach between the English crown and the papacy. There was, of course, nothing anomalous in the pope sending legates *a latere* to England. Pius II had sent an energetic though unsuccessful legate to the courts of Henry VI and Edward IV to compose the wars of the roses ; [1] another had been sent by Innocent VIII to the court of Henry VII in 1486 to dispense with the canonical obstacles to the marriage of Henry and Elizabeth of York [2] ; and there was nothing peculiar about Campeggio's appointment as legate to Henry VIII in 1518 to plead for financial assistance against the Turks. For these were really legates *a latere* : they came from the papal curia ; they were the pope's ambassadors. But Wolsey, as men noted at the time, had never been to Rome, and could not therefore come from the pope : he was not only the subject, but the principal minister, of Henry VIII, to whom he was now accredited as the special representative of Rome. A childish imposture was even devised to maintain the hollow pretence : whenever Wolsey received a fresh commission, either for himself alone or in conjunction with Campeggio, as legate *a latere*, he absented himself from court and then appeared and was received as though he were really an ambassador arriving from Rome.[3] The serious implications in the situation can

when Wolsey himself succeeded Bainbridge as cardinal-archbishop of York; but his real objection in Feb. 1514 (the answer, *ibid.* no. 2928, to this letter refers to 7 Feb. as its date) is to be found in his commission to Silvester de Giglis to obtain for Wolsey himself the appointment as legate *a latere* (see above, pp. 22-3).

[1] Scofield, *Edward IV*, i. 72 n. 4.

[2] *Tudor Studies*, ed. Seton-Watson, p. 35.

[3] 'We have begun to show the precedent how one may be *legatus a latere*, and not be sent from Rome,' *L.P.* iv. pp. 2558, 2560 ; cf. Hall, pp. 593, 629 ; *Venetian Cal.* 1509-19, pp. 450-1, 504, 585.

best be realised by imagining a modern British government appointing as its representative at Washington a plenipotentiary who was not only an American citizen but had never been to England and was actually the president's secretary of state. Wolsey may have thought that by assuming the part of papal ambassador he would evade the dangers of ministerial responsibility ; but in effect he forfeited diplomatic immunity and ultimately subjected the papal legate to the penalties of English law. The task he set himself, when he combined the functions of papal vicegerent with those of an English prime minister, was to run with the hare and to hunt with the hounds.

Even that ambiguous feat has occasionally been achieved with success ; but Wolsey attempted to convert an occasional feat into a lifelong pursuit. Hitherto legates *a latere* had been something special ; they were not ordinary but exceptional representatives. They were appointed *ad hoc* and had a special commission for a special and temporary purpose. Wolsey transcended all these limitations. Appointed at first on 17 May 1518 simply as a colleague to watch and control Campeggio, he kept that colleague in England until he had extorted from Leo X a commission extending beyond Campeggio's both in time and scope.[1] From three years the period was then extended to five and from five to ten, until at length Wolsey exacted from Clement VII a grant for life ; and the special envoy from Rome became a contradiction in terms and a papal fixture in England. The scope was a matter of greater difficulty. In earlier times it had been held that the presence of a legate *a latere* automatically suspended or at least superseded the jurisdiction of the *legatus natus ;* and archbishop Chichele's was in fact suspended by Beaufort's commission from Martin V.[2] But the theory was then that

---

[1] See below, pp. 179-82.

[2] See *D.N.B.* on Beaufort and archbishops Chichele and Kemp ; Makower, *Const. Hist. of the Church of England*, p. 292 ; Maitland, *Roman Canon Law*, pp. 25, 117, 119 n. 2 ; *Eccles. Courts Comm. Report*, ii. 130. Cowell's *Law Dictionary*, ed. 1727, which is followed by the *Encyc. Brit.*, is wrong in saying (a) that a *legatus natus* was exempt from the jurisdiction of a *legatus a latere ;* and (b) that archbishops of York were not *legati nati* (cf. Stubbs, *Const. Hist.* iii. 310, and Makower, *op. cit.* p. 234).

the legate *a latere* was a special and temporary expedient ; and no one but Wolsey could have hoped to suspend for the term of his life the whole authority of the archbishop of Canterbury. The legate *a latere* was, moreover, a special commissioner : he might be a plenipotentiary, but he would only have full power to act within the terms of his special commission ; and Wolsey's efforts were largely directed towards extending the scope of the pope's successive concessions. He was never satisfied, but was extorting fresh bulls and complaining of their inadequacy until the year in which he fell ; and the exact scope of his legatine powers has never been precisely ascertained.[1]

That Wolsey wanted some ecclesiastical reformation is fairly obvious, and his expressed intentions won warm commendations from Foxe and other enlightened bishops as well as from humanists like Erasmus and More. But there is no evidence that he desired any doctrinal change, nor that his ideas of reformation went beyond the increase of learning, the reform of monastic morals, extending to the suppression of the lesser monasteries, the erection of new bishoprics, and 'an overture for taking away the first-fruits' ;[2] and it is more certain that he wanted power for

All such generalisations are, moreover, apt to be misleading because a *legatus a latere* had, as such, no powers at all : they all depended upon the special commission he received, which varied according to circumstances. As for *legatus natus*, it seems to have been simply the papal phrase for an archbishop, who acknowledged his position as a delegate of the pope by accepting his pall from Rome. But, while the death of a pope terminated the commission of all legates *a latere*, it had no effect on the position of the *legatus natus*.

[1] It varied from year to year with the endless amplifications Wolsey sought and apparently sometimes anticipated. ' We have begun,' gibes Palsgrave, ' to have the whole power of the pope ' (*L.P.* iv. p. 2559) ; ' si concedatur,' prophesied de Grassis of Wolsey's legacy in 1516, ' curia Romana destruetur ' (Creighton, *Papacy*, v. 316).

[2] Strype, *Eccl. Memorials*, I, ii. no. 23 ; Pocock, *Records*, i. 95 ; *L.P.* iv. p. 1821. This overture was not made till 1528 ; it came to nothing, and its purport is as doubtful as its purpose. It was made in the effort to constrain Clement VII to grant the divorce, but the pope's reception of it shows that it was not confiscation. ' I took occasion,' writes Gardiner, ' to make him an overture for taking away the first-fruits, telling him it was a suggestion made by the said bishop [Nix of Norwich]—

itself than that he wanted power simply to effect a reformation. Clearly he could not effect a reformation without obtaining the power to do so ; but he was far more
successful in securing the power than in effecting the
reformation ; and it was the concentration of the means
rather than the achievement of their purpose that con-
stitutes Wolsey's importance in English history. Even
with regard to the monasteries, his immediate object was
less to reform them than to abolish the exemption they
enjoyed from all but papal jurisdiction ; and one of his
first efforts was an attempt to reduce the extensive liberties of
Westminster abbey as a sanctuary for criminals.[1] Similarly
he secured the complete surrender by Oxford and Cambridge
of their privileges and statutes to him for reformation ;
but, while he founded lectureships at Oxford, his reformation of university statutes came to practically nothing.[2]

He was far more intent on asserting that all reformation
belonged to him as papal legate and not to archbishops,
provincial convocations, or universities, than he was on
carrying out the reformation itself. The first use he made
of his independent legatine commission was to threaten
Warham with præmunire for having summoned a convocation of his province to consider its reformation, apparently on the ground that Warham's allegation of the
royal consent to its summons was untrue.[3] But however
slight might have been the results of Warham's reforming
convocation, they could hardly have been less than those
of the legatine council by which Wolsey proposed to supersede it ;[4] and the constitutions which he had enacted a
little earlier for his province of York consist merely of

without letting him know that we had any instructions. His holiness
began to inquire about them, and how they might be redeemed. The
project pleased him and the cardinals, and he said he would gladly concur
in it.'

[1] See above, p. 53 *n*.

[2] *L.P.* ii. 934, 4960, App. 46 ; iv. 963, 6377 ; Fiddes, *Collections*,
pp. 34, 122 ; E. L. Taunton, p. 103 ; Creighton, p. 145. His legatine
powers enabled him apparently to interfere frequently with the appointment of proctors at Oxford (*L.P.* iii. 2267, 2604).

[3] Wilkins, *Concilia*, iii. 660.

[4] *L.P.* iii. 77 ; *Hereford Reg.* ii. 65-7, 74 ; Burnet, ed. Pocock, iii. 86-7.

selections from his predecessors' legislation.[1] He looked
upon Warham, not as a colleague in the work of reform,
but as an impediment to his authority. He contemplated
his own succession to the see of St. Augustine and resented
Warham's persistent longevity as a personal grievance.
As early as 27 February 1518, in demanding from Leo X
the deprivation of 'that infamous cardinal' Hadrian, Wolsey
had requested leave to hold the bishopric of Bath and Wells
along with his present 'or any other archbishopric'; and
he can have had none other than Canterbury in his mind.[2]

He had to be content with York, the abbey of St. Albans,
and one bishopric *in commendam* at a time, though Bath
and Wells was exchanged for Durham on Ruthal's death in
1523, and Durham for Winchester on Foxe's death in 1528.
He also, in virtue of his legatine authority, enjoyed the
spiritualities of all English bishoprics during vacancy,[3] and
'farmed' the three bishoprics of Salisbury, Worcester, and
Llandaff occupied respectively by five non-resident aliens,
Campeggio (1524-34); Silvester de Giglis (1504-21),
Giulio de Medici (1521-2), and Ghinucci (1522-35); and
Ateca (1517-36),[4] who merely received fixed stipends from
their sees.[5] Each of these accumulations was a fresh addition to the mass of ecclesiastical abuse which Wolsey was
pretending to reform. It was almost unprecedented for an
English archbishop to hold an English bishopric *in com-
mendam*,[6] and it was a still more flagrant abuse for a secular

---

[1] Wilkins, *Concilia*, iii. 662-81.

[2] Martene and Durand, iii. 1277; *L.P.* ii. 3973; Warham was then
nearly seventy.

[3] *Ibid*. iv. 5313.

[4] Rymer, xiii. 587; Theiner, p. 519; this Spaniard owed his bishopric to the fact that he had been Catherine of Aragon's confessor, the
Italians owed theirs to their services at Rome. On Ateca see *Erasmi Ep.*
iii. 547-8.

[5] *L.P.* iii. 1334; iv. 4824; Cavendish, p. 29. Wolsey, on various
pretexts denied, or at least delayed, possession of Worcester to Ghinucci
(*L.P.* iii. 2791, 2866). Objection was taken at Rome to ' so many sees
being held *in commendam*' (Campeggio to Wolsey, *ibid*. iii. 1187).

[6] St. Oswald held the bishopric of Worcester with the archbishopric
of York from 972 till his death in 992; and Stigand attempted to combine
the tenure of Winchester with Canterbury and several abbeys from 1058
to 1070. But he is said to have been excommunicated by five successive

priest like Wolsey to hold such an improper *commendam* as St. Albans, said to be the richest abbey in England ; and, while Wolsey thus aggravated the need for reformation, he weakened the powers of resistance, for an incidental result of his accumulation of bishoprics and their conferment on aliens was to reduce the episcopal vote in the house of lords, when the Reformation parliament met in 1529, from twenty-one to fifteen.

What would have happened had Wolsey been spared the trial of Warham's longevity is mere speculation. The combination of York with Canterbury would have been no greater a novelty than its combination with Winchester and St. Albans ; [1] and he might thus have completed his control of ecclesiastical administration as in 1523 he completed his control of ecclesiastical legislation by amalgamating the two convocations into a legatine council under his presidency. This sort of national papacy might conceivably have weaned him from Rome, but as late as in 1529 he was still hankering after the supreme pontificate. In January he was discussing a suggestion that Clement VII might resign ; [2] on the 21st, John Casale wrote from Venice to Wolsey that the pope was dead. [3] On the receipt of the news Wolsey at once drafted instructions, which were signed by the king, [4] to his four English agents at Rome pressing his claims as the only cardinal whose election could restore the holy see and avert the manifold dangers impending over it, and emphasising the numerous spiritual promotions which his elevation would liberate for the recompense of those who might support his election. The French king, it was said, had spontaneously offered to use his influence on his behalf, and du Bellay was dispatched post haste from his embassy in London to further Wolsey's candidature at Rome. To

popes, was eventually condemned by a legatine council at Winchester, and imprisoned for the remainder of his life (Freeman, *Norman Conquest*, ii. 607 ; iii. 643 ; iv. 333).

[1] Nicholas Wotton held both deaneries together under all the Tudors save Henry VII ; he was appointed to Canterbury in 1542, to York in 1544, and died in 1567.

[2] *L.P.* iv. 5179.   [3] *Ibid.* iv. 5194 ; cf. 5238.

[4] *Ibid.* iv. 5270 ; the gist of the matter is contained in Wolsey's more private letter to Gardiner in Fiddes, *Collections*, pp. 211-12.

Gardiner Wolsey communicated 'the kings minde and mine concerning my advancement unto the dignity papalle,' impressing on him 'as well the state wherein the church and all Christendome doth stand now presently, as also the state of this realme and of the kings secret mater, which if it shulde be browght to passe by any other meanyes than by the authority of the church, I account this prince and realme utterly undone.' But on the date of this letter du Bellay heard at Clermont that the pope was alive, and Wolsey had to content himself with repeating his instructions to Gardiner and his colleagues in case the pope died after all or resigned.[1]

Wolsey's election would have been a happy release from the quandary in which he was involved by reliance on a policy, which he now saw could only succeed by his own elevation to the papacy. Whether he would have proved more amenable in St. Peter's chair than Thomas à Becket in St. Augustine's is by no means certain, and the probable effects of his election on the history of the papacy and the reformation are extremely problematical. Any consideration of what might have been is commonly regarded as an idle speculation lying entirely outside the purview of the historian. Yet no judgement on what men actually did is worth the paper on which it is written, unless it is based on some consideration and comparison of alternative policies and their probable consequences. No man can be condemned for not attempting the impossible or for succumbing to the inevitable ; and criticism of Wolsey's policy rests on the assumption that it was a gamble on highly improbable futures. No Englishman but one had ever ascended the papal throne, and Nicholas Breakspear had spent but his boyhood in England and was chosen pope before national states had been formed or national rivalries had intruded on papal elections. Adrian VI, his successful rival at Wolsey's first contest, was the last non-Italian to overcome Italian prejudice or patriotism ; and he had been tutor to Charles V who ruled over more Italian soil than anyone else. The papacy had become an Italian state before the

[1] *L.P.* iv. 5274, 5314. For the expenses of messengers sent to Rome on this rumour, see *ibid.* v. p. 309.

church in England became an English church ; and that fact was fatal to Wolsey's prospects. In spite of the flattering assurances [1] of his agents, his name only appeared in one of the eleven scrutinies which preceded the election of 1522, and then he received but seven votes in a conclave of thirty-nine cardinals ; while in 1523 he received no vote at all. The papacy was Italian property tempered by the territorial influence in Italy of other than Italian sovereigns ; neither support was at the disposal of English candidates, and Wolsey's diplomatic attempts to redress the balance by means of other men's swords left him at the mercy of the agents he sought to employ. He resorted to a catholic jurisdiction to settle a question of canon law in what he regarded as national interests, and he encountered an insuperable obstacle in rival Habsburg interests and in the constraint which Charles V could exert over Clement VII.

But the most pessimistic view of English history since 1529 hardly justifies Wolsey's anticipation that 'this prince and realm' would be 'utterly undone' by the decision of the divorce of Catherine of Aragon elsewhere than at Rome. He was thinking rather of the prospects of papal jurisdiction in England and of its particular repository ; he had always identified himself and, so far as he could, his king and his country with the interests of Rome and those interests with his own. 'He alleged,' wrote Campeggio on 28 Oct. 1528, 'that if the king's desire were not complied with, fortified and justified as it was by the reasons, writings, and counsels of many learned men who feared God, the speedy and total ruin would follow of the kingdom, of his lordship, and of the church's influence in this kingdom.' [2] 'I cannot,' wrote Wolsey himself three days later, 'reflect upon it and close my eyes ; for I see ruin, infamy, and subversion of the whole dignity and estimation of the see apostolic. . . . The

---

[1] See above, p. 127 ; and *L.P.* iii. 1952, 1960, p. 806, 1981, 1990 ; *Spanish Cal.* 1509-25, pp. 389-91. The fear of the papacy being transferred elsewhere was used at Rome as a reason or an excuse for not electing a non-Italian pope (*L.P.* iii. 3331).

[2] Laemmer, *Mon. Vat.* p. 30 ; *L.P.* iv. 4881 ; repeated on 22 May 1529 (Ehses, p. 96).

sparks of that opposition, which have been extinguished with such care and vigilance, will blaze forth to the utmost danger of all here and elsewhere.'[1] Wolsey was here a better prophet of the future than judge of his past administration ; for his 'care and vigilance' as legate, so far from extinguishing the sparks of opposition to papal jurisdiction in England, had fanned them into a flame in which it was soon to be consumed.

Never had Roman jurisdiction been brought home to Englishmen so effectively and so intensively as it was by Wolsey. He had advantages over preceding legates other than those conferred by his extensive powers and lifelong commission. For, being chancellor, he controlled the secular arm, so far as the law was concerned, and the issue of all the king's writs. The courts christian, which had become in effect the courts of the cardinal, had no need to fear those prohibitions which had impeded, if not paralysed, the course of the canon law in the days of archbishops Peckham and Winchilsea. The crown seemed to have laid down its secular weapons and acquiesced in the translation of the *regnum* into the hands of the *sacerdotium*.[2] Wolsey, moreover, was on the spot, and his action as resident legate *a latere* was far more regular and insistent than that of intermittent papal envoys or the distant and deliberate course of justice at Rome. All sections of society felt the difference between a papal jurisdiction, indirect, remote, and rarely exerted at Rome, and the same jurisdiction deputed to a legate who could supplement the coercive defects of courts christian out of the plenitude of his power in chancery, in the council, and in the star chamber. A new form of terror, if not a new polity, was portended when by the same agency not only was Buckingham beheaded, a Speaker sent to the Tower, and parliament superseded, but the archbishop of Canterbury was threatened with præmunire and summoned to account for his 'disobedience' to the archbishop of York, the bishop of Coventry and Lichfield was charged

---

[1] *L.P.* iv. 4897.
[2] This is one of the principal complaints of Tyndale, Simon Fish, Skelton, and the ballad writers (see below, pp. 227-9, 359-60).

with treason,[1] bishops Foxe of Winchester and Nix of Norwich were excepted by name from the general and usual act of pardon passed in the parliament of 1523,[2] and Stokesley, soon to be bishop of London, was sent by Wolsey to the Fleet.[3] It is hardly surprising to find Warham's chaplain referring to Wolsey in 1519 as 'this great tyrant'[4] or du Bellay ten years later accounting for Wolsey's surrender to the king on the ground that he preferred the mercy of Henry VIII to that of his episcopal victims.[5]

The general cause for this particular hatred was, of course, the extensive supersession of episcopal authority by Wolsey's legatine powers. Mediæval English bishops had been as a rule by no means averse from papal jurisdiction; they looked to it, rather, to check the encroachments of their more immediate 'sovereigns,'[6] the archbishops of Canterbury and York. Thomas Cantilupe bishop of Hereford, died in Italy while prosecuting an appeal to Rome against archbishop Peckham who had excommunicated him and became a saint hardly less popular than Thomas Becket. But the crushing effect of Wolsey's commissions combining as they did the special jurisdiction of a legate *a latere* with the normal authority of an archbishop of York, provided a cause of resentment that was common to the archbishop of Canterbury and the bishops of both the provinces. In 1515 bishop Fitzjames, in imploring Wolsey's assistance over the case of Richard Hunne, had protested that, if the cardinal could help the clergy in their weakness, they would be bound to him for ever. The legate *a latere* converted that devotion into an episcopal and clerical hostility which paralysed the corporate action of the church, promoted Wolsey's fall, and provoked a reformation at the hands of parliament and the crown.

[1] Hall, p. 655. *   [2] *Rot. Parl.* vol. vii. p. xciii.
[3] Roper, *More*, p. 38 ; Tyndale (*Practice*, p. 309) only says he was 'thrust out of court.' Possibly Roper was thinking of Stokesley's later troubles (*L.P.* 1538 i. 1095). On the other hand, Roper specifically attributes to Stokesley an active part in Wolsey's fall in revenge for his treatment (*cf.* Chapuys in *L.P.* v. 62, x. 752).
[4] *L.P.* iii. 77 (6).   [5] See below, pp. 215, 258.
[6] See below, p. 318 ; and Maitland, *Roman Canon Law*, pp. 115-31

The ecclesiastical despotism which produced this violent reaction was not created at a stroke by Wolsey's appointment as legate *a latere* on 17 May 1518. He then, apart from full powers for the remission of sins,[1] received but a common commission with Campeggio to negotiate on behalf of the pope for peace between European princes and a crusade against the Turks.[2] But this commission was only designed by Wolsey to open the door for other purposes, and he insisted that it should include a suspension of the faculties Warham enjoyed as *legatus natus*.[3] The next step was to obtain from Leo X on 27 August 1518 a bull empowering the two legates to reform the monasteries. Silvester de Giglis, in forwarding it from Rome, remarked that it did not contain the provision, which Wolsey wanted, for reforming the secular clergy as well, because that was the business of bishops : he anticipated considerable opposition even to the monastic jurisdiction, and said that great care would be needed in visiting nunneries as so many errors would be found in them.[4] But Campeggio neither desired nor was desired by Wolsey to remain long in England ; and on 25 March 1519 Wolsey asked that he might retain his own dignity with increased faculties, not for extorting money but 'that I may be able to accomplish some good in the Lord's vineyard and be profitable to all christendom.' If he was now to be deprived of it, he would rather never have had it ; its loss would be anguish and torture to him—*me maxime angit et torquet*. He and Campeggio, he continued, were expecting the bull for the reformation of the clergy which had been withheld in 1518.[5] Silvester had, on Wolsey's instructions, been pressing the pope to 'remove the prohibitions to his legatine authority' ; but Leo X still

---

[1] Rymer, *Fœdera*, xiii. 609, 621-2.
[2] He insisted, however, that he was 'first' legate and that only his cross should be borne before them ; and, while at their public reception Campeggio sat on a seat raised three steps above the floor, Wolsey's was double that height (*L.P.* ii. 4170 ; *Venetian Cal.* 1509-19, p. 464).
[3] Martene and Durand, col. 1284 ; *L.P.* ii. 4073.
[4] *Ibid.* ii. 4399.
[5] Martene and Durand, cols. 1288-9 ; *L.P.* iii. 137, 149.

resisted his 'importunity.' The pope resented the non-payment of the sums, in the hope of which he had made Wolsey legate, and was not impressed by Wolsey's claim to credit for inducing Henry VIII to admit Campeggio as papal legate 'contrary to all the usages of the realm.'[1] He granted to Wolsey alone, however, on 10 June the powers to reform the monasteries after Campeggio's departure, and Wolsey promptly demanded, on 1 August, the legacy for life : he could not abide any limits.[2]

Campeggio left England on 24 August 1519 and on 1 September Silvester reported that, while the pope could not accede to Wolsey's demands, he promised to continue his commission before it expired and renew it as often as need be. Campeggio, who had been given cardinal Hadrian's forfeited house in Rome and had been promised the bishopric of Salisbury, returned to Rome 'an excellent trumpeter,' as Silvester called him, of Wolsey's virtues, and protested that Wolsey's demands 'had no regard whatever to his own interests, but only to the more authoritative reformation of the monks and clergy.'[3] Leo replied that he wished that 'majestas illa serenissima et reverendissima Eboracensis'[4] kept his promises better, but agreed to prolong his legateship for two years and grant some fresh indulgences.[5] On 6 January 1521 Leo granted another two years' extension, making five years in all from the date of Campeggio's departure (i.e. till 24 August 1524),[6] and on 1 April amplified it with powers to legitimatise bastards, reform secular clergy however eminent they might be, reduce them to a more honest

---

[1] *L.P.* iii. 298, 407, 431, 439.

[2] Martene and Durand, cols. 1293-4; *L.P.* iii. 475, 510, 693.

[3] *Ibid.* 444, 533, 645; Polydore Vergil, p. 656. Hadrian's English house in the Borgo had been built by Bramante and was ominously destroyed in the sack of 1527 (Ehses, p. 102 *n*).

[4] Fiddes is at some needless pains to excuse the university of Oxford from the charge of servility in addressing Wolsey as 'your majesty.'

[5] *L.P.* iii. 557, 600, 647.

[6] Rymer, xiii. 734. On 13 Jan., however, Mendoza reported from Rome that Wolsey had asked to be made legate for life and that Leo had appointed him for ten years (*Spanish Cal.* ii. 335). See above, p. 124 *n*. 3.

manner of living, correct, chastise, and punish them himself or by deputy ; grant degrees in theology, arts, and medicine ; dispense with canonical impediments to holy orders ; appoint to ecclesiastical benefices ; absolve from excommunication and all other ecclesiastical sentences and penalties, notwithstanding all limitations and restrictions previously imposed on legatine authority.[1]

There were exceptional reasons for this unusual delegation of papal jurisdiction, but they had little to do with the interests of morality or the reformation of the church. Leo had cast in his lot with Charles V and was striving with every nerve to make as catholic as possible the coalition against Francis. 'As the French,' wrote the future Clement VII, 'could not win over the pope to their purpose, they had recourse to irregular means by seizing one of his towns. This insolence must be chastised, or they will proceed further. The pope has resolved to liberate himself at all hazards from this intolerable slavery, and hopes that Henry will show the same good mind towards him and his confederates that he has always done. Wolsey may secure the honor of England and his own reputation, and recover for the emperor his own, by promoting this design ' which ' is set on foot not merely for the liberation of the holy see, but of Italy, from the fangs of the wolf.'[2] Leo X's successor, Adrian VI, was pestered by Wolsey to extend these powers before he left Spain for Rome ; but the new pope replied that he must consult his college of cardinals, and a few days later wrote that he desired peace between christian princes : he promised to renew Leo X's grant of the legateship for five years, but would not accede

---

[1] Rymer, xiii. 739-42. The phrase about reducing the clergy *ad honestiores vivendi mores reducendi* was incorporated by Wolsey in his summons to both convocations to meet under his legatine presidency in 1523 (*Hereford Episcopal Reg.*, Booth, ii. 142 ; Wilkins, *Concilia*, iii. 700) and gave great offence to the clerical representatives ; the twenty-ninth article of impeachment against him was ' slandering the clergy of England by writing to Rome that they had given themselves *in reprobum sensum* ' (Herbert, p. 299 ; *L.P.* iv. p. 2713). See below, p. 259.

[2] *L.P.* iii. 1209 ; cf. *ibid.* iii. 1369.

to Wolsey's demand for its life-long extension nor add the fresh faculties he requested.[1]

The Medici Clement VII cared less than Adrian for a catholic coalition against the Turk, but a great deal more for the family fortunes in Florence ; and within a few weeks of the new pope's election Wolsey's agents in Rome were able to write on 9 January 1524 that they had secured 'the prorogation of Wolsey's legateship for life, with the faculties he had and those he wished for . . . which was never heard of before.'[2]   They were unduly optimistic, and three months later the bishop of Bath was warning Wolsey that he must be content to come to the consummation of his power gradually.[3]   He was able, however, on 22 August, to send Wolsey bulls 'for the ampliation of the legateship, for the jurisdiction, and the faculties.'[4]   Clement felt most compunction about handing

---

[1] *L.P.* iii. 2260, 2298, 2521, 2713-14, 2766, 2771 (p. 1167), 2891 ; Rymer, xiii. 795-6.

[2] *L.P.* iv. 14-15, 115, 119; *State Papers*, vi. 256-7 ; Theiner, nos. 939-42 (all wrongly assigned to Adrian VI). Even this did not completely satisfy his demands : 'The pope,' continue Wolsey's agents, 'hesitates to grant such faculties *pro non familiaribus* as he has already done *pro familiaribus*. They still sue for it, but without great hopes.'   The obstacle was the impoverishment of the papal *curia* by Wolsey's proposed diversion from Rome of the profits of promotions.   He complained bitterly of this fly in his ointment : 'I esteem somewhat more strangeness to be showed unto me than my merits require, in that there hath been difficulty made to amplify my faculties *per non familiares* [*L.P.* iv. 126 has *pro non familiaribus*] and such other things to be contained in my instructions given to my lord of Bath.'   It was only in documents intended for public consumption that Wolsey made any pretence that his instructions were Henry VIII's.   He went on to assert that his legateship 'with all its faculties, whatever people may report, will not be worth 1000 ducats a year' : in point of fact, 1000 marks were paid for probate on a single estate (Sir W. Compton's), and 1000 marks was just about 3000 ducats ; and the half of all profits on probate in the province of Canterbury which Wolsey received by his arrangement with Warham, came to him in virtue of his special legatine commission.   Wolsey's revenues were thought by other people to be 'about equal to those of the crown (Fiddes, p. 351 ; Gasquet, *Monasteries*, i. 88).   See below, pp. 320-5.

[3] *L.P.* iv. 252.

[4] *Ibid.* iv. 585, 587 ; the text of one only is printed in Rymer, xiv 18-20, but it apparently removes all the impediments to Wolsey's pleni

over the friars to Wolsey's uncovenanted mercies, not that he thought that they stood in no need of reformation but that he feared the tumult they would raise. He again, writes the bishop of Bath, asked him to urge Wolsey 'for Godds saake to use mercye with thois friars, sayeng that they be as desperatt bestes past shame, that can leese [lose] nothyng by clamors.'[1] Wolsey replied that he would use his legatine authority with such moderation that no complaint should arise. The appropriate comment on his undertaking is a resolution of the Black monks, assembled a few months later in London by Wolsey's order, in which, although less vocal than the friars, they beg him to mitigate the reformation of their order 'so as not to drive the weak into flight, apostasy, or rebellion'; for, they went on, 'in the present times, now the world is drawing to its end, very few desire to live an austere life.'[2]

The end of the world for the monks was the conversion of monasteries into cathedrals, and Wolsey's last and most ambitious proposal was to erect thirteen new episcopal sees on monastic foundations. This was merely purgatory compared with the damnation which 'reformation' meant for more than a score of smaller religious houses, suppressed by Wolsey without the consent of themselves or their founders' heirs,[3] partly in the interests of his colleges at Oxford and Ipswich; for the new foundations were to be like the double Benedictine chapters of Bath and Wells, Coventry and Lichfield, half secular and half religious, with

tude of power which might arise out of previous ecclesiastical constitutions from those of Otto and Ottobon downwards.

[1] *L.P.* iv. 610, 759. For further bulls authorising the dissolution of particular monasteries see *ibid.* iv. 697.

[2] *Ibid.* iv. 477-8, 953; cf. 1063, 1137, 1397, 1470, 1521. Among the most strenuous opponents of Wolsey's visitation were the Friars Observants, and nineteen of them 'were accursed at Paules crosse by one of the same religion called Friar Forest' in Jan. 1525 (Hall, p. 691).

[3] See lists in *L.P.* iv. 697, 1137, 1833; and Gairdner, *Hist. of the Church*, 1509-58, p. 419. These lists appear to be very incomplete; at any rate Mr. Salter gives 39 as suppressed before 1526 in the diocese of Lincoln alone (*Lincoln Subsidy*, Oxf. Hist. Soc. pp. xi-xvi); but he includes churches like the two St. Michael's at Oxford.

the bishop as *ex officio* abbot.[1]   There was great opposition
at Rome, where Wolsey's influence was declining under the
growing power of Charles V; and his scheme only led
twelve years later to Henry VIII's erection of six new
bishoprics on a purely secular foundation after the complete
dissolution of the monasteries.   The last of the general
dissolutions, that of the order of St. John of Jerusalem,
had, however, been suggested in Wolsey's time.   After the
fall of Rhodes in 1522 Henry VIII had summoned the
English members of the order home, and when the prior,
Sir Thomas Docwra, died in 1527 it was rumoured that
his lands and those of his order would be confiscated by
the crown.[2]   A successor was, nevertheless, elected and the
order retained its property till he died in 1540.   Wolsey's
latest actual acquisitions of legatine power seem to have
been a bull empowering him to degrade criminous clerks,[3]
and the extension of his legatine authority to Ireland.
There he proposed to reduce the number of archbishops
from four to two, and of bishoprics from thirty to nine or
ten, and to reserve them exclusively for Englishmen.[4]   As
his sub-delegate he appointed his most unpopular agent,*
John Allen, who was made archbishop of Dublin and lord
chancellor of Ireland, thus reflecting Wolsey's own combination of papal and royal, ecclesiastical and secular authority.
Allen, however, came to a more violent, though not perhaps
more unnatural, end than his master: he was assassinated
by native Irish in July 1534.

The reluctance with which successive popes yielded

---

[1] Taunton, *Wolsey*, pp. 119-20;   *L.P.* iv. 5235, 5608.   The pope
or the papal chancery had wished clauses *de consensu quorum interest* and
de consensu fundatorum to be inserted in Wolsey's bulls; but he resisted,
apparently with success (*L.P.* iv. 2418, 2630, 3562, 5226).   Cf. Hall,
p. 694, who says that Wolsey's commissioners 'founde [i.e. by inquests
ex officio] the kyng founder, where other men were founders'; and Roy,
Rede me (p. 113):

> What monasteries he hath broken
> With out their fownders consentis.

[2] *L.P.* iv. 2915, 3036.   Wolsey had built Hampton Court on land
belonging to it; see below, p. 325 *n.* 2.

[3] 12 May 1528, Rymer, xiv. 239; *L.P.* iv. 4257.

[4] Taunton, *Wolsey*, pp. 123-7; *L.P.* iv. p. 1077.

to Wolsey's exorbitant demands was justified by other
considerations than doubts of the circumspection with
which he would wield the powers he obtained; for the
delegation of life-long papal authority to a legate, whose
responsibility to Rome was slight compared with his
responsibility to the secular sovereign whose chief minister
he was, amounted to papal abdication and led straight
towards a disruption of the catholic government of the
church. Leo X's initial objection to Wolsey's importunity
had always been that, if he granted so much to Henry VIII's
chancellor, Charles V and Francis I would be content with
nothing less for their own; papal jurisdiction, not to mention papal finance, would be divided among the gentiles;
and the papacy would only have triumphed over the
disruptive tendencies of the conciliar movement in the
fifteenth century to fall a victim to the ministers of new
monarchs, whose nationalism was as wine to the water
of that which a century before had inspired English
and German, French and Spanish ecclesiastics at Constance
and Basle. Adrian VI had no particular local or family
affections and offered some resistance to the centrifugal
tendencies; but his pontificate was a brief interlude
between those of two Medicean popes who ruled from
1513 to 1521 and from 1523 to 1534 and did more to
precipitate disruption by their Florentine prepossessions
than by their addiction to the balance of power. Wolsey's
national legateship was the price paid for Henry VIII's
support of the efforts of popes to avoid becoming chaplains
to Charles V or Francis I.

But while delegation to Wolsey portended disruption at
Rome, it effected no liberation in England. There was no
relief of the grievances of the laity with which Wolsey had
been confronted in the parliament of 1515; and instead
of a recovery of ecclesiastical self-government there was
simply a *translatio imperii* from a less oppressive pope to a
far more exigent legate. The cumulative effect of the series
of bulls which Wolsey extorted from successive pontiffs was
to establish an unprecedented ecclesiastical despotism in
England, to concentrate in Wolsey's hands a monopoly of

legislative, executive, and judicial authority over the English church, and to supersede its mediæval constitution. The two convocations were first superseded by Wolsey's legatine council, and then the legate was enabled to dispense with council or counsel and act on the monarchical authority derived from his papal bulls. For the time being the very forms of ecclesiastical self-government were suspended, and the annals of convocation were seldom, if ever, so scanty and barren as they were under Wolsey's oppression. Wilkins' 'Concilia' is a very imperfect record, but the loss of archives is not the reason why some forty pages[1] suffice for the convocation documents of the decade of Wolsey's legateship, while those of the next fifteen years fill one hundred and sixty. Wolsey's domination had the same effect on legislation by representative bodies both in church and state; he was as antagonistic to convocation as he was to parliament, and both revived the moment the incubus of his presence was removed.

The absence of parliaments, save in 1523, between 1515 and 1529, involved of course the absence of convocations summoned for parliamentary purposes; but the abstinence was arbitrarily extended to provincial convocations which the archbishops could summon for purely ecclesiastical legislation. Wolsey never in person visited his metropolis or any other of the half-dozen sees of which he was bishop; and scanty as are the records of the southern province during Warham's eclipse, those of the northern convocation are an absolute blank while Wolsey was legate *a latere*.[2] The

---

[1] The alleged destruction of the records of convocation in the fire of London in 1666 has been greatly exaggerated. Tunstal's register is extant and so is Warham's; and the reasons which reduced Wilkins to relying so largely on occasionally accessible episcopal registers elsewhere are obscure. The only episcopal registers which have been printed for this period are, I think, those of Hereford, St. David's, and Winchester (1528-30).

[2] See *Records of the Northern Convocation*, Surtees Soc. 1906, which contain nothing for Wolsey's time after his 'constitutions' of 1518. He had in 1514 appointed, as his suffragan for York, John Yonge, master of the rolls and titular bishop of Negroponte; and, when Yonge died on 25 April 1516, Wolsey asked Leo X to appoint Richard Wilson, who was prior of Drax and afterwards bishop of Meath (Theiner, p. 518; *L.P.* i.

papal legate would not condescend to the duties of a mere archbishop in his province, and he prohibited Warham from aspiring to a provincial reformation as an infringement of the monopoly of ecclesiastical reform in England entrusted to himself.[1] Some bishops met at his house in 1519 to consider proposals which have not survived, and at least one diocesan synod was summoned to consider them.[2] But Wolsey maintained that the reformation of abuses was solely a matter for the legate, and it is in this light that we have to regard the view that 'it seemed for the moment as if the era of provincial councils was about to close' and a return made to national councils.[3] For, if the composition of mediæval convocations remains a matter of doubt, that of a 'national' council under Wolsey is even more obscure. Apart from the convocations of 1523, which were summoned as part of the parliament of that year by the usual parliamentary writs, Wolsey never summoned more than a handful of bishops, without any other prelates or representative clergy, to council: a legatine council simply consisted of such as the legate took into counsel and he would have been the last to call it national. Of any constitutional principles of composition or method of summons nothing is known.

The assembly of 1523 stands on a different footing but illustrates the same constitutional anomaly. The writs were duly issued in the normal way: that is to say, on 6 February the king issued a writ to Warham to summon the bishops and clergy of his province to meet at St. Paul's or wherever else he thought expedient;[4] and on the 7th the archbishop directed his mandate to Tunstal, bishop of

(index) and iii. 2838: the *D.N.B.* article on Yonge mentions neither his titular bishopric nor his suffraganship to Wolsey). He afterwards complained of ' the oversight, despoil, and evil behaviour of such as I did trust' (see below, p. 277).

[1] See above, p. 172.

[2] *L.P.* iii. 63; Wilkins, *Concilia*, iii. 661, 682-8; *Hereford Episcopal Reg.* (Booth), ii. 57, 65-7, 74.

[3] Dr. Armitage Robinson in the *Church Quarterly Rev.* Oct. 1915, pp. 136-7; and cf. Sir Thomas More's opinion, below, p. 192.

[4] Printed in Burnet, ed. Pocock, iv. 8 from Tunstal's register, f. xxxii *b*.

London (as dean of the province), to execute the summons, fixing St. Paul's as the place and 20 April as the date of meeting.[1] Parliament met on Wednesday, 15 April, and on Saturday the commons chose Sir Thomas More as their speaker. 'Asto the convocation amongs the prests,' writes a correspondent on 14 May to the earl of Surrey,[2] 'the furste daye of their apparence assone as masse of the holie gooste at paulis was done, my lorde Cardinall assited [ad- cited] all theim t'appere before hym in his convocation at Westm^r ;[3] whiche soo did : and there was a nother masse of the holie gooste : and within vi or vij dayes, the prests proved that all that my lord Cardinalls convocation shuld doo, it shuld bee voyde, because that their somons was t'appere before my lorde of Cauntirbury ; whiche thing soo espied, my Lord Cardinall hath addressed out of newe citations into every cuntrey commaunding the prests t'appere before hym viij dayes after th'Assencon ; and then I thinke they shal-have the iij^de masse of the Holie Gooste. I praye god the holie gooste bee amongs theim and us bothe. I doo tremble to remember the ende of all thies hye and newe entrepreses : for often tymes it hathe bene that to a newe entreprise there folowethe a newe maner and a strange sequele. God of his mercie sende his grace of such facion that it may bee all for the beaste.' Hall puts the novelty more clearly and openly : 'and in this season the Cardinall by his power legantyne dissolued the conuoca-

---

[1] *L.P.* iii. 2819 (2), from Lambeth MS. xiv. 942. Similar writs were directed to Wolsey to summon the northern province (Wilkins, iii. 698). According to bishop Booth's *Hereford Reg.* (ii. 138) his summons to parliament was dated 23 Jan. whereas the king's writ to Warham for convocation was only dated 6 Feb. No summons to this parliament are given in Dugdale, Rymer, or the *Letters and Papers.* Bishop Booth obtained leave to appoint as his proxies for parliament bishops West, Standish, and Veysey, and lord Ferrers, and for convocation the same three bishops (*Reg.* ii. 139).

[2] Ellis, *Original Letters*, I, i. 221-2 ; calendared in *L.P.* iii. 3024, where the last two sentences are badly summarised as 'is much afraid of the result.' The signature has been torn off.

[3] According to Wilkins the northern convocation was first summoned to meet on 22 March at St. Peter's, York, and then on 22 April at York House, Westminster.

cion at Paules, called by the Archebishop of Cantorbury, and called hym and all the clergie to his conuocacion to Westminster, which was neuer seen before in England.' [1]

The documents needed to elucidate these high-handed proceedings are sadly defective. Papal legates *a latere* had no office or official machinery in England, and Wolsey presumably gave effect to his desires by simply commandeering, in virtue of his papal commission, the machinery of the archbishop of Canterbury. It seems to have been merely by a legatine word of mouth that he dissolved the convocation of Canterbury duly summoned by Warham in pursuance of the king's writ; and it must have been by the sheer extrusion of Warham from his proper function that Wolsey, through Tunstal as dean of the southern province, summoned another convocation of Canterbury with fresh powers to meet with that of York before him as legate in the abbey of Westminster, which was exempt from Warham's jurisdiction.[2] The obscurity extends to our knowledge of what actually happened: Surrey's correspondent gives eight days after Ascension (22 May) as the date for Wolsey's combined convocation; his writ in the Lincoln register is dated 7 May and gives 2 June for the meeting.[3] That in the Hereford register is dated 2 May and gives 8 June for the meeting;[4] while Burnet, apologising for the errors which, 'implicitly following some writers that lived in that time,' he had committed in his first account, roundly declares in his 'Supplement' that 'the true account of that matter' is that Wolsey's re-summoned convocation never met or did nothing.[5] Some support to this view is given by the fact

---

[1] *Chron.* p. 657; 'whereof,' he continues, 'master Skelton, a mery Poet, wrote:

> Gentle Paule, laie doune thy sweard
> For Peter of Westminster hath shauen thy beard.'

Polydore Vergil, on the other hand, says Warham agreed to Wolsey's plan, foreseeing its failure.

[2] As far back as 1314 the bishops had objected to meeting in Westminster abbey on this ground (Dr. Armitage Robinson, *loc. cit.* p. 114).

[3] Wilkins, iii. 700; *L.P.* iii. 3013.

[4] *Hereford Reg.* ii. 142; Burnet, ed. Pocock, i. 52.

[5] Burnet, *Reformation*, ed. Pocock, i. 52-3; iii. 87-8.

that the grant of taxation, recorded in Tunstal's register, is made solely by and in the name of the convocation of Canterbury, 'assembled at St. Paul's on 20 April and continued until 14 August.'[1]

Objection had at once been taken by the clergy to Wolsey's proposal to tax them in his legatine convocation,[2] and it was well grounded : in 1484 the judges of both benches and the barons of the exchequer, assembled in the exchequer chamber, had declared that no grant had ever been or could ever be made by the whole clergy of England, but only by the two provinces.[3] It is clear that all the resistance to Wolsey came from the province of Canterbury : Fisher of Rochester and Foxe of Winchester opposed his demands, but the lead, says Polydore Vergil, was taken by Dr. Rowland Philips, prolocutor presumably of the southern and not of the joint convocation.[4] Probably this resistance was offered between 22 April, when Wolsey's joint session began, and 2 May when he summoned a fresh assembly—the six or seven days mentioned by Surrey's correspondent ; and it may have been inspired as much by Wolsey's unprecedented demands for taxation

---

[1] Burnet, *Reformation*, ed. Pocock, iv. 11-12 ; Wilkins, iii. 699 ; *L.P.* iii. 3239. No reference to this correction of his views is made in Brewer and Gairdner, and it appears to have been generally ignored. 'Continued' does not mean continuous session, but simply that convocation was 'held together,' i.e. not dissolved (see above, p. 34 *n.*).

[2] This is clearly stated by Polydore Vergil (*Historia*, ed. 1555, p. 676) who, as archdeacon of Wells, was almost certainly present on the occasion and can, says Brewer (*L.P.* iii. p. cclxx), be trusted 'for the facts '— though Brewer calls him dean of Wells. A letter from him to Erasmus is dated London, 3 June 1523 (*Erasmi Epistolae*, ed. Allen, v. 289-90).

[3] Tottel's *Year Books*, Michaelmas, 2 Ric. III, f. 4*b*.

[4] For Philips see *D.N.B.* xlv. 182, and also *Hereford Reg.* ii. 211-16 ; *List of Proc. Court of Requests*, p. 94 ; Leadam, *Court of Requests*, pp. civ, cxv. ; *L.P.* iii. 1188, 1204, pp. 1535, 1539, 1544 ; iv. *passim*. He was vicar of Croydon and Brewer calls him ' the most eloquent preacher of his age ' (cf. Tyndale's reference in *The Practice of Prelates*, p. 302, to 'a friar Forest or a vicar of Croydon ') ; but Polydore says 'permagnam suae fecit innocentiae jacturam ' by submitting to Wolsey's dictation and abstaining from further proceedings in convocation. Philips and Polydore Vergil were colleagues in the Hereford chapter ; hence perhaps the information contained in the Hereford register and in Polydore Vergil's history.

s by his equally unprecedented treatment of convoca-
ion. Taxation may have been discussed in the later
oint session, if it was held ; but Wolsey made no
nention of finance in his second summons which merely
eferred to the reformation of the clergy, a matter which,
ae explained, could be more effectively dealt with by
he two convocations in joint session. In any case, the
actual grant [1] was couched in the customary provincial
erms ; and implicitly if not explicitly its description of the
convocation at St. Paul's as having been continued until
4 August denied that it had been dissolved by Wolsey's
ummons to meet at Westminster on 22 April. This
continuation of the convocation of Canterbury until the day
after parliament was dissolved (13 August) was normal procedure. Taken with the absence of any record of proceedings in Wolsey's re-summoned joint convocation, it
einforces Burnet's doubt, whether that legatine council
ever met to reform the clergy : taxation was nearer to
Wolsey's heart than the *honestiores vivendi mores* he alleged
as the object of his united convocation ; and he may well
have thought that the atmosphere engendered by the
quarrel over taxation and provincial autonomy was un-
avourable to the prospects of harmonious self-reformation. [2]

He made no further attempts to reform the church with
its own consent, and relied henceforth on papal bulls authorising him to degrade unwilling clerks and dissolve rebellious
monasteries, protesting vehemently and successfully when
he papal chancery introduced into these bulls such common
safeguards as *de consensu quorum interest* and *de consensu
fundatorum*. [3] The church in England was thus reduced
rom government by conciliar consent to government by
legatine autocracy. Sir Thomas More provides Wolsey
with some excuse : if the clergy, he writes, 'did assemble
often, and there did such things for which such assemblies

---

[1] See above, p. 181.
[2] Polydore Vergil makes no mention of this second assembly, remarking
imply that Wolsey ' remisit patres ad aedem Pauli, ipse vero ad suum
onsessum resedit,' and implying by his narrative that Wolsey intimidated
he prolocutor of Warham's convocation.
[3] *L.P.* iv. 2418, 2630, 3562, 5226 ; cf. Gasquet, *Monasteries*, i. 106.

of the clergy in every province through all Christendom from the beginning were instituted and devised, much more good might have grown thereof than the long disuse can suffer us now to perceive. But all my days, as far as I have heard, nor (I suppose) a good part of my father's neither, they came never together to convocation but at the request of the king, and at such their assembles, concerning spiritual things, have very little done. Wherefore that they have been in that necessary part of their duty negligent, whether God suffer to grow to an unperceived cause of division and grudge against them, God, whom their such negligence hath, I fear me, sore offended, knoweth.'[1] But their negligence was not improved by Wolsey's : the inability of convocation to reform itself when Wolsey had, pleading the urgency of reform, gathered all the powers of reformation into his hands, was due to the legate and not to convocation ; and the inference naturally drawn by Henry VIII. from the double failure of legate and convocation was that reform could only come from the crown in parliament.

But if the bishops were negligent of their legislative opportunities in convocation, they were certainly not indifferent to their episcopal jurisdictions ; and Wolsey's invasion of their courts gave them far greater offence than his supersession of their councils. His view was that his legateship made him a resident pope in England with power to perform, in person or by deputy, whatever functions he chose to take out of the hands of his subordinate or insubordinate episcopate :[2] he had no doubts over the vexed

[1] More, *Apologye*, 2nd ed. 1533, fol. 241, *apud* Burnet, ed. Pocock, iii 43. Cf. the complaint, in *L.P.* v. 49, that ' provincial synods are not held.' Dr. Armitage Robinson has shown (*loc. cit.*) how unsubstantial was the representative character of diocesan synods in the middle ages but the representative character of parliaments has been exaggerated also

[2] Wolsey, writes one of his clients, ' can revoke all the bishop's proceedings by his legatine authority, if he pleases ' (*L.P.* iii. 2838). On 12 July 1521 Ghinucci writes to Wolsey that Warham's vicar in the diocese of Worcester has acted very rigorously and excommunicated the monks of the cathedral who resisted his visitation, thus touching the honour of Wolsey, who has the care of that bishopric, and of de Medici who has been appointed to it. Wolsey must therefore take means that the vicar be removed (*ibid.* iii. 1411).

question how far a legate could delegate to others authority
committed to himself; and if he permitted English bishops
to continue the exercise of their jurisdictions, it was an act
of grace on his part, often qualified by financial exaction.

He extended this claim to the jurisdiction of archbishop
Warham, who complained as early as 26 February 1519
that Wolsey's officers were by their inhibitions disturbing
the jurisdiction which appertained to him, especially in his
court of audience, in virtue of his position as *legatus natus*.
There was no novelty in the supersession of that jurisdiction by a legate *a latere*,[1] but Wolsey was *a latere* only by
fiction, and he had several times promised, as Warham
reminded him, that he would take away no part of the
jurisdiction of Canterbury : if Wolsey, as a permanent legate
a latere persisted in this disturbance, Warham's jurisdiction
would, he wrote, be 'extincted,' and this, he contended, was
'contrary to the law.'[2]   Three weeks later he complained
again that[3] 'not only al mine officers of my courts of the
Arches and the Audience, but also the commissaries of my
diocese in Kent and I myself, not only in matters of suite
of instance of partys, but also in cases of correction depending before me and them, be continually inhibityd by your
officers.' He would, he continued, if Wolsey persisted,
'have nothing left for me and my officers to do ; but
should be as a shadow and image of an archbishop and
legate, voyd of authority and jurisdiction, which would be
to me a perpetual reproach and to my church a perpetual
prejudice.'   Wolsey did persist, even appointing as his
general commissary the notorious Dr. Allen[4] against whom

---

[1] See above, pp. 170, *n.* 2, 179.

[2] *L.P.* iii. 98. Art. 28 of Wolsey's impeachment says he had promised
that ' by his legacie no man should be hurted nor offended ' ; cf. Skelton,
ii. 61, who refers to Warham's register as his authority.

[3] Fiddes, *Collections*, pp. 178-9 ; Ellis, *Original Letters*, 3rd ser. ii.
41 ; *L.P.* iii. 127. Ellis dates the letter 17 and Fiddes 18 March ; the
year is assigned in *L.P.* which notes also an argument in B.M. Cotton MS.
Cleopatra F. i. 262 ' to show the limits of the rights of the archbishop
of Canterbury, as *legatus natus*, touching testamentary jurisdiction, citing
a number of authorities.'

[4] Polydore Vergil (*Historia*, p. 656) asserts that Allen had recently
been convicted of perjury before Wolsey himself as chancellor of England :

Warham had specifically protested ; and six years later, on 24 February 1525, he repeated his fear lest 'finally the jurisdiction of the prerogative should be extinctyd ; and also al testamentary causes shal only depend upon your Graces pleasure, and no mannys will to take any effect but as it shall please your Grace. . . . I would your Grace knew what rumor and obloquy is both in these partys and also in London that no testamentes can take effect otherwise then your Grace is content.'[1]

Wolsey's greed in the matter of testamentary jurisdiction was one of the details which did most to provoke the subsequent reformation. For not only did such exactions as that of a thousand marks for proving Sir William Compton's will exasperate the laity, but his claims alienated bishops and clergy, because in this respect Wolsey was more papal than the pope. For, oddly enough, the exclusive jurisdiction of the ecclesiastical courts in matters of probate was a peculiar English custom confirmed by the legislation of Edward I, but grounded neither on the *jus commune* of

the charge was made earlier, in 1528, by W. Roy (*Rede me̦*, p. 57) and Simon Fish (' Supplicacyon for Beggars ' in Foxe, iv. 663) and has documentary confirmation : in 1517 Allen and Dr. Christopher Plummer were fined 500 marks ' under *præmunire* ' (P.R.O. Lists and Indexes, *Star Chamber Proc.* xiii. 8 ; *L.P.* ii. 3741 ; Fish says £500), and Wolsey applied the money to his extension of the star chamber buildings. Plummer was chaplain to Catherine of Aragon (*ibid.* i. 82 (p. 41), 3499 (10) ; ii. 4702). One of Palsgrave's charges against Wolsey in 1529 is that he had ' begun a new building at Westminster with the forfeitures against the statute of præmunire ' (*ibid.* iv. p. 2557). Hudson, in his treatise on the star chamber (*c.* 1620) mentions Allen's and Plummer's fines and the use to which they were put (*Engl. Hist. Rev.* Oct. 1922, p. 517 *n.* 4). Allen's intrusion by Wolsey into a living, the advowson of which belongs to a religious house, was one of the counts on which Wolsey himself was condemned for præmunire in the king's bench (see below, p. 252 *n.* 1). He had, however, been a protégé of Warham before he entered Wolsey's service (see *D.N.B.* and *E.H.R.* Jan. 1928, p. 159).

[1] Fiddes, *Coll.* pp. 177-8 ; *L.P.* iv. 1118.

[2] 1000 marks = £666 13s. 4d. Brewer (*L.P.* iii. preface, p. cclxxii) multiplies by ten to give the modern equivalent ; but he was writing in 1867 and multiplication by fifteen would be nearer the mark to-day. Compton had made Warham supervisor of his will, but the copy in the P.R.O., which runs to 26 pp., has a title-page written in Wolsey's hand (*L.P.* iv. 4442 ; Nicolas, *Testamenta Vet.* pp. 591-4).

the church nor on positive legislation by the pope.[1] Polydore Vergil, an Italian who had visited many countries, comments on the English singularity and applauds Henry VIII's statute of 1529 limiting probate fees[2]; and it was an extraordinary usurpation on Wolsey's part to pretend legatine authority over jurisdiction vested in English bishops by English statute and by canon law, and not claimed by the papacy there or anywhere else. Warham trusted, he wrote to Wolsey on 6 March 1525, 'that none of your Graces counsail whiche is groundly learned hath or wol persuade unto your Grace that by vertue of your legacy . . . ye may procede severally in knowledge of testamentarie causes whiche heretofor have only apperteyned to the jurisdiction of my prerogative; and . . . if any lerned wol affirme and prove the same, suerly he hath seen other lawes or other understanding of lawes than I could ever know or perceyve, and yet I have taken some payne to loke for such matiers.'[3]

Warham's case was somewhat prejudiced by the facts that, in other than in testamentary jurisdiction, he laid no less stress on his position as *legatus natus* than Wolsey did on his as legate *a latere*; that he had before Wolsey's rise to supremacy been engaged in long and bitter disputes with his suffragans on the question;[4] and that he had in January 1523 made a compromise with Wolsey which many, he says, regarded as 'a great oversight in me' and he now regretted himself.[5] For Wolsey had not kept his part of the compact. Its terms[6] were that, in order to save executors the needless expense of having to attend the courts of both Wolsey and Warham—due to Wolsey's establishment of legatine courts—(i) the legate and the archbishop should have joint commissaries to act by the authority

---

[1] Cf. Stubbs, *Seventeen Lectures*, p. 348, it 'was an exception to the rule of the rest of Christendom'; and Maitland, *Roman Canon Law*, pp. 42, 59; Polydore Vergil, pp. 656-7, 'sicuti moris est apud Anglos. . . . Consuetudine hac non facile aliae, quod sciam, nationes utuntur.'

[2] 21 Henry VIII, c. 5.   [3] Ellis, III, ii. 45.

[4] See *L.P.* i. new ed. 1780, *et passim;* Wilkins, *Concilia*, iii. 654-6; Burnet, ed. Pocock, iii. 85-6.

[5] Fiddes, *Collections*, p. 178.   [6] *L.P.* iii. 2752.

of both in the province of Canterbury, (ii) Wolsey alone should have commissaries in the province of York, and (iii) where the testator had goods both within and without liberties like Westminster, St. Albans, Bury St. Edmunds, and Beaulieu [1]—which were in the province of Canterbury but exempt from Warham's episcopal jurisdiction—Wolsey alone, as legate *a latere*, should have a commissary within, but there should be joint commissaries without, the franchise. There was no question of division in the province of York, and the composition aptly expressed the fact that what was Wolsey's was his own, but of what was Warham's half belonged to Wolsey. Even this compact, 'sealed with your Grace's seal and signed with your Grace's hand,' was not observed, and Warham was soon complaining that Wolsey was sending his commissaries to act independently of Warham in Warham's province. [2]

Warham, in spite of Wolsey's threats of præmunire, could afford to offer more resistance than mere bishops. West of Ely, an old friend and ally of Wolsey's, begged to be allowed to retain his jurisdiction in his own hands, but offered Wolsey 'the whole or part of the money arising therefrom.' [3] Booth of Hereford was let off with a composition by which he had to pay Wolsey only a third of the profits arising from ecclesiastical jurisdiction in his diocese. [4] Nix of Norwich compounded with Wolsey's agents, Allen and Toneys, on terms which do not appear, but on 23 May 1529 he complained to Wolsey of the wrongs done him by the legate's officers. He had paid the sum due at Michaelmas and was asked for it again; Wolsey had appointed a commissary to exercise jurisdiction in the arch-

---

[1] The MS. has 'Bewley,' the correct phonetic spelling of Beaulieu. Brewer suggests Beverley, but Beverley was wholly in Wolsey's province, and there is much correspondence in *L.P.* vol. iv. about Wolsey's jurisdiction over the town as well. The extent to which exemption might go is illustrated in Warham's letter to Wolsey (Ellis, 3rd ser. ii. 29-31) : in the eleven deaneries nearest to Canterbury, he says that ' al the chiefe benefices be appropried to religiouse houses,' and ' be hooly exepte from my examination at this tyme, and the examination of them al is reserved to youre Grace.'

[2] Fiddes, *op. cit.*, p. 178.　　　　[3] *L.P.* iii. 599 ; iv. 1258

[4] *Hereford Reg.* ii. 189.

deaconry of Norfolk which the bishop had paid Wolsey for
permission to retain ; and he had extorted from one of his
clergy £57 13s. 4d. belonging to the bishop, threatening
the unfortunate clerk with imprisonment in the Fleet and
the loss of his office unless he surrendered the money.[1]

Archdeacons as well as bishops and archbishops had to
pay tribute to Wolsey for leave to exercise their jurisdictions.[2]
'There is never a poor archdeacon in England,' runs
the 18th article of the lords' impeachment, 'but that he
paid yearly to him a portion of his living' ; and there is
little if any exaggeration in Hall's summing up of the
matter : 'the Cardinall of Yorke, being Legate, proued
testamentes and did call before hym all the executors and
administrators of euery dioces within the realme, so that
the bishops and ordinaries did proue no great willes in
their dioces except he wer compounded with, not to their
little disauantage.'[3]   The means by which they were constrained to compound are illustrated by Warham's correspondence : even during the negotiations for his own

---

[1] *L.P.* iv. 5589 ; for countercharges against Nix, see *ibid.* iv. 5492,
5511.

[2] Warham to Wolsey, 12 Jan. 1523, Ellis, III, ii. 39-40.

[3] *Chron.* p. 655.   In Warham's composition the figure at which a
'wille' became 'greate' was fixed at £100 (*L.P.* iii. 2752) ; and, if Hall
is correct, an obscurely worded clause in Warham's composition must
mean that even he surrendered to Wolsey probate of all wills over that
sum in the province of Canterbury.   Polydore Vergil (pp. 656-7) as a
churchman is more eloquent than Hall, and writes of Wolsey's 'vulgus
apparitorum per pagos et vicos vagantium qui odorarentur morientium
funera, testamentorumque executores citarent ut ad curiam legati testamenta probanda mature curarent . . . non sine maximo haeredum detri-
mento.'   Wolsey's scent for probate had early been illustrated in the case
of his predecessor Bainbridge (see above, pp. 21-2) ; and lord Darcy charges
him with acquiring in this way much of the goods of Bainbridge's predecessor, archbishop Savage ; of Wolsey's own predecessors in the bishoprics
of Lincoln (Smith), Durham (Ruthal), and Winchester (Foxe) ; and of
his archdeacon of Richmond (Dalby), of his agent, Robert Toneys, 'and
many others' (*L.P.* iv. p. 2548).   The inventory of Wolsey's household
stuff taken after his attainder (*ibid.* iv. pp. 2763-9) contains a considerable amount of goods 'bought of the executors' of Ruthal, Fitzjames,
Toneys, and Hannibal.   Darcy's charges formed the basis of art. 30 in
Wolsey's impeachment (see below, 259 *n.* 2).

composition he complained that 'Wolsey's officers dealt hardly with executors and administrators, which he hoped Wolsey would not have allowed while the matter was in suspense'; and he only made his agreement to avoid the threats of those who 'would have put me and my officers, and other men also, in jeopardy of a *præmunire*.' [1] He concludes with a significant caution on that point : *oportet considerare praesentia, et caute praevidere futura.* Warham had more prevision than Wolsey ; [2] both in the end were threatened with præmunire, but Warham did not, like Wolsey, invoke that penalty, invite retaliation, and then inveigh against it.

Hardly less irritating to the bishops and clergy, though not so offensive to the laity, was the use Wolsey made of his legatine powers to visit the dioceses of both provinces and usurp ecclesiastical patronage. Each visitation involved a levy of 4 per cent on the value of every benefice and religious house concerned, though Foxe in remonstrating with Wolsey claimed that in the whole of his twenty-six years at Winchester he had never demanded it from religious houses. [3] In the vacation between Easter and Trinity terms 1524 Allen visited seventeen London churches and religious houses, and returned the sum of £189 8s. 5d. as due to Wolsey ; and his visitations elsewhere during a somewhat longer period produced £439 12 2¾. [4] From the London visitation St. Mary Overies and St. Thomas' hospital had

---

[1] *L.P.* iii. 2633, 2647. The conflict of jurisdictions extended to Wolsey's commissaries in the two provinces. His commissaries in Warham's province sat in London, those in Wolsey's own at York. His ' subjects,' complained the dean of York, ' are commonly called to appear in London, before his officers . . . sometimes at the promotion of light persons, without reasonable cause '; ' the people murmur at it so much that he is weary of hearing them '; and he asked Wolsey to order his commissaries at York to cease, and allow the others in London to serve for both the provinces, as his subjects did not know which to obey (*ibid.* iv. 2835-6).

[2] 'Cantuariensis,' says Polydore Vergil, ' sapientissimus ad conjecturam futurarum rerum ' (*Historia*, p. 676).

[3] *L.P.* iv. 3815.

[4] *Ibid.* iv. 964. The 25th article of impeachment against Wolsey was that he ' took from religious houses one twenty-fifth of their livelihood at visitations ' (*ibid.* iv. 6075); see below, p. 259.

been respited on account of 'the prevention[1] of the bishop of Winchester'; but Wolsey took peculiar pleasure in visiting the dioceses of his former official superiors in Warham's province, and was not to be prevented by any prior claim. Foxe, for instance, had visited Winchester college in December 1526; in the following March Wolsey sent the offensive Allen to repeat the visitation.[2] This was followed by a general visitation of the diocese, apparently after Foxe's death on 5 October 1528. Normally the right of visitation *sede vacante* belonged to the archbishop of Canterbury; but Wolsey's claim as legate *a latere* to precedence in a joint exercise of the right resulted in an

---

[1] I.e. previous (Wolsey would not admit that it was prior) claim of Foxe. Similarly Laurence Stubbs, Wolsey's receiver-general (*L.P.* v. 386), writing on 6 Aug. 1527 (Ellis, 3rd ser. ii. 62; *L.P.* iv. 3334) to thank Wolsey for his 'restoration' to the presidency of Magdalen in place of 'Mr. Burges, the latly pretendid to be elect' (whom Stubbs accuses of detaining £75 'of the college mony to defend hymself'), says 'my lord of Wynchester myndid to have preventid your visitacion ther.' Foxe was the proper visitor of Magdalen as successor to its founder, Waynflete bishop of Winchester. Stubbs was one of Wolsey's chief financial agents; his letter contains an interesting account of an outbreak of sanctuary-men in Westminster with the idea of attacking York Place and killing Cromwell.

[2] *Wolsey's Winchester Reg.* (Cant. and York Soc. 1926), p. xxvi. A year later would agree better with the dating (*L.P.* iv. 3583, 3623, 3815) of Foxe's complaints to Wolsey on the subject. In the first of these, dated 17 Nov. and assigned to 1527, Foxe asks Wolsey to liberate his chancellor, detained in London by Wolsey 'in consequence of sinister information, and because he has laid claim to a parish church and prebend that Mr. Dowman had.' 'He wants,' continues Foxe, 'his chancellor daily, and especially for the keeping of his consistories . . . and for a visitation in the new college of St. Mary beside Winchester.' Dr. John Dowman had been one of Wolsey's commissaries and archdeacon of Suffolk; on his death in 1526 Wolsey had secured the archdeaconry at least for his illegitimate son, Thomas Wynter; Le Neve, ii. 488-9, says Wynter was appointed on 2 Nov. on Dowman's resignation, but his will, dated 8 Nov., was proved on 6 Dec. (*L.P.* iv. 2694). In his second letter, dated 1 Dec., Foxe complains that Wolsey has not complied with the request. In the third, dated 18 Jan., he thanks Wolsey for being gracious to his chancellor, and replies to the misdemeanours of which he himself and his chancellor were accused. His answer to the charge of undue severity certainly seems conclusive; he had not, he claims, been severe on the secular clerks, except for fornication and adultery, and had never deprived anyone in any of his dioceses.

effective, if not exclusive, predominance for himself; and disputes with any future bishop of Winchester were eliminated by Wolsey's own appointment to the see. To that, as to all his other bishoprics, he was papally provided and not elected by the chapter.

Any kind of election, in the modern sense of the word,[1] was in fact abhorrent to him; and he did much to extirpate the remnants of capitular and conventual election in the church. The former had long gone by the board, and Wolsey merely confirmed the practice of royal nomination and papal provision. But monasteries still enjoyed a considerable amount of choice with regard to their heads; and in many cases there were still open to them, as to papal conclaves, the three recognised methods of ecclesiastical election *per viam acclamationis* (or *spiritus sancti*), *scrutinii*, and *compromissi*, by acclamation, ballot, or committee.[2] The unanimity implied in acclamation or inspiration was not unknown, nor was the equally proper ballot; but the practice of committing the choice to a few opened the path to abdication. The surrender of electoral rights to a domestic oligarchy was followed by its surrender to outsiders, and Wolsey through his legatine commissaries dictated the choice of all the four religious houses which fell vacant in the diocese of Winchester during his brief tenure of that see.[3] That this usurpation was personal and peculiar is shown by a comparison with his predecessor's practice: of the nineteen vacancies which occurred under Foxe, fourteen were filled by acclamation and only three were compromitted. No other register of Wolsey's episcopate than that of Winchester has yet been printed, and it is possible that his record in that diocese represents the climax of his despotic tendencies. But it is clear from the scattered notices available that he used his legatine powers to manipulate conventual elections in his other dioceses and in other

---

[1] I.e. that election implies voting by a number of persons. Primarily, it means 'picking out' which may be done by a single person: hence the difference between 'the elect' of divinity and 'the elected' of democracy.

[2] *L.P.* iv. App. 230; *Wolsey's Winchester Reg.* p. xiv.

[3] *Ibid.* pp. xi-xv.

dioceses than his.   By his direct orders or by the intrigues
of his agents elections were determined at Athelney,[1]
St. Augustine's (Bristol),[2] Butley, Glastonbury, Milton
(Dorset),[3] Newnham,[4] Selby, Wilton, Worksop,[5] and Peterborough.[6]   At St. Augustine's his commissaries wrote 'we
scarcely dared to enter the chapter for fear of the assemblaye,
retainers of noblemen and others.'   At Butley,[7] which was
in the diocese of Norwich, bishop Nix wrote that the
convent was on the point of electing a new prior 'and had
said their service when they received Wolsey's letters of
inhibition and sequestration.'   They thereupon compromitted it to Wolsey, although, said Nix, their cellarer
'would have been chosen unanimously *per viam spiritus
sancti.*'   The abbot of Glastonbury[8] was 'elected by
Wolsey in the chapel of York Place,' the election having
been, it is said, unanimously compromitted to him by the
whole forty-seven monks : why, in that happy state of
unanimity, they could not have elected an abbot themselves
is not explained.   At Selby, the dean of York, in remitting
the choice to Wolsey, deprecated the appointment of a
stranger.[9]

The vacancies themselves were often created by Wolsey's
action.   At St. Benet's Holme the duke of Suffolk protested
against Wolsey's deprivation of the abbot : all the ' wor-
shipfull of the cuntre' would, he wrote, depose to the
abbot's innocence of the charges brought against him, and
he had cleared off a large part of the debts of the house.[10]
The abbot of Chester, who had been sequestered by Wolsey,
was restored by Henry VIII, who also desired that the prior
of Reading who had been imprisoned should be liberated.[11]
The abbot of Hyde, urged by Wolsey to resign, refused and
hoped that Wolsey would not 'experiment any sharper
means' to remove him.[12]   The prior of Lewes was more

[1] *L.P.* iv. 3027.
[2] *Ibid.* iv. 1544, 1828.
[3] Spelt Myddylton in *L.P.* iv. 1291.
[4] *Ibid.* iv. 1228.
[5] *Ibid.* iv. 5964.
[6] *Ibid.* iv. 4047, 4056, 4081.
[7] *Ibid.* iv. App. 230.
[8] *Ibid.* iv. App. 22.
[9] *Ibid.* iv. App. 73.
[10] Ellis, *Original Letters*, 3rd ser. i. 200 ; *L.P.* iv. 3772.
[11] *Ibid.* vii. 854 ; below, p. 350.
[12] *Ibid.* iv. 2394.

amenable,[1] but the abbot of Peterborough resisted himself and caused the prior of Spalding to resist, 'not,' wrote bishop Longland to Wolsey, 'like a wise or kind man, but to keep you from your honourable pleasure and purpose.' Wolsey's pleasure was a contribution of at least £400 to his college at Oxford, which the abbot was said to have promised; but when it came to the point, he suggested 400 marks and would not rise above 500. Ten months later Longland, finding the abbot was determined to keep his office and his money, came to the conclusion that he was 'very impotent' and ought to be removed; and the election of a successor was compromitted to Wolsey.[2] Liberal subscriptions to Wolsey's colleges were in fact often aids to achieve promotion as well as means to prevent deprivation. Announcing to Wolsey the probable death of the prior of St. Bartholomew's in Smithfield, the president of Magdalen writes:[3] 'the frends of the cellerer of the same house, callid William Fynch, hath ben with me and offered to gi your Grace ccc^{li} towards the beldinge of your honorable college in Oxford, or to such other use as it may like your Grace to apply it, for your gracious favor towards hym and hys preferment to the priory when it shelbe voide, allegynge that the convent ther will be glad to elect hym afore any other if thei may have there fre eleccion.' Similarly on 18 July 1528 the bishop of Lincoln writes to Wolsey offering him £200 for his college if he will be a good lord to him and his nephew, Richard Pate, and allow the latter to keep a prebend with his other preferments.[4]

The most notorious of Wolsey's acts as trustee of conventual suffrages was to select as abbess of Wilton a nun who was the reputed mother of two children by two

[1] L.P. iv. 3277.

[2] Ibid. iv. 2378, 2391, 3175. After a year's pressure, Longland writes that he cannot get the prior of Spalding to resign: 'He says he will die prior. He is himself very good and gentle, but is led by others' (ibid. iv. 4081, 4796; no. 4081, in spite of being endorsed '1527,' belongs to 1529 and is misplaced in L. and P. Compare it with no. 5210 which is certainly 1529).

[3] Ellis, 3rd ser. ii. 64-5; L.P. iv. 3334; cf. Wolsey's Winchester Reg. p. xiv.

[4] L.P. iv. 4514, 4527; Pate was afterwards bishop of Worcester.

different priests and mistress of a third.[1]   The notoriety
arises not from her ill-fame but from the fact that Wolsey
made the election in spite of the protests of Henry VIII,
and thus drew down upon him a royal rebuke and warning
which Wolsey would have been wise to heed : [2] 'Ah, my
Lord, it is a double offence both to doe ill and colour it too.
. . . Wherefore, good my Lord, use noe more that way with
me, for there is no man livinge that more hateth it. . . . And
bicause I dare be bolder with you then a great many that
mumbell it abroad,' he went on to deal with Wolsey's
methods of getting money for his college.   'Surely it is
reckoned that much of the good that buildeth the same
should not be the best acquisite and gotten, reckoninge it
to come from many a religious house unlawfully, bearinge
the cloake of kindnes towarde the edifyinge of your col-
ledge.'   'They say,' he reiterated a few days later,[3] 'not

---

[1] *L.P.* iv. 4477 : the nuns had compromitted the election to Wolsey
on 17 June 1528 (*ibid.* iv. 2549).

[2] See the full text in Fiddes, *Collections*, pp. 174-6, summarised in
L.P. iv. 2507. Wolsey made the matter worse by pretending ignorance
of Henry's wishes, whereupon the king quoted word by word the letter
in which they had been conveyed.

[3] Text in Herbert, *Henry VIII*, ed. 1672, p. 164, summarised in *L.P.*
iv. 2509. Lord Herbert describes this letter as 'written all with his own
hand, as we find it in our records.' Neither it, nor the preceding letter,
printed by Fiddes, appears now to be extant. The king assumed that
Wolsey's agents were responsible : 'I trust verely that if anythinge be
amisse, it is more longe of them then of you. Notwithstanding I am
sure you know that *in talibus ignorantia non excusat peccatum*' (cf. Saint-
German, ii. cap. xlvi., 'where ignorance of the law excuseth in the laws
of England, and where not'). Nearly a year before, Dr. Knight, then
secretary, had written to Wolsey : 'I have herd the Kyng and noble
men speke thinges incredible of th'actes of M. Alain and Cromewell'
(Ellis, 3rd ser., ii. 101 ; *State Papers*, i. 261 ; in *L.P.* iv. 3360, the
meaning is altered, without shortening the sentence, into 'incredible
things are spoken respecting the conduct of Alayn [Allen] and Cromwell,
as I have heard from the king and others.' Still earlier, in Feb. 1525,
Sir Thomas More had communicated to Wolsey on Henry's behalf complaints that had reached the king's ears (Ellis, 2nd ser., ii. 18-20 ; *L.P.*
iv. 5533). Hall (p. 694) attributes Wolsey's dissolutions to a desire to
enrich his college at the expense of others : 'wherefore sodainly he
entered by his commissioners into the saied houses and put out the Religious and tooke all their goodes, moueables, and scarcely gave to the poore
wretches any thyng except it wer to the heddes of the house.'

that all that is ill gotten is bestowed upon the college, but that the college is the cloak for covering all mischiefs. . . . One thing more I perceive by your own letter, which a little methinketh toucheth conscience ; and that is that you have received money of the exempts for having their old visitors. Surely this can hardly be with good conscience. For, and they were good, why should you take money? and if they were ill, it were a sinful act. Howbeit your legacy herein might peradventure *apud homines* be a cloak, but not *apud Deum*.' Wolsey made a humble submission, and Henry assured him that 'there remaineth at this hour no spark of displeasure towards you in my heart. And thus fare you well and be no more perplext. Written with the hand of your loving sovereign and friend.' Wolsey's enemies were less forgiving ; and among forty-four articles of impeachment brought against him in parliament by the lords was a twenty-fourth which affirmed that 'the same lord cardinal, at many times when any houses of religion have been void, hath sent his officers thither and with crafty perswasions hath induced them to compromit their election in him ; and that before ere [*sic*] he named or confirmed any of them, he and his servants received so much great goods of them that in manner it hath been to the undoing of the house.'[1]

While Wolsey was thus reducing conventual elections to a mere matter of legatine nomination, he was no less active in absorbing the patronage over secular benefices whether the advowson belonged to a bishop or to a religious house. The fact that all English bishops were degraded to the position of Wolsey's commissaries[2] did not protect them from molestation at the hands of the legate's other and inferior agents. He revived by his legatine authority the practice of papal provision to English benefices which popes themselves had tacitly long aban-

[1] Herbert, *Henry VIII*, p. 298 ; *L.P.* iv. 2713.
[2] For references to the bishops of St. Asaph, Bath and Wells, Ely, Hereford, Lincoln, London, and Salisbury acting as Wolsey's commissaries, see *L.P.* iii. 1690, 1863 ; Fiddes, *Collections*, p. 176.

doned ;[1] and his crowd of apparitors in the provinces kept
as watchful an eye on benefices about to come vacant as on
wills which would need to be proved : both brought grist
to the legate's absorbing mill.   He had, writes Cavendish,
glorying in his master's greatness, 'also in every diocese
through this realm all manner of spirituall ministers, as
commissaries, scribes, apparitors, and all other necessary
officers to furnish his courtes ; and presented by prevention whom he pleased unto all benefices throughout all this
realme and dominions thereof.'[2]   Tunstal's register records
under the date of 10 December 1526 that Wolsey had
presented to eight benefices within that diocese without
asking the bishop's consent ; and a marginal note added
later mentions that the giving and accepting such institutions by the legate's authority involved the clergy in
præmunire from which they were subsequently obliged to
redeem themselves.[3]   On 26 March 1524 Warham complains that a chaplain of Wolsey's had been intruded into
All Hallows, Lombard Street, which belonged to the monks
of Canterbury, thus depriving them of their advowson and
Warham of his jurisdiction in giving institution and in-
duction ;[4] and a similar complaint about St. Keverns,
Cornwall, comes from the bishop of Bangor and relates to

---

[1] 'Quamvis istud pontificis jus jamdiu in Anglia obsolevisset'
(Polydore Vergil, pp. 657-8) ; Vergil is here referring to parochial and
not to episcopal benefices.   Henry VIII kept a tight hand on the royal
right of conferring the baronies which constituted the endowment of
episcopal sees.   Vergil mentions advowsons *quae episcoporum vel nobilium
propria essent*, but it does not appear that Wolsey often ventured to intrude
upon the latter (see below, p. 251).

[2] P. 27.   'Provisions' are frequently called 'preventions' in the early
sixteenth century, and the latter word is the more expressive : the legate
anticipated and thus prevented presentation by the legal owner of the
advowson. Cf. lord Darcy in *L.P.* iv. p. 2551, 'how many times he
hath therein offended in giving of promotions by prevention,' and the
seventh article of impeachment against Wolsey (Herbert, p. 295 ; *L.P.*
iv. p. 2712). The claim to have jurisdiction 'over all the said king's
dominions' was made by Wolsey himself (*L.P.* iv. 4444).

[3] Tunstal's *Reg.* fol. 31, cited by Burnet, ed. Pocock, iii. 88-9.

[4] *L.P.* iv. 193 ; cf. the abbot of Ramsey's suit against Wolsey, *ibid.* iv.
6486

a benefice appertaining to Beaulieu of which that bishop was abbot.[1]

But the liveliest account of these legatine proceedings occurs in a letter, written to Cromwell on 11 May 1529, from Ruthyn by one Edward Johns or Jones, rector of North Crawley in Buckinghamshire, which illustrates the length of Wolsey's legatine arm and the elasticity of clerical residence.[2] For the Buckinghamshire rector was Wolsey's commissary in Wales and came into conflict with the bishop of Bangor whom we have just seen writing from Beaulieu in Hampshire about a benefice in Cornwall.[3] The rector remarks that Wolsey gave him, on leaving London, 'a large commission concerning his preventions, and he has incurred great anger of the ordinaries. Two small benefices fell in the diocese of Bangor on 6 May. He prevented them both in my lord's name within two hours of the incumbent's death. Within three days after came a chaplain from Dr. Glyn, who would have entered in the bishop of Bangor's name, 'but he was put by, and some had broken elbows.' Before Christmas my lord gave, by prevention, a poor benefice not worth £5 ; on which the bishop gave Dr. Glyn a commission to dispose of all benefices in his diocese ; 'and the said doctor hath commissioners in every bush, but I have disappointed them now,

[1] Ellis, 3rd ser. ii. 61 ; *L.P.* iv. 5726.

[2] *Ibid.* iv. 5533. The rector had in 1526-7 leased his parsonage with all its tithes to one William Johnson ; a portion was subsequently claimed by the dean of Wolsey's college, and on Johnson's disputing the claim Wolsey committed him to the Fleet for twelve weeks. On this incident is grounded the 41st article in his impeachment (Herbert, pp. 300-1).

[3] This otherwise obscure prelate first appears in public documents as Thomas Patexe *alias* Thomas Skevington, abbot first of Waverley and then of St. Mary the Virgin, Beaulieu, Hants (*Cal. Pat. Rolls*, 1495-1509, p. 569). He succeeded John Penny (translated to Carlisle) as bishop of Bangor just before the death of Henry VII ; but almost his only appearances in the state papers of Henry VIII are on the commissions of the peace for Hampshire, Shropshire, and Warwickshire (*L.P.* i. new ed., pp. 1537, 1542, 1545). He died in June 1533 ; his heart was buried in Bangor cathedral, his body in Beaulieu abbey. He may have been brother of the more famous Sir William Skeffington, lord-deputy of Ireland (*d.* 1535).

and will do, with God's grace.' My lord must do something to check the haughtiness of these bishops. My lord of Bangor has not been in his diocese these fourteen years, but sets his bishopric to farm to Dr. Glyn.[1] He is indicted in divers places of his diocese for lack of visitation. He has been bishop these twenty-one years, and never commissioned any one to give away benefices till now to debar my lord of his preventions. Hopes my lord will be even with him, to his pain. 'He shall not sit at Bowley [sic] and compare with my Lord's Grace. *Poena unius debet esse metus multorum.*' Dr. Glyn, too, may be punished.' Johns then produces a list of charges against Glyn calculated to ensure that consummation; and continues: 'I am right glad if my lord's Grace may have a substantial matter against the bishop, for he is the richest monk of England.[2] Also, I have a great bede-roll of abbots and priors, and surely my lord's Grace shall do much good amongst them, and also his Grace shall have a large pot of wine.' Finally, Johns discusses his own prospective gains and how much he will have to contribute to Wolsey's college, remarks that he has to ride on to St. David's and Llandaff to execute Wolsey's commission, and asks for authority to put those who resisted Wolsey's preventions 'in irons till my lord send for them.'

There is abundance of colour and contrast in this miniature of the state of the church painted six months before Wolsey's fall by one of the less notorious of his agents. It may be that the colour is reflected rather from Cromwell, the correspondent to whom it was addressed, than from the papal legate whose commissary the writer was; and Johns' gloating over his 'great bede-roll of abbots and priors' suggests the hammer of the monks rather than the legatine reformer of the monasteries. But Wolsey was to have the 'large pot of wine'; and from Cromwell and Leigh, who is also recommended in this letter,[3] downwards the agents of the dissolution were nearly

---

[1] Dr. John Glynn, dean of Bangor from 1509 to 1534.

[2] Wolsey, although he held the abbey of St. Albans, was not, of course, a monk.

[3] To advise with Bonner on methods of proceeding against Glynn.

all trained to their work in Wolsey's school. There are two sides to the picture : the need for reformation is not more glaring than the disfigurements in the reformer. The absentee bishop of Bangor is to be castigated by the legate who set eyes on none of his own cathedrals ; a prelate who let out one bishopric to farm is to suffer at the hands of one who farmed half-a-dozen. The 'preventer' of benefices in his own diocese is himself to be forestalled by the wholesale provider in all ; and 'the haughtiness of these bishops' is to be curbed by 'the haughtiest man in all his proceedings alive.' The retiring abbot of Beaulieu must not 'compare' with the cardinal, legate, archbishop, and chancellor, nor 'the richest monk of England' with the secular priest who became a millionaire in the discharge of his official duties.

There is something to be said for Wolsey. What the abbot of Beaulieu did with his wealth we do not know, but Wolsey's 'spoliations and robberies,' as his friend du Bellay termed them, did not all go into his palaces at Hampton Court, the More, or Tittenhanger ; and there was probably more social justice in Wolsey's courts of equity than in those of the common law, and in his novel assessments for probate than in 'the laudable custom' of old, which commended itself to the conservative lord Darcy.[1] To modern eyes, however, the chief redeeming feature in Wolsey's supersession of episcopal jurisdiction by legatine power is the respite from the stake which it afforded heretics ; and it has been claimed,[2] apparently with justice, that not a single English man or woman perished in the flames so long as he controlled ecclesiastical jurisdiction. It does not follow that he was a better man than the bishops who had been condemning heretics to the stake before 1515 and resumed the practice after 1529 ; for toleration may arise merely from indifference, and Wolsey was essentially what the next generation of Frenchmen called a *politique*.[3] His concern was with

---

[1] *L.P.* iv. p. 2551 ; see below, p. 338.

[2] E. L. Taunton, *Wolsey, Legate and Reformer*, 1902, p. 129.

[3] See Tavannes, *Mémoires*, ed. Buchon, 1884, p. 269 : 'Le nom de politique a esté inventé pour ceux qui préférent le repos du royaume, ou

heretics as probable disturbers of secular peace and authority, and his severity was mitigated by their limited capacities in that direction. He had no mercy for a duke of Buckingham, but the humble scholars who read and annotated bibles were at worst imprisoned in the Fleet and at best preferred to the cardinal's college.

The facts, however, that Wolsey was succeeded as chancellor by Sir Thomas More and that the substitution of the finer for the grosser character was followed by a revival of the flames of religious persecution, have led to so much fallacious comparison that some account of the legal conditions, under which both of them dealt with heresy, is required. Confusion mainly arises from remembering that both were chancellors but forgetting that one was the highest ecclesiastic in the land, while the other was only a layman. That was the essential difference : Wolsey could have burnt as many heretics as he wished, and it is to his credit that he refrained ; but the law gave no jurisdiction in heresy to laymen, however exalted. More had to obtain leave from his bishop before he could even read heretical books in order to refute them ; and he was far too sound a catholic to trespass as a layman upon a sphere of jurisdiction strictly reserved for courts that were christian. The issue that had smouldered since 1515 was whether lay judges could even deal with crime committed by clerks ; and no lay court had yet ventured to adjudicate on matters of the faith. More, therefore, had and could have legally nothing to do with any sentence to death for heresy.

He was, however, as chancellor, the highest magistrate except the king, and a statute of Henry V[1] had required

de leur particulier, au salut de leur âme, et à la religion, qui ayment mieux que le royaume demeure en paix sans Dieu qu'en guerre pour luy.'

[1] 2 Henry V (Stat. 1) c. 7 ; *Statutes of the Realm*, ii. 181-4. It should be noted, however, that the chancellor is not mentioned lower down with the justices of the king's bench, of the peace, and of assize, who are commissioned to inquire about heretics, their books, and sermons. The same point arose over an Academy picture in 1928, representing the lord chancellor with a black cap ; and it was shown that, while the commissions at the central criminal court and at assizes are addressed to the lord chancellor, he is not among those appointed to execute them (Sir Herbert Stephen in *The Times*, 11 May 1928, p. 17).

the secular authorities from the chancellor downwards to take an oath on admission to office to assist the church by arresting and presenting heretics for trial and carrying out the judgements of the spiritual courts. But all responsibility for deciding whether the heretic, condemned after relapse by the church, should suffer the *poenas in jure expressas* and be burnt or not by the secular arm, had been denied to the state by the 'Sext' of Boniface VIII in 1298,[1] was disclaimed by Henry IV *par advis des seigneurs temporels en parlement*,[2] and was finally repudiated by the notorious statute *de hæretico comburendo*.[3] It required the sheriff, or other king's officer, to attend the ecclesiastical court on the bishop's summons when judgement was to be given, receive the condemned prisoner, and thereupon have him burnt *coram populo in eminenti loco*; and the subsequent statute of Henry V imposed on the sheriff a specific oath to discharge this duty.[4]

---

[1] Maitland, *Canon Law*, pp. 176-7; Lyndwood, *Provinciale*, p. 293.

[2] *Rot. Parl.* iii. 459 *a* [29].

[3] 2 Henry IV, c. 15; *Statutes of the Realm*, ii. 125-8; *Rot. Parl.* iii. 466-7. The clearest statement of the law is still Blackstone's (*Commentaries*, ed. 1773, iv. 46-9) which has not, I think, been impugned by any legal writer. His remark that by this statute 'lollardy was also made a temporal offence and indictable in the king's courts' must not be construed as meaning that heresy was 'triable' in the king's courts.

[4] 'That is the cause,' writes Fitzherbert (*New Natura Brevium*, ed. 1677, p. 595), '(as it seemeth) that that writ is not put in the new registers, because that writ ought not at this day to be sued forth, but is as it were void by reason of the said act.' Foxe himself describes the act as 'the cruel statute ex officio' (iii. 239-40), though, like Arundel's register, he first gives it in full under 1410 instead of 1401. The act was a petition of the bishops and clergy granted by Henry IV 'de consensu magnatum et aliorum procerum regni sui' without any reference in the rolls of parliament to the consent of the commons, though a prayer of the commons is introduced into the version inscribed on the statute roll. No action seems to have been taken upon it until 1410. In January of that year the commons presented a petition for its repeal, which the king rejected, and the act was then put in force against Badby. The advisability of a royal writ in this case was obvious. Makower (*Const. Hist.* p. 188) whittles down the meaning of the act in saying that 'the necessity of a royal order is not laid down'; for the whole point of Foxe's description of it as 'the cruel statute *ex officio*' is that, as Blackstone says, it made the burning of heretics an *ex officio* duty of sheriffs. The fuller title of the Roman inquisition was 'the holy office of the inquisition' and the duty imposed

Reference to the crown in council and the necessity for a writ out of chancery were thus eliminated. The statute did not, of course, prohibit the crown from supplementing the law by special orders to carry it out ; two or three such writs bear witness to Henry IV's and Henry V's zeal for theological orthodoxy, fear of Lollard intrigues, or anxiety for the support of the church ;[1] and on 20 October 1521 there issued a royal mandate from the new defender of the faith to mayors and others to assist bishops in executing justice on heretics.[2]

Sir Thomas More's persecuting activities were therefore legally restricted to issuing writs for the arrest of heretics as well as other offenders, which was obligatory under the Lollard statutes, and the doubtful and superfluous function of issuing writs *de heretico comburendo*. In the discharge of the former duty, reasserted in a proclamation of 6 March 1529, he may have arrested the martyr John Frith, and have inflicted the minor penalties he admits ; and before he became lord chancellor he and Tunstal, as ambassadors at Cambrai, commissioned Stephen Vaughan to search out English heretics

---

on oath by 2 Henry V, c. 7 gave the ' *ex officio* oath ' much of its sinister and unpopular significance in the sixteenth century. Makower also treats the requirement of a royal writ by 25 Henry VIII as a confirmation of his interpretation, but that act was a repeal of 2 Henry IV, c. 15, and was the beginning of the policy of insisting on lay concurrence and consent to the burning of heretics. ' Now,' continues Fitzherbert, ' by the statute made *anno* 25 H. 8, cap. 14 . . . the ordinary ought not for to commit him [the relapsed heretic] to the lay power to be burnt without the king's writ first obtained for to burn him.' On 29 Aug. 1536 lord chancellor Audley consulted Cromwell before granting what appears to have been the first application made to him for a writ *de haeretico comburendo ;* and a treatise of that time refers to the ' expired power of the ordinaries ' in that respect (*L.P.* xi. 85, 369). ✻

[1] Apart from Henry IV's writ for the burning of Sawtre (before the statute was passed), the only undoubted instance of such a writ seems to be that in Badby's case (Rymer, *Fœdera,* viii. 627 ; Foxe, *Acts and Monuments,* iii. 235-9 and, for a list of Foxe's errors, *ibid.* iii. 821-2). Foxe's second case (iii. 584) is more dubious. He refers to, but does not give, a writ ' in the records of the Tower,' represents the condemnation as taking place after the receipt of the writ, and dates the writ the same day as the execution.

[2] *L.P.* iii. 1692.

in the Netherlands and make them give security to appear in London or go to prison.[1] How far More usurped the function of issuing writs to burn depends upon Foxe's casual and contradictory remarks that writs were received before the burning of some of the half-dozen martyrs who suffered that death during More's chancellorship.[2] The absence of any

[1] *L.P.* iv. 5823.

[2] Wriothesley mentions five of these (*Chron.* i. 16-17), whose execution took place between Aug. 1531 and April 1532 ; and Foxe (v. 25) mentions another at Exeter on 10 Jan. 1532,* Sir T. Denis being sheriff (*P.R.O. List*). Foxe alleges a writ in this case, assumes one in Bilney's case (iv. 42-3) but says nothing of one when he comes to the actual execution (p. 52), while there is nothing about one in the records of the inquiry which followed (unpaged documents at the end of vol. iv.) ; and denies a writ in Tewkesbury's (iv. 694). In no case does he produce one, while Richard Bayfield, he says, was burnt on 4 Dec. 1531 (iv. 687-8), ' without any writ in that behalf obtained, but only by virtue of the bishop's letters, by the statute of king Henry IV in that behalf provided and directed unto them [the sheriffs] under the bishop's seal.'

It was, however, natural enough that Foxe should think one necessary, because the repeal in 1534 of 2 Henry IV, c. 15 made the receipt of a royal writ indispensable for the burning of a heretic (25 Henry VIII, c. 14 ; *S.R.* iii. 454-5). The act of 1401 was, however, with the other statutes, re-enacted twenty years later (1 Phil. and Mary, c. 7) and writs again became unnecessary : three heretics were burnt at Beccles in May 1556 without any writ, on Foxe's own testimony (viii. 146). But there was clearly a growing reluctance to give effect to the re-enacted Lollard statutes without specific royal writs. In July 1557 four sheriffs, the mayor of Rochester, and the bailiffs of Colchester were required by the privy council to explain, not their disobedience to a royal writ, but their stay of execution after the bodies had been delivered to them by the ordinary (*Acts P.C.* 1556-58, pp. 135, 144). At Lichfield the sheriff delayed execution until his successor came into office (Foxe, viii. 403). At Salisbury Sir Anthony Hungerford refused to carry out the sentence of the ecclesiastical court, and was advised by Mr. Justice Browne (so Foxe says, viii. 509) that he was entitled to do so until he received a royal writ ; Foxe also says that when the writ did arrive, the under-sheriff burnt it instead of the intended victims, one of whom was vicar of Marlborough when Foxe wrote. The reason for this reluctance is clear enough, especially towards the close of Mary's reign. The principle that coercion should not be applied without the specific consent of royal authority had taken deep root. Præmunire had been invoked not merely against Wolsey and all the clergy but against the laity ; and sheriffs felt that, without a specific royal writ for their discharge, they might, when Elizabeth succeeded, find themselves in the same quandary. Even so, there is little evidence of these writs, and the form

confirmation of Foxe on this point suggests that he is wrong. The above-mentioned proclamation of 1529 had just reminded sheriffs and others of their statutory duty to execute the sentence of the ecclesiastical courts without reference to royal writs ; and Fitzherbert, whose 'New Natura Brevium' first appeared in 1534, treats the royal writ *de comburendo* as obsolete and improper. On 13 May 1532 moreover, Chapuys writes that Henry VIII 'wishes bishops not to have the power to lay hands on persons accused of heresy, saying that it is not their duty to meddle with bodies and they are only doctors of the soul.' 'The chancellor,' continues Chapuys, 'and the bishops oppose him ' ; and that remark indicates More's real responsibility for religious persecution. 'The king,' observes Chapuys, ' is very angry, especially with the chancellor and the bishop of Winchester, and is determined to carry the matter.' Three days later More resigned, and Henry VIII achieved part of his purpose by the statute of 1534, repealing that of 1401 and requiring a royal writ before a heretic could be burnt.[1]

Wolsey as chancellor was restricted like More ; but it was as legate *a latere* that he dealt with cases of heresy. The second main feature of the statute of 1401 had been to enable a mere diocesan synod, as well as a provincial convocation, to condemn heretics to death ; and it was usually in diocesan consistories, before 1518 and after 1529, that protestant martyrs were made. But Wolsey's legatine authority overrode episcopal jurisdiction ; it was in his legatine court that heretics were condemned in penalties which were often

of one, which is given by Foxe as addressed to Bonner (viii. 532), is reprinted by Wilkins (*Concilia*, iv. 177), and is cited by Makower (p. 188), is not in Bonner's register (Foxe, viii. App. p. 786). It does not, of course, follow that it was not sent ; but the more drastic methods Mary employed to secure executions were the appointment of special commissions and even the requirement of the presence of privy councillors at burnings. Royal writs, of course, became obligatory again with the Elizabethan settlement, under which Foxe was writing.

[1] See below, p. 356. The relation of the two acts is illustrated by Audley's remark (*L.P.* ix. 90) that the later one was unnecessary for Ireland because ' the statute of Henry IV was never put in execution there.'

preliminary to the harsher fate they encountered when the bishops recovered their liberty ; and the diocesan courts of Stokesley in London, Nix at Norwich, and Veysey at Exeter account for all the burnings during the chancellorship of Sir Thomas More. Wolsey earned papal commendations for his holocaust of Lutheran books in May 1521 ; but the future Clement VII opined that heretics rather than their books deserved committing to the flames, and Warham cautioned Wolsey about the prevalence of Lutheran views at Oxford.[1] Wolsey's own college became seriously infected ; but while the records of his legatine court teem with cases of penance, confession, abjuration, and imprisonment, there is no instance of the extreme penalty being inflicted during Wolsey's legacy by the cardinal himself, his commissaries, or the diocesan synods whose jurisdiction he effectively superseded.[2] The protestants whose translations of the bible were burnt were not very grateful for the substitution of their books for their bodies, and Tyndale, Roy, Simon Fish, and others rivalled Skelton in their vituperation. They regarded the burning of bibles as the more heinous crime : [3] the blood of martyrs was the seed of the church, but scripture was the irreplaceable source of truth and the only means by which they could combat error ; they would rather be robbed of lives than see their weapons destroyed. Yet there was unusual expectation when some of them appealed to Wolsey's 'usual clemency,'[4] and a plausible

---

[1] *L.P.* iii. 1193, 1197, 1210 ; iv. 4125.

[2] There is reference in *L.P.* iii. 3062, under April 1523, to the burning of two heretics, but they had been burnt some years before (see Foxe, iv, 124, 219, 245). For illustrations of Wolsey's personal treatment of heretics see *L.P.* iii. 1922 ; iv. 1962, 4029, 4175, 4444 ; and for their confessions, etc., see *ibid.* iv. 4218, 4242, 4260, 4418, 4545, 4850. In iv. 4254 is a curious reference to hereditary heresy : ' nota quod iste oritur de stirpe vitiata, quia avus patris sui erat ob haeresim concrematus, ut dicitur.' This would constitute a link between lollardy and protestantism, and since the man's name was William Bocher, possibly with a yet later heretic, Joan Bocher.

[3] In this betrayal of the scriptures Roy (*Rede me*, pp. 117-20) makes Standish play the part of Judas while Wolsey only
> Spake the wordes of Pilat
> Sayinge, I fynde no fault therin.

[4] *L.P.* iv. 4396.

ground for the final charge against him by his accusers in
the parliament of 1529 'that the said lord cardinal, besides
all other his heinous offences, hath been the impeacher and
disturber of due and direct correction of heresies, being
highly to the danger and peril of the whole body and good
christian people of this your realm.'[1]

That article is but one of many which reveal episcopal
influence in the final attack on Wolsey's position and explain
du Bellay's remark in October 1529[2] that, when required
to answer before the king's bench or in parliament, the legate
'thinking, what is quite true, that the bishops had already
chosen judges after their own liking for the said parliament,
preferred to put himself in the mercy of the king,' and appear
by his attorneys before the court of king's bench.   For, bitter
as was the enmity Wolsey had excited in the minds of judges
by his contemptuous treatment of the common law and subjection of their courts to his discipline in chancery, it was
as nothing compared with resentment aroused in English
bishops by his comprehensive supersession of their jurisdiction and depletion of their revenues.

Wolsey had, indeed, superseded the mediæval constitution of the church in England and revived and
intensified English dislike of papal centralisation by the
ruthless vigour with which he used his legatine powers to
interfere with most of the courts christian, religious houses,
and benefices in the realm.   Whatever might be in store for
them, English bishops desired no more papal legates *a latere*.
As between Wolsey and Henry VIII, they preferred the
king, even when he shocked them with his royal supremacy.   For the supreme head himself did not supersede
convocations or diocesan synods ; he might control but
he did not extinguish the jurisdiction of his bishops ; and

[1] Herbert, p. 301.   There is here no evidence of sympathy with
Lutheranism.   Wolsey had other motives for inhibiting the two bishops,
whose intended visitation of Cambridge university provided the material
for this charge ; and the proclamation of March 1529 had repeated the
terms of the Lollard statutes, though it might be possible to attribute this
step less to Wolsey's influence than to its decline.

[2] Du Bellay to Montmorenci, 22 Oct. 1529 (*L.P.* iv. 6018).   For
the meaning of du Bellay's phraseology see below, p. 258.

he left their revenues almost untouched. The monasteries, which suffered most, were exempt from bishops' authority and not therefore their principal concern. There were ecclesiastical pastures into which no layman, not even Henry VIII, ventured to trespass; there were none from which Wolsey, as legate *a latere*, was debarred. But for Wolsey, the breach with Rome would have been longer deferred and the reformation would assuredly have taken a different course; it was he who converted the hierarchy in England to at least acquiescence in a change from what it had undergone at the hands of the only man who had, uncontrolled by parliament, combined despotic authority in the state with the sole control of the English church. He always drove furiously; and as legate *a latere* of the pope he rode papal jurisdiction in England to its death.

CHAPTER VI.

THE NEMESIS OF POWER.

Wolsey's legacy was the culmination of his power, and, had it been devoted to a single-hearted effort for the reformation of the church, it might have been the crowning glory of a marvellous career. But his heart was never wholly in the reformation which had been alleged as the reason for his extraordinary legatine authority. Foreign policy, secular administration in the chancery and star chamber, the acquisition of wealth and ostentation of power, severally occupied far more of his energy and attention than did the purification of morals, the remedy of ecclesiastical abuses, or the defence of the faith. In the early days of his supremacy, the procuring of incense for himself and his master had been described as his sole object in life ; and his dissolution of monasteries resulted mainly in a college, on nearly every stone of which, wrote Chapuys in 1529, were blazoned the cardinal's arms.[1] The pinnacle of his every edifice was himself, and the penalty of his eminence was his isolation. There had been no love lost between the laity and the clergy when Wolsey achieved his power ; but the church could have resisted the coming attack with more success had its cohesion not been loosened by the dissolvent effects of Wolsey's acid superiority. The aloofness of a papal legate, who objected to a brother-archbishop addressing him as a brother and robbed his episcopal colleagues of their independence and prestige, left him with hosts of servants but hardly a genuine friend in the spiritual house to which he belonged. Neither in church nor in state did he think he needed men's affection so long as he enjoyed that of the prince in whom he put his trust ; and a

---

[1] *Spanish Cal.* 1529-30, p. 326 ; W. Roy, *Rede me*, p. 54.

king, however sincere his affection might be, could not forever let it outweigh his reasons of state.

Wolsey in fact fell a victim to the nemesis of all centralising autocracy. Such autocracy as had existed during the middle ages was tolerated because of the absence of centralisation. It was dilute, not because it was distributed in many hands, but because it was derived as of right from many independent sources. There were the liberties of the church, based on law superior to that of the king ; there was a law of nature, graven in the hearts of men and not to be erased by royal writs ; and there was the prescription of immemorial local and feudal customs stereotyping a variety of jurisdictions and impeding the operation of a single will. There was no sovereignty capable of eradicating bondage by royal edict or act of parliament, regulating borough franchise, reducing to uniformity the various uses of the church, or enacting a principle of succession to the throne. The laws which ruled men's lives were the customs of their trade, profession, locality, or estate and not the positive law of a legislator ; and the sum of English parliamentary legislation for the whole of the middle ages is less in bulk than that of the single reign of Henry VIII.[1]

So, too, the tribunals which enforced these rules represented heterogeneous authorities ; and the jurisdictions with which most men came into contact and therefore into conflict were not for the most part royal. The crown was not, unless the conflict led to crime, involved in the discontent with oppression by gild or municipal courts, by feudal lords and overmighty subjects, or by ecclesiastical judges, whose more or less wholesome rigour provoked the ironical mediæval debate whether an archdeacon could possibly be saved. The object of peasants' animosity in 1381 was the manorial court-roll, and they looked for a moment to

---

[1] In the ' Statutes of the Realm ' legislation from Henry I's charter to 1485 occupies 896 pages ; for Henry VII's reign it occupies 196 and for Henry VIII's 1032. But most of the mediæval statutes are given in two languages, whereas a single English text suffices for the reign of Henry VIII.

Richard II to lead them as German peasants looked in 1524 to Charles V.[1] There was conflict enough between barons and the crown ; but it was contact with the crown in the king's court that led to rebellion in the field. There was strife between feudal factions for the control of the crown culminating in the wars of the roses ; but there was no civil war between the king and his people until the new monarchy had destroyed feudal liberties, which had stood between the crown and the mass of its subjects, and had insisted on the simplicity of the single state in which all jurisdiction came from a single monarchical source.

It thus removed the buffers which softened the impact of popular disaffection, and by claiming a monopoly of loyalty invoked a concentration of discontent. Feudal liberties were converted to the use of the ' independent monarchy ' of James I ; local streams of disaffection trickled into the river of parliamentary revolt ; and royal supremacy over the church concentrated on the crown the lightnings of blasphemy which had played harmlessly over the multitudinous archidiaconal body. For the church was centralised like the state on the foundation of *une foi, une loi, un roi*. Royal supremacy entailed ecclesiastical uniformity ; national religion destroyed the various uses, the local shrines, the side-chapels, and the particular altars of mediæval veneration ; and the aristocracy of saints submitted to the absolute monarchy of monotheistic doctrine just as the estates of the realm and the liberties of feudal magnates succumbed to the dogma of the sovereign state. The great rebellion was inevitably preceded by the new sovereignty ; and the act of parliament, which had most to do with the execution of Charles I, was the act of 1534, which made the supreme head a stumbling-block to protestant religion and to independent members of the body of the church. Strafford evoked the secular hatred of the landed gentry ; but it was Laud's administration of the royal supremacy that brought

---

[1] Cf. *The Anonimalle Chronicle*, ed. Galbraith, 1927, p. 144, ' nous ne voillioms avoir autre roy qe vous,' and their petition ' qe nulle homme ne deveroit estre nayf,' with the demands of the German peasants (*Cambridge Mod. Hist.* ii. 184-5).

into the struggle the puritan spirit which substituted a
martyr's for the royal crown of Charles I ; and Wolsey's
history came into public favour when men discerned in him
a prototype of Laud.[1]   There was something in that
association of ideas ; for the concentration of jurisdictions which produced the monopoly of the crown was
largely Wolsey's work, and he in particular was responsible
for the union of ecclesiastical with secular authority which
Henry VIII proceeded to establish on a statutory basis ;
though Wolsey had nothing to do with the invoking of
parliament, which made the royal supremacy subject to
parliamentary interpretation and an occasion for civil war.
Nevertheless, his accumulation of jurisdictions, dignities,
and powers, and his trespasses upon the rights and liberties
of parliaments and convocations, feudal magnates and
bishops, judges and municipalities,[2] were the effective
means of provoking the heterogeneous coalition which led
to his fall.

Rumours of tentative combinations to obtain his
removal began to spread with the growth of Wolsey's
unpopularity, which dates from the pressure of taxation
owing to the French war of 1521-23 and the failure to
reap any apparent return even from the total defeat and
capture of Francis at Pavia.   It developed rapidly when
Wolsey's peace with France appeared a mere prelude to
war with Charles V ; and Wolsey's nervousness on the
subject was illustrated by his committing to the Fleet John
Rowe or Roo, a serjeant-at-law of twenty years' standing,
for a masque produced at Gray's Inn at Christmas 1526, in
which the cardinal discerned an attack on himself.[3]   But

---

[1] Cavendish's *Life of Wolsey* was first published in 1641, in a mutilated
form, while Prynne was emulating Tyndale in his *New Discovery of the
Prelates' Tyranny* (1643), and *Canterburie's Doom* (1646).

[2] L.P. iv. 3486, 5107, App. 6.   See below, p. 319.

[3] Rowe had been justice of the peace for Devon since 1504 (*Cal. Patent
Rolls*, Henry VII, ii. 424, 636), was serjeant-at-law in 1512 (*Rot. Parl.*
vii. p. xxxii *b* ; *L.P.* i. new ed. 3049 [20]), and of the counsel in the
star chamber in 1516 (*ibid.* ii. 1856 ; cf. Leadam, *Star Chamber*, ii.
117).   In 1519 he was participating in judicial deliberations in the exchequer chamber (Tottel, *Year Books*, 12 Henry VIII, Trinity, f. iii *b* ;

the first to gather, and repeat in writing, details of the
opposition was somewhat naturally Iñigo de Mendoza,
bishop of Burgos, who had succeeded de Praet as Charles V's
ambassador.   Writing on 18 May 1527, he reports that
pasquinades were nightly circulated 'so hostile to the king
and especially to the legate that there was a general rumour
that the king intended to relieve the legate of [? part of]
his share in the administration, taking from him either the
foreign or the home affairs and leaving him only one
department.'   Warham he describes as Wolsey's rival and
an opponent of war with Spain, but he 'never comes to
court.'[1]   Wolsey's chief abettors were his secret enemies
who hoped to destroy him thereby, 'for they would not be
satisfied with turning him out of office, but seek his entire
ruin.'   Besides Warham, he mentions Norfolk and Tunstal,
who was considered a likely successor to Wolsey as chancellor.
Wolsey himself he describes as ' universally hated . . . . . so
great is the abhorrence felt for the legate in this kingdom
that it has hitherto proved an actual check upon his wicked
designs.'[2]

Five months later Anne Boleyn had appeared on the
scene and complicated affairs.   She was already prejudiced
against Wolsey, who had disappointed her father of office

cf. Dyer, *Reports*, 6 H. 8, f. 2 *b*, and 32 H. 8, f. 47 *b*).   The fullest account
of the incident is given by Hall (*Chron.* p. 719) who says Wolsey also
deprived him of his coif, and that one of the actors, Thomas Moyle (probably the Speaker of 1542, see *D.N.B.*) was also sent to the Fleet.   Warham, in a letter to his chaplain Henry Gold on 6 Feb. 1526-27 (*L.P.* iv.
2854), says he has heard that Rowe is committed to the Tower and ' is
sorry such a matter should be taken in earnest.'   According to Foxe
(iv. 657) the leading part in the acting was taken by Simon Fish, after all
others had refused it ; but he escaped abroad where he joined Tyndale.
Rowe was apparently soon released (*ibid.* iv. 3213 [18]).   In 1539 he
was appointed an original member of the council of the west (see his letter
to Cromwell in *L.P.* 1539 i. 686 and C. A. J. Skeel in *Trans. Royal Hist.
Soc.* 1921, pp. 63-4, 77, 79).   He was still acting as serjeant-at-law in
1548 (Gladys Bradford [Mrs. Temperley], *Star Chamber Proceedings*, pp.
264-6 ; Tanner, *Const. Docs.* p. 270).
[1] *Spanish Cal.* 1527-29, pp. 190-2 ; cf. Skelton's poem, ' Why come
ye nat to court ? ' in *Works*, ed. Dyce, ii. 26-7.
[2] *Ibid.* pp. 193, 207, 209, 274-5.

and herself of a suitor[1] and was now scheming to marry
Henry VIII to the French queen's sister; and on 26 October
1527 Mendoza represents Norfolk and the Boleyns as the
heads of a league against Wolsey and Wolsey himself as
'now trying all he can to prevent the divorce' for fear of
Anne becoming queen.[2] From that time onwards Wolsey
was suspected of playing a double game in the matter. He
was, indeed, on the horns of a dilemma : his relations with
Catherine had never been good ; she naturally disapproved
alike of Wolsey's lax morality and of his Francophil policy ;
'she identifies herself,' says Mendoza, 'entirely with the
emperor's interests.'[3] Wolsey had now embarked on his
crucial contest with Charles V for control of the papal curia ;
his avowed object was to convert the Anglo-French entente
into a perpetual alliance, and the surest way to commit
Henry VIII to that course was the divorce of the emperor's
aunt. Alone it might suffice, but Wolsey hoped to
supplement the Spanish divorce with a French marriage.
Matrimony was a fleeting foundation for permanent policy,
but it might forestall the danger from Anne Boleyn. Just,
however, as Wolsey's ecclesiastical ambition was partially
foiled by Warham's longevity, so his marriage scheme was
frustrated by the persistence of Henry's passion for Anne.
He was divided in mind ; if he achieved the divorce, he
paved the way for his domestic enemies, Anne, her father

[1] Henry had in 1515 promised Sir Thomas Boleyn the treasurership
or controllership of the household on Sir Thomas Lovell's death or retirement, and had renewed the promise on Boleyn's departure early in 1519
as ambassador to France. On 14 May he wrote from Poissy reminding
Wolsey of these promises, but Wolsey put him off for another three years.
The refusal was connected with a general removal from court of Francophil courtiers, which disturbed Francis I and caused a good deal of comment (*L.P.* iii. 223, 235, 249; *Venetian Cal.* 1509-19, pp. 524-5 ;
Rawdon Brown, ii. 270-2 ; Tyndale, *Works*, i. 239 ; Hall, p. 598).
Wolsey may also have been responsible for the delay in Boleyn's peerage,
which although announced in a letter of the solicitor-general of 28 April
1523 (*L.P.* iii. 2982 ; Gairdner in *D.N.B.* v. 322a, calls it a 'private'
letter), was not apparently conferred until 28 June 1525. Henry, lord
Percy, afterwards sixth earl of Northumberland, had been Anne's suitor
in 1523.   [2] *Spanish Cal.* 1527-29, p. 432.

[3] *Ibid.* p. 194 ; cf. above, p. 105 *n.* 2; and Lord Acton, *Lectures*,
p. 137, 'she led the opposition to Wolsey, the author of the change.'

(now viscount Rochford), and her uncle, the duke of Norfolk ; if he abandoned the divorce, he would offend his French friends without reconciling Charles V or Catherine. How far the dilemma really affected the genuineness of his efforts to obtain the divorce cannot be ascertained ; but to the end of his embassy Mendoza continued to harp on Wolsey's fear of Anne becoming queen ; 'in secret,' he writes on 18 September 1528, 'all know that he is working in Catherine's favour ' ; [1] and Francis I gave similar warnings to Henry VIII. In February 1529 Mendoza brings Suffolk into the Boleyn-Norfolk combination against Wolsey, but remarks that 'hitherto they seem to have made no impression on the king, save that the cardinal is no longer received at court so graciously as before.' He thought it unlikely that Henry's 'displeasure would take any other form for the present,' although the king was complaining that the cardinal did not fulfil his promises.[2]

Henry had in fact relied too implicitly on Wolsey's wizardry, and Wolsey had promised more than he could perform. His colleagues somewhat weakly accused him, after the event, of having often stifled discussion in the council by staking his head that their forebodings had no foundation, and complained with more justification that he monopolised the sources of information on which alone they could form a judgement. A good deal of this correspondence was between the legate and the holy see which might plausibly be withheld from a mere council of state. The king himself long left it to Wolsey. When Ammonius died in 1517 his nephew, Peter Vannes, succeeded him both as Wolsey's secretary and as Henry's Latin secretary, the language in which the king's correspondence with the papacy was naturally conducted. It is Wolsey's voice we hear in the royal compliments to him and his administration which his secretary penned for papal consumption ; [3] and just as the legate relied on the impression he conveyed to Rome of his power in England, so his alleged influence over the papal curia was the means by which Wolsey

persuaded the king that he could obtain his divorce and
guarantee him against the risk from the consequent enmity
of Charles V. His other reason for confidence lay in his
intimate relations with Louise of Savoy, the queen mother of
France ; but this correspondence was also not for the eyes of
the council or even those of Henry himself. It, too, proved
a broken reed : after more than a year's imprisonment,
Francis I paid fleeting attention to the serious task of
saving Italy and the papacy from the clutches of Charles V.
France was nearly as weary as England of a struggle which
Wolsey required to save his policy and himself from destruction. Luther and the Turks between them afforded France
some relief and tempered the emperor's exploitation of his
victories in Italy in 1528-29 ; he was constrained to forgo
the most onerous terms of the treaty of Madrid and turn to
the correlated tasks of raising the sultan's siege of Vienna
and restraining the German reformation. Both Henry VIII
and his subjects were relieved to get out of the European
cockpit with only financial losses, and revert to domestic
problems, which had been burked by the papal legate but
now claimed the attention of the first long parliament in
English history.

Wolsey's failure abroad naturally brought to a head at
home the heterogeneous discontent which his conduct of
affairs had evoked. Nothing short of his compelling power
could have driven so motley a host together in opposition ;
and his enemies ranged from the staunchest of catholics to
the keenest of protestants, from the greatest of feudal
magnates to the poorest of unemployed craftsmen. Lord
Darcy was the first of Henry's council to commit to paper
a comprehensive indictment of Wolsey's misdeeds,[1] and the

---

[1] *L.P.* iv. pp. 2548-54. The original in the P.R.O. is in Darcy's
hand and is dated by him 1 July 1529. It is headed : 'hereafter followeth
by protestation articles against the cardinal of York, showed by me
Thomas Darcy, only for to discharge my oath and most bounden duty to
God and the king, and of no malice.' Darcy was 62 years old at the time
and had rendered long and distinguished service at home and abroad to
Henry VII and Henry VIII (see *D.N.B.*). His consistent conservatism
carried him farther in his eventual opposition to Henry VIII than in his
action against Wolsey. His ' articles ' fill fifteen pages, range from

name that stood at the head of the parliamentary articles of impeachment was that of Sir Thomas More. Yet both lost their heads on the scaffold, Darcy for his share in the Pilgrimage of Grace, and More for rejecting the royal supremacy. Bishops could not constitutionally reveal their minds by demanding Wolsey's head, but Warham and Nix, Tunstal and Veysey were at one with the secular lords who presented the accusations ; and they did but repeat what was written and said of Wolsey by lawyers and men of letters, courtiers and protestant refugees. The forty-four articles of Wolsey's impeachment in parliament re-inforce the forty-seven stanzas of an anonymous ballad composed in 1528 ;[1] the satirical

domestic and foreign policy to personal grievances, and illustrate the anti-clerical feeling of the catholic laity, the anti-bureaucratic feeling of the feudal nobility, and the discontent in the north with Tudor centralisation. Except for a few details, the charges can be supported by other contemporary documents. Darcy concludes by suggesting methods of bringing Wolsey to account, and coping with the defensive action he was expected to take, e.g. by packing the approaching parliament. For Darcy's later petition see above, pp. 91-2 n. 1.

[1] Furnivall, *Ballads from MSS.* 1868-72, i. 352-61. It begins with a contrast between St. Thomas of Canterbury and Thomas of York (cf. Tyndale's 'neither is Thomas cardinal's life anything save a counterfeit of St. Thomas of Canterbury,' *Practice of Prelates*, p. 292, and Skelton in 'Colin Clout,' *Works*, i 317-18), denounces Wolsey's 'inordinate appetite,' 'usurped authority,' pomp and pride, extortion 'in all places probate,' dissolution of monasteries, ruin of Buckingham, destruction of churches, planning dissension 'betwixt the noblest *hunc* and *hanc*' Henry and Catherine, cf. Roy, *Rede me*, p. 52 ; and *ibid.* p. 57 for Wolsey's 'golden shoon'], restraint of trade ; threatens him with a fall like that of Lucifer, Simon Magus (see above, p. 101 n. 1), the Despensers, and Mortimer, and with the vengeance of the commons ; says all are looking to the king for a remedy and reformation ; and urges Wolsey to repent

> And do like the peacock for thine avail,
> Look on thy feet, and down with thy tail,
>   And off with thy golden shoon !
> And lay down thy pillars, poleaxes, and crosses,
> By the which this land hath had great losses
>   And pill the people no more !

There are three other contemporary ballads relating to Wolsey in Furnivall's volume : (1) 'The Ruin of a Realm' (pp. 158-66), more general and less pointed ; (2) 'Of the Cardnall Wolse' (pp. 333-5), a brief denunciation of the 'butcher's cur' and of the subservience of the nobility ;

jottings of John Palsgrave [1] supplement the heartfelt philippics of Tyndale ; while the censures of the historians Hall and Polydore Vergil are pale reflexions of Skelton's and Roy's poetic invectives.

For the moment these discordant and diverse interests were massed for a joint attack. Wolsey's exuberant and aggressive personality afforded ground that was common to all, and Tyndale and Roy agreed with Warham's catholic entourage and with Darcy's feudal following in representing the papal legate as the great tyrant. His financial exactions touched them all and offended them most by the modernity of his methods : never a tyrant, writes the indignant translator of the New Testament, did such a thing as Wolsey had done in requiring men to swear on oath what they were worth for taxation ; judges, he says, should not 'break into the consciences of men.' [2]   Assessment was better than inquisition, and the lord chancellor's campaign against perjury appeared to have a distinctly financial motive. So had his dealings in probate, which all men reprobated ; though feudal lords and ecclesiastical reformers detected a special

and (3) 'The Complaynt of North' (pp. 336-9; noticed in *L.P.* iv. App. 244), probably by Edward afterwards first baron North (see *D.N.B.*) who was pardoned on 24 January 1525 (*L.P.* iv. 1049) after imprisonment for a book against Wolsey. Furnivall says ' it looks as if the writer meant to make an acrostic on Wolsey's name. But neither in this poem nor in the next is there one.' Yet the first letters of the lines in the second read 'God preserve Thomas lord legate and cardynal.' * A fourth (pp. 281-90), against the English Lutherans, probably dates from late in 1529 ; its allusion ' the Turk cometh now at hand ' is far from being, as Furnivall suggests, nothing ' more than the old bogey cry,' and is to the siege of Vienna, Sept.-Oct. 1529 (see Hall, p. 770). The adjuration to Henry VIII to protect the realm from heresy suggests a date soon after Wolsey's fall (see below, pp. 349-50).

[1] See above, pp. 17, 71, 91. Palsgrave's indictment is far more comprehensive, though less bitter, than Darcy's, and consists of three documents (calendared in *L.P.* iv. pp. 2555-62) which were found in two searches of his rooms and were certainly never intended for publication (compare his remarks on Bessie Blount, p. 2558, with his letter to the lady on p. 2595). When, by whom, and by whose orders the searches were made, does not appear : Palsgrave was acting at the time as tutor to the duke of Richmond at Sheriffhutton in Yorkshire ; see his letters to Henry VIII, Sir T. More, and Cromwell (*ibid.* pp. 2593-96).

[2] Tyndale, ' Obedience of a Christian Man ' (*Works*, i. 187, 203).

objection to it as a fresh endowment of the clergy and of
Wolsey in particular. For the unreformed church was not
exempt from the common acquisitiveness of the age ; and
fees for probate, mortuaries, and other perquisites of their
profession were the means by which the clergy strove to keep
in step with the explorations and exploitations of an incipient British empire. 'No penny, no *paternoster*'[1] expressed
the ecclesiastical counterpart of the secular economy which
converted into private capital the common rights of men.

Here, of course, the protestant peeped out, but only in
his anti-clerical habit. That, however, cloaked a multitude
of diversities in the days of Wolsey's tribulation. The
catholic Darcy demanded, as loudly as the indifferent duke
of Suffolk or the virulent author of the ' Practice of Prelates,'
that ' never legate nor cardinal be in England ' ; and asked
in feebler English Tyndale's question, 'is it not a shame
above all shames, and a monstrous thing, that no man should
be found able to govern a worldly kingdom, save bishops
and prelates ? ' 'The hypocrites,' continues Tyndale, ' say
unto the kings and lords ' these heretics would have us down
first, and then you, to make all common.' . . . The kings
and lords are down already. . . . We would have them up
again and restored unto the room and authority which God
hath given them.'[2] Like Luther after the failure of the
peasants' revolt in 1524-5, Tyndale was a political conservative ; and he was almost as shocked as Darcy that Wolsey
should ' call earls and barons his subjects and servants.' No
one, save Wolsey's agents, had a word to say for the dissolution of monasteries as practised by him ; and the pope
himself was involved in the unpopularity of his legate. Darcy
not only denounced temporal government by bishops, but
complained of the papal ' entry ' Wolsey had effected, of his
jurisdiction in probate and 'prevention' of benefices, and
urged that the weapon of præmunire should be employed
against him.[3]

[1] ' After the common saying ' Tyndale, *Works*, i. 245).
[2] *Ibid*. pp. 206-7, 247 ; Darcy's articles in *L.P.* iv. p. 2553.
[3] *Ibid*. iv. p. 2550 : ' Memorandum, at his entry to authority this
realm was at peace. . . . Item, then and above a hundred years before,

Darcy, who had commanded forces sent to Ferdinand's aid in 1511-12 and had accompanied Henry on his campaign of 1513, was less free than Tyndale to denounce the cardinal's adventurous foreign policy; but he probably sympathised with Tyndale's suggestion that 'the king ought to count up what he hath spent in the pope's quarrel since he was king. The first voyage cost upon £1,400,000,' and Tyndale reckons that the total was four or five millions. 'The king,' he goes on, 'ought to make the clergy pay every farthing and restore the money to the commons again; not that only which the cardinal and his bishops compelled the commons to lend . . . but also all that he hath gathered of them . . . or else by consent of the commons to keep it in store for the defence of the realm.'[1] Tyndale's excursion into political pamphleteering is of interest not merely because Henry VIII acted on so many of his suggestions, but because it adumbrates views of English history which Shakespeare has made permanent in English literature. 'Behold,' he writes, 'king Henry the Vth whom they [the bishops] sent out for such a purpose as they sent out our king that now is . . . To set one realm at variance with another, and to cause 20,000 men to die in a day,[2] is but a trifle and a pastime with them. . . . War and conquering of lands is their harvest.' 'Consider,' he goes on, 'the story of king John. . . . I suppose they make the chronicles themselves.' Tyndale

the best prelate within this realm ever content with one dignity of a bishopric only. . . . Item, then no abbeys nor houses of religion . . . pulled down, nor noble founders' wills broken, nor Magna Carta . . . nor sanctuaries violated. . . . Item, then the pope's holiness had none entry, gift, nor use of any spiritual promotion [cf. above, p. 205 n. 1] nor levying of any money within this realm contrary to the king's prerogative. . . . Item, then every man, spiritual and temporal, and cities and towns disposed and gave their own promotions and offices without any interruption of legacy, faculties a latere. . . . Item, then none of high or low degree durst enter into the danger of the praemunire, but that for example of others they were punished accordingly, and also by him' (see above, p. 194 n.).

[1] Tyndale, *Works*, i. 335-6. See above, p. 131 n. 2 and below, p. 355.

[2] Cf. Roy, *Rede me*, p. 54:

> Of twenty thousande fyghtynge men
> Scant returneth home agayne ten,
> In good state and perfect lykynge.

reviewed them, and converted the blackest of monastic portraits into a forerunner of the gospel according to kings.
'This,' Henry VIII is reported to have said when he read
it, 'is a book for me and for all kings to read.'[1]

That was not until a year or two after Tyndale's book
was written and published and Henry's mind was beginning
to move away from its moorings. Tyndale was enamoured
of kings as they ought to be and not of kings as they were :
'the emperor and kings,' he wrote, 'are nothing nowadays
but even hangmen unto the pope and bishops.'[2]   The
writers of prose and verse are full of what Henry ought to
do but did not ; and they marvel at the supineness, which
some attribute to his indolent love of pleasure and others
can only explain by Wolsey's art which they liken to that
of Simon Magus.[3]   Still, they had hopes of the king but
none of the clergy ; and their common prayer is that he
may rid himself and his subjects of their thraldom to 'such
wily tyranny which increaseth more and more daily.'[4]

Henry VIII, however, had hitherto been as staunch and
sincere a papalist as Wolsey, and it was not till the pope
refused to divorce him that he began to distinguish between
what he called 'good Englishmen' and 'Englishmen papisti-
cate.'[5]   He had defended the papal states by his sword and
the papal faith by his pen ; and his services had been rewarded
by the papal grant of a title which still encircles the heads
of his successors with a somewhat ambiguous halo.   For a
king, he was no mean theologian ; and, being a king and a

---

[1] See Strype, *Eccl. Memorials*, I, i. 173.   The protestant reformation
made some curious 'contemporary' history of the twelfth and thirteenth
centuries ; and the glorification of king John as England's protagonist
against the pope, which began with Tyndale and the ballad writers in
1527-28, led up to the destruction of the shrine of St. Thomas à Becket
in 1538, to the story that his bones were disinterred and burnt for con-
tumacious heresy to the state, and to Shakespeare's play. Cf. below, pp.
355-6.

[2] *Works*, i. 242. See below, pp. 335, 359-60.

[3] Furnivall, *Ballads from MSS.* i. 357 ; cf. *ibid.* pp. 158-9, 163, 166,
333-5, 358 ; and Skelton, *Works*, ii. 17, 21, 39, 40, 45, 47-8.

[4] Tyndale, *op. cit.* p. 240.

[5] Henry VIII to Bennet and Carne, 6 Dec. 1530, *State Papers*, vii
269 ; *L.P.* iv. 6760.

Tudor, his theology naturally took a bent towards casuistry concerned with his own particular case. Did not the validity of his marriage and consequently the legitimacy of his children, nay, even his own legitimacy and title to the throne, depend upon papal dispensations?[1] How then could he permit himself or others to deny the plenitude of papal power?

It would have been strange, indeed, if Henry, with this mentality, had failed to discover a theological reason for the singular fatality which attended the issue of his marriage. Several children perished on their way to birth, though Henry was particularly careful of his queen at what experience led him to call ' her dangerous times ';[2] and of the sons who were born only one lived as long as six weeks. There is no doubt of his genuine anxiety : a local tradition persists that he trod barefoot and in secret a Norfolk road on a pilgrimage to pray for the flickering life of that infant ; and he certainly vowed to lead a crusade in person against the Turk if the last of his expectations produced an heir to the throne.[3] Nothing availed ; and, while no one, as Tyndale objected, could promise him a son by another wife,[4] it was certain by 1525 that he would have none by his brother's widow.[5] Deuteronomy seemed to be right and the papacy wrong : at least the dispensation of Julius II had not been effective for the practical purposes of the succession to the throne. There was, indeed, a daughter ; but what woman had ever sat in

---

[1] A papal dispensation had been considered necessary to remove the obstacle of consanguinity to the marriage of Henry VII and Elizabeth of York (Campbell, *Materials*, Rolls Ser. i. 392 ; my *Henry VII*, i. 35-41). Henry VIII had also been led to believe that his ' imperial ' crown depended upon papal grant (see below, p. 331).

[2] See my *Henry VIII*, pp. 173-9.

[3] Henry VIII to Leo X (Martene and Durand, *Collectio*, 1724, vol. iii. cols. 1297-9), ' si ante expeditionem suscipiendam, miseratione ejus qui ex lumbis Abrahae eduxit populum in hereditatem Israel, contigerit nos optatissimam suscepisse prolem.'

[4] *Practice of Prelates* (Parker Soc.), p. 333.

[5] In July 1525 Tunstal, Wingfield, and Sampson justified to the emperor Henry's refusal to send Mary to Spain as Charles' bride on the ground that she was his only child and he could hope for no further issue from Catherine (*L.P.* iv. p. 662).

the seat of English kings? Matilda had tried to mount its steps, but the effort, after costing a civil war, had failed; and, if women could rule, Henry VII and Henry VIII himself had usurped the throne of their mother and grandmother, Margaret Beaufort, who was still alive at her grandson's coronation. Henry was so convinced that he and his realm needed a son to succeed him that in 1525 he gave his illegitimate son the titles of Richmond and Somerset which he, his father, and his Beaufort forbears had borne, and began to prepare his path to the throne. What scruples of law or conscience or policy frustrated this idea, we do not know. Possibly Wolsey suggested that, where Julius II had done wrong, Clement VII might be persuaded to do what was right. Julius had doubted, or professed to doubt, his power to dispense; Clement VII had no doubt that he could annul his predecessor's dispensation. Cardinal du Bellay wrote to Francis I from Rome on 15 March 1534, 'no one will be bold enough to maintain in consistory that the dispensation ever was valid';[1] and Sixtus V 'afterwards declared that Clement deserved the calamities that befel him, because he had not dissolved so unholy a union.'[2] Clement agreed with Wolsey that only Rome could decide, and Henry fell in with the idea. What was the point of Wolsey's legatine eminence and influence at Rome if he could get whatever he liked for himself, but not the one thing that was wanted by his sovereign?

The lion in the path was Charles V. Henry was inclined to think that obstacle overrated: Charles, he pointed out, had seen one sister driven from her throne in Hungary and another from her throne in Denmark without lifting a finger to restore them.[3] Why, then,

[1] *L.P.* vii. App. 12.
[2] Lord Acton, *Lectures on Modern History*, p. 137.
[3] *Spanish Cal.* 1529-30, p. 506. Salviati had used the same argument in March 1528, and Wolsey in October (Ehses, pp. 255-6; *L.P.* iv. 4881), but it was not so relevant to the cardinal's policy. Charles V would not, and did not, make war on Henry for the sake of Catherine (cf. *L.P.* viii. 182, 189; x. 575); but he did make war in Italy to retain his dominions and his influence over the papacy. The argument was

anticipate greater affection for an aunt? In point of fact this forecast was justified; and when the emperor perceived that Henry had not the remotest intention of making the divorce a preliminary to, or pretext for, a joint attack with France upon the empire, he did little more for Catherine than he had done for Mary, queen of Hungary, or Isabella, queen of Denmark. But Wolsey's policy was different: the divorce was to him a means and not an end. He and not Henry VIII was, in his eyes, the principal in the duel with Charles V; and Charles was of the same opinion. The Anglo-Spanish breach in 1528 was Wolsey's and not Henry's war;[1] and its objective was the control of Italy and the papacy. Rome was essential to the papal legate but not to the English king. Thence came Wolsey's pride of pomp and power; Henry's depended upon firmer but more insular foundations, and those foundations did not trouble Charles, though they troubled his successors. The emperor cared for Italy more than he cared for Catherine; and he needed a papal coronation and papal co-operation before he could turn north to wrestle with the German reformation and defend the empire against the Turk. Henry, on the other hand, cared more for the divorce than he did about Italy, and he was beginning to doubt his need of the pope. There was thus room for accommodation between Henry and Charles. The emperor, as he told his brother Ferdinand, was sure that Henry would marry Anne Boleyn with or without the pope's consent, and he was above all things anxious to avoid a conflict with England.[2] The divorce, he said, was a private matter: he did not regard it as a case for war, and he steadily evaded papal invitations to undertake the execution of papal decrees against Henry, who on his part carefully avoided giving Charles any other ground of offence.[3]

sound for Henry's defensive policy, but quite unsound for Wolsey's attempt to substitute Anglo-French for imperial influence in Italy and Rome.

[1] See above, pp. 157-9.

[2] Charles V to Ferdinand, 11 Jan. 1530, in Lanz, *Correspondenz des Kaysers Karl V* (Leipzig, 1844-46), i. 360; *Spanish Cal.* 1529-30, pp. 405-6.

[3] *L.P.* vi. 568.

The issue with Wolsey was another matter. There could be no compromise between him and Charles at Rome. As legate *a latere* of an independent pope, or of a pope who was amenable to English discipline, Wolsey held a strong position in England ; as legate of Charles V's chaplain he would have no value for Henry VIII. For Wolsey, as for Charles, so much was at stake that the issue could only be fought to a finish. The end came in 1529 : on 16 April Mendoza reported from London that there was great vexation 'at the famous Italian league being dissolved or nearly so.'[1] The battle of Landriano (21 June) completed tne process of dissolution. Clement abandoned the cause at the treaty of Barcelona (29 June), and Francis I at that of Cambrai. Du Bellay protested against this last desertion : it would, he declared, be 'the cause of Wolsey's total ruin' ; he would be called a Frenchman and a traitor, for Henry had only been induced to embark on the enterprise by the assurances of French fidelity Wolsey had given in his efforts 'to break off for ever the alliance with the emperor.'[2] Wolsey hoped by another visit to France in May to re-establish his influence in the French government ; 'he is,' wrote du Bellay, 'in the greatest pain he ever was.'[3] Henry would not let him go, and sent Suffolk instead. Presently Wolsey was complaining that the duke had 'put him out of favour with Francis,' and Francis was warning Henry not to trust too much in the cardinal over the divorce ; Wolsey had, he said, 'great intelligence' with the pope and Campeggio, and Henry had better look to his own affairs himself.[4] Wolsey also wanted to go to Cambrai to repeat his earlier triumphs of 1521 and 1527 ; but Henry

---

[1] *Spanish Cal.* 1527-29, p. 981.

[2] *L.P.* iv. 5582, 5679; Le Grand, iii. 324.

[3] *L.P.* iv. 5580; cf. Salviati's letter of 20 May in Ehses, p. 264.

[4] *Ibid.* iv. 5635. Francis I had told Salviati in January that Wolsey was repenting of his share in the divorce, and Campeggio wrote to the same effect (Ehses, pp. 69, 261). Clement had expressed a 'desire to have a secret understanding' with Wolsey as early as 1524 (*L.P.* iv. 296). Wolsey wrote, while Campeggio only signed, their joint letters (Ehses, *Römische Dok.* p. 66) ; Campeggio's correspondence (1521-30) is printed in H. Laemmer, *Monumenta Vaticana*, 1861.

distrusted his intimacy with Louise of Savoy.[1] He may also have had doubts of Wolsey's return and fears of what he might do if he went to Rome to take his place in the college of cardinals.[2] In February Mendoza had been 'certain that . . . the pope will have the case brought before his own court and recall Campeggio'; and on 22 June Wolsey himself wrote to Rome that its advocation would 'utterly destroy him for ever.' That blow fell on 23 July:[3] 'now,' burst out Suffolk in the legates' court at Blackfriars, 'I see that the old said saw is true, that never a cardinal or legate did good in England.'[4]

It was the only remark of Suffolk's that anyone ever remembered. For once in his life he had given public expression to public opinion in a way to make it decisive. Wolsey's power was gone. He had himself warned the pope on 24 June that the avocation of the suit would utterly alienate the king and the realm from Rome and be ruin for himself.[5] Gardiner, who had been his chaplain and secretary, entered on his new duties as secretary to the king on 28 July and remained in constant

[1] *L.P.* iv. 5753, where Wolsey tells Louise that Henry had intended to send him, but owing to shortness of time was sending Tunstal and More.

[2] Darcy (*ibid.* p. 2549) reports Wolsey as saying that if all else failed, he would get the pope to summon him ' as straitly as may be to appear at Rome, and there he to remain.'

[3] The case had been advoked to Rome by Clement VII on 16 July (*Venetian Cal.* 1527-33, p. 224; Ehses, pp. 120-2; *L.P.* iv. 5780, 5785); but this, of course, was not known in England when on 23 July Campeggio adjourned its hearing until after the vacation. Henry and Wolsey, however, had known that it threatened before 22 May (Ehses, pp. 95-7).

[4] Wolsey's alleged rejoinder to Suffolk that but for him, the duke would have no head upon his shoulders, rests solely on Cavendish, who professes thirty years later to give a verbatim report, running to 300 words, of what Wolsey said. Chapuys (*Spanish Cal.* 1529-30, pp. 235-6), Hall (p. 758), and the author of the *Life of Fisher* (E.E.T.S. pp. 65-6), who report Suffolk's remark, have nothing about Wolsey's rejoinder; and the idea that Henry VIII had any thought of executing Suffolk for marrying Mary Tudor seems to have no other foundation than Wolsey's desire to remove a rival (see above, p. 109 *n.*).

[5] *State Papers*, vii. 189.

attendance throughout the rest of the year : [1] he would,
thought du Bellay, have much to do with the government
especially if he would consign his clerical garb to the dust
heap ; [2] and he was the first of Henry's secretaries whom
Wolsey had not found opportunity or occasion to remove
to other spheres of influence. But Wolsey was not yet
deprived of office, and as late as October Chapuys, the
new ambassador from Charles V, wrote, 'not many days
will elapse before we have a new government in this
country, and then we shall have to sail before the wind.' [3]
According to Darcy, Wolsey was trusting to divide the
nobility, make a strong party in the forthcoming parliament, and defeat his foes. Henry's cautious and secretive
mind looked before it leapt and appeared to be sudden in
action only because it kept its counsel close. He had
long relied upon Wolsey, and was not at all sure how far
he could depend on anyone else. He was determined, if
he could, to escape both from his matrimonial bonds and
from the closeness of the alliance with France in which
Wolsey had involved him. But he would not completely dispense with Wolsey until he had ascertained
that the Franco-Spanish negotiations at Cambrai implied
no danger of Francis I siding with Charles V, and until
the separate treaty between himself and Charles V [4] made
it evident that the emperor would not regard the divorce
as a *casus belli*. Released from the foreign imbroglio, he
could, and indeed, must, deal with domestic affairs without the legate's help or hindrance. He was satisfied on

---

[1] *L.P.* iv. 3835, 3340, 3918, 5018, 5798, 5819 ; Müller, *Life of
Gardiner*, 1926, pp. 28-32. Wolsey had described him to Clement VII
in Feb. 1528 as *mei dimidium*, 'my other half' (*L.P.* iv. 3912).

[2] ' Je voy que le docteur Stephen sera fort avant au manyement des
affaires, principalement s'il veult jetter le froc aux horties ' (Le Grand,
iii. 378).

[3] *Spanish Cal.* 1529-30, p. 278.

[4] Proclaimed on 27 August (Steele, *Proclamations*, vol. i. no. 117 ;
Venetian Cal. 1527-33, pp. 229, 237). 'This blessed peace,' the one is
called by du Bellay in a letter to Montmorenci (Le Grand iii. 347), and
the other by Henry VIII in conversation with Chapuys (*Spanish Cal.*
1529-30, p. 253).

both points during August and spent the rest of vacation in determining how to deal with Wolsey.

The daws were already beginning to pluck at the cardinal's plumage. Henry had given the revenues of the vacant see of Durham to Anne Boleyn's father, viscount Rochford, as from Michaelmas 1528; but Wolsey's officers had retained the money, and on 1 August Rochford ventured to demand the half-year's rents due the preceding 25 March, reckoning them at £1200.[1] William Roy had crept back to England in June;[2] in August Rowland Philips, the popular vicar of Croydon, reporting to Wolsey that the abbot of Wigmore would gladly have accepted his offer of a pension in return for his resignation, says that now he refuses, trusting to 'a great change and especially the extinction of your authority'; and on 5 September one of Cromwell's correspondents 'hears that there is a new abbot of St. Albans.'[3] Chapuys, who arrived in London in the last week of August, reported on 1 September : 'it is generally and almost publicly stated that the affairs of the cardinal are getting worse and worse every day. For some time past the king has forbidden any applications to be made to him by foreign ambassadors, those of France not excepted who have at all times found refuge in him.' Three days later he specified Suffolk, Norfolk, and Rochford as 'the king's most favourite courtiers and the nearest to his person, who transact all state business.' 'Formerly,' he continues, 'no one dared say a word against the cardinal, but now the tables are turned, and his name is in everybody's mouth ; and, what is still worse for him, libellous writings, I am told, are being circulated about him.'[4]

Henry had been at Durham Place when Campeggio broke off the hearing of the divorce on 23 July. He removed to Greenwich on the 28th and thence on 2 August to Waltham, where Cranmer made his suggestion of an appeal to the

---

[1] L.P. iv. 5816; see below, p. 311.
[2] Ibid. iv. 5667 contains a lively account of the efforts of Wolsey's emissaries to capture him and his fellow poet, Jerome Barlow.
[3] Ibid. iv. 5898, App. 237.
[4] Spanish Cal. 1529-30, pp. 189, 195.

universities of Christendom.[1] Wolsey offered to entertain the king and defray his expenses at his palace at the More ; but Henry declined, pleading fear of the plague,[2] and continued his progress by way of Hunsdon, Barnet, Tittenhanger, Windsor, Reading, and Haseley to Woodstock, where he remained from 25 August to 14 September. Gardiner had been his chief official companion during this progress, but Norfolk and Suffolk joined him on 28 August at Woodstock and More by the 31st. Tuke was there by 7 September, and there du Bellay and his brother were received in audience. They advised Francis I to acknowledge the good offices of Norfolk, Suffolk, and Rochford : Wolsey, they remarked, was at the More (where he had been for a fortnight), and 'does not seem likely to come hither.'[3] He begged for a personal interview on 10 September on the ground that he could not conveniently write what he had to say. Gardiner replied on Henry's behalf with an awkward refusal which indicates some compunction on the part of both.[4] On the 14th Chapuys had his first interview with Henry and reported that although Wolsey had ' long been asking permission to re-appear at court,' he was still ' under sentence of exile, ordered to reside three miles away from it and not to appear unless summoned.'

Campeggio at length 'though not without great difficulty'

---

[1] See my *Cranmer* (2nd ed.), pp. 38-9. Henry's movements during the summer can be traced in the treasurer of the chamber's accounts, printed, under the following year in *L.P.* v. pp. 311-17 ; from November onwards some further information can be obtained from the privy purse expenses, 1529-32, ed. Sir H. Nicolas (1827). In B.M. Lansd. MS. 1 f. 210 (*L.P.* iv. 5965) there is a list of places visited by Henry VIII during this ' progress,' but it is a later compilation, not one of the official ' king's giestes,' and needs correcting and supplementing from the dating and other evidence in the contemporary correspondence. On 1-4 Sept. Henry paid a flying visit to Langley. The dating of the letters in *L.P.* is defective ; e.g. iv. 5864, which its writer wrongly dated 4 Aug., is assigned to 24 Aug. but should be 4 Sept.

[2] *L.P.* iv. 5825.

[3] *Ibid.* iv. 5911 ; More remained till the 13th (*ibid.* 5941).

[4] *State Papers, Henry VIII*, ed. 1830, i. 343-5 ; the calendar (*L.P.* iv. 5936) has ' relieve the king from this agitation ' for ' quyet his mynde and cogitation.'

obtained leave for Wolsey to come to court; and the king consented to receive both legates at Grafton on Sunday 19 September, but only on condition that they came 'without any sort of pomp or ceremony, without their crosses preceding them as usual, or that arrogant display which the two cardinals were wont to shew in public.'[1] According to Chapuys they had 'as poor a reception as could be,' and Wolsey cannot have been encouraged by an incident which Cavendish witnessed. Discussing at dinner proposals for the approaching parliament, Wolsey remarked 'the king should do well to send his bishops and chaplains home to their cures and benefices.' 'Yea, marry!' retorted Norfolk, 'and so it were meet for you to do also.' Wolsey expressed his willingness to go to Winchester. 'Nay,' said Norfolk, 'to your benefice at York, where is your greatest honor and charge.'[2] But to Wolsey's entourage his reception appeared a triumph, refuting the reports that were circulated against him: he had, wrote the keeper of his wardrobe,[3] been repeatedly consulted by the king during the vacation; at his going to, and return from,

---

[1] *Spanish Cal.* 1529-30, pp. 214, 235, 253, 257. Erasmus had heard in September that Wolsey was in prison (*L.P.* iv. 6090).

[2] P. 152. Cavendish repeats this remark of Norfolk's on p. 197 as made to Cromwell for communication to Wolsey (see below, p. 271). The suggestion had already been made by Darcy (*L.P.* iv. p. 2555).

[3] See T. Alvord's letter to Cromwell, 23 Sept. (Ellis, *Orig. Letters*, 1, i. 307-10; *L.P.* iv. 5953). Alvord was writing from St. Albans; Campeggio makes no allusion to Wolsey in describing his interview with Henry VIII (*L.P.* iv. 5995). Cavendish naturally gives the same impression as Alvord: 'many great wagers,' he says, 'were laid,' that the king would not see the cardinal; and Henry's reception of Wolsey 'blancked his enemies very sore and made them to stirre coals.' The rumours had reached Paris (*ibid.* 5946). Some confusion has been caused by locating this interview at Greenwich: Alvord's letter (Cotton MS. Vitellius, B. xii. 173) is mutilated; Sir H. Ellis prints 'Grene . . .' and extends it in a note to 'Grenewych,' which is adopted in *L.P.*, although it had been corrected in the 1852 ed. of Cavendish, p. 157 *n.* Cavendish is confirmed by Chapuys (*Spanish Cal.* 1529-30, pp. 253, 257) and other evidence in giving Grafton in Northamptonshire, whence Henry returned (24-29 Sept.) by way of Buckingham, Notley, and Bisham to Windsor. There is no doubt of the courtesy of Henry's reception, though Suffolk, according to Chapuys, had taken care that Wolsey should find no lodging in the court, and he is confirmed by Cavendish.

the court he was treated by the nobility and gentry as usual ; the king had talked with him privately for over two hours 'till it was dark night' ; on Monday he had seen Henry again and sat with the council all the forenoon. Wolsey tried to keep up appearances even with his friend du Bellay, who stayed with him two days (Wed. to Friday, 15-17 Sept.) before the interview : 'he spoke much,' writes du Bellay on 18 September, 'of the practices of this court, not showing himself so much vexed with them as I am sure he is. I have less hope than before of his influence, from the conversation I have had with him ; for I see he trusts in some of his own *protégés* who, I am sure, have betrayed him. I should never have believed that they would have been so wicked, and the worst is that he does not understand it.' [1] For more than a fortnight du Bellay is silent ; then in a postscript to a letter of 4 October to Montmorenci he writes 'I forgot to tell you that I see clearly Wolsey is to lose his influence entirely in this parliament. I see no chance to the contrary.' [2]

The last straw which broke the back of Wolsey's fortunes may have been added to his burden at Grafton. Cavendish [3] there overheard Henry ask him 'How can that be : is not this your owne hand?' and he 'pulled a letter or writing out of his bosome and shewed the same to my lord.' The king had three months before been warned by Francis I of Wolsey's private intelligence with Campeggio and the pope ; and documentary evidence seems to have been provided by Gardiner after his arrival from Rome

[1] *L.P.* iv. 5945. Gardiner is certainly, and Brian Tuke probably among those to whom du Bellay alludes ; More may have been a third. The words, which the *L.P.* renders as *protégés*, are *aulcuns faits de sa main* (Le Grand, iii. 356). Du Bellay's following words, *lesquels, je suis seur, luy ont tourné la robe*, show that he meant persons, not things ; but 'creatures' might have seemed a more natural translation than '*protégés*.'

[2] *Ibid.* iv. 5983. 'I have stated my reasons,' continues the calendar, 'in writing to Francis.' That letter to Francis I is not in Le Grand ; and, as calendared in *L.P.* iv. 5982, it contains no reasons for Wolsey's fall. It would appear that the reasons relate, not as implied in the calendar, to Wolsey's fall, but to the negotiations over the *fleur de lys* with France.

[3] Pp. 151-2.

on 22 June.[1] But, however incriminating that document may have been, it was irrelevant to the legal proceedings which now threatened Wolsey ; and it can only have been decisive in the sense of at last determining Henry to sanction an attack which had long been in preparation and owed its momentum to a comprehensive combination of political forces. Discontent had already found expression in general complaints of taxation and unemployment, in the correspondence of catholic bishops and tirades of protestant reformers, in the verse of poets and popular ballads, and in nobles' intrigues at court, and commons' insurrections in the country.

The lawyers were less vocal in print but more deadly on parchment. In an undated letter [2] to Dr. William Claiburgh, Cromwell beseeches him 'as ever you intend to do my lord [Wolsey] pleasure or service, that ye with all diligence seek out the register of Mr. Toneys, and also all other registers with also the bulls of my lord's legacy, to the intent the same may be shewed this night to the king's attorney, for such causes as I declared unto you at my last speaking with you.'

[1] A French diplomatist at Henry's court in Thomas Cromwell's time reported that several persons had told him that Gardiner, when sent to Rome by Wolsey, had received ' a double commission, to pretend one thing and work for another, which instruction he betrayed to the king, out of which flowed hatred and mistrust between the latter and Wolsey ' (F. von Raumer, *Illustr. of History*, 1835, ii. 64).

[2] Merriman, *Life and Letters of Thomas Cromwell*, i. 326 ; *L.P.* iv. 5812. Brewer and Gairdner place it at the end of July, and Professor Merriman adopts that date. Probably it is later ; the preceding letter (iv. 5810), also undated, almost certainly belongs to 23 Oct. In it Claiburgh asks Cromwell to come to Kingston with all the books and writings of Wolsey's two colleges at Oxford and Ipswich. Wolsey had just been deprived of the great seal and sent to Esher, and was greatly alarmed at the proceedings against him in the king's bench and their probable consequences. These documents relate to the same circumstances, and are more naturally connected with the October proceedings. The correspondents concerned do not appear to have been in Surrey in July ; nor was Wolsey himself. If the letters really belong to July, the plan of campaign against Wolsey must have started the moment Campeggio broke off the hearing of the divorce. Dr. Robert Toneys and Claiburgh (or Claybroke) had been among Wolsey's most active agents. Claiburgh was protonotary of the legates' divorce court. Toneys had died in 1526 (see *Erasmi Epist.* iv. 332).

Claiburgh replied by return [1] that he had never had custody of Toneys' registers 'or any other concerning preventions,' but would do all he could to find them, and wished Cromwell to meet him at Blackfriars the following day, when he would tell him 'of the communication between the lords and others.' The references to the king's attorney and to the communications between the lords 'and others' portended legal process against the legate ; and Claiburgh's mention of 'preventions' indicate the specific ground upon which an indictment would be framed.

The lords and others were no doubt the council which Hall says the king summoned to begin at Westminster on 1 October.[2] Its proceedings were kept remarkably secret: the king remained at Windsor; and councillors met at Wolsey's lodgings on Sunday, the 3rd, to discuss French business with du Bellay. Wolsey was also present when they met again on Wednesday the 6th to receive Chapuys,[3] but that was his last recorded appearance. On 29 September Gardiner had written from Windsor to Wolsey requiring him to send to the king the parliamentary writs for Nottingham and Derby shires, which he intended to be dispatched 'by the hand and advice of the duke of Norfolk' ; Wolsey was also to send the writs for Buckingham and Bedford shires, Hampshire, and Southampton.[4] Some inkling had apparently reached the king that Wolsey might turn to parliament for support, and in the first week of August Gardiner had sent to Ralph Pexsall, clerk of the crown in chancery, for a list of parliamentary boroughs. Hearing that Pexsall was not with Wolsey, he wrote on 6 August from Hunsdon to the chancellor himself.[5] Three days later, the king's signed bill ordering Wolsey to make out writs for a general election was enrolled on the close roll.[6] There was nothing

[1] I.e. on the back of Cromwell's letter and by the bearer who had brought it, as Cromwell had requested.
[2] *Chronicle*, p. 759.
[3] *L.P.* iv. 5982 ; *Spanish Cal.* 1529-30, pp. 276-7.
[4] *L.P.* iv. 5993.   [5] *Ibid.* iv. 5831
[6] Rymer, *Fœdera*, xiv. 302-4, from close roll 21 Henry VIII, m. 10 *dorso*. The signed bill apparently was not dated ; and, curiously

abnormal in the interval between 9 August and 6 October, which was apparently required by the clerks in chancery to prepare the writs ;[1] but the removal of the writs from Wolsey's control was a clear indication that Henry intended henceforth to deal with his parliaments by other means, and that a new chancellor would preside over that which was summoned to meet on 3 November.

Henry, however, had no intention of leaving Wolsey to parliament ; the law was a more convenient method. 'At present,' writes du Bellay on 4 October, 'the king takes the management of everything himself ' ;[2] and apparently on 8 October he came secretly to London.[3] The law courts were to be open on the 9th, and Wolsey, who had been encouraged by the receipt of his own writ of summons to parliament and by his continued admission to council, 'came into Westminster hall with all his trayne the first day of the Terme : but none of the kynges seruants would go before, as they were wont to do ; and so he sat in the Chauncery, but not in the Starre chamber, for all the lords and other the kynges counsail were gone to Wynsore to the Kyng.'[4] Worse was to happen that day ; for, while the chancellor sat in chancery, the attorney-general preferred a bill of indictment for præmunire against him in the king's bench ; and Wolsey went home to write a pitiable appeal to the king

enough, is placed in the calendar under 2 Nov., nearly three months after the enrolment (*L.P.* iv. 5837 and 6042).

[1] The order for the writs of Henry's first parliament is dated 17 Oct. 1509, but parliament was not to meet until 21 Jan. 1509-10 (*L.P.* i. new ed. 205) ; that for his second, to meet on 4 Feb. 1511-12, is dated 28 Nov. 1511 (*ibid.* no. 963) ; that for his third, to meet on 5 Feb. 1514-15, is dated 23 Nov. 1514 (*ibid.* no. 3464). It is more significant that no directions for summoning the fourth parliament (1523) seem to have been enrolled, and that the word ' parliament ' does not occur in the index to that volume (iii) of the ' Letters and Papers.' Wolsey's indifference to parliaments extended to the editors of his correspondence.

[2] Le Grand, iii. 361, ' qui est celuy qui à present prent l'addresse de toutes ses affaires.'

[3] The only reference to this visit is in du Bellay's letter of 12 Oct. (*L.P.* iv. 6002), in which he says : ' The king hardly made any stay here, but returned to Windsor.'

[4] Hall pp. 759-60; Cavendish, p. 159, ' after which day he never sate more.'

for mercy 'from your most prostrate poor chaplain, T. Cardinalis Ebor. miserimus' [*sic*].[1]

He felt the blow all the more severely because of his faith in his legal immunity. He had protected even Warham from a suit in the court of common pleas lest it should appear that 'the common pleas should have superiority upon the chancellor'; and he held that chancery 'hath jurisdiction to command the law in every case.'[2] With no less consistency and fervour he had maintained the catholic principle that the Lord's anointed were not justiciable at the hands of laymen; and the subjection of a legate *a latere* of the pope to such indignity was the death-blow, not merely to his personal pride and glory, but to the whole system of church and state in which he lived and moved and had his being. He had foretold disaster himself.[3] But he had used similar diplomatic threats so often that they probably made even less impression on his own mind than they did on those to whom they were addressed; and the fulfilment of his prophecies found the prophet unprepared. There was never a fall so complete, so simple in its method, and yet so devastating in its effects.

No unseemly haste disfigured the legal proceedings.

---

[1] The letter is naturally more vivid printed *in extenso* in *State Papers*, i. 347, than calendared in *L.P.* iv. 5999. It has neither date nor place, but in the *L.P.* it is placed under 8 Oct. More probably it followed the indictment on the 9th, and did not precede Wolsey's progress 'with all his train' to Westminster hall to open the law courts. The most likely date appears to be Sunday the 10th, which Cavendish says Wolsey spent at home.

[2] *L.P.* iii. 751; Cavendish, ed. 1852, pp. 188-9. The effects of this immunity were inconvenient to others and added to Wolsey's unpopularity. Among the avalanche of creditors' claims which descended with his fall from power, the following little bill from William Botrye, mercer of London, tells its tale with the briefest clarity: for various fabrics 'from 24 May 1512 to 6 Oct. 1515. Total, £40 11s. 10d. Paid by William Bolle, 14 Aug. 1514, £2 6s. 8d. Due, 13 Oct. 1529, £38 5s. 2d.' (*L.P.* iv. 6006). The Greshams follow with much larger sums, and the total would amount to at least £50,000 in modern currency. The canonical doctrine of the 'just price,' moreover, forbade the charging of interest and called it usury.

[3] 'Che ne seguiria presta et total ruina del Regno, di sua Sign. Rev., et della reputatione ecclesiastica in questo Regno' (above, p. 176).

On the day that the indictment was presented, Henry licensed Wolsey to appoint two attorneys to represent him in lieu of a personal appearance in court. But Wolsey hesitated to avail himself of the 'privilege.'[1] To him it was not so much a privilege as the surrender of the key to his ecclesiastical fortress; for the appointment of attorneys in the king's bench involved an acknowledgement that he was responsible to that court for things he had done as papal legate; and du Bellay, who visited him during the following week, found him in woeful agitation: 'il m'a remonstré son cas en la plus mauvaise rethorique que je viz jamais, car cueur et parolle luy failloient entierement; il a bien pleuré et prié que le roy et madame [Francis I and Louise] voulsissent avoir pitié de luy.'[2] Norfolk and Suffolk were constantly passing to and fro between Windsor and London; a further bill of indictment was presented on the 20th; and at length Wolsey was offered the choice of answering either before the king's bench or parliament.

This drove him to make his great surrender to the common law. He preferred the king's bench to parliament not merely for the reason du Bellay gives, that he would sooner fall into the hands of the king than into those of the bishops,[3] but because the maximum penalty for the offences, for which he had been indicted in the king's bench, was total loss of goods and imprisonment for life, whereas an act of attainder might well involve his life. On the 22nd he

[1] Dr. Gairdner regards Wolsey's condemnation in his absence as an additional injury; but Chapuys writes: 'The sentence, it is true, was pronounced in his absence, for in this particular his enemies were quite ready to please him' (*Spanish Cal.* p. 306); and for some two years Henry's agents at Rome were pleading that the king should not be summoned to make a personal appearance before the papal curia in the divorce case. Wolsey had as little desire to exhibit in person his responsibility to a secular court as Henry had his to the court of Rome.

[2] Du Bellay to Montmorenci, 17 Oct. (Le Grand, iii. 370; *L.P.* iv. 6011). Darcy had, among other remarks of Wolsey's, reported his saying that he would appeal to 'the French king to sue for him' (*L.P* iv. p. 2549).

[3] Above, p. 215.

signed an acknowledgement[1] that, on the authority of bulls obtained by him from Rome, he had 'unlawfully vexed the greater number of the prelates of this realm and other of the king's subjects, thereby incurring the penalties of præmunire, by which also he deserved to suffer perpetual imprisonment at the king's pleasure and to forfeit all his lands, offices, and goods.' The indictments, which were found good in the king's bench, more specifically charged him with making presentations to livings belonging to other patrons, with causing the wills of persons dying in other dioceses than his own to be proved before his commissioners, with holding legatine visitations, and with surreptitiously procuring for himself by his legatine authority divers large pensions from abbots. He was formally attached and the sheriff was ordered to produce him in court on the 30th. At length on the 27th he appointed his attorneys, who appeared on the 30th and submitted on his behalf to the king's mercy.[2] His lands and goods were declared forfeit and his person placed out of the king's protection.

This condemnation of the most powerful impersonator of papal jurisdiction in England by a simple and almost routine process in the court of king's bench is so crucial an episode in the development of the English constitution that it requires closer examination. The conventional statement that Wolsey was condemned for being papal legate is

[1] *L.P.* iv. 6017. There is a copy of the proceedings against Wolsey in Westminster Abbey MSS. (*Hist. MSS. Comm.* 4th Rep. App. p. 194*b*). See also the recitation of the proceedings in Rymer, xiv. 350-2 and 402-4.

[2] The précis of the controlment roll given in *L.P.* (iv. 6035) appears to assign all these proceedings to the 30th; but Chapuys, after a letter dated the 25th, adds a postscript specifically dated the 27th, saying 'two days after the above was written the cardinal was judicially and definitively condemned.'* He adds, 'by the great council of the king,' which may be merely a foreigner's misinterpretation of the king's bench. On the other hand, constitutional development has consistently been ante-dated, in the interests of constitutional reform, by Coke and others who wished to exclude from the king's bench the king himself and every one not a professional member; and it would be rash to deny the possibility that, on this and other occasions in the sixteenth century, an expanded session of the king's bench might be made to look like the king's council.

legally so absurd that it can be dismissed in a few words. It was no offence by any law then obtaining in England to be papal legate. Every archbishop of Canterbury or York for centuries had been a papal legate—even Cranmer took the title in 1532 ; English law drew no distinction between a *legatus natus* and a legate *a latere ;* and the specific statute under which Wolsey was condemned [1] makes no mention of legates at all. It appears, indeed, impossible to condemn anyone in any English law-court for 'being' anything at all. The courts christian came nearest to that possibility in their condemnation of heretics ; but even there the heresy had to be proved by confession, by specific expressions of opinion in spoken, written, or printed words, or by specific acts of commission or omission. Loosely we speak of a man being condemned as a traitor ; but the legal charge is always a specific act of treason which has to be assigned to a specific place and date and proved by specific witness. To say that Wolsey was condemned for being a papal legate is as meaningless as to say that a policeman, condemned for taking bribes, is condemned for being a policeman.

It was not for being a legate that Wolsey was condemned, but for what he did as a legate ; and the further point of the royal licence, as commonly put, is irrelevant. A judge or a home secretary is not licensed by the king to break the law, even in the discharge of his official duties, because he is appointed by the king. Wolsey was not appointed legate by the king, but Henry undoubtedly agreed to his original appointment ; the articles of his impeachment in parliament, indeed, specifically assert that fact.[2] But that

---

[1] 16 Richard II, c. 5. Nor is the word used in the act of parliament (*Rot. Parl.* App. p. clxiv) reciting Wolsey's attainder in the king's bench.

[2] I find no evidence that Henry agreed to the amplifications of his authority which Wolsey was charged with procuring from Clement VII. The 28th article runs : ' Also, where the said lord cardinal did first sue unto your grace to have your assent to be legate *de latere*, he promised and solemnly protested before your majesty, and before the lords, both spiritual and temporal, that he would nothing do or attempt by virtue of his legacy that should be contrary to your gracious prerogative or regality, or to the damage or prejudice of the jurisdiction of any ordinary, and that by his legacy no man should be hurt or offended ; and upon that condition and no other he was admitted by your grace to be legate within this your

was no licence to commit the deeds which formed the grounds of Wolsey's indictment. He was not accused of exercising legatine powers, but of 'purchasing' bulls from Rome and illegally exercising his powers under those bulls in such a way as to usurp the legal rights of others by making presentations which did not belong to him, appropriating the testamentary and visitatorial jurisdiction of his fellow-bishops, and extorting bribes from abbots. Wolsey claimed [1] to 'have the king's licence in my coffers under his hande and broad seale for the exercising and using thereof in the most largest wise.' But assuredly it did not cover his comprehensive breaches of the common law ; and, even if it had done so, the licence was not available at law. In 1486 the judges had laid it down that the king could pardon an offence after its commission but could not license it beforehand, and that even then the pardon only extended to the offence against the king and not to its effects upon the rights of others.[2]   Still earlier, in Richard III's reign, they had declared that the king could license the importation of papal bulls so far as they affected the crown, but not if they affected other parties.[3]

Equally unsubstantial are the pleas put forward by himself and his apologists that he did not know he was breaking

realm ; which condition he hath broken, as is well known to all your subjects' (Coke, *Fourth Institute*, p. 92 ; Herbert, pp. 298-9 ; cf. Skelton, *Works*, ed. Dyce, ii. 60-1). The prevalent misconception, however, arose at once : on 17 Nov 1529 a correspondent writes, as calendared, to Cromwell, 'it is proved that my lord cardinal obtained both his legacy and cardinalship without the king's licence, and for this he is cast in a *præmunire*' (*L.P.* iv. 6058 ; see above, pp. 22-4, 55 for Wolsey's methods of obtaining the cardinalate).

[1] According to Cavendish, p. 181. To account for its non-production, a later story represents Henry as having instigated Cromwell to steal it (Richard Hall, *Life of Fisher*, E.E.T.S., extra series, cxvii. p. 76). This would have been before Cromwell entered Henry's service, and in spite of the admission of its existence by the accusing lords in parliament.

[2] Tottel, *Year-Books*, 1 Henry VII, Hilary, f. 10*b* ; 'car le pardon ou relesse le roy apres le forfaiture est bone, mes nemy deuaunt, quod nota bene.' Cf. *ibid.* Michaelmas, f. 2*b* ; my *Henry VII*, iii. 292-3.

[3] *Ibid.* 2 R. III, Michaelmas, f. 12 : 'Et similiter rex potest dare licentiam alicui ad deferendas litteras apostolicas infra regnum, ubi tantum regem tangat, sed non ubi tangat partem.'

the law, and that præmunire was an obsolete and forgotten prohibition only revived for his particular ruin. In July 1528 Henry had warned him that *in talibus ignorantia non excusat peccatum*,[1] and ignorance of the law was a poor excuse for a lord chancellor. As a matter of fact he had himself in 1514 urged Silvester de Giglis to prosecute their common enemies before the papal curia, and had told him that he was 'quite at liberty, without breach of the king's laws,' to cite Clerk (the future bishop of Bath and Wells) to appear at Rome.[2] It was not that he was ignorant of the law, but that he thought his influence with the king entitled him to dispense with the law and guaranteed him against the legal consequences : he recked as little of common law compared with his legacy as a soldier does compared with his orders. In 1518 he had kept Campeggio knocking at the gates of Calais for three months on the plea that it was not 'the rule of this realm' to admit legates *a latere*.[3] So far from præmunire being obsolete or forgotten, it had continued since its enactment an acute question of controversial politics. Convocation had complained in 1447 that the common lawyers were using it to make ecclesiastical jurisdiction impossible ; and it hung like a shadow over the career of cardinal Beaufort. Edward IV had, indeed, in 1462 granted the church a charter of liberties which seemed to exorcise the danger ;[4] but the king's bench was considering cases of præmunire in 1484,[5] and early in Henry VIII's

---

[1] Above, p. 203 *n.* 3.

[2] Tottel, *Year-Books*, i. new ed. pp. 1460-1. Three royal licences to obtain bulls from Rome, notwithstanding the act of 16 Richard II (which is recited in each case), were granted on 7 Aug. 1512, 3 Nov. 1513, and 23 Nov. 1514 (Rymer, x. iii. 340, 383, 469). I have found no others in that volume which extends from 1502 to 1523, and am unable to explain this sudden emergence and disappearance.

[3] *L.P.* ii. 4034, 4072. The king, wrote Wolsey on this occasion, was bound on oath to observe these *municipalia jura*, but they would be relaxed if Wolsey were joined in Campeggio's legacy : by this means Henry thought Campeggio would be prevented from breaking them (*ibid.* ii. 4055)

[4] See above, p. 167 and *n.* 1.

[5] Tottel, *Year-Books*, 2 Richard III, Michaelmas, ff. 17b-18b, on an appeal from the court of audience to Rome. Coke, referring apparently

reign the principle became a dominating issue in the relations of church and state.

In 1512 a bailiff of Cambridge, excommunicated by the vice-chancellor, sued for a writ of præmunire against the university, and the vice-chancellor wrote apparently with success to Sir John Fyneux, chief-justice of the king's bench, to parry the attack.[1] A year or two later Richard Hunne brought his famous suit of præmunire; and in 1515, in spite of Wolsey's own protests, all those who assisted convocation in its proceedings against Standish were declared by the judges liable to its penalties.[2] Wolsey, while objecting to its use by others, was an adept in its use himself. He fined Allen and Plummer for offences under that head and used the fines to extend the buildings of the star chamber;[3] he argued in the exchequer chamber that the use of papal bulls that were void was an offence against præmunire;[4] and he threatened Warham and Nix with its penalties.[5] Skelton made the legate's employment of that weapon one of the counts of his indictment in 'Colin Clout';[6] and the popular belief that 'Hunne was made a heretic because he sued out a præmunire,' which became an item in the controversy between Tyndale, Simon Fish, and others on one side and Sir Thomas More on the other, may have been stimulated by Wolsey's action, and may have suggested the turning of the weapon against himself. Three months before the legate's own indictment in the king's bench Darcy pointed to præmunire as the appropriate means of dealing with his offences.

to unprinted year-books, says (*Third Inst.* p. 120) that in 5 Edward IV it was held that the ecclesiastical courts in England came within the meaning of the *curia Romana* of 16 Richard II; and in Michaelmas 11 Henry VII that a suit in an ecclesiastical court for a temporal cause was a case of præmunire.

[1] Cooper, *Annals of Cambridge*, 1842, i. 294; *L.P.* i. 1526.
[2] See above, pp. 32, 48.   [3] See above, pp. 194 *n.*, 228 *n.*
[4] Keilwey, *Reports*, ff. 184*b*, 190*b*, 191*b*.
[5] See above, pp. 172, 198.
[6] *Works*, ed. Dyce, i. 315, 352. He thought:
    That the premenyre
    Is lyke to be set a fyre
    In theyr iurisdictions
    Through temporall afflictions

As in so many other respects, so in the interpretation of præmunire, Henry VIII was the pupil of Wolsey; and under their hands the doctrine achieved an elasticity worthy of the English constitution. By a quaint kind of Irish bull Scarpinello the Milanese ambassador in England in 1530 terms præmunire 'a purely English word'[1]; and half a century later Nicholas Ormanetto, who had been cardinal Pole's 'auditor' during Mary's reign and was afterwards papal nuncio to Spain, reporting to the papal secretary on the prospects of a conquest of England, writes: 'they have laws most prejudicial to the apostolical authority and the liberty of the church, and among them one called *premoneri* which is most bestial; to which laws they hold on tooth and nail, as the saying is, and I can bear good witness thereof, for there was daily to do about the matter. If these laws could be abolished when by God's grace we get the upper hand, it would be a most holy thing.'[2]

Præmunire was, indeed, a legal expression of the insularity which formed and conditioned English nationality: the statute of Richard II, under which Wolsey was condemned, emanated from the age of the morning star of the reformation and of the first glimmerings of a dawn, which ultimately revealed an Anglican church, either (or both) catholic or (and) protestant, and an English state revelling in splendid isolation and in wielding the balance of power. While Henry VIII was applying to Wolsey the doctrine of præmunire, he was also explaining to others that, friendly as he was to France, he desired liberty of action in his foreign policy. Præmunire implied a similar independence. Ecclesiastical tribunals were disliked, not so much because they were courts christian as because they were catholic and looked towards Rome: their doors opened on to a broad highway, along which the king's subjects were tempted to err and stray from the king's allegiance. The king's courts allowed

---

[1] *Milanese Cal.* p. 527. On Scarpinello see Erasmus, *Epistolae*, ed. Allen, iv. 413, and below, pp. 295-6.

[2] Ormanetto to the cardinal of Como, 19 Dec. 1575, *Cal. State Papers*, Rome, 1572-8, p. 242; *D.N.B.* s.v. 'Pole, Reginald,' p. 44b.

no such licence or leakage : the wider their jurisdiction, and the closer the watch they kept on steps that tended to roam, the broader would grow the sphere of the king's great seal, and the more English England itself. Richard II claimed to be 'entire emperor' in his realm and to have all laws locked in his breast. Henry VIII was not less imperial, and præmunire was the weapon by which he asserted his supremacy over the church. The king would have but one law to govern all his subjects by ; [1] and, if that law was not exclusively English, the jurisdiction should at least be exclusively royal.

The specific charges on which Wolsey was indicted involved a breach of the statutes both of provisors and of præmunire. Provision, commonly called at that time 'prevention' and occasionally 'anticipation,' was premature presentation by ecclesiastical (generally papal) authority to an ecclesiastical benefice before it was vacant or before the owner of the advowson exercised his legal right ; and of Wolsey's offences under this head the most vivid illustration is afforded by Johns' proceedings in North Wales.[2] But these were also infractions of præmunire, because advowsons had always been considered a form of real property and therefore a matter for the exclusive cognisance of the king's courts ; and Wolsey's 'preventions' in virtue of his legatine authority brought them under his legatine jurisdiction. He had, it was alleged, invaded the rights of lay as well as of ecclesiastical patrons and even the king's ; [3] but by an ingenious selection, possibly designed to widen the breach between the legate and his fellow-churchmen, the two instances put in the forefront were both usurpations of the rights of religious houses : he had given away the living of Stoke-next-Guildford, Surrey, the advowson of which

---

[1] See below, p. 359.
[2] See above, pp. 206-7. The attorney-general's indictment, as calendared in *L.P.* iv. 6035, is chronologically inaccurate in representing Wolsey as having procured and published bulls from Clement VII on 28 Aug. 15 Henry VIII : Adrian VI did not die until 14 Sept. Wolsey's letter acknowledging Clement VII's ' bull of legacion now granted to me ' is dated 28 Feb. [1523-4] (*State Papers*, vi. 257).
[3] *Spanish Cal.* 1529-30, p. 305, and above p. 205 *n.* 1

belonged to the prior of St. Pancras, Lewes, and that of Galby in Leicestershire which belonged to the master and brethren of the hospital of Burton Lazars in that county.[1]

There was a further point in this second case. The offence had been committed on 2 December 1523: Adrian VI had died on 14 September, and for weeks Wolsey had been pressing his own claims on the papal conclave. Clement VII was elected on 18 November, but the news did not reach Wolsey until 6 December,[2] and no bulls of the new pope arrived until 1524. On 2 December 1523 he was wittingly using the bulls of a pope whose death had made them void. Furthermore, he had on 10 November 1519 declared in the star chamber that 'cestui qui voit emprendre sur luy de mitter tiel bulle en execucion est merement deins le cas de premunire'.[3] He was then speaking of bulls which were only void *quia contra legem terrae* : the bulls, in virtue of which he acted on 2 December 1523 were doubly void by the law of the land and the law of the church ; and Wolsey by his opinion in 1519 had 'provided' his own condemnation in the court of king's bench. Possibly he thought to protect himself when he extorted from the new pope the extension of his legation *ad vitam suam* ; but no pope could bind his successor.

The other counts in the indictment were legally less serious. Singly they would have been trivial ; but, systematically repeated on Wolsey's colossal scale, they were weighty enough. More substantial than the excuse of triviality was Wolsey's plea that they proved no malice against the king. But Wolsey forgot, in his excessive royalism, that the law did not exist solely to protect the king, and that, even if his intrusions on the rights of episcopal colleagues from Warham downwards, and of patrons great and small, were entirely benevolent, the benevolence did not extend to his agents and was no justification in law. His condemnation in the king's bench

---

[1] Wolsey conferred the latter on his unpopular agent Allen.*

[2] See Wolsey's letter to Henry VIII in Burnet, ed. Pocock, vi. 15-16.

[3] Keilwey, *Reports*, f. 191b.

was the heated retort of the common law to Wolsey's trespass on its property.[1]

Henry, however, admitted the absence of malice, and tempered the common law with some grains of equity ; the penalty actually exacted fell far short of the imprisonment and total loss of goods which the law imposed. Wolsey was not imprisoned at all, but allowed to retire with no small household to Esher, a palace which he had begged from Foxe as bishop of Winchester,[2] had then acquired as Foxe's successor in that see, and now occupied by leave of the king into whose hands it had fallen by Wolsey's attainder. He had, indeed, to forgo the abbey of St. Albans, the temporalities of Winchester, and York House which Henry turned into Whitehall and habitually used during sessions of parliament.[3] But he was restored to the archbishopric of York, kept the spiritualities of Winchester with a thousand marks yearly pension, and was given by Henry, in lieu of his forfeited goods, a sum in cash and plate of over seventy thousand pounds in modern currency.[4] The king was probably astonished at his own moderation in withholding so much less than he might have withheld from what Wolsey had originally received

---

[1] Gardiner's interesting comments on the case (Foxe, vi. 43) are marred by the fact that, writing from recollection eighteen years later, he has mixed up the indictment in the king's bench with the subsequent charges in parliament.

[2] *L.P.* iii. 414. ' Use it,' wrote Foxe on 14 Aug. 1519, ' all ways, as often and as long as it shall please you, right as your own, and make it a cell to Hampton court, as the king that dead is, whose soul God pardon, made Hampton court and it cells to Richmond.' Cf. Shakespeare, *Henry VIII* Act iii. sc. ii. 232 : 'To Asher-house, my lord of Winchester's '.

[3] St. Albans was given to Robert Catton, prior of Norwich, who died two years later. There are four Cattons of Norwich in the *D.N.B.* but not Wolsey's successor at St Albans. *

[4] The actual amount was £6374 3s. 7½d. The indenture between Wolsey and the king and its enrolment on the close roll are in the P.R.O., dated 17 Feb. 21 Henry VIII. The enrolment is printed in Rymer, xiv. 371 (cf. *L.P.* iv. 6220). Fuller details of Wolsey's property are to be found in the returns of the commissioners appointed on 14 July 1530. The commissions are given in Rymer, xiv. 402-4 ; their returns are only catalogued in *L.P.* iv. 6516.

from him. But, while he took his pickings, the main object of Wolsey's indictment was not spoliation, but the destruction, once and for all, of the ecclesiastical supremacy which, in Wolsey's person and by means of papal delegation, had dominated English affairs. 'My legacy is gone,' cried Wolsey: that was the trouble, as it appeared to him. The more important fact was that papal legacy had gone altogether, and without a word of protest from Rome.

Compared with the legal revolution effected in the court of king's bench, Wolsey's consequent loss of political place and power was a minor event. It required no legal procedure, and still less any constitutional alteration, to dismiss a lord chancellor. Wolsey, indeed, was inclined to resist: he had not yet been condemned when, on Sunday 17 October, Norfolk and Suffolk appeared at York House and demanded the surrender of the great seal; and he refused to recognise a commission 'by word of mouth' and claimed[1] to hold his office for life by the king's letters patent. They debated the matter, says Cavendish, 'with many great and heinous wordes,' in which the dukes were seemingly worsted. They rode back to Windsor without the great seal, but returned the next day not only with the king's letters for Wolsey but with orders to make public his deprivation. Wolsey may also have reflected that even a patent for life would not avail against an impending conviction in the king's bench. He delivered the great seal to Dr. John Taylor, master of the rolls, who carried it on the 20th to Windsor where Henry personally affixed it to certain documents.[2] Meanwhile, on Tuesday the 19th, the two dukes came into the star chamber and announced that the king had appointed them, lest people should complain for lack of justice, to sit in the star chamber and, with the assent of the other lords, to hear and determine causes indifferently; and 'so that weke they sat in the star chamber and determined causes.'

Wolsey's successor was still in doubt. Warham had re-appeared at court and is said to have been offered again,

---

[1] According to Cavendish, p. 161; cf. Coke, *Fourth Institute*, p 87.*
[2] *L.P.* iv. 6025; Rymer, xiv. 349.

and to have declined, the office from which he had been driven by Wolsey fourteen years before.[1]   Old age would account for his refusal, but the anti-clerical mood of the court for the moment was a stronger deterrent.   In the star chamber on that Tuesday, the 19th, there sat twenty-six lay, but only four spiritual, members of council and the prior of St. John's ; and, for the first time in its history, the laymen were placed on the right hand of the chair and the churchmen on the left.[2] On Saturday the 23rd the king came up to Greenwich ; and, says Hall, 'there muche consulted with his counsaill for a mete manne to be his chauncellour, so that in no wise he were no manne of the spiritualtie.'   'I expect,' writes du Bellay on the 22nd, 'the priests will never have it [the great seal] again, and that in this parliament they will have terrible alarms.'[3]   Suffolk was suggested, but Norfolk objected to the great seal being placed 'in such high hands' : [4] the lord high treasurer thought he had suffered enough from one over-mighty colleague, and he had no wish to see the second of the 'two obstinate men,' who were said to govern

---

[1] *Spanish Cal.* 1529-30, p. 296.   Chapuys (*ibid.* p. 324) says that when the 'estates' met they 'elected at first the archbishop of Canterbury to be their speaker ; but, being a churchman, he was not agreeable to the king, who rejected him on the plea that he was too old.'   Dr. Gairdner (*D.N.B.* s.v. 'Warham') makes this statement unnecessarily obscure by assuming that 'estates' meant the house of commons.   Darcy (above, p. 92 *n.* 1) calls the chancellor 'the speaker of the high court of parliament.'   Erasmus has the same account as Chapuys (Ellis, 1, ii. 48) ; ' archiepiscopus Cantuariensis vocatus, imo revocatus, est ad cancellarii munus, quo non aliud in Anglia majus ; sed is excusavit aetatem jam imparem tanto negotio.'   Ellis oddly identifies the archbishop with Cranmer (*ibid.* p. 47).   In the same letter (not in *L.P.*) Erasmus mentions Wolsey's imprisonment of Pace and threats to Warham.

[2] B.M. *Lansd. MS.* 1, Art. 44, f. 108*b*.   The original council records for the period have disappeared, and this is only a late sixteenth-century transcript ; but it has on it a note, *concordat cum recordo*, in the hand of William Mill, clerk of the council in the star chamber when the transcript was made.   Mill's note may have been due to the unusual nature of the contents of the record.   In 1510 the spiritual lords sat on the right and the temporal on the left (Leadam, *Star Chamber*, ii. 11), and there were seven ecclesiastics, if we include the prior of St. John's, and nine temporal members.

[3] Hall, p. 760 ; Le Grand, iii. 378 ; *L.P.* iv. 6019.
[4] *Spanish Cal.* 1529-30, p. 326.

everything in 1514,[1] succeed the first. Tunstal had also been suggested in 1527, but was now ruled out as a bishop, and recourse was had at last to a layman and common lawyer : on Monday, 25 October, the great seal was delivered to Sir Thomas More, whose eminence cast no reflection on dukes, whilst his common-law training commended him to the judges and his virtues to all men except the insurgent protestants.[2] On Tuesday the 26th he publicly took the oath as lord chancellor in Westminster Hall, and on Wednesday, 3 November, he took his seat on the upper woolsack at the opening of the 'reformation' parliament.

The main idea in the lords, if not in the commons, was the reformation of Wolsey's government ; and the new chancellor, who had the first voice but, as a commoner, no vote in the upper house, began with a speech in which he likened the king to a good shepherd who had long been led astray by the greatest of his sheep, but had at length 'seen through him' and administered 'a gentle correction.'[3] The correction was too gentle for the chancellor and other lords of parliament, and, 'constrained by necessity of our fidelity and conscience,' they set to work to produce on 1 December an indictment consisting of forty-four articles. The attainder in the king's bench had been limited to

[1] See above, p. 108.

[2] Tyndale's theological controversy with More had completely blinded him to More's real position in politics. He had always disliked Wolsey's foreign policy, especially when it involved war and, above all, war against England's traditional ally. He was imperialist rather than French in his sympathies Personally the gentlest of men, he was theoretically more hostile to heresy than the politic cardinal ; and Tyndale's view of More as little better than Wolsey's jackal was simply bred of ignorant suspicion (see below, p. 264).

[3] More's uncompromising attack on Wolsey on this occasion has proved a stumbling-block to the apologists of both. Brewer ignores it in his lengthy introduction to vol. iv of the *L. and P.*; and there has been a tendency to ascribe the report in Hall to malignant imagination. But Chapuys, writing on 8 Nov. five days after its delivery, gives a substantially similar account of the speech (*Spanish Cal.* p. 324) ; even the bare official record (*Rot. Parl.* Suppl. p. cli) says More discoursed at length on the errors and abuses, their causes and occasions, for the 'reformation' of which parliament had been summoned. For Darcy's reference to the speech, see above, p. 92 *n.* 1.

Moor L'Chancelour

SIR THOMAS MORE

(*Reproduced by gracious permission of H.M. the King*)

THOMAS CRANMER

specific breaches of the law committed by Wolsey in virtue of his legatine authority. These, writes du Bellay, were 'robberies and exactions, but would not be mortal offences. They say that at Amiens he agreed to admit the duke of Ferrara into the league without the knowledge of the king, that he delivered to Francis a bond under his [the king's] hand without authority, that he made intimation of war on the emperor.... The least of these things, they say, will cost him his head.'[1] There were other charges which could not be made public in parliament or openly stated. He was said, for instance, to have sent 150,000 angelots without Henry's knowledge to John Zapolya, who under the ægis of the Turks was disputing Ferdinand's kingdom of Hungary.[2] 'His enemies,' continues du Bellay, 'insinuate that he has always had, both in peace and war, secret intelligence with Madame,[3] from whom during the war he received large presents, and that this was the reason why, when Suffolk was at Montdidier, he did not help him with money which would have enabled him to take Paris. This they talk of in a whisper, that I may not be apprised of it. As to the said presents,[4] he hopes Madame will not do him an injury if it be spoken of.' He saw 'no means of safety unless Francis and Madame will help him,' and he begged that they would intervene in his favour as 'the instrument of this perpetual amity, so renowned throughout christendom.

---

[1] *L.P.* iv. 6018.

[2] *Spanish Cal.* 1529-30, pp. 304, 329, 798; Ehses pp. 70-1, 88-9; cf. *Cam. Mod. Hist.* ii. 198, 206 *sqq.* Tyndale refers to the harm done to England by the report that ' by help of our money Ferdinand was driven out of Hungary ' (*Practice*, p. 340), though he hardly credits the story. There is, however, no doubt of Wolsey's support of Zapolya 'for all means must be used to check the tyranny of the emperor and his brother' (*L.P.* iv. Introd. pp. dclxvi-xx; App. 144; *State Papers*, i. 206).

[3] This charge, at least, was not an invention of 1529: 'many people believe,' wrote de Praet in Jan. 1524-25, 'that he has had a secret understanding with Louise throughout the war,' and that he had done other things without Henry's sanction (*Spanish Cal.* 1525-26, pp. 24, 42); and it was for such statements that Wolsey ordered his arrest on 25 Feb (*ibid.* pp. 50-1). See above, p. 138 *n.* As early as 1522 Skelton was accusing Wolsey of taking bribes from both sides (*Works*, ii. 32).

[4] The 100,000 crowns; see above, p. 149 *n.* I.

. . . This was the most reasonable of all his requests. . . . If the king and Madame think this advisable, they will have withdrawn a faithful servant from the gates of hell. But he begs above everything that this king be not informed that they have been asked to do it.'[1] He repeated this request and caution a few days later and asked Francis and Louise 'to send a gentleman hither in all diligence . . . without . . . giving the least intimation that it was at his request, otherwise it will be immediate death to him.' Du Bellay hoped they would consent, but feared to press the point, 'knowing that where affection and pity reign the judgement is apt to be biassed.'[2]

Neither affection nor pity reigned in the house of lords. The bishops, whom du Bellay—himself bishop of Bayonne —regarded as the legate's particular enemies, could have nothing to do with a capital charge ; but according to him they had chosen 'judges after their own liking for the said parliament.' Possibly he meant the triers of petitions, possibly the committee of both houses which drafted the forty-four articles. There were thirteen triers of petitions, of whom only four had been triers in Wolsey's parliament of 1523. Wolsey himself had been replaced by Warham, and the other new triers included Suffolk and Rochford and six other temporal peers : the triers of 1523 had consisted of five spiritual, three temporal, lords and two judges ; those of 1529 consisted of three spiritual, nine temporal, lords and one judge.[3] The committee on the articles consisted of the lord chancellor, twelve temporal peers, two judges and two members of the house of commons who were also officers of the king's household—Sir William Fitzwilliam, treasurer and knight of the shire for Surrey,

---

[1] Le Grand, iii. 370-5 ; L.P. iv. 6011.

[2] Ibid. iv. 6018. Du Bellay was in effect the liaison-officer between Louise of Savoy and Wolsey, who between them had forged the 'perpetual friendship' between France and England. See Gilbert Jacqueton, La politique exterieure de Louise de Savoie, 1892, and Bourilly and Vaissière, Ambassades en Angleterre de Jean du Bellay, 1905. According to Chapuys du Bellay was 'greatly vexed,' when ordered in October 1529 to abstain from communication with the cardinal (L.P. iv. p. 2683).

[3] Rot. Parl. Suppl. pp. lxxvi, cli.

and Sir Henry Guilford, controller and knight of the shire for Kent.[1]   Besides the triumvirate of Norfolk, Suffolk, and Rochford, the committee included Northumberland and Darcy who had already compiled lists of charges from which it could select;[2] and, if these judges were really to the bishops' liking, the fact illustrates somewhat strikingly the co-active force of their dislike to Wolsey.

All these diverse elements in the coalition contributed to the torrent of accusation : the forty-four articles to which it amounted were, said their subscribers, 'but a few in comparison of all his enormities, excesses, and transgressions against your grace's laws.'   The church came first, as in Magna Carta, with an article on its liberties ; but it was tinged with a Tudor bias, and the injured liberties of the church were also those of the crown : the papal legate had 'not only hurt your said prescription ' but ' also hath usurped upon all your ordinaries . . . much part of their jurisdiction.'   Later articles complained that he had slandered the whole body of the clergy by accusing them of unmentionable vice (29)[3] ; had pillaged religious houses (13, 19), vexed them with visitations (25), and robbed them of free election (24) ; had deprived bishops and archdeacons of their testamentary jurisdiction (17) and of their advowsons by preventions (18) ; had embezzled the goods of his predecessors in the sees of Lincoln,[4] York, Durham, and Winchester (30) and impeded their efforts to check the progress of heresy (43).   Then came offences against the king and state, ranging from unauthorised treaties and bonds (2, 3) and usurping equality with the king (4, 5, 8, 34) to stamping his cardinal's hat on the coinage (40) and involving the king in the risk of contagion from the cardinal's disgraceful diseases (6).

---

[1] Herbert, *Henry VIII*, p. 302.

[2] Possibly it was by the order of this committee that Palsgrave's study was searched for his charges.

[3] See above p. 181 *n.* 1 ; his accusers identified Wolsey's phrase with St. Paul's ' reprobate mind ' (Rom. i. 28).

[4] This was William Smith, co-founder of Brasenose, Oxford, whose bequests ' appear never to have come into the possession of the college. They were probably appropriated by Wolsey ' (*D.N.B.* liii. 140*b*). Cavendish had often seen them in Wolsey's house (see below p. 322 *n.*).

The council he had offended by withholding information on foreign affairs (9, 10, 12),[1] burking discussion (15), and acting without warrant from his colleagues (11). The nobles complained that, while they swore their servants to be true liegemen first to the king, the cardinal swore his to be faithful only to him (5) and sought by 'crafty and untrue tales to make dissention' between them (32). The judges averred that he examined in chancery matters already determined at common law (20), granted injunctions by writ and dispossessed men of their lands and tenements (21, 38, 42), suspended papal pardons (22), extruded farmers from their patents (23), delayed justice (16, 26), removed indictments from the law courts into chancery (31), prevented his victims in the star chamber from suing the king for pardon (37), and inflicted illegal imprisonment (41). The poorest suffered from his increase of rents and fines (14) and his illegal demands for cartage and purveyance (33, 35), while all were offended by the greed, extravagance, bribery, extortion, cruelty, iniquity, affection, and partiality, by which he had 'subverted the due course and order of your grace's laws' (27, 34, 44).

In a letter to Cromwell Wolsey answered that most of these articles were untrue, and that those which were true showed no malice or untruth to the king's person or to the good of the realm. But his only specific points are a complaint of 'the wrong information of the earl of Northumberland' and a suggestion that stamping his cardinal's hat on the coinage of the mint at York was in accordance with precedent.[2] He found a better defence in

---

[1] Articles 8 and 10 accuse Wolsey of having made ambassadors and agents coming from abroad call on him before the king and punished those who did not. Sir T. More, apologising to Erasmus for not obeying his request to call on Fisher as he returned from Flanders in Oct. 1517, remarks, 'nam hoc solenne est apud nos, a legatione redeuntem recta regem petere, nec obiter ad quemquam divertere' (*Erasmi Epist.* iii. 132).

[2] *State Papers*, i. 354; *L.P.* iv. 6204. This original is mutilated, but before mutilation a full précis was made (apparently by or for Lord Herbert) and is now among the MSS. of Jesus College, Oxford (*L.P.* iv. 6076, p. 2715). Northumberland was one of the signatories to the articles; for his personal grievances against Wolsey see *D.N.B.* s.v. 'Percy, Henry Algernon, sixth earl.'

the king who had already on 18 November taken him into
the royal protection, forfeited in the king's bench,[1] and sent
him other tokens of good-will.   Henry, writes Chapuys, had
'from the beginning determined that his case should not be
brought before parliament ; for, had it been decided against
him, he could not, in face of such a decision, have pardoned him as he intended to do, and has since done,
as I will relate hereafter.'[2]   The articles are not, in fact,
couched in the form of a bill of attainder or act of parliament ;[3] they accuse Wolsey neither of treason nor felony
and neither ask for nor authorise his execution : they
merely request that 'he be so provided for, that he
never have any power, jurisdiction, or authority hereafter to trouble, vex, and impoverish the commonwealth.'
They were presented to the king, probably on 1 December,
the day on which they were signed ; and then, Wolsey's
confession and subscription having been obtained, they
were brought down into the commons' house and read.
There was apparently no question, and there is no record,
of any assent being asked or given ; it was simply a matter
of communicating what had been done to the commons,
like 'the writing' sealed with Wolsey's seal and giving
the king his lands and goods which was also exhibited in
the house.   The story of Cromwell having inveighed
against the bill 'so discreetly, with such witty persuasions

---

[1] Rymer, xiv. 351.   [2] *Spanish Cal.* p. 448.
[3] Contrast them with the 'quaedam billa formam cujusdam actus
convictionis et attinctionis continens' against the duke of Buckingham in
1523 (*Rot. Parl.* Suppl. pp. cv-cxxi).   The original document, which Coke
says he had seen and had in his custody (*Fourth Instit.* ed. 1797, pp. 88-95),
has apparently disappeared.   The *L.P.* only prints a summary from White
Kennett who took them from Herbert.   Coke, however, transcribed the
articles '*de verbo in verbum* without omission of anything' on the ground
that they were untruly rehearsed in chronicles and had not, so far as he
knew, been printed.   Herbert also transcribed them from the original,
with a similar remark about the chronicles.   Coke's third and fourth
Institutes were not published till 1644, and Herbert's *Henry VIII* not
till 1649.   Fiddes (*Coll.* pp. 215-23) refers both to Coke and Herbert;
there are copies, the second imperfect, in B.M. Cotton MSS. Julius F.
vi. 31b-36, and Vespasian F. ix. 190-3.   There are a few verbal discrep-
ancies between Coke's and Herbert's transcripts.

and depe reasons, that the same could take no effect' rests solely upon Cavendish, whose recollection, when he wrote in 1557, of what had happened in 1529 was so confused that he gives the failure of the 'bill' in the house of commons in December as the reason for Wolsey's indictment for præmunire in the king's bench on the preceding 9 October.[1]

Whatever the precise details, there is no doubt about Henry's general attitude. He was just escaping from the domination Wolsey had exercised over his mind, but he did not want his hands to be tied by anyone else. He meant to keep himself as free as he could, not only with regard to his foreign but also his domestic policy. He would not be subject to any particular minister as he had been to Wolsey. But Norfolk was already being described as 'the most powerful man in the kingdom':[2] till Henry knew how the duke would behave in his novel eminence, and how far he was competent to fill the part of principal minister, it might be well to keep Wolsey in view as a possible alternative. Moreover, he had too much insight into the mind and politics of his country to think that he could govern it by his simple *ipse dixit*. 'Little by little,' he explained to Chapuys, 'he hoped to be able to introduce reforms and put an end to scandal';[3] but the extent of his power would depend upon the degree to which he could hold the balance between opposing parties. His Tudor fear of feudal influence had led him to give all his support to the hammer of the nobility. Wolsey had proved almost too effective, but the balance might be tilted equally far in the other direction

[1] Cavendish (p. 180) is followed by Herbert (p. 302). There is no journal of the house of lords for this session nor, of course, for the house of commons. Hall, however, was a member and gives a very full account of the debates and proceedings in the lower house : he says nothing of any debate on the 'articles' and does not mention Cromwell's name until Jan. 1531. Nor have I found any reference to the alleged incident in Cromwell's own correspondence or any other source earlier than Cavendish. Chapuys' account, which is the earliest, seems also to be the simplest, and it is confirmed by the silence of Hall.

[2] *Spanish Cal.* 1529-30, p. 416 ; cf. *ibid.* p. 369.

[3] *Ibid.* p. 350.

by his total destruction. The lords had shown their hand when they subscribed the articles ; Henry need not further weight that scale nor help parliament to depress the cardinal beyond recovery. Hence his partial restoration : he had some chances even now, and the last phase in his career was still marked with a note of interrogation.

CHAPTER VII.

THE LAST PHASE

'I BELIEVE,' writes du Bellay two days before judgement was pronounced on Wolsey in the king's bench, 'that the king will leave him with some part of his goods and treat him no worse. If that is the case, and these lords fall out, as I imagine they will, he may recover in time. . . . And if so be that he recovers, he will feel himself bound to Francis'.[1] From his refuge in Flanders a very different observer derived a somewhat similar view of the situation, though Tyndale thought that the trouble was merely a screen behind which Wolsey sheltered himself from the storm aroused by the failure of his war against Charles V and his efforts to obtain the divorce. He believed that the new chancellor was put on the woolsack merely to keep the seat warm till Wolsey returned to power, that even the reformation parliament had been summoned 'to blear men's eyes withal,' and, in short, that the whole comedy was the latest example of 'the practice of prelates.'[2]

Whether this view was derived from Tyndale's English correspondents and the English community at Antwerp or from the diplomatic correspondence of the agents of Charles V and Margaret, his regent in the Netherlands, it was a complete misapprehension. Nevertheless, Wolsey himself recovered almost at once some hope of his restoration.

---

[1] To Montmorenci 27 Oct. 1529 in Le Grand, iii. 380. Campeggio limited himself to saying that Henry 'non correrà a furia et non farà sì non consideratamente in quello come suole ne l'altre sue actioni' (Theiner, p. 588b).

[2] Tyndale, *Works* (Parker Soc.), ii. 334-8 : 'This is also nothing save a cast of his old practice . . . and he had learned also of his necromancy, this would be a jeopardous year for him.'

When the great seal was taken from him and he was required to leave York House, Sir William Gascoyne, his treasurer, remarked : 'I am sorry for your grace, for ye shall go straightway to the Tower, as I heard say ' ; and Cavendish further reports that, as he took to his barge at York stairs, the Thames was crowded with boats filled with people who 'joied very much' at that prospect. His first relief came with the knowledge that Esher and not the Tower was his destination ; and he was extravagantly overjoyed when, disembarking at Putney, he was met by Henry Norris with a message from the king that he was 'as much his favor as ever you were, and . . . you knowe well, he is able to recompense you againe, and to restore you to twise so much.' The promise was confirmed by the gift of a ring 'which ringe,' quoth he, 'the king saith you know very well.' Sir John Russell came with another ring and a similar assurance on the night of 1-2 November, after the judgement in the king's bench ; and Wolsey, addressing the servants whom he had to dismiss on All Saints' day, assured them that he had no doubt 'but that the kinge . . . will shortely restore me to my living.' [1]

The buoyancy of Wolsey's hopes did not, however, induce patience in adversity or restrain his expectations within a reasonable compass. He had never been satisfied in the days of his prosperity with the amplitude of power delegated to him by the pope or left him by the king. He was ever asking for more or taking it without the asking ; and now he put a generous interpretation on his 'living,' and read too much into the 'favour' of the king. 'It is generally believed here,' writes Chapuys, 'that the king bears no hatred to the cardinal. If there has been ill-will it has been against the wealth he has amassed and property, and not against his

[1] Cavendish, pp. 164-8, 175, 177-8. *L.P.* iv. 6024 places Wolsey's acknowledgement (undated as usual) of Russell's message under 24 Oct. and Chapuys refers on 25 Oct. to the sending of a ring (Bradford, *Corresp. of Charles V*, p. 291 ; *L.P.* iv. 2683 ; *Spanish Cal.* 1529-30, p. 304). But, if Cavendish is right, the October message must be Norris's, not Russell's, and Wolsey's acknowledgement should be dated 2 Nov.; it is clearly after the judgement in the king's bench. This Russell was afterwards first earl of Bedford.

person'; and Chapuys thought no great injury had been done him, 'especially since from the moment he began to suspect his disgrace up to the time of his fall he kept repeating that the king could not do him a greater favour than to take away and appropriate to himself everything he possessed in this world, proceeding as it did from the royal bounty.'[1] But Wolsey, as Cromwell used to remark,[2] was hated for his ' many words without deeds ' ; and, so far from expecting any resignation of his to be taken seriously, he subsequently asserted that he had only surrendered at all on the understanding that all would be restored.[3]

The 'incessant complaints and tears and sighs,' into which Chapuys says ' all his bravadoes have been turned,'[4] were, however, a genuine expression of the ignominy of having to bow to necessity and to choose between imprisonment and the surrender of exorbitant wealth and power ; and, if he felt like breaking, it was because his neck was uncommonly stiff and he was unaccustomed to bend. He gave no sign of contrition : if he had offended at all, his offences were trivial, and were not committed against anyone for whom he had any respect. He was the 'first great prelate,' he wrote to the lord chief justice, 'that ever was committed in the præmunire for using of the authority of the legate *de latere* within this realm ' ; and to Gardiner he complained that ' he did not deserve to have lost Winchester and St. Albans, having done no offence to the king.'[5] He saw nothing abnormal and nothing to repent in his unprecedented accumulation of ecclesiastical property and use of

---

[1] *Spanish Cal.* 1529-30, pp. 368, 448.

[2] *L.P.* v. 1027. Cf. Skelton (*Works*, i. 283) on Wolsey's ' largesse in words.'

[3] *State Papers*, i. 355 ; *L.P.* iv. 6181. Wolsey here asserts : ' As God is my judge, I never thought . . . at the making of my submission to depart from any of my promotions.' But two months later he was telling Cavendish, ' I had rather confesse the matter, as I did, and to live at large, like a poor vicar, than to live in prison with all the goods and honors I then had ' (Cavendish, p. 215).

[4] 'Toutes ses braveries furent changées en extremes plaintz, pleurs, et soupirs, et ce sans cesser nuyt ne jour ' (Bradford. *Corr.* p. 291 ; *L.P.* iv. p. 2683 ; *Spanish Cal.* p. 304).

[5] *L.P.* iv. 6182, 6575.

legatine power. After his fall and when his former possessions were in question, he ventured, according to Cavendish,[1] to remind the king that there was such a thing as conscience and even such places as heaven and hell ; but it needs little conscience to think of hell for other people, and Wolsey showed as yet no other sign of grace.

He professed to du Bellay in October that he cared for none of the things he had lost : ' he does not desire legateship, seal of office, or influence—is ready to give up everything, to his shirt, and go and live in a hermitage, if this king will not keep him in disfavour.'[2] But not all the king's rings and messages, not the protection he accorded in November, nor even the restoration of his archbishopric and the gift of a pension out of Winchester and great sums of money could convince him of Henry's favour. He complained that 'having now but York . . . I cannot tell how to live and keep the number of poor folks which I have,' and adjured Gardiner to remember ' how now, approaching to death, I must begin this world again.' He held that he should have not less than £4000 a year, which he thought the least on which he could live, considering his degree.[3] In January he fell ill,[4] and the king sent him no fewer than four of his physicians, with Dr. William Butts at their head,[5] and strict instructions not to return to court until he was out of danger and to accept no fees for their service

[1] Pp. 181, 189.

[2] Le Grand, iii. 371 ; *L.P.* iv. 6011 ; cf. *Spanish Cal.* p. 370.

[3] *L.P.* iv. 6204, 6224.

[4] ' Or, as some will have it, feigned illness in the hope that the king would go and see him ' (Chapuys to Charles V, 6 Feb. 1530, *Spanish Cal.* pp. 444, 449 ; *L.P.* iv. 6199 ; Bradford, p. 307). Cavendish (pp. 190-4) gives a long description of this illness without any medical information : Wolsey himself writes of ' being entered into the passion of dropsy ' (Ellis, 1, ii. 7 ; it is undated, but was written early in January, and is misplaced in *L.P.* (iv. 6224) under 17 Feb.). On 19 Jan. Agostini asks for Dr. Butts and some leeches and says ' no time must be lost ' (*ibid.* iv. 6151).

[5] The others were More's friend John Clement, Edward Wotton, and Cromer the Scot. All except Cromer became presidents of the Royal College of Physicians and are in the *D.N.B.* But Wolsey, says Cavendish, ' trusted more to Dr. Cromer than to all the rest ' because he was Cromer's patron.

which Henry himself would reward. He recovered towards the end of the month and at his own request was allowed to remove from Esher to Richmond. Butts and Chapuys agreed that the king's tokens of favour and his promised pardon had more to do with Wolsey's recovery than medical advice; but Wolsey continued to the end writing abject appeals for mercy. Nothing would demonstrate Henry's good-will but Wolsey's return to power : for the king to do without him was a merciless dispensation.

It was not so much the favour for which he craved as for its practical demonstration; he judged things by their tangible fruits. Nor did he doubt that he had recovered Henry's good-will : to Cavendish he justified his surrender in October on the ground that otherwise the king's favour 'would never have bin by me recovered.' But he thought the king was prevented from giving effect to his inclinations by the malign influence of the 'night-crow,' Anne Boleyn, and her relatives. He had so long dominated Henry's mind that he could not believe the king was acting on his own initiative; and he thought that once those earth-born clouds were dispersed, he would bask again in the royal sunshine. The favour of kings was a breath of his nostrils, and no demagogue hungered more keenly for vulgar applause than Wolsey panted for 'the holy water of the court.'[1] He had drunk so long and deeply of that dram that life seemed not worth living without it : he even urged Cromwell that 'all possible means must be used to attain the favour' of Anne Boleyn,[2] and in the misery of his deprivation and in despair of satisfaction by legitimate means he turned to others which involved him deeper in disgrace.

His first hope had been in Francis I and Louise of Savoy, and his consciousness of the peril of his appeal for

---

[1] Cf. *L.P.* iv. 6325, ' the king departed, casting a little of the holy water of the court.' It had already come to mean delusive promise, and Wolsey, after his fall, hoped that neither he nor Cromwell would be deluded by it (*ibid.* 6262; cf. 'holywater-sprinklers,' *ibid.* i. p. 1511, and *N.E.D.* s.v. ' Court-holy-water,' where the earliest instances quoted are from Golding (1583), Florio (1598), and Shakespeare (1605).

[2] *L.P.* iv. 6114.

foreign assistance is shown by his remark to du Bellay that it would be his death if it were known. The French king and his mother responded to his appeal and du Bellay's advice ; and in the first days of January sent to England, Giovanni Giacomo di Passano, now sieur de Vaux, whose reputation as a 'worker of diplomatic miracles' is frequently acknowledged by his imperial rival Chapuys.[1] But it was not to his intervention that Wolsey owed the royal pardon on which he congratulated himself as the first step in his rehabilitation.[2] France was interested less in Wolsey's personal fortunes than in his value as an ally, and that depended upon two considerations—his political influence and the policy of the English government. There was no need for Frenchmen to put themselves out for Wolsey's sake, if England was going to be friendly in any case ; they had no use for him unless he could influence English policy, and any intervention in a purely domestic question might cause resentment and would certainly be attended by risks. Chapuys opined that the French might console themselves for his continuance in retirement by saving the costly pensions he would otherwise require, and by reflecting that he was the cause of the renewal of war after the peace of Madrid and of the slaughter of Lautrec and the French nobility in Italy.[3] Chapuys also discovered as early as November that the new government 'smacked of the French school of diplomacy,' and in December du Bellay reported that he had 'never seen the king and his council in such a favourable mood.' [4] De Vaux came, not as Chapuys thought at first, to reinstate Wolsey, but to discover whether it was worth while making the attempt.

He had ample opportunity of exploring the ground. At the end of January, 'though still,' says Chapuys, 'unwell and under the hands of his physician,' Wolsey

---

[1] Above pp. 137-8 n.; Spanish Cal. 1529-30, pp. 391, 450, 514.

[2] Cavendish, pp. 214-15. Coke (Third Institute, p. 235) said that the pardon to Wolsey was one of the two ' most large and beneficiall pardons by letters patents that we have read and doe remember.'

[3] Spanish Cal. pp. 331, 384.

[4] L.P. iv. 6109, 6227 ; cf. Le Grand, iii. 383, 445.

sent that physician, Agostini, to stay with de Vaux 'four
or five days.' In spite of the consolations the French
sought in his fall, Chapuys had 'no doubt that if they
only found the means of reinstating him, they would spare
no trouble to bring him into power again. . . . Were the
affair properly conducted, the result would be greatly
to their advantage ; but if they fail in the attempt, as
seems probable, it will only serve to irritate those now in
power and at the head of affairs, whose very lives are at
stake.'[1] Agostini, however, produced little effect on the
French ambassador, and Wolsey endeavoured to persuade
de Vaux to visit him at Richmond whither he had removed
from Esher early in February. The urgency of the
cardinal's request was due to his approaching departure
for his diocese ; but, while he still begged for the continuance of 'the kind and affectionate interference' of
Francis I and Louise in his affairs, his principal object
was an appeal to their charity on the plea of his poverty.
'I found him,' writes de Vaux, 'so completely resigned,
and so armed with patience that there was hardly any need
for me to advise such a course.' He had need of greater
persuasion to extract from Wolsey quittances for three
half-years of his French pension ; for Wolsey was as
reluctant to acknowledge his receipts as he was to pay
his debts, and de Vaux had to depart with promises :
receipts for the payments for May and December 1528
were sent within a week, but that for May 1529 was still
lacking when de Vaux wrote again on 4 April.[2] To obtain

---

[1] Bradford, p. 307 ; *Spanish Cal.* pp. 448-9 ; *L.P.* iv. 6199 omits the
last phrase. Cavendish (p. 190) has almost the same wording : 'They
feared him more after his fall than they did in his prosperity, doubting
his retourne againe into authority by the kings favour ; whereby they
might rather be in danger of their lives.' Chapuys and Cavendish also
report in almost identical terms Norfolk's threat to hasten Wolsey's departure for York (*Spanish Cal.* p. 450 ; Cavendish, p. 200).

[2] Le Grand, iii. 410-16. Le Grand remarks on the second of these
two letters, which runs from 2-4 April, 'le commencement de cette
lettre semble manquer.' It appears to have been intercepted and copied
for the benefit of Charles V. At any rate, the editor of the Spanish state
papers calendars (pp. 485-7) a copy of a letter from de Vaux to Francis I,
running from 27-29 March without any comment on the anomaly of

them was probably the real cause of his visit, unless his cold comfort of resignation was intended as a polite intimation that Wolsey could not look to France for assistance in any political aspirations : when a papal nuncio arrived in England in September 1530 he found that relations between Wolsey and de Vaux were strained.

Wolsey accepted the hint and turned to the emperor. But there was an interlude during which his adversity seems to have purged, for the time at least, the material dross from his heart and mind. His illness may have helped him ; but Cavendish puts the change immediately after the final order to betake himself to his diocese. Hitherto he had clung as close as he could to the court that he might keep in touch with his foreign and other friends and perhaps by a personal interview re-establish some hold over Henry's mind ; and when Cromwell, coming from court, informed him of Henry's or the council's decision that he must 'go home to his benefice,' he replied, 'well then, Thomas, we will go to Winchester.' If he must have a cure of souls, it should not be too far removed from the possible cares of state. Cromwell referred the question to Norfolk, and Norfolk repeated his insistence on York. Still Wolsey tarried. 'Cromwell,' said Norfolk, 'methinketh that the cardinall thy master maketh no haste to goe north-warde. Tell him if he goe not away but shall tarry, I shall teare him with my teethe. Therefore I would advise him to prepare himselfe away as shortly as he can, or else he shall be sent forwarde.'[1] Norfolk had asked Russell 'whether he did not think Wolsey still cherished the hope of returning to power,' and Russell had replied, 'that the cardinal's courage and ambition were such that he would never draw back were there a chance of re-entering office, and that this chance might present itself should the king require his counsel and assistance in any matter which he had formerly been in the habit of transacting.'

such a dispatch appearing in the correspondence of Charles V. Owing to Napoleon's depredations there are many Simancas MSS. at Paris ; there are believed to be very few Paris MSS. at Simancas.

[1] See above, p. 238 ; Cavendish, pp. 197, 200, and *Spanish Cal.* pp. 449-50.

Chapuys reports on 16 March the same impression, gathered from Agostini who had come to see him about the payment of Wolsey's Spanish pensions ; but the cardinal was now convinced that he must relinquish the advantages of proximity to the court and turn his attention to his spiritual duties in the north. Lent had begun on 2 March, and Wolsey had removed about that time from the Lodge to rooms in the Charterhouse at Richmond, which Colet had built and where he had died.[1] Possibly the association recalled the sermon the dean had preached nearly fifteen years before, and Wolsey at length remembered that he who abased himself should be exalted.[2] He resorted, says Cavendish, 'every day to the Charterhouse there, and in the afternoones he would sit in contemplation with one of the most auncient fathers of that house in their celles, who converted him and caused him to despise the vaine glory of the world, and gave him shirtes of hair to weare, the which he ware diverse times after. And thus he continued for the time of his abode there in godly contemplation.'[3] The poet has perpetuated these emotions of the moment :

> Never so truly happy, my good Cromwell.
> I know myself now : and I feel within me
> A peace above all earthly dignities
> A still and quiet conscience.   The king has cur'd me
> .   .   .   .   .   .   Farewell
> The hopes of court ! my hopes in heaven do dwell.

And 'such an honest chronicler as Griffith ' says :

> His overthrow heaped happiness upon him ;
> For then, and not till then, he felt himself,
> And found the blessedness of being little.

That is the legend of piety and romance. The cardinal was, indeed, at last *curatus :* the cure of other souls might

---

[1] Cavendish, pp. 204-5 ; *L.P.* iv. 6249 (misplaced under March ; nos. 6261-2, both dated from Esher, are also misplaced under March).

[2] See above, p. 57.

[3] P. 206. Cavendish (p. 181) represents Wolsey as having already in the autumn told the judges he repented of having been ' alwaies contented and glad to please the king before God, whom I ought most chiefely to have obeied.'

well have cured his own ; and conversion was a seemly
prelude to that going up to York to suffer exile which the
consummate actor began in his master's Passion week.[1]
But his ruling passion, strong in death, was of another
order ; and his other preparations were less appropriate to
the simple life of godly contemplation.   He sent Cromwell
to court to tell Norfolk he 'would most gladly go north-
ward, but for lack of money, wherein he desired his help
to the king.'   The council debated how much he should
have, and eventually advanced him a thousand marks out of
his pension from the bishopric of Winchester.[2]   Henry was
more generous, sent for Cromwell, and added £1000 out
of his privy purse, with a message to Wolsey to be of good
cheer and an assurance that he should not lack, which
messages and money Cromwell delivered to him at Richmond.   Having dipped into Henry's purse, Wolsey explored
those of Francis I and Charles V ; Agostini applied to
Chapuys for the cardinal's pensions from Spain and Wolsey
in person to de Vaux for those out of France.   Private
sources were also tapped : Sir W. Paulet and the master of
the Savoy each lent him £100, and prebendary Kellet of York
a hundred marks, while Robert Browne of Newark lent him
£124.   These are mere notes of sums borrowed after his
fall and unpaid at his death : the total claims of his creditors
came to £4265, between £50,000 and £60,000 in its
modern equivalent.[3]   Some of this debt may have been
incurred before his fall : he had concealed its extent in
order to make a fair show at the moment ; and, as Gardiner

---

[1] Passion Sunday in 1530 fell on 3 April. Cf. Cavendish's very scriptural account of Wolsey's dinner on 1 Nov. 1530, his betrayal by Agostini,
and Wolsey's interpretation thereof (pp 234-7)

[2] It was paid on 18 March (treasurer's accounts in *L.P.* v. p. 318).
Cavendish, p. 197, says : 'The lordes who were not his friends, per-
ceiving that my lorde was disposed to plant himselfe so nighe the kinge,
thought then to withdrawe his appetite from Winchester, and then moved
the king to give my lord a pension of four thousand markes out of Winchester.' But the indenture, printed in Rymer, xiv. 371 (two other copies
in *L.P.* iv. 6220) only mentions an annual pension of 1000 marks, apart
from York and the gift of £6374. It is dated 17 Feb. *

[3] *L.P.* iv. 6748 [15]. See below, pp. 320-5, for the details of Wolsey's
income and its relative value.

bluntly said, if he was in financial straits, it was his own fault, for the king, in taking over Wolsey's original debts as well as his assets, had had to pay eight times as much to creditors as Wolsey had allowed.[1] The £1000 and the thousand marks he received in March were inadequate to clear him, and Wolsey instructed Stubbs that no one was to be paid except his household servants.[2]

With what remained, with what he could beg, and with what he obtained on credit, Wolsey set to work to provide for the train of a hundred and sixty horse who rode north with him, the three hundred workmen he took to repair his neglected and dilapidated residences in the diocese, and the convoy of ships which carried most of his goods by sea.[3] Cavendish was dispatched to London to procure fresh liveries for his reviving household; hangings of arras and masses of plate were obtained from city merchants;[4] and the king was approached for letters under the privy seal recommending Wolsey to the consideration and hospitality of lords and others on his route to his diocese, to which he was entitled as a cardinal and archbishop. With his usual complaisance towards Wolsey Henry allowed him and his friends to draft and correct these letters themselves;[5] they did not lack in the warmth of their recommendations, and in one at least Wolsey was described as 'our right trusty and right entirely welbeloued.' 'The king,' wrote Wolsey a little later, 'has advertised Nor-

---

[1] L.P. iv. 6204, 6545.

[2] Ibid. iv. 6390; for Stubbs see above, pp. 199 n., 202.

[3] Ibid. iv. 6343-4   In one letter (iv. 6182) he complained that York had decayed by 800 marks a year, in another (6224) he puts it at £800.

[4] Ibid. iv. 6748 [15].

[5] Ibid. iv. 6294. One draft in the P.R.O. is corrected by Wolsey and another by Cromwell, while there is a clean copy in the hand of Brian Tuke; this was to the abbot of Peterborough. Other privy seals were sent to the earls of Northumberland and Westmorland and the dean of York, while a special letter was addressed to lord Dacre, warden of the West Marches, bespeaking for Wolsey 'the loving and favourable assistance of the noblemen and others in those parts' (Ellis, III, ii. 172-3; cf. L.P. iv. 6076 6295, 6345; the last should be placed in Sept. not in April).

thumberland, Sir Robert Constable, and others that he will not be dissatisfied with those who show me favour and treat me as my dignity requires and assist me in all my causes.' Other letters written in Wolsey's own name or by his instructions were somewhat more exigent and were less well received. Owing to the disrepair of his own palace at Southwell, Wolsey wanted to borrow the house of arch-deacon Magnus at Sibthorpe; but Magnus pleaded that he was bound, by the new act requiring residence, to put in some time at his own benefice; and in spite of the recommenda-tions to the abbot of Peterborough, Wolsey was soon complaining to Gardiner of the charges he had there to sustain.[1] A guest, encumbered with a hundred and sixty retainers and a debt amounting to thousands of pounds, might well strain the charity and the resources of even the abbot of Peterborough. Wolsey was glad to remove to Sir William Fitzwilliam's neighbouring house at Milton manor, where 'he was joiously received and had worthy and honorable entertainement at the onely costes and charge of the said Mr. Fitzwilliam all the time of my lord his being there with him.'[2]

He had started from Richmond on Tuesday 5 April and proceeded by way of Hendon, Rye House, Royston, and Huntingdon, spending a night at each, to Peterborough where he remained from the 9th over Holy week and Easter (17 April) until the 21st. On Maundy Thursday

---

[1] *L.P.* iv. 6299.

[2] Cavendish, p. 212. This Sir William Fitzwilliam 'senior' must be distinguished from Sir William Fitzwilliam 'junior' who afterwards became earl of Southampton. Both were knights in 1526 and both were of Henry VIII's 'counsel' (*Lansd. MS.* 160 f. 311*b*). The elder was treasurer of Wolsey's household, the younger of Henry VIII's. Both are noticed in the *D.N.B.* which does not, however, give Cavendish's reasons for the elder's friendship with Wolsey, viz. that Fitzwilliam was 'main-tained' by Wolsey in his quarrel with the city of London, 'against whose malice my lord bare him much'—in spite of Wolsey's severity against 'bearing' by others (see above, p. 75): the fine imposed upon him by the city was remitted and his franchise restored by a star chamber decree on 10 July 1511. Viscount Milton is still the second title of his descendant, earl Fitzwilliam (see G. E. C.'s *Complete Peerage*, new ed. v. 520 *n.* (*a*)).

he washed the feet of fifty-nine [1] poor men and bestowed on each a royal largesse of 'twelve pence in money, three ells of good canvass to make them shirtes, a paire of new shoes, a cast of red herrings, and three white herrings. . . . Upon Easter day he rose to the resurrection, and that day he went in procession in his cardinalls vesture, haveing his hat on his heade, and sang the high masse there himself solemnely. After his masse he gave his benediction to all the hearers with cleane remission.' On Good Friday, however, he was not too busy with his devotions to write a letter to the captain of his convoy complaining of the ships' delay at Wivenhoe and inferring that the crews were spending their Easter at home with their wives and children instead of conveying Wolsey's goods to Hull.[2] After spending four days with Fitzwilliam at Milton manor, he proceeded on Monday the 25th to Stamford, 'where he lay all night at the signe of the bull'; on Tuesday night he stayed with Francis Hall of Grantham [3] and journeyed on

[1] Cavendish, p. 210. The number was supposed to denote the age of the person officiating, and this would place Wolsey's birth in 1470-1. Cavendish is now supposed to have been mistaken and Wolsey to have been four years younger (D.N.B.). At Henry VIII's Maundy, however, in 1512 (8 April; L.P. ii. p. 1455) there were twenty-two beneficiaries, and on 28 March 1532 (L.P. v. 863) there were forty-two, though Henry, having been born on 28 June 1491, was only twenty years and nine months old on the former, and forty on the latter occasion. Similarly on 8 April 1531 there were forty-one beneficiaries and each received 41d. (ibid. v. p. 325). * The number taken for Maundy purposes seems to have been the number of years, incomplete as well as complete, in which the benefactor had lived. Wolsey's number of fifty-nine is therefore not incompatible with his having been born as late as 24 March 1472[-73]. He would thus, in April 1530, have lived in fifty-nine years, although he was only fifty-seven years and eleven months old. Giustiniani, reporting to the Venetian senate on 9 Oct. 1519, says Wolsey was 'about 46 years old,' which gives the same result. * The abbot of Winchcombe's letter of 26 Aug. 1514 (L.P. i. 3925), on which the D.N.B. relies for Wolsey's birth in 1474-5 because it congratulates him on becoming archbishop before he was forty, must be discounted by its flattering implication that archbishops at forty were as rare as bishops, created at sixty or seventy, were common.

[2] L.P. iv. 6343.

[3] Grandfather of the ' first translator of Homer into English,' see H. G. Wright's Arthur Hall of Grantham, 1919, which does not, however, mention this incident in Francis Hall's career.

Wednesday to Newark castle where he lodged till Thursday afternoon the 28th. He then rode the short four miles into Southwell and, in doing so, entered for the first time the province, of which he had been metropolitan since August 1514.

He wrote a painful letter to Henry VIII to signalise his arrival. The misappropriated proceeds of his predecessor's will, which Pace had hoped would go at least to repairing the dilapidations of his see, had with other gains been spent on other palaces—at Hampton court, the More, Tyttenhanger, and York Place; and the money which Wolsey had borrowed to repair his palace at Southwell had not yet achieved its purpose. 'He was compelled,' says Cavendish, 'to lie in a prebendaries house, over against the bishoppes place, and there kept house untill Whitson-tyde.' 'According to your pleasure,' wrote Wolsey to Henry,[1] 'I have come into my diocese unfurnished, to my extreme heaviness, of everything that I and my poor folks should be entertained with . . . I have neither corn nor cattle, ne any other thing to keep household with, nor know where to borrow anything in these parts towards the provision of the same. My houses be, by the oversight, despoil, and evil behaviour of such as I did trust, in such ruin and decay, as well in the roofs and floors as in all other implements of household that a great parti of the portion assigned unto me to live with for one year will scantily, in a very base and mean fashion, repair and make the same mete to be inhabited.' His creditors are impor-tunate and he cannot satisfy them. His baggage, which he sent by sea, has not arrived. He is 'wrapped in misery and need on every side; not knowing where to be succoured or relieved, but only at your highness' most merciful and charitable hands . . . beseeching your royal majesty graciously and benignly to consider the premises, and to have pity and compassion on your poor cardinal, who is and ever shall be, his life during, your faithful and most obedient creature, daily beadsman, and slave.'

The thousand marks from Winchester were, he wrote,

[1] *L.P.* iv. 6344.

'clearly gone and spent';[1] he had added 'with all that I could borrow besides,' but thought it better to strike that passage out, either because he did not wish Henry to know the fact or because it was not true. For no sooner was he installed in his palace at Southwell (4 June) than, says Cavendish, 'he kept there a noble house, where was bothe plenty of meate and drinke for all comers, and also muche almes given at the gate to the poore of the town and country. He used much charity and clemency among his tenants, and other of the king's subjects . . . for now he was very much familiar among all persons, who then accustomably kept him company, and glad at any time when he might doe them any goode. He made many agreements and concordes between gentleman and gentleman, and betweene some gentlemen and their wives, and other meane persons, the which had been long before asunder in great trouble ; making for every of them, as occasion did serve, great assemblies and feastes, not sparing his purse where he might make a peace and amity ; which gat him much love and friendshippe in the contry.'

Wolsey was an accomplished and inveterate courtier ; and, if he might not court the king, he would court his people. But the money, with which Wolsey was retaining a host of followers, restoring his palaces, and purchasing his new popularity, had been given by the king, borrowed from his subjects, or withheld from creditors, who for these and other reasons regarded his conduct with resentment and suspicion. Having fulfilled the letter of his instructions by getting within the verge of his diocese, Wolsey showed no inclination to probe any further into his province or remove to greater distance than he need from London ; and he remained at Southwell until the end of August keeping in

---

[1] The £1000 he had received from Henry had not apparently come into Wolsey's hands, but had been entrusted to Laurence Stubbs with strict orders to use it only in paying Wolsey's clamorous creditors. Even so, Stubbs 'was unable to pay James Nedam in full, but the king examined him [Stubbs] as to whether he had spent the whole £1000, and, finding that it was so, paid Nedam the remainder of his debt' (Stubbs to Wolsey, 17 May 1530, *L.P.* iv. 6390). Wolsey had made Stubbs promise him the non-existent balance.

constant touch with friends at court and abroad, wading deeper and deeper into the treacherous stream of political opposition and intrigue, and paying no heed to the warnings he received of the peril of his course. It was hoped that he would at least strive to follow the example of Warham and Foxe, both of whom, after official careers more extended than Wolsey's, had on their retirement from secular office done their best to atone for their long neglect of their spiritual duties. But Wolsey's correspondence yields not a trace of interest in anyone's spiritual welfare, not even his own until death looked him in the face. When his friend Giberti retired from the papal curia to his bishopric at Verona, Wolsey had reproved his 'untimely eagerness for a quiet life.'[1] He had peace sometimes in mind but never at heart : the old Adam survived his fall ; he clung to the gates of the paradise he had lost and cherished the mirage of redemption by means of the cunning which had betrayed him.

Foolish friends encouraged his lingering and backward glances. 'Heard you,' he inquired of Cavendish after his visit to London to purchase the new liveries for his master's servants, 'no communication of me? I pray you tell me.' And Cavendish told him of some who 'lamented your decay and fall very sore, doubting much the sequell not to be good for the commonwealth. And also they mervailed much that you, being of such excellent witt and of such high discretion, would so simply confesse yourselfe guilty unto the king, as you did.'[2] Three weeks later, on 12 May, William Tresham reported to him the saying from London that 'peradventure in time to come, the king would call your grace near unto him.' On the 29th another clerical sympathiser wrote to Bonner, then one of Wolsey's chaplains, 'my lord cardinal is communed of, and among lords of the council specially. They fear that they shall of

---

[1] *L.P.* iv. 3906 ; see three articles in *Engl. Hist. Rev.* 1903, pp. 24, 266, 439. Wolsey's motive in laying himself out to reconcile enemies and make friends in the north was not more spiritual than his vigorous administration of justice in chancery and the star chamber.

[2] Cavendish, p. 214.

necessity be compelled to call for my lord cardinal's grace again. God continue their minds in that behalf.'[1] Chapuys' comments are more detached. 'The cardinal,' he wrote on 16 March,[2] 'has not yet gone to York; probably he does not wish to remove so far from the court, as he would then have less facility for watching his opportunity and returning to it, the hope of which he has not yet relinquished, as I gather from his physician, who came the other day to speak to me.' 'The Duke of Norfolk tells me,' he remarks in the same dispatch to Charles V, 'that he himself obtained the cardinal's pardon and that he hopes to be able to prevent his coming again into favour, lest he should, as formerly, try to sow discord between the king his master and your majesty.'

Chapuys had already expressed the opinion that Norfolk's life would be endangered by Wolsey's restoration; and that fear was more lively than Norfolk's anxiety for the friendly relations between Henry and the emperor. But others, less vitally interested, discerned only portents of evil in the news which came of the cardinal's conduct. 'It has been reported in the court,' writes the vice-chamberlain, Sir John Gage, to Cromwell on 13 April,[3] 'that he rode in such sumptuous fashion that some men thought he was of as good courage as in times past, and that there was no impediment but lack of authority. Certain people came to him, some for debt, and some for things wrongfully taken by him; to which he answered that the king had all his goods, and he could neither pay nor restore. Thinks it would be wisdom for him to have himself in good await what words pass him.' 'Would to God,' exclaimed another counsellor, Heneage, who had been in Wolsey's service,[4] 'that your grace would content yourself with that you have, and there is no doubt but that the king will be good and gracious to your grace'; and a former secretary of the cardinal's, Peter Vannes, writing on 1 July,[5] 'adds a little news as to public affairs, not from any desire to turn his mind to these things from his present devotions,' and 'hopes that Wolsey will persevere

[1] *L.P.* iv. 6377, 6411.   [2] *Spanish Cal.* p. 476.
[3] *L.P.* iv. 6335.   [4] *Ibid.* iv. 6447.   [5] *Ibid.* iv. 6496.

in his present mode of life, and not be agitated by public events, as this is the only means left him of mollifying the temper of the king and the nobles and preserving their affections.' 'You are much bound to God,' writes Cromwell on 18 August,[1] 'that you have obtained the good wishes of the people in those parts, and the report of it here has augmented the good opinion of many towards you ; yet, notwithstanding, your charitable demeanour is misinterpreted here by your enemies. Yet follow all such things that shall stand best with the pleasure of God and the king. Some allege you keep too great a house and are continually building. I beseech you, as I have often done before, to consider the times and refrain from all building more than necessity requires. . . . I think you happy that you are now at liberty to serve God and banish all vain desires of the world which bring men nothing but trouble and anxiety. Wherefore in my opinion, your grace being as you are, I suppose you would not be as you were, to win a hundred times as much as ever you were possessed of.'

These counsels, critical, ironical, and friendly, produced no effect ; and on 17 October Thomas Arundel, who had been sent by Wolsey to press various suits at court, reported in more ominous terms.[2] He had declared to Norfolk all Wolsey's 'good fashions and manner of living,' and 'tried to persuade him how little you aspired to any authority ' ; but the duke could refrain no longer and said no man should make him believe that, and that, 'though I list to be blinded, I should blind no man here ; for, he said, he had both your grace's hand to the contrary and knew three messages sent by three divers persons of your grace to the king,[3] whereby it might well appear that ye desired as much authority as ever ye did.' Nevertheless, although Wolsey's restitution 'is

---

[1] Ellis, III, ii. 181-8 ; Merriman, *Life and Letters of Thomas Cromwell,* i. 331-4 ; *State Papers,* i. 365 ; *L.P.* iv. 6571.

[2] *Ibid.* iv. 6688.

[3] Chapuys reports Norfolk as making a similar statement in July (*Spanish Cal.* p. 630).

considered not available by law,' Arundel opined that Wolsey need not fear the king or any other 'as concerning the estate that ye be now in.'

Chapuys was better acquainted with Wolsey's ideas of that 'estate' in October 1530 than Arundel or even Norfolk. One of the aspects of the cardinal's conversion was his change of mind with regard to that great *opus manuum vestrarum*,[1] the perpetual amity with France ; and that in turn affected another design with which he had been principally associated, the divorce of Catherine. It is not impossible that conscience may have led him to regret the part he had played therein, and even convinced him of the truth of the story he told on his death-bed of his having from the first begged Henry, on his knees and with tears in his eyes, to refrain from moving in that matter. But the divorce of the emperor's aunt had been the cornerstone of his 'perpetual amity' with France ; and assuredly his faith in that foundation did not break down until the superstructure failed him as a refuge and support. He had in his trouble turned instinctively first in that direction, and appealed to Francis I and his mother to protect him. He may have had doubts of their zeal, and in any case he invoked other assistance. During the winter of 1529-30 envoys came to London to plead his cause from duke George of Saxony and from the German elector and primate, Albrecht, whom Luther called 'the devil of Mainz' and Wolsey had selected in 1527 as his sub-delegate for Germany in case he were himself made vicar-general of the catholic church.[2] Now Albrecht, although he contemplated taking a wife and secularising his ecclesiastical fief—like his cousin and namesake, the grand master of the Teutonic order—did not believe in divorce ; and duke George wrote in a similar sense to Henry VIII.[3] Probably their views had less effect on Wolsey than his declining faith in the French

---

[1] Gardiner to Wolsey, *L.P.* iv. 5918.

[2] See above, p. 154 *n.* 4; *Spanish Cal.* 1527-29, p. 437 ; for George and the two Albrechts, see *Cam. Mod. Hist.* ii. 121, 163, 169-70, 195, 211, 238, 251 (the index is defective) ; and the *Algemeine Deutsche Biographie*.

[3] *L.P.* iv. 6519; for other German negotiations in London in 1529-30, see *Spanish Cal.* pp. 444, 451-3, 468.

court and his knowledge that the only adequate compensation for the loss of French support was to secure the favour of Charles V.

To Charles he slowly turned, but the curve in his course was sharp. For the sake of his perpetual amity with France he had made himself Charles V's peculiar enemy ; and the emperor had advertised the fact in the singular manifesto which he published to the world in 1528. If there was to be reconciliation, followed by assistance from that quarter, it could only come by way of the emperor's aunt and a change of mind about Catherine's divorce. She had naturally regarded Wolsey as her principal enemy and had on the ground of his partiality repudiated the jurisdiction of his and Campeggio's legatine court. Wolsey, on his part, had long regarded her as an obstacle to his policy, and significance has even been attached to the coincidence between Wolsey's rise to power, the alliance with France, and the first suggestion of a divorce in 1514.[1] But Wolsey's loss of favour, coupled with Henry's persistence in the divorce, modified her attitude. By September 1529 she had come to believe that the case 'originated entirely' in her husband's 'iniquity and malice,' and in December she 'had shown some pity for the cardinal's fall.'[2] They

---

[1] See above, p. 19 *n.* 2; and Mr. Brodie's preface to the new ed. of vol. i. of the *L. and P.* p. xxi. Among his various superstitions, Wolsey believed that his fall would come through a woman (* R. Hall's *Fisher*, p. 51) ; cf. his curious discourse to Cavendish (pp. 202-4) on the figure of a 'dun cow' in Richmond Park and on the couplet :—

> When the cow rideth the bull,
> Then, priest, beware thy skull.

That his relations with Catherine were not very friendly is indicated by Pace's letter of 12 April 1518 (*L.P.* ii. 4074), when she was expecting her last and most critical confinement, 'praying God heartily it may be a prince, to the surety and universal comfort of the realm,' and begging Wolsey to 'write a kind letter to the queen.' One of the priests whom Wolsey had fined for breach of præmunire in the previous year was Catherine's chaplain, and she was always the chief support of the pro-Spanish party at court (see above, pp. 105 *n.* 2; 222 *n.* 3 ; and Le Glay, *Negociations*, i. 513, where Wolsey couples her with Charles V and Margaret of Savoy as opponents of his French policy).

[2] *Spanish Cal.* pp. 236, 368

had found a common and virulent enemy in Anne Boleyn
and a common object to pursue in her removal from court.
Wolsey was not slow to reciprocate Catherine's feelings,
and his natural enmity to his supplanters was no less naturally reinforced by his dislike of the parliamentary measures
against the church which he had all along foreseen and endeavoured to forestall. So soon as occasion served, he
began to give the queen the benefit of his private advice;
his chaplain, Bonner, became one of her secret counsel,[1]
and means were found of establishing communications with
Chapuys.

The imperial ambassador had need, however, to tread
warily. His master had, since his victory at Pavia, gone
on from strength to strength, but he was now faced with the
greatest of his herculean labours. In the same year, 1529,
the Turks first laid siege to Vienna and the Lutheran
'protest' of Speyer cleft in twain the catholic church.
Wolsey was a very diminutive object to Charles V when, for
the last time, a Holy Roman emperor received the imperial
crown from a pope, and then made his way up from
Bologna through Alpine passes to deal with problems presented by Solyman the Magnificent and Martin Luther.
The cardinal's fall was a feather in Charles' cap and seemed
to afford an additional security against fresh disturbance
from Francis I. Even the divorce was a minor question.
Charles was obliged for decency's sake to do what he
could for his aunt, and he made more serious efforts
to safeguard her daughter's place in the succession; but
'though,' as he said, he was 'bound to the queen, this
was a private matter, and public considerations must be
taken into account.'[2] Nor could Wolsey look for much
support at home. Fisher was the rock of the English
opposition to the divorce; but there is not a trace of
co-operation between him and Wolsey, and the enmity

---

[1] On 30 Jan. 1532 Chapuys, informing Charles V of Bonner's dispatch
on a mission to Clement VII, says he was 'formerly one of the queen's
council [? = counsel], but has since been suborned' (L.P. v. 762; cf.
Gairdner in D.N.B., s.v. 'Bonner').

[2] See my Henry VIII, p. 310, and references there given.

between them is reflected in catholic tradition.[1] There was as little understanding with the new opposition growing in More and Darcy and the catholic bishops who felt in their turn the weight of præmunire. Wolsey was plough-ing a lonely furrow and seeking a purely personal restora-tion : his egotism was as devastating to comradeship in opposition as it had been when he sat above all but the king in the seats of the mighty. Only disaster could therefore attend his back-broken efforts to creep into power once more by seeking the favour of those who had ample cause to distrust him.

It was probably from him that Chapuys received on 28 December 1529, by well-concealed and circuitous means, a warning that Henry and Francis were scheming to assist the Lutheran princes : the information came from some one who 'feigned to be unwell' and sent for the queen's physician ; but she thought it important enough to dictate in Spanish and communicate to the ambassador in order that he might send it in cipher to Charles.[2] But it was not until March 1530 that Wolsey, convinced that nothing could come of de Vaux's mission from France, sent Agostini direct to Chapuys, ostensibly to beg for the continuance of his pensions from Spain.[3] These, like those from France, had been grounded on political services and ceased when friendly relations were interrupted ; and the only meaning this application could have was that Wolsey was prepared to prefer the imperial service to that of France. Definite assurance was forthcoming in April : 'he has sent,' writes Chapuys to the emperor on the 23rd, 'his physician to me on three different occasions to vindicate his past conduct and to offer his services to your majesty, declaring that . . . knowing so thoroughly as he does the nature of men and the condition of things in this country, he thought his advice might be of use. He begged me to intercede that he might be restored to your majesty's favour and grace.' Chapuys promised to write but suggested that Wolsey should give

[1] See especially Richard Hall's *Life of Fisher* (E.E.T.S., extra series, no. cxvii), pp. 34-6, 45-51, 58-9.
[2] *Spanish Cal.* pp. 392, 419.   [3] *Ibid.* p. 476.

some proof 'whenever the opportunity offers' of the
genuineness of his professions. 'It can do no harm,' he
continues, 'to temporise with him for a while and see how
he behaves and what he will say or do, which can easily be
done without his enemies getting wind of it. He has still
great hope of being taken into favour again. It was
thought here at one time that he would have been murdered by the people of his diocese, and that in spite of his
great reputation he was quite afraid of going thither; but
it appears on the contrary that he was very well received
at York. He is not at all sorry for Wiltshire's failure.'[1]

Wolsey's satisfaction at the failure of Henry VIII's
embassy to Charles V and the pope at Bologna[2] indicated
his desire to satisfy the emperor; and Agostini's information about his reception 'at York' was designed to show
that he still possessed some influence and value. Most
of the documentary evidence of Wolsey's new-found popularity emanates from Wolsey himself, though he undoubtedly exploited Henry's letters of recommendation with
some success; but in point of fact, when Chapuys wrote,
Wolsey was still enjoying the hospitable shelter of Fitzwilliam's house in Northamptonshire and he never got to
York at all. Chapuys' dispatches from 10 May to the
middle of June are unfortunately missing, but on the 15th
of the latter month he quotes a letter[3] from Agostini in
which the cardinal's physician somewhat obscurely indicates
that 'his master not knowing exactly the state *of the queen's
affairs, cannot give any special advice upon them;*[4] that if
he could get fuller information he would give counsel and
directions as though paradise were to be gained through it,
for his happiness, honour, and repose depended on that, and
that it seemed to him that now was the time *to take stronger
measures and call in the assistance of the secular arm.'*
Chapuys approved, and suggested to Charles that the best
means to hasten matters 'would be the removal' of Anne
Boleyn from the court, '*in which opinion the cardinal also*

[1] *Spanish Cal.* pp. 514-15. [2] *Ibid.* pp. 522, 533.
[3] *Ibid.* p. 600.
[4] The words in italics were put by Chapuys in cipher.

coincides, saying that when that is accomplished, the management of affairs may be left to those who know best how to act, *by which he means himself.'* A few hours after Chapuys dated this letter two gentlemen from the king's chamber [1] roused Wolsey from his slumbers in Southwell palace, and showed him a 'great parchment' already bearing many seals and signatures, 'the which my lord sealed and subscribed his name with his own hande, and delivered the same againe unto them.' It was the well-known memorial from prelates, temporal peers, and others to Clement VII begging him to meet the king's wishes in the matter of the divorce and dwelling on the evils of further delay : Wolsey's name heads the list, which does not contain those of Henry's lord chancellor or bishop Fisher.[2]

Wolsey was not abashed by any contradiction between his public acts and his secret correspondence. 'The cardinal,' writes Chapuys again on 27 June, '*sent the day before yesterday to inquire how the queen's case was progressing, and to urge strong and immediate action in it*, as I had

[1] William Brereton, afterwards executed as an accomplice of Anne Boleyn, and Thomas Wriothesley, afterwards lord chancellor and earl of Southampton.

[2] Cavendish never learnt what the document was, or he would hardly have described at such length the scene of its signature and sealing by Wolsey (pp. 217-20), or been so innocently emphatic about the cardinal's opposition to the divorce. His story is confirmed by Brereton and Wriothesley's account of their expenses in the latter half of June travelling north, west, and south to obtain seals and signatures to the letter (*L.P.* iv. 6489) ; and incidentally their account explodes the idea that seals and signatures afford any proof of the collective presence of signatories to documents. The letter, which was discussed on 12 June (*Spanish Cal.* p. 598) and finally dated on 13 July after the signatures had been obtained, is in the P.R.O., was first printed by Herbert (pp. 331-4), then by Rymer (xiv. 405) and others (cf. Ehses, *Röm. Dok.* pp. 153-6, 161-4). The *L. and P.* (iv. 6513, 6638) give an adequate summary of Clement VII's answer on 27 Sept., but not of the representations to which he was replying. * More was in some danger of losing the great seal owing to his refusal to sign (see Chapuys in *Spanish Cal.* pp. 599, 727, 762). Warham signed as well as Wolsey and twenty-two abbots but only four bishops—Sherbourne of Chichester, Rawlins of St. David's, Kite of Carlisle, and Longland of Lincoln, a very invertebrate representation. Chapuys says that More and other opponents of the divorce were not present at the council on this occasion.

occasion recently to write to your majesty. He is showing great hospitality and leading so religious, quiet, and humble a life among those with whom he now is, that he is wonderfully loved and respected and is beginning to win universal praise.'[1] But he was getting impatient in August : 'the cardinal,' says Chapuys once more, 'sends *daily to inquire* how the queen's cause is progressing, and *why it is not more energetically pushed.* He dislikes delay above all things, for he thinks that, this business once settled, he has a good chance of returning to power.'[2] His chance was a gamble with heavy risks ; and if Wolsey did not know it, it was not for lack of warning. He had not kept that guard on his lips which Sir John Gage had recommended in April ; and in May Cromwell wrote that the king, acknowledging the receipt of Wolsey's letters, 'shewed me how it is come to his knowledge that your grace' had uttered words which 'should sound to make sedition between him and my lord of Norfolk.'[3] The duke himself had in July given Chapuys the information he subsequently repeated to Arundel in October, that Wolsey had attempted by means of three different agents to undermine his position, and that they had told him all about it ;[4] and Chapuys had capped the information with the remark that probably the bishop of Tarbes,[5] Guilliaume du Bellay,[6] and others 'had been scheming for the cardinal in France and elsewhere.' Rumours of Wolsey's political activities had spread. On 1 September, as Wolsey left Southwell, the English ports were suddenly closed, 'an unprecedented measure since the time when these people wanted to get hold of the duke of Buckingham.' 'Some say,' continues Chapuys, 'this is being done lest the cardinal should escape . . . but there is not much show of probability in any of these conjectures.' His scepticism was justified, but the

---

[1] *Spanish Cal.* p. 619.   [2] *Ibid.* 20 Aug. p. 692.

[3] The abstract of this letter, with others from the Jesus Coll. MSS., is put in *L. and P.* (iv. p. 2715) under 1 Dec. 1529, though its date 17 May [1530] is also given. It is obviously from the same letter as the extract (*ibid.* iv. 6391), which is there placed under its proper date.

[4] *Spanish Cal.* p. 630.   [5] Grammont.   [6] The ambassador's brother.

rumour could only have arisen from a suspicion that Wolsey was engaged in other than purely pastoral cares.[1]

His voice, if not his arm, had in fact once more reached Rome. 'He used,' writes Chapuys, '*to keep me well informed of all his movements, begging me to find out whether the nuncio had not instructions concerning him*,' and assuring me that he was again on the road *to his former position*.' 'The pope,' wrote Mai to Charles V from Rome on 18 July, 'agrees, and the cardinal approves, that the king shall be admonished to separate in the meantime from the woman on account of the scandal of such an intercourse. . . . The pope is now sending to England as nuncio the baron del Borgo.'[2] The baron arrived in London on 8 September ; he subsequently stated that his instructions with regard to the cardinal were to be guided by de Vaux's advice, but that, as de Vaux was not on good terms with Wolsey, he himself had not been able to broach the matter. Clement VII, in fact, saw no reason to put his hand into the fire in order to pull out chestnuts for Wolsey. He wanted to escape responsibility and avoid incurring any more enmity than he need. He had prevented sentence in the divorce being given in England, but was in no hurry to give it at Rome. Del Borgo advised him from London that the case should not be proceeded with, if the king promised to remain inactive, and suggested that its suspension for ever might be a good expedient.[3] Catherine might die, and Henry might then marry Anne without offence to anyone. Where would the pope stand then, if he had ordered Anne's removal from court? He desired, no doubt, to satisfy Charles, but Charles' own representative at Rome told the emperor that the specific allegations, on which Wolsey's proposed papal order was grounded, were baseless.[4] It was not until 15 November 1532 that the pope felt himself justified in sending Henry that order to cease cohabitating with Anne

---

[1] *Spanish Cal.* pp. 708, 711.   [2] *Ibid.* pp. 647, 804-5.
[3] *Ibid.* pp. 712, 719.

[4] 'There is no positive proof of adultery,' wrote Mai on 10 Jan 1530-31, 'none having yet been produced here at Rome, but on the contrary several letters proving the contrary' (*ibid.* IV, ii. 8).

which Wolsey had begun to demand two and a half years earlier in order to facilitate his return to power.[1]

Clement VII feared lest he might, in stopping a breach of morals, open a schism in the church. While the papal curia was debating whether to prohibit Anne's presence at Henry's court or to prohibit their marriage, Francis I was urging on Henry the latter course and engaging to see him through the consequences.[2] With Henry's financial assistance and diplomatic support, he had reclaimed his children from the clutches of Charles V and was hoping to make something out of the emperor's difficulties with the Lutherans and the Turks. But before he could indulge in further adventures in Italy or novel adventures in Germany, he must feel secure at least against an alliance of Henry with Charles. Henry's bigamous marriage with Anne might serve him as well as, ten years later, the bigamous marriage of Philip of Hesse served the emperor.[3] Jean du Bellay returned once more to England to reinforce de Vaux in August ; and an important council at Hampton court considered their proposal that Henry, relying on the opinions obtained from the universities of Europe, should obtain his divorce in England and marry Anne without waiting for the interminable delays of the papal curia.[4] Clement VII himself had more than once privately urged this course, though it met with his official reprobation ; but only Norfolk and Wiltshire were found to support it in Henry's council.[5]

The same council considered Wolsey's case. There was no truth in the rumour of his projected flight, but he had left Southwell about the end of August and was slowly moving towards York by way of Newstead, Rufford, and

---

[1] *L.P.* v. 1545 ; *D.N.B.* xxvi. 84*b*. Cranmer, writing on 17 June 1533 says Henry married Anne about 'St. Paul's day last' (25 Jan. ; see my *Cranmer*, p. 60 *n.* 1), and queen Elizabeth was born on 7 Sept. following.

[2] *Spanish Cal.* p. 708.

[3] See *Cambridge Modern History*, ii. 240-2.

[4] *Spanish Cal.* pp. 690-2.

[5] *L.P.* iv. 3802, 4120 (p. 1822), 6290 ; *Spanish Cal.* p. 708 ; Friedmann, *Anne Boleyn*, i. 120.

Blithe abbeys to Scrooby where he stayed until Michaelmas. Thence he proceeded to Cawood, taking with him, remarks Chapuys, 'no less than six hundred horsemen in his train, which has by no means improved his case.'[1] How much the council knew of his secret approaches to Rome is uncertain ; but Henry's agents, Bennet and Carne, were instructed to search for evidence there,[2] and on 12 September a proclamation was drafted[3] stringently prohibiting the 'purchase' from Rome or elsewhere, and the divulging or publication, of 'anything' 'containing matter prejudicial' to the royal authority and jurisdiction. This proclamation, says Hall, 'was muche mused at and every woorde of thesame well noted. Some sayd that it was made because that the quene had purchased a new bull for the ratification of her mariage, other sayd that it was made because the cardinall had purchased a bull to curse the kyng if he would not restore him to his old dignities, and that the king should suffer him to correct the spiritualtie and he not to meddle with thesame.' Chapuys at first could discover no reason for the proclamation, unless it was 'to spite the pope,' being published, he says, 'on the very day that the nuncio had his first audience with the king ;' but later on he learnt from del Borgo that the sole object was to forestall measures against the king on the queen's behalf.[4] Henry, however, consented to the prorogation of parliament, and with it further consideration of the divorce, from the 2nd until the 22nd of October, and thence till the next year, much

---

[1] *Spanish Cal.* p. 805. Cavendish's account of Wolsey's progress is detailed, but not precise with regard to dates, which can, however, be supplied to some extent from Wolsey's correspondence. Cavendish (pp. 220-2) has an interesting alibi for Wolsey against Chapuys' charge for one stage of the journey. He was afraid of the impression the concourse would produce at court, and secretly altered his route. But he would not announce his reasons lest his adherents 'should leave their accustomed access to him, which was much to his comforte.'

[2] *L.P.* iv. p. 3024 ; Hall, p. 773.

[3] *L.P.* iv. 6615 ; *Spanish Cal.* p. 726 ; *Venetian Cal.* p. 259 ; *Milan Cal.* p. 528. Hall says it was proclaimed in London on the 19th ; cf. Steele, *Proclamations*, i. no. 124.

[4] *Spanish Cal.* pp. 726, 735.

to the satisfaction of people at Rome who were less inclined than ever to intervene on Wolsey's behalf.[1] The threatened proceedings against the English bishops for præmunire were also postponed, Cromwell informing the cardinal that 'another way' had been found.[2]

This prorogation betrayed Wolsey into another unfortunate incident. He had, without waiting for a regular royal mandate, summoned a convocation to meet at York on 7 November; and Tunstal, who had been sent north in July, not only as bishop of Durham but as 'chief of the king's council in the north parts,'[3] to watch if not to control the cardinal's proceedings, sent him on 16 October a warning hint. He had, he wrote, informed his diocesan clergy of Wolsey's command, but told him that parliament had been prorogued until the 22nd and that men doubted whether even that date would hold. Moreover, he went on, the 'old custom'—with which he was familiar as ex-dean of the province of Canterbury—'has been to see what the province of Canterbury first assented to, and then for the province of York to consent or dissent, as the case may be.' If Wolsey adhered to his convocation of 7 November, Tunstal begged leave to be absent until 30th, when he would have to be at York—not for Wolsey's convocation but 'for the king's commission'—as president of the council in the north.[4] It was a polite reminder that things had changed since the days when Wolsey was bishop of Durham as well as archbishop of York, and the council in the north was packed with Wolsey's servants.

What Wolsey did about the summons of his convocation

---

[1] Probably these were 'the good results obtained in England' which Mai says (*L.P.* iv. 6700) were indicated in a dispatch (missing) from del Borgo; the original phrase is 'en él vera Vᵃ Magᵈ los buenos fines que allá se tienen,' but the *Spanish Cal.* (p. 779) translates 'in which your majesty will be able to judge of the king's good intentions'; cf. *ibid.* pp. 719, 758.

[2] *L.P.* iv. 6699.

[3] Rachel R. Reid, *King's Council in the North*, p. 113 *n*. 1.

[4] P.R.O. State Papers, Henry VIII, vol. 58, f. 133, calendared in *L.P.* iv. 6687. Tresham had informed Wolsey of this prorogation in a letter dated 11 Oct. (*ibid.* iv. 6679).

we do not know. But he had fixed his enthronement as archbishop in York minster for that same Monday, 7 November ;
and he persisted in that arrangement. According to Hall,
he ' sent to all the lordes, abbottes, priors, knights, esquiers,
and gentlemen of his dioces to be at his manor of Cawood
the vi day of Nouember and so to bring him to Yorke with
all maner of pompe and soleṁnitie ' ;[1] and the constitutional differɛnce between the assembly gathered for that
occasion and a convocation of the province would depend
more upon what was said and done when it met than upon
the personnel of the meeting. We have no answer to
Tunstal's question, and the wildest rumours prevailed in
London about the cardinal's intentions and instructions.
' By the king's command,' reports the Milanese ambassador
Scarpinello on 20 October, ' the cardinal has gone to York
. . . it is said to be in order to incline the people there to
some things which his majesty has in view.' ' By the
king's consent,' says the Venetian ambassador Falier on
the 29th, ' Wolsey has convoked the English bishops and
prelates about holding a *parlamento*.'[2] Later on Scarpinello heard that the cardinal had actually entered York with
eight hundred horse. The rumours of October are only
of importance as indicating the prevalence of a vague
idea, corresponding with the assurance Wolsey had given
Chapuys, that he was again on the road to his former
state. But a popular impression of that sort would be
wormwood and gall to his successors who were suffering
under some uncomplimentary comparisons between their
ability and the cardinal's, to which Henry is said to have
given vent in council.[3]

[1] *Chron.* p. 773.

[2] *Cal. of Milan State Papers*, 1913, i. 525 ; *Venetian Cal. 1527-33*,
no. 629. The editor of the latter translates *parlamento* by ' convocation ' ;
in no. 584, where it means the law-courts, he translates it ' parliament ' ;
in reality it is as vague as ' assembly,' though in Florence it came to mean
a particular kind of assembly. Here it would almost imply that Wolsey
was thinking of a legatine council ; but no stress should be laid on the
word. Falier's dispatch is not extant, and this is only a précis which
Sanuto registered in his voluminous diaries.

[3] *Spanish Cal.* p. 819.

Their apprehensions, however, would not alone have accounted for the blow which fell on Wolsey on Friday 4 November, three days before his anticipated enthronement at York. Few can have seen in Wolsey the stormy petrel of a pilgrimage of grace; nor could the arrest of a chaplain of his, with incriminating correspondence, as he was seeking to cross the Channel a few days earlier, have provided more than a last straw in the way of evidence.[1] The arrangements must have been made at least a week before and determined even earlier. For it was after those deliberations and arrangements that Walter Walsh, a groom of the king's chamber who had recently married Sir William Compton's widow, set out from the court at Greenwich on 1 November with a joint commission for himself and the earl of Northumberland to effect the cardinal's arrest;[2] and it would seem that the determining factor was the coincidence of Tunstal's news of Wolsey's unauthorised convocation with the report which reached Henry about 23 October[3] that a papal brief had been issued against him at Bologna. This simply forbade his marriage *pendente lite*; but the pope had also talked of excommunicating Henry and ordering him to dismiss Anne Boleyn from court, and the publication of any papal brief at Wolsey's enthronement and convocation at York was a threat which, if Wolsey contemplated, Henry must prevent. Norfolk denounced the proposed excommunication as a most outrageous measure on the ground that Henry had always been a dutiful son of the church and had never intentionally offended the pope.

How much influence Norfolk, the king, and the council attributed to the representations Wolsey had made to Rome

[1] *Venetian Cal.* pp. 263, 267; *Milan Cal.* pp. 528-9.

[2] *L.P.* iv. 6072 [13]; Cavendish, pp. 233-7.

[3] This appears from a dispatch of Chapuys (*Spanish Cal.* pp. 832-3), dated 4 Dec., in which he states that the king had known and complained of the brief to the nuncio 'more than six weeks ago.' This brief was 'affixed in the chancery of St. Peter's and secretly in St. Petronius', and has been sent to Madame for publication in the Low Countries' (*L.P.* iv. 6635 [ii.]). As to the brief for the separation of Henry and Anne, Mai had on 2 Oct. only obtained a promise (*ibid.* iv. 6661) which was not fulfilled until two years later.

is mere inference; but it is certain that the evidence, on which Wolsey's arrest was made, was not the confession extracted from Agostini a fortnight after it had taken place. 'They say,' writes de Vaux to Montmorenci on 10 November,[1] referring to Norfolk and Suffolk, 'they have many important causes against him; and the king says he has intrigued against them, both in and out of his kingdom, and has told me where and how, and that one and perhaps more of his servants have discovered it and accused him.' The 'particularities,' which Henry communicated to his ambassador in France in letters dated 11 November, 'did chiefly concern presumptuous sinister practices made to the court of Rome, for reducing him to his former estate and dignity.'[2] Either Agostini must have betrayed him or have been himself betrayed by the intermediary who conveyed his communications to Chapuys; for Walsh singled out Agostini when making Wolsey's arrest, called him a traitor and sent him, bound to his horse like a traitor, in advance of Wolsey to London. But this was probably due to the interception of his correspondence: 'it is undeniable,' writes Scarpinello, 'that a few days before the arrest certain letters from this same physician, Messer Agostino, were intercepted, containing a few lines in cipher'; and besides Agostini, there was Wolsey's arrested chaplain whose letters, however, were 'understood not to have been of much importance.' Both were examined, but it was Agostini who, either because he knew more or was less able to resist the blandishments of his captors, provided the fuller information. Chapuys was, however, relieved to find that Agostini had apparently 'when interrogated, denied having any understanding or acquaintance with me' or with their intermediary.[3] The government

---

[1] *L.P.* iv. 6720; Le Grand, iii. 527.   [2] *State Papers*, vii. 212.

[3] *Spanish Cal.* p. 820. The usual statement that Agostini 'betrayed' Wolsey is a convenient ambiguity. It may mean simply that, his letters having been intercepted and himself arrested and imprisoned, he was unable to clear himself and turned 'king's evidence,' thus involving Wolsey. This is practically certain, but that fact does not support, and still less prove, the assumptions based on it, that Agostini had forged the whole correspondence with Chapuys, de Vaux, and del Borgo and invented the conduct of which Wolsey was accused. In Oct. 1529 du Bellay thought

seems to have been more suspicious of de Vaux : the king
and council assured him that they had unbounded confidence
in his personal integrity ; but they arrested two Genoese,
'great friends' of his, and seized their papers, keeping the
papers for examination but releasing their owners on the
ambassador's undertaking to stand security for them.[1]

For our knowledge of the actual charges against Wolsey
we have to depend on what Scarpinello calls 'vulgar
rumours' but obviously believes, and on Chapuys' report
of what de Vaux told Falier of Agostini's confession ; but
there is substantial agreement between them.[2] De Vaux,
writes Chapuys on 27 November, 'told the Venetian ambassador that by the physician's own confession the cardinal
had solicited the pope at Rome to excommunicate the king
and lay an interdict on his kingdom, unless he immediately
dismissed the lady from court and treated the queen with
proper respect. By which means he hoped to cause a

him the only servant of Wolsey's who had remained faithful. The
secrecy, to which he was bound (*L.P.* iv. 6763) under a heavy fine to
observe with regard to his confession 'written with his own hand in a
book,' was not enforced because his information was false, but because it
involved the ambassadors of Francis I and Charles V with whom Henry
wanted to keep on good terms ; and, Wolsey being dead by the time of
the bond, there was no need of the evidence for judicial purposes. Agostini, who was a native of Venice and a nephew of Ghinucci, bishop of
Worcester, is described by Chapuys as a man of wit and sense ; he had
entered Wolsey's service about 1527, was given by him the prebend of
Wetwang in York cathedral, and was naturalised in 1530 He became
in 1532 physician to Wolsey's old colleague Campeggio, was a friend of
Sir T. Elyot, kept up a correspondence with Cromwell, and referred to
Wolsey as *heros meus felicis memoriae* (*L.P.* v. 283, 910, 1666, etc).*
Cavendish, in his 'life' of Wolsey, represents Agostini as Wolsey's Judas
and the cardinal's ruin as entirely due to the machinations of his enemies ;
but in his 'poems' (ed. Singer, ii. 15) he makes Wolsey confess that he

> To farrayn potentates wrote my letters playn
> Desireing their ayd, to restore me to favor againe.

[1] *L.P.* iv. 6720 ; *Spanish Cal.* p. 805.

[2] Only fragments of Falier's correspondence survive, and they do not
include his dispatches on this subject. In his report on his embassy,
made on 10 Nov. 1531, he says : 'The cardinal, having had such a fall
and being brought so low, commenced plotting with the pope against the
crown' (*Venetian Cal.* 1527-33, p. 301).

rising throughout the country, and in the midst of the confusion seize again the reins of government.' The charge about hoping to foment a rising and seize the reins of government seems highly improbable.[1] All that is certain is that Wolsey intended to make his enthronement an imposing demonstration and the government determined to prevent it. It was Wolsey's pathetic belief that, were Anne once removed, Henry would automatically revert to his inveterate faith in the cardinal ; though how she was to be removed with the help of a papal excommunication and interdict, but without confusion if not a rising, is not apparent. But apart from these excrescences and the reference to an interdict, there is nothing in the report of Agostini's confession which Chapuys had not for months been putting in his own dispatches ; and independently of either Agostini or Chapuys, de Vaux had given a similar account to the French government.[2]

Before the charges could be judicially formulated, and before it was even decided whether Wolsey should be put on his trial or not, he had passed out of Henry's jurisdiction. Arrested at dinner on Friday, 4 November, it was not until late on Sunday that the arrangements for his

[1] Wolsey himself gave ground for suspicion by his request in July to be allowed to appoint leaders of his Winchester ' manrede ' at musters and to visit that diocese (L.P. iv. 6544 ; the appointment for musters belonged, as Paulet replied, to the king alone).

[2] ' Sir,' writes Sir Francis Bryan, the English ambassador at the French court to Henry, ' as farre as I can perceive, the relation made unto the kinge your brother by Monsr de Vaux, his ambassadour, was of verye good sort, in disclosinge the mysdemenour of the sayd cardinall ' (State Papers, vii. 213). The meaning of this is obscured in the L.P. précis (iv. 6733). ' I think that de Vaux . . . has done well in disclosing the misdemeanour of the cardinal,' which might mean that de Vaux had done well to disclose it, and that he had disclosed it to Henry VIII, instead of to Francis I. Nor can de Vaux' report have been based on Agostini's confession. Henry's letters to Bryan, announcing Wolsey's arrest, were dated 11 Nov. and reached Bryan at Blois, where the French court was, at 7 a.m. on the 19th. De Vaux' report had already been received when Bryan discussed the matter with Montmorenci and Francis I a few hours later, and must have been written at least as early as Henry's. It was not until 27 Nov. that Chapuys was able to say anything about Agostini's confession, though he had written on the 13th announcing his imprisonment in the Tower.

departure from Cawood were complete. He had refused to recognise Northumberland's commission but admitted Walsh's authority as a gentleman of the privy chamber ; [1] he told Cavendish that his enemies 'would not suffer him to have indifferent justice but would seek sinister means to dispatch him,' and according to Hall, protested the immunity of his order.[2] That night he lay at Pontefract abbey and the next at the Whitefriars, Doncaster.* On Tuesday he reached Sheffield park, where the earl of Shrewsbury, on Henry's orders, hospitably entertained him for sixteen days (8-24 Nov.).[3] He told the earl 'there is no man alive that loketh in this face of mine, who is able to accuse me,' and protested that he had 'no assured friends in all the world but the king's grace.' He could not therefore have gone about to betray him without 'lack of bothe grace, wit, and discretion . . . for he is the staff that supporteth me . . . having no other refuge . . . but only under the shadow of his wings.' He repeated to Shrewsbury his conviction that his enemies intended to 'dispatche me rather than I should come before his presence,' and the earl promised to forward to Henry his request 'for the triall of your truthe.'

So matters stood until Tuesday the 22nd, Shrewsbury often inviting Wolsey to hunt in Sheffield park but always being refused. On that day Sir William Kingston, constable of the Tower and captain of the guard, arrived with a body of twenty-four, most of them Wolsey's old servants. Wolsey was, or fell, ill. One of his superstitions was that Kingston would be fatal, and it is said that he would never ride through it, although it was on his shortest route from his house at Esher to court.[4] "Mr. Kingstone' quoth he,

---

[1] Cavendish, p. 242 : 'and also you are a sufficient commissioner in that behalfe, in as much as ye be one of the king's privy chamber.'

[2] 'You haue no such power, sayd ye cardinal, for I am both a Cardinal and a Legate de latere and a pere of the College of Rome and ought not to be arrested by any temporal power, for I am not subject to that power' (p. 773).

[3] Cavendish says 'eighteen days' (p. 252) and 'a fortnight' (p. 256).

[4] Fuller, *Church History*, 1656, v p. 178 ; Cavendish, p. 259. Wolsey seems, however, to have passed through Kingston on his way from Esher to Richmond about 2 Feb. 1530; cf. his reference to what Stubbs 'promised at Kingston' (*L.P.* iv. 6390).

rehearsing the name once or twice ; and with that clapped his hand on his thighe, and gave a great sighe.' Shrewsbury, seconded by Cavendish, assured him that the guard was only come to convey him honourably to the king's presence in accordance with his own request ; but ' he most lamentably, as he was accustomed to do, aunswered him.' Even when Kingston came and knelt before him ' with humble reverence ' and gave the king's message that ' he beareth unto you as much good will and favour as ever he did ; and willeth you to be of good cheere,' he replied, ' Mr. Kingstone, all the comfortable wordes, which ye have spoken unto me, be spoken but for a purpose to bring me into a fooles paradise : [1] I knowe what is provided for me.' His prophetic soul or uneasy conscience did not deceive him : in the accounts of the treasurer of the king's chamber occurs the item : ' To Sir W. Kingston . . . sent to the earl of Shrewsbury with divers of the guard for the conveyance of the cardinal of York to the Tower, 40*l*.' [2]

He had little faith in his cause, or less in the deity under the shadow of whose wings was his only refuge. His sickness grew worse, and it was not until Thursday the 24th that he could ride again. He got that day to another house of Shrewsbury's, Hardwick Hall ; [3] on Friday he reached Nottingham, and on Saturday Leicester abbey. There ' continued he, sicker and sicker.' On the morning of Monday the 28th his ' ghostly father,' Dr. Palmes, bade Cavendish ask if the cardinal would be shriven. "What have ye to doe to aske me any suche question ? ' quoth he, and began to be very angry with me for my presumption.' In the afternoon came David Vincent, who had been one of the grooms of Wolsey's privy chamber [4] with letters from

---

[1] Tyndale also has this phrase (*Works*, ii. 337).

[2] *L.P.* v. p. 322.

[3] In Nottinghamshire : not to be confused with ' Bess of Hardwick's ' more famous Hardwick Hall in Derbyshire (see G. E. C.'s *Complete Peerage*, 1st ed. vii. 140-1 ; *D.N.B.* s.v. ' Talbot, Elizabeth ').

[4] *L.P.* iv. 4198, v. p. 325 * ; he was appointed ' keeper of the king's wardrobe at Greenwich ' on 21 Feb. 1532 (*ibid.* v. 838 [31]). The missing amount would be about £20,000 in modern currency.

the king : a sum of £1500, entered in the inventory taken at Cawood, could not be found ; and Vincent, suspected of secreting it, had been at first imprisoned in the Tower and then sent to Wolsey to investigate. Could Wolsey, asked Kingston, give them any information ? The cardinal was indignant at the implication he detected : rather, he declared, than deceive the king of one penny, 'I would it were moulten, and put into my mouthe.' He had never, he continued, regarded anything as his own but as the king's, 'having but the bare use thereof during my life, and after my death to leave it wholly to him.' He proceeded to specify the friends from whom he had borrowed the money, beseeching the king to repay them. 'There is no doubt of the king' said Kingston, '. . . But, sir, I pray you, where is this money?' 'I will not conseale it from the king,' replied the cardinal, 'but will declare it unto you or I dye, by the grace of God. Take a little patience with me, I beseech you.' Kingston said he would trouble him no more for the time, 'trusting that ye will tell me to morrowe.' 'Yea, that I will,' repeated Wolsey.

Kingston came for his answer at six a.m. on the 29th ; the cardinal had been at confession for an hour, and told Sir William that he 'tarried but the pleasure of God, to render up my poore soule into his handes.' Kingston said he made himself worse by his needless fears. 'I see,' retorted Wolsey, 'the matter maketh you much worse than you should be against me : howe it is framed I knowe not. But if I had served God as diligently as I have done the king, he would not have given me over in my grey heares.'[1] He then proceeded, according to Cavendish, to deliver a speech, which occupies four of Cavendish's pages, warning Kingston of Henry's obstinacy and self-will ; declaring that he himself had from the first tried to divert the king from the divorce ; urging Henry to 'depresse this new sorte of Lutherans ' ; attributing to Wycliffite heresies the peasants' revolt of

[1] Some ten years earlier Skelton (*Works*, i. 290) had made his dethroned ' Magnificence ' lament

> In welthe to beware, yf I had had grace,
> Never had I bene brought in this case.

1381, the ruin of Bohemia,[1] and the rebellion of Sir John
Oldcastle, and the 'pretence to have all things in common';
and foretelling that 'if these be not plain presidents and
sufficient persuasions . . . then shall ensue mischiefe upon
mischiefe . . . to the utter ruine and desolation of this
realme.'

The prophet must needs be a prophet at death; but
not one word of the fifteen hundred pounds! 'And in-
continent the clock struck eight, and then he gave up the
ghost, and thus he departed this present life. And calling
to remembrance howe he saide the day before, that at eight
of the clocke we should lose our master, as is before rehearsed, one of us looking upon another, supposing that
either he knewe or prophesied of his departure, yet before
his departure, we sent for the abbot of the house to annoyle
him.' He died with the last of his promises unfulfilled.
'And if he will not tell the truthe,' Cavendish had advised
Kingston the night before, 'there be [those] that can satisfy
the king's minde therein.' Wolsey had told Kingston that
the money was 'in an honest man's keeping, who will not
keep a penny from the king.' A week later Cavendish was
telling Henry about this honest man, his master, and his
money : 'Sir, if it please your highness, after the departure of
David Vincent from my lord at Scroby,[2] who had the custody
thereof, leaving the same with my lord in divers baggs, he
delivered the same unto a certaine priest safely to kepe to
his use. . . . The priest shall not be able to deny it in my
presence, for I was at the delivery thereof ; who hath gotten
divers other rich ornaments into his hands, the which be not
rehersed or registered in any of my lords books of inventory
or other writings, whereby any man is able to charge him
therewith, but only I.' Was Cavendish moved by his
biblical inspiration to deny his master also? He follows
with an account of how he and Kingston conspired to disown
all knowledge of the cardinal's dying words and confound

---

[1] Bishop Fisher had used Bohemia as a terrible warning in his attack
on the reform bills sent up by the house of commons in the parliamentary
session of Nov.-Dec. 1529 (Hall, *Chron.* p. 766).

[2] In Sept. on Wolsey's journey from Southwell to Cawood.*

the yeoman of the guard 'that saw and heard him talk and die,' posted from Leicester to the king, and told the truth.

Cavendish's final page moralises on 'the mutability of vaine honors, and brittle assurance of abundance ; the uncertainty of dignities, the flattering of feigned friends, and the fickle favor of worldly princes' ; and he concludes with the 'wise man's' warning against the accumulation of riches, 'that another, whom peradventure he hated in his life, shall spende it out, and consume it.' We do not know whether Henry recovered the fifteen hundred pounds which Wolsey was still secreting at death ; but Cavendish's analogue has a far wider and deeper meaning than he saw. Henry was heir to much more than Wolsey's wealth, and Wolsey had taught him other things than to dissolve monasteries, build palaces, and grasp at riches. He had shown him a vision of that unity of jurisdiction and monopoly of power, which, whether vested in a single person, in a popular assembly, or in that composite entity, 'the crown in parliament,' is the essence of our ideas of sovereignty and of the modern state. Wolsey, indeed, had no conception of parliamentary government ; but, with that fundamental exception, Henry's royal supremacy was Wolsey's work. The king received from the cardinal not only his methods and ideas, but even the mausoleum which had been designed by Wolsey for himself, but remained symbolically incomplete when Wolsey was hastily buried ere dawn on the morrow in the 'tyrants' grave' at Leicester.[1]

[1] Richard III had been buried there and Chapuys, writing on 4 Dec. says : 'et gissent tous deux en une mesme eglize, la quelle l'on commence desja appeller la sepulture des tyrans' (Bradford, p. 331 ; *Spanish Cal.* p. 833 ; *L.P.* iv. 6757).

CHAPTER VIII.

CHARACTER AND ENVIRONMENT.

It has been said of Wolsey that he should be judged less by what he did than by what he chose to do ; [1] and it will probably be admitted that the test of a man's character lies rather in his aims than in his achievements. He has at least more choice with regard to what he attempts than with regard to the success of his endeavours. But, if it is not in mortals to command success, there was in the fifteenth century no wide range from which a boy, sprung from the lower middle class, could select a path to greatness. Neither army nor navy yet provided a career ; the common law was a possibility, but the ranks of society, from which the king's judges were recruited, have not been precisely ascertained ; and it is probable that that avenue, like commerce, was open only to sons of the gentry, like Dick Whittington, [2] or of prosperous merchants in great cities such as London, York, and Bristol. For other professions the church was the obvious portal, and for the son of a butcher in Ipswich a career was hardly a matter for self-determination. However secular his mind might be, his profession must be clerical ; [3] and the doors of the church were open to all without much discrimination. Precocity paved his way to the university, and his college

[1] Creighton, *Wolsey*, p. 2.

[2] Son of Sir William Whittington of Pauntley, Gloucestershire, and his wife Joan, daughter of William Mansell, sheriff of that county (*D.N.B.*).

[3] It is rather to Thomas Cromwell's credit than otherwise that he should have taken a more independent, albeit disorderly, course in his youth. But he was born some fifteen years later than Wolsey, and seems to have had a wider choice of occupation; see *D.N.B.* and Merriman, *Life and Letters of Cromwell*, 1902.

would see to it that a fellow was not merely a clerk but a
priest as well.   He might still have specialised in canon or
civil law ; but these were learned professions, and Wolsey
early divined that learning was not a primrose path to
preferment.

Choice began to operate and character to tell.   Wolsey
was ambitious and his business was to arrive.   He must
catch the train of some one who went to court ; and the
marquis of Dorset and his numerous sons were a godsend.
He just missed the possible patronage of Morton who
died in 1500, but caught a connexion with his successor
and became archbishop Deane's domestic chaplain in
1501.   He was unfortunate in Deane's death two years
later, and probably regarded his attachment to Sir Richard
Nanfan as a makeshift.   Nanfan, however, was greatly
impressed by his ability, and amply rewarded his services
by the strength of his recommendation to Henry VII ;
and Wolsey achieved a chaplaincy to the king in 1507.
Financial rather than clerical influence clouded Henry's
last years, and his episcopal councillors were politically
overshadowed by Empson and Dudley.   They came to
their own under Henry VIII, and with the aid of their
noble colleagues sent the financial upstarts to the block.
But Wolsey attached himself less to archbishop Warham
than to the more statesmanlike Foxe, under whose wing
he crept into the confidence of an exceedingly trusting
sovereign.

It is easy to understand the young king's subjugation.
Foxe was old and somewhat stiff and upright, Warham
more so.   Wolsey was not yet forty, buoyant, pliant,
brilliant, and convivial—'a gay finder out of new pastimes,'
as Tyndale called him.[1]   He was a past master of graceful
flattery : 'loth I would be,' he once wrote to Henry,
'that, your grace being so expert in archery, the emperor
should have more strings to his bow than ye.'[2]   He was
'as subtle as the Sinon that betrayed Troy,' and 'as

----

[1] *Practice of Prelates*, p. 307 ; cf. Cavendish, p. 18, 'and so fast as the
other counsaillors counselled the king to leave his pleasure and to attend
to his affaires, so busily did the almoner persuade him to the contrary.'

[2] *L.P.* iii. 2450.

eloquent as subtle.'[1]   Above all, he had a 'courage,'
better rendered in modern English by 'heartiness,' which
appealed to the high-spirited youth who reigned but had
not yet learnt to rule.   If cock-fighting had attained its
later vogue, Wolsey might have been described as Henry's
favourite bird ; he thought its performances superb, so
long as the spectacle pleased and no serious question of
maintenance arose.   'I defend myself,' wrote the friendly
du Bellay, ' with beak and claws, yet in the end he will
come at me again.'[2]

Wolsey, albeit a bad loser, was a born fighter encumbered
by clerical garments and spiritual professions to which he
had no vocation, but to which he was condemned by the lack
of other outlets for his mental and physica¹ exuberance.[3]
He rose above the underworld of crime which peopled the
country with criminous clerks ; and, if he transgressed the
proprieties of his profession in his private and public life,
there was a common cause in the system which forced into
the church the able-bodied and ambitious servants of the
state : a celibate civil service, unaccustomed to the surgical
operations of the later Roman empire, was probably worse
than a celibate priesthood ; and one of the premonitory
symptoms of the reformation, for which Wolsey himself
was responsible, was a secular act of parliament passed in
1523 to release the 'six clerks' of chancery from their
unnatural inhibition.[4]   Wolsey had long ignored his own

[1] Tyndale, *loc. cit.* ; cf. above, p. 101 *n.* 1.   Cavendish also speaks of
Wolsey's ' speciall gifte of naturall eloquence,' though elsewhere he calls
it ' ornate,' and his ' filed tongue ' (ed. 1908, pp. 13, 16).

[2] *L.P.* iv. 5701.

[3] Tyndale (*op. cit.* p. 307) describes him as ' a man of lust and courage
and bodily strength to do and suffer great things.'   But he was always
dosing himself with physic.   Congratulating him on his good health (by
the hand of Sir T. More on 5 July 1519) Henry VIII ' saith that ye
may thank his counsaile thereof by which ye leve the often takyng of
medecines that ye were wont to use ; and while ye so do, he saith, ye
shall not faile of helth ' (Ellis, 1, i. 197-8).

[4] 14 and 15 Henry VIII, c. 8.   The act recites the old custom that all
clerks ' writing to the great seal ' should remain unmarried ' except only
the clerk of the crown,' but states that ' now the said custom ' only
obtained in ' the office of the said six clerks ' and proceeds to remove that
disability.

obligation to chastity, and about the time of his rise to
power he formed a liaison with 'the daughter of one
Lark.'[1] The practice was common enough among prelates, and the polite phraseology is to say that Wolsey was
'uncanonically married' and to call Thomas Wynter his
son instead of his nephew.[2] It is to his credit that he
seems to have been faithful to the lady[3] until he passed
her on, in canonical marriage, to one Lee or Legh of
Adlington in Cheshire, with a dowry the extortion of
which from Sir John Stanley formed one of the articles
in his impeachment;[4] for, while references to this connexion with Lark's daughter abound in the letters and
papers and literature of Wolsey's day, none have been
traced to any other; and her relatives profited from his
family partiality to the exclusion even of Wolsey's own
brothers.

The ablest of her brothers, Thomas Lark, became
Wolsey's own confessor and chaplain to the king, and was
given a canonry of St. Stephen's on 10 November 1511,
when Wolsey had just established his influence at court.
Writing to Erasmus on 26 June 1515, Ammonius describes this Lark as 'omnipotent' with the archbishop of

[1] Possibly the Peter Lark, innkeeper of Thetford, whose pardon for
certain offences comes next in *L.P.* i. (new ed.) 3499 [39 and 40] to the
earliest reference to Wolsey as *intimus consiliarius* of the king. Cf.
Skelton on 'a lusty lark' in *Works*, i. 269, 276; ii. 258.

[2] *D.N.B.* lxii. 343a. Bishop Clerk, however, calls Wynter Wolsey's
nephew in 1526 (*L.P.* iv. 2568); and Wolsey can hardly have regarded
the lady's subsequent marriage as bigamy.

[3] This is the most charitable theory. Dr. Gairdner (*D.N.B.*) says
'the cardinal's after life was certainly not pure' (cf. Skelton, *Works*, ed.
Dyce, ii. 33, lines 221-3; and William Roy in Furnivall, *Ballads from MSS.*
i. 73 and ed. Arber, p. 58).

[4] Article 38 in Coke's *Fourth Institute*, p. 93, Herbert, p. 301, and
L.P. iv. p. 2713; cf. Leland, *Itinerary* (ed. Toulmin Smith, v. 26) 'Le of
Adlington, a mile from [north of] Prestby [Prestbury], a man of 100 mark
land.' * The Sir John Stanley who was despoiled, after a year's imprisonment by Wolsey in the Fleet, was the elder illegitimate son of James
Stanley, bishop of Ely (see *D.N.B.*). His treatment led him to become a
monk at Westminster, where he died. From him descended the Stanleys
of Handforth, Cheshire; and from Lee's family came Charles Lee, the
American major-general (Ormerod, *Cheshire*, i. 466-7; *D.N.B.* xxxii. 343).

York ; and in April 1518 Silvester de Giglis, bishop of Worcester, writing to Wolsey from Rome, sends his compliments to Lark, and says that every one talks of his modesty and virtue : Erasmus wrote him a letter in 1516, and in August 1520 Charles V's ambassador also testified to his influence. He was master of Trinity Hall, Cambridge, from 1520 to 1525, when he was succeeded by another of Wolsey's *protégés*, Stephen Gardiner.* He was with Wolsey at Southwell and died there in July 1530.[1] Another brother, Peter, was found employment in the household of Wolsey's friend, John Kite, archbishop of Armagh, and, after his death, in Gardiner's ; and a third, William, became a draper.[2] Of Wolsey's own brothers we know little apart from the remark in Giustiniani's report, on 10 October 1519, to the seigniory of Venice that he had two, ' one of whom holds an untitled benefice, and the other is pushing his fortune.'[3] One of them was possibly the ' Mr. Wulsey of the privy chamber,' to whom an occasional reference is found,[4] but neither got very far on the path to preferment. The ability of the family was clearly concentrated in the cardinal, and he lavished his favours on his only son ; his daughter, who was born about Michaelmas 1512, was named Dorothy, fathered on one John Clansey, and sent to the nunnery at Shaftesbury.[5]*

---

[1] Erasmus, *Epistolae*, ed. Allen, ii. 267, 320, vi. 265-7 ; Le Neve, *Fasti*, iii. 679 (where his name is given as Robert Lark) ; *L.P.* i. 969 [50] ; ii. 629, 4068 ; iii. 955 ; iv. 6534.* In 1525 Norfolk, writing to Wolsey, refers to ' your bedchamber at Mr. Lark's house' (*ibid.* iv. 1265). J. J. de Vaux was harboured in Lark's house when he came on his secret mission to Wolsey in 1524 (Hall, p. 704 ; cf. de Vaux' letter to Lark in *L.P.* iv. 1233).

[2] *Ibid.* iii. 2345 ; iv. p. 412 ; ix. 216 ; 1538, ii. 444, 961 (2).

[3] Rawdon Brown, *Four Years at the Court of Henry VIII* (1854), ii. 314 ; *Venetian Cal.* 1509-19, p. 560.

[4] *L.P.* iv. p. 2726.

[5] Brewer's preface to *L.P.* iv. pp. dcxxxviii ; *ibid.* ix. 228 ; * Ellis, I, ii. 91. A ' poor kinswoman ' of Wolsey's married his servant John Oxenherd, a seaman who was engaged in conveying the cardinal's goods by sea to the north in April 1530, when she was apparently threatened with eviction by Sir T. More and his son-in-law, Daunce (see Wolsey's and Cromwell's letters in Ellis, II, ii. 30-2 ; *State Papers*, i. 366).

The son, called Thomas Wynter, was made as glaring an example of abuses in the church as was his father. He was brought up at Willesden,[1] but first appears in a letter of 29 November 1521 from his tutor, Maurice Birchinshaw, who was rewarded for his pains by various livings in Wolsey's gift. Birchinshaw writes from Louvain that he is glad Wolsey is pleased, and hopes for better results when the boy 'has attained an age more fit for solid education': with regard to his 'speaking less Latin than Wolsey desired,' it was neither his fault nor the boy's, 'but rather that of his plan of study, which, like other things, has a commencement, through which those must pass who wish to succeed.'[2] On 2 December 1523 bishop Clerk writes from Rome that he had left the boy 'sick of a fever in the mountains' near Trent, and that his steward was to convey him to Padua: the physicians said he could not stay in Italy another summer, so Clerk had arranged for his return to Louvain, although the universities were so much disturbed by the wars that he thought students would profit as much or more in other places.[3] On 2 September 1524 Erasmus, writing from Louvain to Wolsey, throws out a hint that he might help in the boy's education.[4]

He was brought into public notice in the autumn of 1525 : the king's son had just been created duke of Richmond, and Wolsey thought it was time the church made

[1] *L.P.* iv. 5503. He has been wrongly identified with the Thomas Wynter, who resigned a corrody in Evesham abbey in Feb. 1511 for it to be re-granted in survivorship to him and William Dyngley (*ibid.* i. 749 [11]), the reversion of which was granted on 11 May 1532 to one Francis Dod (*ibid.* v. 1065). But T. Wynter and a T. Dyngley are found associated in another Evesham grant as late as 1546 (*ibid.* 1546 ii. 332 [7]), and there is no other connexion of either Wynter or Wolsey with Evesham. There was, however, in 1509 another Thomas Wynter of Worcestershire (*ibid.* i. p. 270, l. 3), whose father was Robert Wynter. To these Winters of the West belonged the admiral, the Gunpowder plot conspirator, and the hero of 'Winter's leap' on the Wye (see *D.N.B.* under Winter, Sir John, Thomas, and William).

[2] *Ibid.* iii. 525. Birchinshaw was a B.C.L. of Magdalen, and a master at St. Paul's school in 1515,* *Reg. Univ. Oxon.* i.79, 298 ; *Erasmi Espistolae*, ed. Allen, v. 99 ; Le Neve, i. 85.

[3] *L.P.* iii. 3594.   [4] *Ibid.* iv. 618 ; *Erasmi Ep.* v. 533, 540.

some provision for the papal legate's. On 28 November Dr. Bennet informed Wolsey that he had delivered his letters to the canons residentiary of Wells and declared his pleasure as to the election of a dean at the next vacancy, which they expected not later than Christmas; they had agreed to Wolsey's wishes and 'would choose Mr. Thomas Wynter as dean.' On 28 February 1526 he appears as a prebendary of St. Peter's, Beverley (of which Thomas Lark was a pensioner); 'this,' continues the document, 'is valued at £48, and is the best piece of preferment, with the exception of the provostship, which is 100 marks.'[1] On 26 March Wynter received from Garter king a grant of arms,[2] which informs us that, in addition to being dean of Wells and prebendary of St. Peter's, Wynter was already provost of Beverley, archdeacon of both York and Richmond, and chancellor of Salisbury, besides holding the prebends of Lutton (Wells),[3] Strenshall (York), Bedwin (Salisbury),[4] Milton (Lincoln), and Norwell (Southwell),[5] and the rectories of Rudby[6] (Yorks), and St. Matthew's, Ipswich. Dispensations on the ground of age, non-residence, and plurality were of course necessary; and Clerk wrote to Wolsey from Rome that the omission from his drafts of a dispensation *super defectu natalium* would also have to be remedied.[7]

[1] *L.P.* iv. 1790, 2001.

[2] Supplied by John Anstis to Fiddes, *Collections*, pp. 227-8; the summary in *L.P.* iv. 2054 omits the cathedral churches in which these prebends were held. There is, says Fiddes (p. 531), 'a near affinity' between Wolsey's arms and Wynter's; and Lupset, writing to Erasmus from Padua on 23 Aug. 1525, remarks that Wynter was not less dear to Wolsey *quam si ex eius paternitate natus esset (Erasmi Epp.* ed. Allen, vi. 146).

[3] I.e. Lytton.

[4] Campeggio was then bishop of Salisbury, which was one of the sees Wolsey 'farmed' for foreign prelates.

[5] Wynter had received Norwell Palishall on 2 June 1522 and exchanged it for Norwell Overhall on 22 Aug. following (Le Neve, iii. 438, 442); the latter was 'the richest of all' and was valued at £40 a year (*L.P.* iv. 2922); but Milton was valued at £48 in 1526 (*Lincoln Subsidy*, 1526, Oxf. Hist. Soc. p. 259).

[6] *L.P.* misprints this Rugby: Fiddes has it correctly.

[7] *Ibid.* iv. 2482. This list of preferments is only complete down to its date in 1526; among others he held Shirburn hospital and Winwick,

Meanwhile, the boy was pursuing his studies in Paris, where Dr. John Taylor, afterwards master of the rolls, attended Greek lectures with him, and Francis I promised to do anything for him that Wolsey desired.[1] Every one praises him, writes Sir John Russell on 16 January 1527, for his own deserts and Wolsey's sake. The papal secretaries, Giberti and Sanga, expressed great affection for him ; and Claude Dodieu, secretary to the French embassy in London in April 1527, wrote home asking that a house in Paris might be bestowed on the cardinal's 'bastard son, whom he calls his nephew.'[2] Thomas Lupset, the humanist, was now his tutor, and writes on 4 March 1528 that his 'hopes have been disappointed, his fears more than justified' : the youth 'was spending money at a great rate.' To meet this difficulty, Wolsey leased to his son all the minerals in the bishopric of Durham.[3] In July Longland, bishop of Lincoln, offered Wolsey the archdeaconry of Oxfordshire for Wynter, and Wolsey himself obtained from Henry the gift of St. Leonard's, York, 'for the poor dean of Wells' who would surrender a prebend in Ripon in exchange. He was, however, still short of money, owing partly to his extravagance and partly to the fact that most of his revenues were retained by his father. By August he was also in possession of the archdeaconries of Norfolk and Suffolk.[4] He did not lack for tutors, and about this time another famous humanist, Florence Volusenus (or Wilson), joined Lupset in that capacity. On 5 October died Foxe and on the next day Wolsey, who had already obtained Henry's assent to his own prospective translation to Winchester from Durham, asked that Durham should be given

where he succeeded his uncle T. Lark (*ibid.* iv. 6088 ; App. 61). The references to him in the index to *L.P.* vol. iv. between nos. 2922 and 3955 have dropped out. He also held in 1526 the prebends of Brixworth (Lincoln) and Swynbroke in Salisbury (*Lincoln Subsidy*, ed. Salter, pp. 127, 267).

[1] Roy, *Rede me*, p. 58, even alleges that Wolsey hoped ultimately to make the boy pope by ' the French king's grace.'

[2] *L.P.* iv. 2545, 2568, 2805-6, 2868-9, p. 1407.

[3] Valued at £185 a year in the *Valor Eccl.* (v. 299).

[4] *Ibid.* iv. 4105, 4229 [7], 4514, 4521-7, 4645-6, 4659.

to 'my poor scholar, the dean of Wells': the promotions thus vacated would, he urged, enable Henry 'to avance twenty chaplains' and Wolsey himself to 'fynish my poore college.'[1] Wolsey's audacity sometimes merged into an effrontery which has no parallel in English history; and this last request was too much, even for Henry's complaisance. Durham remained vacant until Tunstal's appointment in 1530, but Wolsey succeeded in drawing the revenues until he was tottering to his fall in August 1529.[2]

In May of that year du Bellay referred to the presence of 'Wolsey's son' in Paris as a security in the hands of Francis I; and in October Chapuys informs Charles V that the cardinal's son, about whom he had previously written, had been summoned to England.[3] His scandalous preferments and the scandalous use made of them by Wolsey to enrich himself had been stigmatised in July by Palsgrave, and were made one of the charges against Wolsey by Sir Thomas More and his colleagues in the house of lords.[4] Bishop Nix seized the opportunity to cite his archdeacon of Norfolk and Suffolk to appear before him in January, 1530: Nix 'is a devilish man,' writes John Curat, who reports the citation and was himself in a similar predicament now that he was

---

[1] State Papers, i. 328; L.P. iv. 4807 n., 4924, 5019.

[2] See above, p. 236.

[3] Le Grand, iii. 315-16; L.P. iv. 5581; Bradford, p. 291; L.P. iv. 6026; Spanish Cal. 1529-30, p. 304.

[4] L.P. iv. p. 2552; Herbert, p. 298, Art. 27, where Wolsey is charged with securing for Wynter revenues amounting to £2700 a year and giving him only £200 a year to live on. The former figure is not far out: Wynter's four archdeaconries would probably bring him between £1600 and £2000, his five prebends £200 or more, and his deanery, chancellorship, rectories, and other benefices would account for the rest. Beverley, in 1536, was worth about £70 a year (ibid. x. 941). Moreover, Lupset in his letter to Erasmus of 23 Aug. 1525 (above, p. 309 n. 2) says the boy already had 7000 ducats a year (= £1555, or c. £20,000 in modern currency). He thought, however, that he would abandon his ecclesiastical preferments and marry the heiress of Henry Bourchier, second earl of Essex; eventually she married William Parr, marquis of Northampton and brother of queen Catherine Parr. Finally Wolsey himself in his letter of 6 Oct. 1528 gives £2000 'or thereabouts' as 'the yearly value' of Wynter's preferments, agreeing for once with Roy who had that year put it at the same figure (Rede me, p. 58).

no longer protected from his bishop by the papal legate.[1]
Wynter lost many of his preferments by his father's fall,
but retained those in the diocese of York. Henry had
adopted him as 'his scholar,' and made him his chaplain ;
and in 1532-4 he was travelling in France and Italy with
three servants and four horses, always outliving his income
and begging from his friends, especially Cromwell.[2] In
1537 Cromwell obtained for him the archdeaconry of
Cornwall, which he promptly leased with all its profits for
thirty-five years to a layman, William Body, who was
murdered by the Cornish insurgents at Helston in 1548.[3]
This scandalous lease led to a good deal of litigation, and
was quashed in the bishop of Exeter's court ; and in 1543
Wynter resigned the archdeaconry which he had regarded,
like his other benefices, solely as a source of income to
be spent abroad. 'I am devoted to letters,' he wrote to
Cromwell on 2 March 1534, 'but desire to keep my preferments,' though he was still evading priest's orders.[4]
He disappears from sight with his resignation of the archdeaconry ; his sister received a pension at the dissolution of
Shaftesbury in 1540, and is said to have survived till 1553.[5]

Wolsey's nepotism, like his legatine authority, almost
attained to papal proportions ; it has demanded attention, not
merely because one of his latest ecclesiastical biographers
ignores it altogether, and another professes himself unable to
determine whether Wolsey had any children at all,[6] but because it illustrates his lack of any ordinary standard by which
to measure and govern his conduct. He emulated popes
and princes without any scruple because he considered himself their equal, and the wrath he provoked was largely due
to the fact that he was not to the manner born. The

---

[1] *L.P.* iv. 6139.

[2] *Ibid.* iv. 6261, 6529 ; **v.** 766 [12] ; vi. 314-15.

[3] Le Neve, i. 399 ; Mrs. Rose-Troup, *The Western Rebellion of* 1549,
pp. 47-63, 172, 415 ; and *P.R.O. List of Star Chamber Proc.* xiii. 45.

[4] *L.P.* vii. 280. For his acknowledgement of Henry VIII's kindness,
see *ibid.* 964.

[5] Brewer, *loc. cit.*, says Thomas survived till 1546, but the references
in vols. **xix.-xxi.** of *L.P.* are to another Thomas Winter.

[6] Creighton and E. L. Taunton, pp. 228 *et seq.*

' butcher's cur ' had to make his way with nothing to help him, except his own qualities, until he won the favour of Henry VIII, who alone seems to have borne him no personal grudge.[1] He would not have won and retained that favour so long, had he not possessed personal attractions as well as political abilities of a remarkable order. Erasmus, who declared, after the cardinal's fall, that he had ' clearly governed more really than the king himself, had been feared by all, and loved by few, if any,' had previously written of his ' rare and unheard of affability,' though he admitted even then that he was not always affable or easy to get on with ;[2] and there is as good evidence for the truth of Shakespeare's lines :—

> Lofty and sour to them that lov'd him not ;
> But, to those men that sought him, sweet as summer,

as there is for the preceding accusation that

>   He was a man
> Of an unbounded stomach, ever ranking
> Himself with princes   .   .   .   .   .
> He would say untruths and be ever double
> Both in his words and meaning. He was never,
> But when he meant to ruin, pitiful.
> His promises were, as he then was, mighty ;
> But his performance, as he now is, nothing :[3]
> Of his own body he was ill, and gave
> The clergy ill example.

Even Tyndale seasons his censure with a grain of reluctant homage : ' his chief study, yea, and all his felicity and inward joy, hath ever been to exercise that ' angel's wit of his ' (as my lord of Lincoln[4] was wont to praise him) in driving of such drifts to beguile all men, and to bind the

---

[1] According to Cavendish (p. 278), the king told him on 6 Dec. 1530 that he would rather have lost £20,000 than Wolsey. Complimentary regrets are not very costly, and Henry's may be set side by side with Charles V's alleged remark (Roper, *More*, p. 95) that he would rather have lost the best city in his dominions than so worthy a counsellor as More.

[2] ' Rara quaedam et inaudita comitas . . . non passim comis aut facilis ' (Ellis, I, ii. 48 ; Elyot, *Boke of the Governour*, ed. Croft, ii. 40-3).

[3] Cf. Skelton, i. 283 : To make fayre promyse, what are ye the worse ?

[4] Bishop Longland.

whole world withal'; [1] and the painful anxiety of his rivals to keep him away from court after his fall affords testimony to the wizardry of which he was accused.

Still more convincing, because unconscious, is the witness his colleagues bear against themselves to Wolsey's personal ascendency in council. They complain in their parliamentary charges that he overbore their opinion and browbeat them into unwilling submission. But it is fairly clear that the dominance was due to a superiority of intellectual vigour and vitality. They acquiesced in his advice before it was collectively tendered on their behalf to the king; for the convention was already at least a century old, that council's advice to the king must be, in form at any rate, unanimous, and the first lord Tiptoft, the father of the 'butcher' earl of Worcester, had in 1428 liberated his reluctant soul with the subscription *nolens volo* to a council minute. [2] Wolsey's colleagues liberated theirs in parliamentary accusations after the event and after Wolsey's condemnation in the court of king's bench. They would be no partisans of a tyranny that was past; but they had given Wolsey his chance, because they were not quite sure whence his counsel proceeded, and because his 'angel's wit' and the animation and passion, with which he supported his schemes, convinced or deceived them as well as himself. [3]

---

[1] *Works*, Parker Soc. ii. 334-5.

[2] Nicolas, *Proceedings of the Privy Council*, iii. 312; *D.N.B.* lvi. 410.

[3] Skelton (*Works*, ii. 32-3) pictures them as being simply cowed:

> He is set so hye
> In his ierarchy
> Of frantycke frenesy
> And folysshe fantasy,
> That in the chambre of starres
> All maters there he marres;
> Clapping his rod on the borde,
> No man dare speke a worde,
> For he hathe all the sayenge,
> Without any renayenge;
> He rolleth in his recordes,
> He sayth, How saye ye, my lordes?
> Is nat my reason good?
> Good euyn, good Robin Hood.

Wolsey did not adopt the maxim, that the offensive is the best method of defence, as a matter of reason and calculation, but because it was his nature to be aggressive. Mere self-defence would not have led the boy from Ipswich very far along the path to the woolsack and to the steps of the papal throne. He needed vehemence and a vehicle; and the trouble about his progress was that, while he possessed a superabundance of driving force, he lacked the means of self-control. Like some other great men, of whom Napoleon was the greatest, he came to a sudden end because he did not know when or even how to stop. His spirit ruled him, not he his spirit; and his spirit was highly explosive. There was a great deal of passion, but little patience, in his soul; and passion provoked him into outrageous breaches of good manners and diplomatic etiquette. He laid violent hands on the papal nuncio Chieregati;[1] he not only intercepted the dispatches of Charles V's ambassador in England, Lois de Praet, when the emperor was Henry VIII's ally, but kept him in prison and prohibited further correspondence with his master because de Praet had presumed in confidential dispatches to inform the emperor of Wolsey's secret dealings with Louise of Savoy and to criticise his conduct of English affairs.[2] At the same time he insisted that the regent of the Netherlands should dismiss one of her principal counsellors, the provost of Utrecht, because Wolsey thought

> Some say yes, and some
> Syt styll as they were dom :
> Thus thwartyng ower thom,
> He ruleth all the roste
> With braggynge and with bost ;
> Borne up on euery syde
> With pompe and with pryde.

[1] *Venetian Cal.* ii. 341 ; Rawdon Brown, ii. 17 ; cf. *ibid.* i. 158. Chieregati was another of Erasmus' correspondents (*Epistolae*, iii. 61).

[2] *Spanish Cal.* iii. 13, 24, 42, 50, 76, 78, 92, 112 ; *L.P.* iv. 186 ; and see above, pp. 138-9. De Praet was a soldier, administrator, diplomatist, and ' one of the foremost figures in the Netherlands during the reign of Charles V.' Erasmus, Vives, and other humanists dedicated books to him (*Erasmi Ep.* ed. Allen, iv. 450).

him too French.[1] In the autumn of 1527, before his declaration of war on Charles V, he urged the French to seize the emperor's chancellor, Gattinara, then on his way to Italy; for he now regarded Gattinara as 'the wickedest man in the world,' and wanted him to be handed over to his own tender mercies.[2] He demanded the imprisonment at Rome of the friars there who had opposed his dissolution of the monasteries;[3] he offered to pay the expenses of a military expedition to overawe the conclave of cardinals in his own interests as a candidate for election to the papacy;[4] and he told the French chancellor in 1521 that Buckingham had had his head cut off for murmuring against his policy and seeking to frustrate it.[5]

Force was ever his favourite remedy for resistance: he imprisoned Pace in the Tower on 25 October 1527 for opposing the divorce; and Casale, another of his agents, who was happily out of his reach, fell ill when he heard of Wolsey's displeasure.[6] He clamoured for the excommunication of Spanish bishops for not paying his pensions out of their sees,[7] and he took the administration of cardinal Hadrian's bishopric of Bath and Wells out of Foxe's hands before Hadrian had been deprived.[8] Annoyed with Venice for not joining England against Francis I, he seized the artillery on Venetian ships in English waters 'out of the love I bear them';[9] and he was not above forging

---

[1] *L.P.* iv. 110, 141, 158, 186, 224. He threatened to break off confidential communications with the regent unless she complied, and complained of her conduct to Charles V

[2] *Ibid.* iv. 3365, 3757, 3940. Mercurino Arbitrio Gattinara (1465-1530), a Piedmontese, succeeded Le Sauvage as chancellor of Castile in 1518 and was made cardinal, as Wolsey was falling, on 13 Aug. 1529. His autobiography, only discovered in the 20th century, was edited in 1915 by C. Bornate (*Erasmi Ep.* ed. Allen, iv. 359; cf. Armstrong, *Charles V*, passim).

[3] *L.P.* iv. 1750.   [4] See above, p. 126.

[5] Le Glay, *Negociations*, ii. 520. Cf. the cases of Sir Robert Sheffield (above, p. 52) and John Roo (p. 220).

[6] See my *Henry VIII*, p. 114; *Erasmi Ep.* vii. 335, 455; *Spanish Cal.* 1527-9, pp. 440-3; Tyndale, *Practice*, p. 317; *L.P.* iv. 2879.

[7] *Ibid.* iv. 2493, 3153, 3263.

[8] *Venetian Cal.* ii. 412.   [9] *L.P.* iii. 2863.

letters and destroying papal briefs and royal letters in favour of other people.[1] The venom which at times affected him he attributed to others; and in 1527 he wrote to Henry VIII that if the pope were taken to Spain 'he would probably be poisoned there.' In that year he threatened the emperor with deposition, and in 1529 the pope with deprivation.[2]

Few men have exerted greater authority than Wolsey, and still fewer have afforded so striking an illustration of the demoralising effects of irresponsible power. It was already a settled principle of English law that the king could not arrest a subject himself; for the king could do no wrong, and if the arrest were unlawful, there would be no lawful remedy.[3] Some minister must therefore take the responsibility; but what if the responsible minister were a cardinal or any clerk in holy orders? From the day when Sir Amias Paulet put him in the stocks, throughout the agitation over the criminal clergy act of 1512, down to his own arrest in 1530, Wolsey had maintained the personal irresponsibility of the Lord's anointed to the secular arm; and of spiritual jurisdiction in England he was himself arbiter, responsible only to a distant, incurious, and helpless pope. He failed to exercise that restraint upon himself which was needed all the more because it could be exercised by no one else; and the exorbitance of his vagaries was not the least of the factors in his career which demonstrated the necessity, and precipitated the final assertion, of the fundamental principle of English law. The old phrase about the 'established' church of England has gone somewhat

---

[1] *L.P.* iv. 2102; Rawdon Brown, ii. 116; cf. Skelton, ii. 47

> For what is a man the better
> For the kynges letter?
> He wyll tere it asunder
> Wherat moche I wonder.

and W. Roy, *Rede me*, p. 105:

> His power he doth so extende,
> That the kingis letters to rende
> He will not forbeare in his rage.

[2] See above, p. 158; *L.P.* iv. 5746.

[3] Tottel, *Year-Books*, 1 Henry VII, f. 4*b*; my *Henry VII*, ii. 10-11.

out of fashion because it has been misunderstood : it was plain enough in the sixteenth century, when it meant that the church in England had been placed on a basis of law, which was English rather than Roman, admitted no rival jurisdiction, and tolerated no clerical ' liberty to sin.' That settlement did not in the least imply that an English churchman could not be an English statesman : there was still room for an archbishop Laud within the terms of the establishment. But it did mean that, in the last resort, English churchmen as well as English statesmen were equally amenable to a law that was common to all.

Wolsey's abuse of his immunity would not, however, have contributed much to that reformation, had it been restricted to violations of diplomatic practice and international law. It was his English victims who counted in his indictment, and they were forthcoming in every sphere in which Wolsey had displayed his indifference to legality and to other liberties than his own. A good deal of the resentment was perhaps rather the expression of a novel independence than resistance to a novel usurpation. Archbishops were still occasionally termed the ' sovereigns ' of their suffragans, and even after the reformation bishops would sometimes talk of their ' subjects.'[1] Wolsey as a cardinal, and therefore a ' prince ' of the church, and still more as a legate *de latere* and therefore a sort of papal viceroy, might well assume a loftier condescension. He treated Charles V as his equal at Bruges in 1521, and was formally admitted to be the arbiter between Henry VIII and Francis I. He naturally expected dukes to hold the ewer and towel while he washed, and earls to tie the latchet of his shoes.[2] But such services did not come naturally from

---

[1] See my *Evolution of Parliament*, p. 228, and Hist. MSS. Commission, *Report on Various Collections*, iv. 225 : ' William Walter herd the bishop of Sarum [Jewel] say that the Maior of Sarum was his maior and the people of Sarum his subjectes.'

[2] *Venetian Cal.* iii. 18, 29 ; *L.P.* iv. p. 2560, ' and temporal lords served us of combe water.' His delay in giving audience annoyed foreign diplomatists, English magnates, and humbler folk alike. As early as 1517 Thomas Allen complains to the earl of Shrewsbury that ' he that shall be a suitor to Wolsey may have no other business but to give attendance

the ducal servitors, because legates *de latere* were somewhat rare and exotic in England and *legati nati* had not presumed to exact them : their legacies had become almost indigenous in their archiepiscopal guise and dukes were lower, but only a little lower, than archbishops. Still, it was not the service which they resented, so much as the spirit in which it was exacted ; they would sooner have rendered it to Fisher, though only a bishop, because they still thought him the holiest bishop in England, while Wolsey was only, in Cavendish's words, 'the haughtiest man alive.'[1]

These might have been only private griefs but for their public and ceremonial exhibition which Wolsey required. Even so, they were of little moment compared with his obvious indifference to the laws, the liberties, and the customs of the country. Within his own archiepiscopal jurisdiction York, Beverley, and Hexham were threatened with the extinction of their 'liberties' ;[2] the mayor of York was deposed, and the city reduced to humbly thanking the cardinal that it was still to remain a city ;[3] and in 1530 Wolsey's reluctance to go north was attributed to his fear of being murdered by his indignant subjects.[4] Wolsey was doubtless unfamiliar with the common law and to a large extent with the statute law. But, in view of his frequent reference to, and employment of, the statutes of præmunire, his alleged ignorance of them is only apologetic imagination : the trouble was not so much that he was ignorant of law and custom as that he thought that they did not matter. Protestants could not, perhaps, protest with much consistency when in 1525 the cardinal quoted the scriptural case of

upon his pleasure,' and says he would sooner be sent to Rome. Lord Dacre's servant had to wait five months in London for an answer—Skelton, has ' perchaunce halfe a yere' (Lodge, *Illustr.* i. 34 ; Skelton, *Works*, ii. 46 ; *L.P.* ii. 3807 ; and the sixteenth article of his impeachment, Herbert, p. 297).

[1] P. 275 ; cf. *Venetian Cal.* iii. 56 : ' He is the proudest prelate that ever breathed.'

[2] *L.P.* iv 2740, 2835, 5107, 5954.   [3] *Ibid.* iv. 1218, 3846.

[4] *Spanish Cal.* 1529-30, p. 515, and *Venetian Cal.* 1509-19, p. 440, where Wolsey is said to be afraid to go to York *sine magno praesidio.* Doubts about his reception increased his eagerness for the king's letters of recommendation ; see above, pp. 274-5, 286.

Joseph as a precedent for his own unparliamentary taxation ;
but lawyers, and even common councillors of London,
were shocked when he argued that the act forbidding
benevolences was invalid because Richard III, under whom
it was passed, was a usurper ; and Wolsey himself cannot
have thought that any law entitled him to threaten those
who refused to pay his demands with the loss of their
heads. The truth was that he had no respect for parliament
or its legislation. He attempted to browbeat the only
parliament he summoned, and he had little more regard for
convocation which he treated in 1523 in much the same
way as the house of commons. Even a papal co nclav
might be legitimately overawed by a military force obeying
in Wolsey's cause an emperor's behest. He had no belief
in any but despotic authority, and only in that so long as it
served his interests. When he was at issue with Charles V,
he proposed the emperor's deposition ; and, when for a
moment he doubted the loyalty of Clement VII to his
legate, he threatened the pope with an English schism.

This egotism exceeded even Tudor arrogance, and it
was exhibited in more than Tudor ostentation. The papal
legate became the richest man in England save the king,
and even that exception has to be qualified by various considerations. The royal revenues were undoubtedly greater
than Wolsey's, but royal expenses included those of national
government which do not in modern times fall on the
privy purse ; while no small part of the expense of Henry's
diplomatic service was incurred in promoting the cardinal's
personal interests. Whatever the relation of their revenues,
Wolsey undoubtedly acquired, between 1513 and 1529,
far more wealth than did Henry VIII. In 1519 Giustiniani
estimated his yearly income at 42,000 ducats,[1] about £9500,

---

[1] The ducat had risen between 1453 to 1512 from 3s. 4d. to 4s. 4d.
(*Venetian Cal.* vol. i. p. lxxi *n.* ; my *Henry VII*, iii. 321) ; it was in
1531 reckoned at 5s. (*L.P.* v. 62) ; 4s. 6d. has been taken as an average value
in Wolsey's time, because it was fixed at this value by proclamation on
6 July 1525 (*L.P.* iv. 1478, 1481). This 42,000 ducats was made up as
follows : York, 14,000 ; Bath, 8000 ; fees from chancery, 5000 ; and
new year's gifts, 15,000. Giustiniani reckons his silver as worth 150,000
ducats, and says that wherever he was he always had a sideboard of plate

or over £100,000 in modern currency. But that was before Wolsey had exchanged Bath and Wells for the progressively richer bishoprics of Durham (March 1523) and Winchester (Oct. 1528), had acquired St. Albans (17 Dec. 1521), the richest monastery in England, was farming three bishoprics for their foreign occupants, had exploited the financial advantages of his legatine jurisdiction, realised the full extent of his value as a pensioner of Francis I or the emperor and as a dispenser of favours to Englishmen, or taken his profit from the dissolution of monasteries. In 1531 Giustiniani's successor, Falier, in making his report on his three years' English embassy, put Wolsey's ordinary income [1] at 150,000 ducats, which would be about £35,000 and at least ten times that amount in present values. In any case, he enjoyed the income of a modern multi-millionaire, though he could not of course dispose of the capital sources from which that income was derived. Still he had acquired it, not like cardinal Beaufort or Edward IV by money-lending and commercial enterprise, and still less like Henry VII by careful economy. It had all come to him by exploiting the favour of Henry VIII and the opportunities afforded him by the discharge of his official duties : he pillaged as papal legate the goods of every bishop he succeeded, made as foreign minister a private financial profit out of every treaty he concluded, and took as chancellor a commission for every favour he conferred.[2]

worth 25,000 ducats (*Venetian Cal.* 1509-19, p. 560 ; Rawdon Brown, *Four Years at the Court of Henry VIII*, ii. 314).

[1] Excluding his French and other pensions and his new year's and other presents (*Venetian Cal.* 1527-33, p. 300). These certainly amounted to much more in 1529 than in 1519, and Wolsey's total income on the eve of his fall cannot have been much less than £50,000, or over half a million in modern values.

[2] The document in which Sforza promised Wolsey 10,000 ducats a year if he were restored to the duchy of Milan is printed in Rymer, *Fœdera*, xiii. 525-6. The growth of his French pension can be traced in the French official accounts, which Bergenroth transcribed for insertion in his *Spanish Cal.* (1509-25, nos. 194, 251, 255, 262, 265, 270, 273, 277, 301, 305); cf. above, pp. 116-17, 148-9. For his Spanish pensions see below, p. 324 *n*. 2. For his seizure of Bainbridge's goods, see above, pp. 21-2, and for other bishops see the inventory of Wolsey's property in *L.P.* iv.

These figures are almost incredible to an age which has been led to believe that, while there was a great spoliation of the church in the reign of Henry VIII, there was not very much to despoil, and that ecclesiastical wealth before the spoliation has been greatly exaggerated. We must not, of course, confuse the wealth of the church with the wealth of particular churchmen ; and the complaint of the Good parliament of 1376 that the church had been endowed by the laity with more than a third of the land in England[1] was afterwards made ridiculous by applying it to the monasteries alone. But so far as Wolsey's wealth is concerned, it is more difficult to realise than easy to exaggerate ; and the figures have little meaning without comparison. In the official 'Valor Ecclesiasticus' of 1535 the archbishopric of Canterbury is valued at £3204,[2] somewhat more than double its present emoluments. The duke of Buckingham was supposed to be the greatest landlord in the country, and his revenues were given in 1521 as £6045.[3] Wolsey, after his fall and while he was talking to Cavendish about being 'a poor vicar'[4] i.e. only archbishop of York, declared that he could not live on less than £4000. Now, as lord chancellor, Wolsey had like his successors the right to present to livings of less than a certain value, and he increased that value by $33\frac{1}{3}$ per cent., either to extend the range of his patronage or, more legitimately, to compensate

6184. Of Lincoln Cavendish says 'he found the means that he gat possession of all his predecessours goods, into his handes, whereof I have diverse times seene some parte that furnished his house' (p. 23).

[1] *Rot. Parl.* ii. 337a. Tyndale has the same complaint that 'the priests have the third foot of all the temporal lords' (*Works*, i. 236). Savine, *English Monasteries*, pp. 76-87, considers the sixteenth century estimates 'fairly trustworthy'; according to them the gross income of the monasteries on the eve of dissolution was about £171,000, and the net income about £135,000 in contemporary values. According to this calculation, Wolsey's income was at least a quarter of the total English monastic revenues of his time.

[2] *Record Comm.* ed. i. 89. This would equal about £30,000 to £40,000, and the present value is given in Whitaker's *Almanack* as £15,000. In 1532 the figure was little more than £2000 (*L.P.* v. 450). But these Tudor figures are for lands only and do not apparently include fees for probate, etc.

[3] *L.P.* iii. 1288.   [4] Cavendish, p. 215.

for the decline in the value of money.   The relevant point is that the increase was from twenty marks (£13 6s. 8d.) to £20 a year ; [1] and its importance consists in the fact that Wolsey could not live as ' a poor vicar ' on less than from two to three hundred times the income from the ' livings ' to which, as lord chancellor, he presented.   In Wolsey's day the poorest of benefices seem to have been about as poor as they are to-day, though pluralities tempered the wind to the shorn but favoured lamb ; for himself five times the present revenues of York [2] seemed the direst poverty. Yet at that moment he was disclaiming all desire for ' the muck of this world ' and pleading for more on the grounds that ' in space groweth grace ' and ' the king cannot gain so much at any man's hand as at mine.' [3]

The poverty was relative to the wealth he had lost. Only the roughest estimate of the details of what Spelman called Wolsey's ' incomparable wealth ' [4] can be formed, though some of the figures are known.   His French pension was 25,000 crowns ' without the extras,' writes Chapuys on 31 December 1529, ' of which not one livre is owing.' [5] This would amount to about £7500 ; and there seems no reason to doubt the substantial truth of the charge that he made about £2500 a year out of Wynter's preferments. [6] York was probably worth £3000 or more ; Winchester in 1535 had lands worth £3820 a year, and St. Albans' lands worth £2102 a year. [7]   It is not likely that Wolsey made less than £1000 a year out of each of the three bishoprics

---

[1] G. W. Sanders, *Orders in Chancery*, i. 10-12.   These figures would be equivalent to about £160 and £240 a year in modern values.

[2] £9000 ; Wolsey's £4000 would now be over £45,000.

[3] *L.P.* iv. 6182, 6226.   [4] *History of Sacrilege*, pp. 204, 208.

[5] *Spanish Cal.* 1529-30, p. 384.   [6] See above, p. 311 *n.* 4.

[7] *Valor Ecclesiasticus*, i. 451 ; ii. 2.   The *Valor* unfortunately gives (v. 1) only the value of York as taxed in 3 Eliz. after the spoliation of Henry VIII's and Edward VI's reigns.   It appears there as £1609; Giustiniani's reckoning at 14,000 ducats would make it £3150 in 1518. Wolsey said that Winchester was not worth much more than Durham (Ehses, *Römische Dokumente*, p. 64).   Rochford's reckoning of the half-year's rents of Durham at £1200 (above, p. 236) would not presumably include its spiritualties, and it is almost exactly half the £2398 at which the total value appears in the *Valor* (v. 299).

he farmed, allowing their occupants what Cavendish calls
'a convenient' pension;[1] and he was still drawing his own
pensions from Spanish bishoprics until the declaration of
war in 1528.[2] Leaving these out of account, there would
remain another £12,000 a year to bring the total up to
Falier's figure; but that is not an excessive sum to expect
from Wolsey's emoluments as lord chancellor, the profits
of his episcopal, archiepiscopal, and legatine jurisdictions,
and the presents which, Giustiniani remarks as early as
1519, he received 'like a king.'[3] As lord chancellor his
salary and allowances, with an additional £50 a term for
sitting in the star chamber, came to little more than a
pound a day; but the substantial emoluments consisted of
fees, which cannot have brought him in less than the £2000
or so a year accruing a century later to each of the 'six
clerks' in chancery.[4] The profits of his legatine jurisdiction can hardly be guessed at: when one estate paid
£666 13s. 4d. for probate and Wolsey was claiming a
shilling in the pound on the value of all wills proved,[5] the

---

[1] Cavendish, p. 29, who also points out that ' all the spirituall promotions and presentations of these bishopricks were wholy and fully in his
domaine and disposion, to preferre whom he liked.'

[2] For these pensions from the archbishopric of Toledo and bishoprics
of Palencia and Badajos, see above, p. 117 n.; Rymer, xiii. 591-2, 714,
725, 769-71; L.P. iii. 709, 958, 1012, 2774, 3032, 3244; iv. 2489,
2493, 2987, 3041, 3263, 3464; and Spanish Cal. ii. 251, 273, 600, and
vols. iii. and iv. passim. The pension from Badajos was 5000 and from
Palencia 2000 ducats.

[3] Venetian Cal. 1509-19, p. 560; cf. Cavendish, p. 18, 'in came
presents, gifts, and rewardes so plentifully that I dare say he lacked
nothing that might either please his fantasy or enrich his coffers.'

[4] This at least was the figure in More's case (L.P. iv. 6079); but
allowances brought the chancellor's salary, without the star chamber,
up to £500 in Edward III's reign (Maxwell-Lyte, Great Seal, pp. 5, 329).
It was considerably higher before the end of the sixteenth century (L.P.
1544, i. 610 [41]; Household Ordinances, Soc. Antiq. ed. 1790, p. 241).
A pound a day was the salary of the lord privy seal (L.P. i. 2197; iv.
331). For the fees of the Six Clerks, see Sir Simonds D'Ewes, Autobiog.
ed. Halliwell, i. 177).

[5] See above, p. 93. In L.P. iv. 2360 is a brief summary of a six-page
document in the P.R.O. containing 110 cases of fees for various ecclesiastical offences; cf. ibid. iv. p. 3047, v. 66, and Spanish Cal. 1529-30,
pp. 326, 362.

proceeds from that source alone would run into thousands. Equally incalculable were his profits from the wardship of wealthy minors like the earls of Derby and Oxford. There were also fees for the granting of denization, the legitimation of bastards, for marriage dispensations, and licences for pluralities, not to mention the commissions Wolsey took for making presentations to livings, visiting monasteries, and consenting to conventual elections.[1]

Wolsey needed it all. Hampton Court has survived as a memorial of his magnificence. But he also built palaces at York Place, the More, and Tyttenhanger[2]; and two of these at least excited more comment than Hampton Court. The More was Wolsey's favourite country house, and du Bellay thought it more splendid than Hampton Court; but it was York Place which Henry VIII coveted most and converted into Whitehall : it is one of the ironies of Wolsey's career that he should not only have unconsciously done so much to build up the modern English state, but should also have unwittingly provided the habitat for its swelling bureaucracy. Then there were his colleges at Oxford and Ipswich to which Wolsey devoted part of the wealth he derived from the monasteries he dissolved.[3]

[1] Cf. Rymer, xiii. 605-6, 788-9; Roy, p. 59; Brodie, *L.P.* i. p. xvii; Lodge, *Ill.* i. 35. For some of his fees charged for monastic visitations see Salter, *Lincoln Subsidy of 1526* (Oxf. Hist. Soc.), pp. vi, 45-8, 93, 166.

[2] Ellis, *Original Letters*, iii, ii. 65. The More and Tyttenhanger belonged to St. Alban's abbey, Hampton Court to the knights of St. John (*L.P.* iv. App. 70).* The prior, Sir Richard Weston, complained after Wolsey's fall that the lease of other lands of his order had passed to Wolsey ' without free assent, and contrary to right ' (*ibid.* v. 335) ; some of them had been extorted by Sir Richard Empson and passed on to Wolsey (Rymer, xiii. 269). His lease of Hampton Court is dated 11 Jan. 1514-15 (Law, *Hampton Court*, p. 343). In 1524-5, stung perhaps by Skelton's gibe (see above, p. 103 *n.* 1), he ' gave ' the lease to Henry, but continued to occupy it till his attainder (Hall, p. 703 ; *State Papers*, i. 150 *n.*; *L.P.* iv. 5754). He then ' gave ' it once more to Henry, this time ' in exchange ' for Richmond (Cavendish, p. 196), and on 5 June, 1531 the prior of St. John's ' granted ' it to certain trustees for Henry's ' use ' (*L.P.* v. 285).

[3] See above, pp. 202-4. Their total yearly value was £1826 13s. 4d. (*ibid.* v. 47).

Parental affection was stamped all over Cardinal's college;[1]
and although Henry VIII's council provided him with the
convenient argument that so great a college was not 'meet
for the common weal,' the king's final foundation of Christ
Church endowed it with lands exceeding in annual value the
whole of Wolsey's dissolutions.[2]   Anxiety for its fate was
one of the redeeming features of Wolsey's last year; but
the college had only fallen into Henry's hands through
Wolsey's own negligence or inability to release his grip on
anything he grasped.   The deeds granting him the lands
of the dissolved monasteries were drafted on his instructions: they granted the lands to him and his heirs in fee
simple for ever, and no 'trust' or 'use' was expressed
therein.   They therefore remained his absolute property,
and the college acquired no legal personality: hence, as the
judges explained, they fell to the crown under the operation
of Wolsey's attainder, a fate from which they would otherwise have been exempt.[3]   Wolsey had not trusted his own
foundation with the control of its endowments because he
could not bear to part with authority: even after his fall he
was still interfering with the election of proctors in the
university of which Warham still was chancellor.[4]

Wolsey, however, contemplated no college that would
have compared in size or splendour with the household he
maintained; and a few comparative figures will illustrate
the exorbitant importance he attached to his position and
to the exhibition of his wealth and power.   At the field of
the Cloth of Gold he had three hundred servants, Warham
and each of the two dukes seventy; and at the subsequent
meeting with Charles V at Gravelines, while they had ten
on horse and ten on foot, Wolsey had fifty of each.[5]   In the
list of household servants assessed for subsidy in 1526,
those of Henry's sister Mary, the ex-queen of France,

---

[1] See above, p. 217.

[2] *L.P.* iv. 6579; 1546, ii. 648 [25]; the details fill ten columns of
the calendar.   The value £2200 appears on p. 337*a*; but the fortunes of
the 'House' under Henry VIII still need elucidation.

[3] See Wolsey's correspondence on the subject with the judges, attorney-
general, and others in *L.P.* iv. 6510, 6575-9.

[4] *Ibid.* iv. 6377; Fiddes, *Coll.* p. 122.   [5] *L.P.* iii. 702, 906.

number forty-four, those of his daughter Mary sixty-five ; Wolsey's number four hundred and twenty-nine.[1] There were at least as many more who were not taxed for subsidy, and the total number of Wolsey's household servants was little if at all short of a thousand. In a state paper attributed to Burghley it is said that 'in his family there were one earl, nine barons and about a thousand knights, gentlemen, and inferior officers.'[2] Even that number seems inadequate to account for the gargantuan scale of its commissariat : a somewhat obscure list of its requirements from 10 October 1528 to 30 September 1529 includes ' 430 oxen, 181 muttons in the month of October ; 728 ditto within November ; 621 ditto between Easter and 1 August ; 363 ditto between 1 August and 30 September.'[3]

To the accumulation of this gigantic mass of worldly goods Wolsey devoted much of his energy during the zenith of his fortunes, and to its remnants he clung with desperate tenacity as the shadows lengthened on his parting day. Getting and spending, he made waste his powers, and laid bare the poverty of his soul. His kingdom was all outside him, and he had little within on which to rely. His courage did not consist in the fortitude of his mind : no great man was ever more pitiably dependent upon externals ; and when he looked upon the travail of his soul he found no satisfaction because there was no sacrifice. His dignity consisted in his dignities, his honour in his honours, and his welfare in his wealth. He could recognise in others, as in Sir Thomas More, the virtue of being slow to ask for favours ; he could never refrain from asking for himself. In this he was typical of a shamelessly acquisitive age, but he shamed himself and his profession by his insatiable appetite for gain ; and in the ruin which he precipitated, he pulled down, not the temple of his foes, but the altars he had made his stepping-stones to fortune.

Yet he had a vision of better things and a mind and

---

[1] *L.P.* iv. 2972, 6185.

[2] *Cabala*, ed. 1715, pp. 97-111 ; cf. Fiddes, *Wolsey*, p. 531, and Burnet, *Ref.* ed. Pocock, iii. 84.

[3] *L.P.* iv. 5967. *

intellect to achieve them, had not the grossness of carnal affections outweighed the promptings of equity, and the wilderness of his spirit laid him open to the temptations of principalities and powers. In this, too, he betrayed the characteristics of an age of self-made men, marked by what modern psychology calls an 'inferiority complex.' We find it in Cromwell as well as in Wolsey, in the first two Dudleys, and to a modified extent in some of the Elizabethans ; and it was not confined to royal courts and aspiring politicians. Both the ancient universities surrendered their privileges and statutes to Wolsey to be reformed before they surrendered to Henry VIII ; and Cambridge declared that 'no cloudlet of envy could ever obfuscate his sempiternal glory, which would testify to posterity that there was once a legate, Thomas of York, who possessed all the excellences that could be found in man.'[1] The symptom is not difficult to explain ; but, unless we explain it, we cannot understand either the men or the age in which they lived. 'None of us all here,' once remarked Cranmer, who possessed the humility without the aggressiveness of the new men and was pleading for the continuation of mediæval facilities for the education of children of lowly origin, 'beinge gentlemen borne but hadd our begynnyng that wey from a lowe and base parentage.'[2] Englishmen of to-day, however humble the circumstances of their birth, have behind them centuries of legal, if not of social and economic, freedom. But the new men of the Tudor period were barely emerging from centuries of servitude ; and the freedmen of history have ever been the aptest servants of a servile state. They have to be freed long before they are free ; an inferiority complex is not to be exorcised by acts of emancipation or deeds of manumission, and symptoms of ancestral serfdom came out in the servility of Tudor statesmen.

[1] *L.P.* ii. 934, 4690, App. 46; iv. 963 ; Fiddes, *Collections*, pp. 34-42 ; Creighton, *Wolsey*, p. 145 ; Taunton, p. 103. Cf. *L.P.* 1543, i. 981 [71]. ' Never,' says More, ' was he saciate of hearinge his owne prayse ' (*English Works*, p. 1221).

[2] *Narratives of the Reformation* (Camden Soc.), pp. 274-5 ; my *Cranmer*, pp. 3-4.

But to them their bondage to the royal estate, just dawning as the English State upon their minds, was not a servitude but a redemption. After villeinage on a manor it was a glorious release ; and service to a throne was heaven to thraldom on a feudal franchise. Wolsey and Cromwell might have been villeins to the petty tyrant of a village : there is not much mystery, and there is more than simple baseness, in their devotion to a monarchy which, if it exacted much, exalted them to lofty heights of influence and power. They were, indeed, tenants at will of the crown, and the custom of the king's court gave them little security ; but their tenure of office afforded that crowning mercy to creative minds, a freedom from ' the meagre, stale, forbidding ways of custom, law, and statute,' and a liberty to build. * The creatures of mediæval bondage became the builders of Tudor palaces and the makers of modern England.

Wolsey's mind was not so much creative as acquisitive. He could acquire jurisdiction, and the extent of his acquisition amounted to the creation of a monopoly ; but it was a purely personal achievement, and did not create an institution. He could not found a dynasty of papal legates *a latere*, nor even establish its custom without dismembering the papal monarchy to which as late as 1529 he was hoping to succeed. But this was an inhibition imposed upon him, not by his lowly origin, but by his place in the Roman Catholic church. His mind took its colour from that environment, and he was singularly free from, or devoid of, those nationalistic impulses which were stirring, or about to stir, to passionate and patriotic self-expression the English laity of his time. It has been noted as if it were an anomaly that, although he sprang from the people, he understood them less than did Henry VIII in spite of his royal education.[1] The navy was one of the few departments of government in which he took little interest, and his vision was never turned across the ocean. He even failed to understand the English attachment to the house of Burgundy or its economic causes. He looked across the Channel consistently enough, but only because

[1] Creighton, p 131.

across it led the path to Rome, towards which his eyes had turned from his earliest advent to power.

We must acquit him of the graver charges of political or ecclesiastical dishonesty which have been alleged almost as though they were his principal claims to statesmanship. He did not aim 'at bringing the church under the royal power as completely as he wished to subject the state,' nor 'use the papal power, not as a means of guarding the rights of the church, but as a means of casting an air of ecclesiastical propriety over their abandonment.'[1] The assumption that whatever he did, he did to please the king, is pressed too far when it extends his servility to the crown to cover treachery to the church. From first to last Wolsey strove to retain for the church all the liberties it possessed. It is true that he compromised its position by the zest with which he concentrated its liberties in the hands of himself, a minister of the crown ; but, that he regarded himself as a mere conveyancer of those liberties to the crown is a theory inconsistent with the fundamental facts of his career. He looked to Rome for all his remedies : he stalled off the agitation over the cases of Hunne and Standish by appealing to Rome and obtaining a papal bull to restrict admission to lower orders, and postponed till after his fall the renewal of the anti-clerical act of 1512 ; he went to the pope for legatine powers to reform the church and dissolve monasteries ; and, even if he originally suggested Catherine's divorce, he insisted on its reference to Roman jurisdiction in the conviction that only papal sovereignty could decide it, and in the hope that a favourable decision would bind Henry VIII still more closely to the Roman see.[2] He instilled into Henry's mind the highest

---

[1] Creighton, pp. 132-3.

[2] Wolsey did, indeed, write in Jan. 1528 that his 'legatine authority might have been sufficient without any reference to the pope' (*L.P.* iv. 3913) ; but this was probably to earn credit with Clement VII for referring it. Sanga asserted in Dec. 1528 that the pope knew for certain that Wolsey had persuaded Henry to ask for a legate 'although the prelates of the kingdom assured him that he could do without one' (*ibid.* 5072). 'Would to God,' he continued, ' the cardinal had allowed the matter to take its course.'

conceptions of papal power : if, as legate, he received his authority from the pope, so had the king received his 'crown imperial,' which, says More, 'I never heard of before'; and More vainly tried to dissuade Henry from asserting the divine institution of the papacy in his book against Luther. 'Nay,' quoth his grace, 'we are so much bounden unto his see of Rome that we cannot do too much honour unto it.'[1] Wolsey protested, indeed, that his personal property should all of it go to the king; but so far from designing such a translation of his legatine jurisdiction, he lamented on the eve of his fall that it would be followed by the subversion of the church. Henry might be the defender of the faith, but Wolsey was convinced that he as legate was the only defender of the liberties of the church. He was at times more papal than the pope.

It was the egotism of that claim that ruined his defence. He could only see salvation in his own despotic power. He had as little faith in ecclesiastical as in political representation, and he could no more work with convocations than he could with parliaments. Amid all the papal troubles of 1525-29 he never suggested an œcumenical council : his expedient in 1527 was a schismatic conclave of four cardinals under himself as papal vicar. Hence the impossibility of his position : his power had neither pride of ancestry nor hope of posterity.[2] The crown had the one, and parliament the other; and between them they might effect a permanent English reformation. But Wolsey had no sense of the 'body-politic' of which lawyers and statesmen were beginning to talk; he might be the head, but he was not a good member of anything. Nor could a papal legate, with revocable powers, achieve a national reformation without the support of either the pope or parliament. He contemplated, in fact, and desired no such reformation as that for which parliament clamoured in 1529, which

[1] Roper, *More*, pp. 65-6; *L.P.* vii. 289 (p. 124); More, *English Works*, p. 1424.

[2] 'Papal government by cardinal-legates,' wrote Creighton (*Papacy*, v. 177) before he dealt with Wolsey, 'could never waken national feeling.'

was not so much doctrinal—Tyndale denounced its earliest measures as hypocritical shams—as a practical pruning of ecclesiastical wealth and jurisdiction. He might convert monasteries into colleges, endow learning, provided it were not of the 'new' variety, and plan to establish new bishoprics ; but he stood in his person for all the ecclesiastical liberties, privileges, power, and riches against which the opposition was massing its forces. His character condemned him to sterility in the face of his environment.

A policy, for which there was no national demand and for which Wolsey sought no national support, can hardly be called national ; and no epithet is less appropriate to Wolsey's cast of mind or scheme of things. He might be called a good European, a good papalist, even a good catholic so far as intention was concerned. But the national isolation, splendid or ignominious, to which Henry VIII, following Henry VII and heralding Elizabeth, turned after 1529, was a reaction against the European and papal policy of Wolsey. No sooner had he fallen than Henry began to dwell, in discourse with Chapuys, upon the fact that he was a small king in a remote corner of Europe and to congratulate himself upon his release from the bonds in which he had been bound to European allies and their wars.[1] It was he who became the insular and schismatic exponent of patriotic nationalism, a protestant in all but his theology and an individualist at that.

Nor was Wolsey's catholicism inspired by lofty principles or projects. He ingeminated peace in 1514 and in 1518 ; but he made war with equal zest whenever it suited his purpose, and his alleged idea of a European settlement of ecclesiastical questions appears to have had no existence. In 1519 Giustiniani could discover no deeper plan in his mind than to 'procure incense for his king and for himself' ;[2] and ten years later he was generally thought to be intent on the disturbance rather than the settlement of

[1] Spanish Cal. 1529-30, pp. 253, 338, 423.
[2] Venetian Cal. 1509-19, p. 505 ; Brown, Four Years at the Court of Henry VIII, ii. 258; cf. above, p. 140; L.P. iv. 1467.

Europe : it was a relief to all parties when he was kept away from the congress of Cambrai, which brought at least a fourteen years' respite from English intervention in the wars of Europe. Like many another man with a marvellous aptitude for accumulating materials—wealth, power, or learning, as the case may be—he was at a loss for adequate purposes on which to spend his acquisitions. He had no idea of building a temple of any kind, and the only use he had for gain was to secure more. Solomon in all his glory was hardly arrayed like Wolsey[1]; but Solomon built a temple that counted for more in a nation's eyes than Hampton Court or even the cardinal's college.

Wolsey lived so wholly for himself and so intensely in the present that he had no eye for the future and little sympathy with his fellow-men. He told du Bellay in 1529 that the welfare of the church in England was bound up in him ; but his moral was not so much that he must save the church as that it was the duty of the church to rescue him : after him might come the deluge, and he never even made a will. He was legate for life, but what security had he provided for the future? He attempted no concordat like that which secured Gallican liberties for the church in France, and apparently he desired none for the church in England apart from his own legatine powers. But they were, like the lands of the monasteries he dissolved, granted to him in person, not as archbishop of York : still less were they conceded to Canterbury or to a corporate church in England. Granted like the papal concordat with France, they might have passed to his successors, become a national inheritance, and formed the framework or at least the bulwark of a national church. Granted to Wolsey as papal legate, they could only perish with him and leave the task of compromise or liberation to the crown. The French concordat was between the crown of France and the papacy ; but, in spite of Wolsey's exceptional influence over successive popes and over Henry VIII, it never seems to have occurred to him that a concordat between the papacy and the crown might have provided a

[1] Cf. Skelton, i. 274 : ' Were never halfe so rychely, as I am, drest.'

better security for catholicism than the transient dictatorship he created for himself.

But such a solution was incompatible alike with Wolsey's position and with his uncompromising character. 'The independence of the Gallican church turns, as a historical question, on the non-reception of Roman decrees, the acceptance of the council of Basel, and the non-reception of portions of the Tridentine canons.'[1] But the whole edifice of Wolsey's legatine authority in England was built up on the assumption that there was no such national right of receiving or not receiving the laws and the legates of Rome. He had been commissioned from Rome to reform the English church, and there the matter ended : convocations, synods, and universities had nothing to do but submit to his pontifical authority, and none thought of any other remedy than an appeal to the source from which that authority was derived, until the whole basis of Roman positive law was destroyed by Wolsey's attainder in the king's bench. The issue had been raised by Standish's case in 1515 ; Wolsey had then repudiated the doctrine of non-reception and gone to Rome for a remedy. He never ceased his recourse to Rome or dreamt of Anglican liberties.

Anglican liberties would have, moreover, like those of the Gallican and other churches, to be the outcome of negotiation and compromise between national *regna* and the catholic *sacerdotium*. When the pope had triumphed over œcumenical councils, he need not trouble about the independence of provincial synods. But kings were kittle cattle, especially when they raided Anagni, ruled in Milan, or invaded Rome. There were persons with whom to negotiate and a basis, if not of concord, at least of concordats. Wolsey thought himself in a happier case : he was himself the English concordat. But he had the defects as well as the qualities of supremacy. 'How,' asked James I, 'can the king grant a *præmunire* against himself?'[2] How could Henry VIII's lord chancellor negotiate with the papal legate

---

[1] Stubbs, *Seventeen Lectures*, 1887, p. 352.
[2] *Political Works*, ed. McIlwain, 1918, p. 334.

a concordat for the liberties of the Anglican church? It should have been simple : it was in fact impossible for Wolsey, because it would have involved a sacrifice of his autocracy. His only plea is that reform was necessary, that only a despot could achieve it, and that the state of the English church was so desperate that, endowed with Anglican liberties, it would have continued to sin.

Some such concordat as that with France, or the later concordats with Spain, Austria, and Italy, would, however, have been welcomed by conservatives like Darcy, Sir Thomas More, and Warham, who were staunchly catholic but detested Wolsey's legatine autocracy and had no particular admiration for papal jurisdiction. It would assuredly have prevented that division in the English church which Wolsey provoked, and might have staved off the breach with Rome and the royal supremacy which ensued. But to a permanent concordat between the crown and the papacy Wolsey preferred a fleeting union of the powers of both in his own person as minister of the king and legate of the pope. So far from transferring ecclesiastical liberties to the crown, he arrogated to himself as legate the influence in ecclesiastical affairs which had been exerted by Henry VII and other English kings ; and in the eyes of Tyndale, Simon Fish, and other indignant protestants conveyed the government of the realm into the pocket of the church.[1] Wolsey's faith in offence as a means of protection provoked a counter-attack on the church ; and the reaction of 1529 did more than reverse that translation of power of which the reformers complained.

Wolsey's one prescription for the evils which he saw around him or forbode was power to prevent them ; but he failed to understand the limitations of his preventive system or to realise that the homœopathic remedy of more power in the hands of ecclesiastical authority was worse than the disease of discontent with what existed. He attempted to

[1] Tyndale, *Works*, i. 242, 247. Fish, *Supplication of Beggars* (ed. Dearmer, *Religious Pamphlets*, 1898, p. 63), says the priests did ' nothing but translate all rule power lordshippe auctorite obedience and dignite from your grace unto theim.'

dam the stream of anti-clerical feeling while he fed the sources from which it flowed ; and the higher he built the bulwark of his authority, the greater the risk of devastation when it broke. Papal jurisdiction fell because he had inter-posed and involved it more completely than ever before in the growing English antagonism between secular insurgence and the restraint of clerical discipline. His whole policy, including his efforts to secure the papacy for himself, was directed towards strengthening his preventive power ; and he was so much engrossed in that acquisition that he had no leisure, if he had the insight or inclination, to think out the principles of any counter-reformation which might have reduced the flood with which he had to contend. He was no prophet of the council of Trent or forerunner of Ignatius Loyola.

His foreign policy was merely a means to this acquisition of authority. His alleged addiction to the balance of power was aggressive and not defensive. England was in no danger when Wolsey came into office ; no potentate coveted a foot of English soil, and Calais was safe enough partly because, as Charles V explained to his council, it was better, both from the point of view of the Netherlands and from that of Spain, in English hands than in French,[1] and partly because both Habsburgs and Valois had their eyes fixed mainly on Italy. But, for that very reason, Wolsey looked in the same direction for influence over the papal curia ; and he played off one against the other in order that, by warlike or diplomatic penetration, he might reach the seats of the mighty at Rome. This led him into his anti-imperial policy. He was antagonistic to France as long as French kings ruled in Milan, and Spain, the Netherlands, and Austria were held in different hands ; but their union with the empire under Charles V, followed by the bitter disappointment of Wolsey's hopes of ascending the papal throne under the emperor's wing, converted him into the author of 'perpetual friendship' with France. 'After that the old king of France [Louis XII],' writes Tyndale late in 1526, 'was brought down out of Italy, mark what

---

[1] *L.P.* vi. 774; *Spanish Cal.* iv, ii. p. 734.

pageants have been played and are still a-playing, to separate us from the emperor, lest by the help or aid of us he should be able to recover his right of the pope, and to couple us to the Frenchmen, whose might the pope ever abuseth to keep the emperor from Italy.'[1] All Wolsey's paths led to Rome and all were eventually blocked by Charles V. In pitting himself against that imperial barrier Wolsey staked his all and lost. His influence in England had depended upon what he could get out of Rome, and the source of his ecclesiastical power was now controlled by the man he had made his particular foe : he had appealed to his chosen gods by his chosen methods and both alike had failed him. Englishmen turned away from the fountain that was dry : 'they were thinking,' wrote Chapuys in 1529, 'of nothing but how to do without Rome.'[2]

This pursuit of power at Rome distracted Wolsey from the use of what he possessed in England and sacrificed for a shadow abroad his more substantial projects for reform at home. No minister with such opportunities left so little trace upon the statute-book, and his single parliament of 1523 was one of the most barren in English history. Legislation by parliament was not, however, to Wolsey's taste ; and it is more to the point that so many of his administrative projects remained but little more, his codification of English law, reform of university statutes, redress of illegal inclosures, re-organisation of chancery, the exchequer, the king's household and his council—not to mention his scheme for ' one manner of grammar throughout all the realm.'[3] The variety of these ideas illustrate Wolsey's intellectual activity ; and, with his extraordinary industry and driving power, there is little doubt that many of them could have been accomplished. The value of his early work in chancery, the star chamber, and the court

---

[1] Tyndale, *Works*, i. 340. [2] *Spanish Cal.* 1529-30, p. 522.
[3] Palsgrave's articles in *L.P.* iv. p. 2558 ; cf. Cardwell, *Documentary Annals*, i. 20 *n.* ; Heylyn, *Ecclesia Restaurata* (ed. J. C. Robertson), i. 74, where Wolsey is said to have contributed to William Lily's Latin grammar, which was issued with Henry VIII's approval and imposed upon all schools by Edward VI's ' injunctions ' of 1547 : it enjoyed this monopoly until 1664.

of requests has been unduly neglected, and much of the activity, which provoked odium and wrath against him, deserves a different judgement in more impartial eyes. There was a sounder idea of social justice in the thousand marks he took for probate from Compton's estate, and in the shilling in the pound he demanded from others, than in the simple fee of half-a-crown for every will, irrespective of its value, which commended itself to the reactionary Darcy.[1] Modern finance, indeed, would hardly view with favour a system of death duties for the benefit of the church and still less for the enrichment of a papal legate ; but it would regard with no more sympathy Tyndale's indignant complaint that never a tyrant did so ill as Wolsey in compelling men to swear what they were worth for taxation.[2] Where his private interests were not concerned he had a high conception of justice, felt a keener sense of such offences as perjury than the common law enforced, and exhibited, if not a very sincere sympathy with the poor who suffered from inclosures and the weak who laboured under oppression, at least a just severity towards the feudal lords who inflicted the wrong.

But the early promise which won unstinted encomiums on his administration from Warham and Foxe, More and Erasmus, Giustiniani and Chieregati, faded into a sere and yellow leaf of 'many words without deeds' and a procrastination, which postponed until too late the achievement of reform. 'Beware of 'Had I wist'' is the burden of a ballad addressed to Wolsey in 1528.[3] Had he but known the result of his papal ambitions and of the futile foreign policy in which they involved him, he might have chosen another path which led to a better end. But, rejoicing in the whirlwind and the storm, he had no ear for the still,

---

[1] *L.P.* iv. pp. 2551, 2554, and above, p. 324.

[2] See above, pp. 75 *n.* 4, 226.

[3] *Ballads from MSS.* (ed. Furnivall), i. 353. But the phrase comes from Skelton's 'Magnificence' (*Works*, i. 232, 270) and is repeated in 'The Image of Ypocresye' (Furnivall, *op. cit.* i. 225), in R. Hill's 'Chronicle' (E.E.T.S. extra ser. ci. ed. Dyboski) p. 47, and in the 'Paradyse of daynty deuises' (1576).

small voices. Perhaps, like Luther, he could do no other.
He was endowed by nature with an unsurpassed ability, an
insatiable appetite for work, and a hunger and thirst, sometimes after righteousness but always after wealth and power :
absorbed in his passion for getting, he lost sight and sense
of the ends for which he got.

CHAPTER IX.

WOLSEY'S PLACE IN ENGLISH HISTORY.

WOLSEY's place in the traditional catholic view of history
was summed up by the eighteenth century inscription on
the anonymous but contemporary portrait at Arras describing him as *l'auteur du schisme*.[1] So far as Wolsey's intentions were concerned, the legend is a libel. Nothing was
further from his mind than the repudiation of papal jurisdiction and the severance of England from communion
with the Roman church. England's rejection of Rome
was deliberate enough, but Wolsey had no part in the
deliberation. That is not to say that he had no responsibility for the event, and his place in English history depends
upon the unrehearsed effects of his career.

The most obvious, immediate, and comprehensive
result of his ambition and success was to provoke a reaction against his methods and his policies and a restoration
of those which had obtained before he rose to power.
The conventional view, in which Cromwell appears as his
immediate successor, and revolution as the instantaneous
consequence of the removal of Wolsey's restraining hand,
ignores alike the fundamental radicalism of Wolsey's position and the conservative character of the administration
which came into power after his fall. There was an
interval, brief but important, between Wolsey's and Cromwell's predominance ; and during that interval, while no
one stepped into Wolsey's shoes, Norfolk and Gardiner
rather than Cromwell and Cranmer were the advisers on
whom Henry relied the most. But the king himself had
no knowledge of how far he would be able, perhaps not

[1] Reproduced as frontispiece to E. L. Taunton's *Wolsey* (1902) and
Ernest Law's *England's first great War Minister* (1916).

even how far he wanted, to go. He boasted in September 1530 that he was both emperor and pope so far as England was concerned, and told Chapuys more modestly that there were certain reforms he meant 'little by little' to attempt.[1] But, with all his self-will and stubbornness, Henry's caution and self-control were stronger than his passion and greater than his greed, and five years of undermining and approach were to elapse before the breach became public property. He knew how to wait and to vary his course with the shifting winds and currents of circumstance ; and he was better aware than anyone else of the composite nature of the ministry which had succeeded Wolsey and of the forces which had brought that coalition into being.

His boast about his power hardly needed further demonstration after Wolsey's capitulation. The plenipotentiary of the pope had, despite his ecclesiastical and diplomatic claims to immunity, been condemned in the king's bench to imprisonment for life and total loss of goods ; and Wolsey was not equal to the part of Becket which some men half expected him to play.[2] The penalty was for the most part remitted because punishment was not the purpose of the condemnation. Its object was to show that the exercise of papal jurisdiction in England, unless confined within limits laid down by English law, involved liability to penalties imposed in that behalf by acts of parliament, and that the most privileged of churchmen could find no security in the law of his church against the ordinary process of the common law of the land. Logically, Clement VII should have donned the panoply of papal prerogative and invoked the plenitude of his power in defence of Wolsey as a prince of the church and a specially commissioned representative of the holy see. Actually, he made not the faintest protest and allowed the case for the liberties of churchmen, if not of the church, to go by default. He had, of course, no reason to be grateful to the cardinal ; Wolsey had been

---

[1] *Spanish Cal.* 1529-30, pp. 350, 734.

[2] Cf. Cavendish (pp. 214-15) on the surprise of his friends at his surrender, and Tyndale's remark about Wolsey's ' counterfeiting ' St. Thomas of Canterbury (above, p. 225 *n.* 1).

an exigent legate, who had diverted a great deal of money from Rome, had monopolised papal jurisdiction in England, and had failed to protect St. Peter's itself from desecration by the troops of Charles V. His fall was no less a relief to the papal curia than it was to the English church. Nevertheless, the pope's acquiescence was a death-blow to papal authority in England ; and Clement condoned the affront by sending a lay papal nuncio, the baron del Borgo, to England in 1530 to represent the holy see as though it were simply a secular power. The royal supremacy was in October 1529 an accomplished and advertised fact : except for the purpose of giving it parliamentary sanction and putting it on a permanent basis, there was no need for the statute of 1534 ; and that act was merely declaratory of the principle, without any pains or executive provisions.[1]

Nothing short of the comprehensive antagonism which Wolsey had provoked could have led to the general acceptance of this breach in the liberties of the church. Fisher was vocal enough in the parliament of 1529 against the bills to limit pluralities, fees for probate, mortuaries, and other attacks on clerical privilege which he ascribed to lack of catholic faith ; but he had nothing to say for Wolsey as its bulwark and the whole bench of bishops was equally silent. They had reasons as good as those of Clement VII : the ruin, which Wolsey had prophesied for the church as a consequence of his fall, seemed to them its liberation. They at least had recovered their jurisdiction and were freed from the tribute Wolsey had levied on what he allowed them to keep. The abbots were for the moment released from fear of dissolution ; for no one, knowing Wolsey's appetite, could have felt much confidence that he would long be content with the dissolution of the smallest monasteries ; and one or two of the abbots who had been deprived by him were restored by Henry VIII.[2] Convocation, too, had with the reassembling of parliament

---

[1] The pains and penalties commonly attributed to it arose from the subsequent act against 'maliciously attempting to deprive' the king of any of his titles, of which 'supreme head of the church' had become one.

[2] See e.g. *L.P.* vii. 854.

resumed its liberty of action without the oppressive presence of an over-ruling papal legate. Reform might not be
to its taste, and clerical representatives grudged for divers
reasons at the various projects proposed in parliament. The
bishops raised no objection to the mortuaries bill, because,
says Hall, ' it touched them little ' ; but they ' both frowned
and grunted ' at the bill for probate, ' for that touched
their proffite.' [1] But while it might be over-ridden in
parliament on exactions from the laity, convocation could
deal with purely ecclesiastical matters. There was no longer
a legate to claim that reform of the church had been
committed to his exclusive authority : the clergy were not
reformed by Henry VIII without their official consent, however reluctant it may at times have been ; and convocation
was seldom more active than it was in the sessions which
followed Wolsey's fall. For the moment it was almost constrained to concur in Edward II's *articuli cleri*, and admit that
' what is found necessary for king and commonwealth should
not be judged harmful to the liberty of the church.' [2]

But if the church reacted against Wolsey's domination, the swing of the parliamentary pendulum was even
more pronounced. Wolsey had reduced the two houses to
an insignificance unknown since the earliest days of their
existence ; and there was no precedent for his fourteen
years of government without a parliament, broken only by
the barren session of 1523.[3] It has been suggested that it
was summoned in 1529 mainly in order to release the king
from his debts ; [4] but that theory affords an inadequate
explanation of the facts that, after those debts were cancelled,

[1] *Chron.* pp. 765-7. Burnet (*Hist. Ref.* ed. Pocock, i. 145) has a
story that Wolsey was present in this parliament ' where he shewed himself as submissive in his fawning as he had formerly done in his scorn and
contempt of all who durst oppose him ' ; but there is no other evidence
for this than the fact that he received a writ of summons, which, says Hall
(*ibid.* p. 760), ' muche conforted hym.' He was kept at Esher during
the whole of the session The *Journals*, of course, are missing.

[2] See above, p. 46.

[3] Coke, *Third Inst.* p. 2, says this was called the ' black parliament.'

[4] Brewer, preface to *L.P.* iv. pp. dcxlvii-dcxlix ; J. Gairdner in
D.N.B. xxvi. 83. In July 1527 Wolsey assured Henry that people showed
no desire to be repaid (*State Papers*, i. 205).

it continued to meet for seven years, and that co-operation between crown and parliament became the cardinal feature of Henry's policy and the basis of the constitution. Its meeting, indeed, gave effect to the only alternative policy possible after Wolsey's ecclesiastical government, and provided an outlet for the pent-up popular feeling which had been accumulating since Wolsey persuaded the king to put a premature end to the parliament of 1515. But it was only by degrees that its members acquired, during its then unprecedented span of seven years, a corporate consciousness and a common knowledge which enabled it to leave a deeper impress than any other on the subsequent history of England.

Compared with this efflorescence of parliament, the feudal reaction against government by a ' new man ' and a churchman was of slight and transient importance. For Cromwell soon became as unpalatable to the feudal nobility as Wolsey had been himself ; [1] and the new polity, in its revolt against the papal legate, was not disposed to go back on its whole existence and return to the middle ages. Wolsey's policy with regard to enclosures was, indeed, suffered to lapse ; and More reversed some of his decisions in deference either to the common law or to his baronial colleagues. But the presence of Darcy and his friends in the coalition is significant mainly as a mediæval protest against the radicalism of Wolsey, which threatened to merge the estates of the middle ages in a single bureaucratic state without a parliament to represent their interests and moderate alike their conservatism and their discontent. It is also important as illustrating the wedge which Wolsey had driven between conservatism and allegiance to the papacy. Darcy had demanded, before Suffolk's exclamation in July 1529, that never again should there be a cardinal or legate in England ; and he had complained almost as bitterly as Tyndale of ecclesiastical tyranny. In 1533 Chapuys remarked that Henry VIII ' used to be the only defender of

---

[1] In July 1534 Chapuys opined that Dacre's acquittal showed the hostility of the nobles to Cromwell and their fear that he ' would follow Wolsey's course ' (*L.P.* vii. 389).

the pope in his court' ; [1] and when in 1536 Darcy took part in the Pilgrimage of Grace, the programme of that movement exhibited no enthusiasm for papal jurisdiction.[2]

For the moment, however, the nobility were in with the flowing tide. The king and lords, of whose depression Tyndale had complained in 1526,[3] were up again to some purpose in 1529. In 1526 the executive committee of the council had consisted of Wolsey as chancellor, Norfolk as treasurer, and Tunstal as lord privy seal : by the end of 1529 Suffolk had been added as president of the council, the earl of Wiltshire had taken Tunstal's place as lord privy seal, and More sat in Wolsey's seat on the woolsack. But the remarkable thing was less the presence of peers than the total absence of churchmen ; [4] and a peculiar significance attached to More's occupation of the woolsack. He was a layman, a common lawyer, and had been speaker of the last house of commons. Though less moved by personal antagonism to Wolsey than his colleagues, he represented in his person three of the principal antipathies to the cardinal, the lay, the common law, and the parliamentary ; he also created a precedent for the succession of a speaker of the house of commons to the presiding office in the house of lords, which was emphasised in 1532 when Audley, his successor as speaker, also succeeded him on the woolsack.[5]

More had been selected 'after long debate' for very good reasons of various kinds. His personal qualities

---

[1] *L.P.* vi. 1510 ; cf. *ibid.* ii. 4257 ; vii. 289.

[2] Divergences of opinion among the pilgrims led to the proposal that the pope should be recognised as head in spiritual matters, but spiritual authority should be given to the archbishops of Canterbury and York ' so that the said bishop of Rome have no further meddling ' (*L.P.* xi. 1182 ; cf. M. H. and R. Dodds, *The Pilgrimage of Grace*, 1915, i. 347-8).

[3] Tyndale, *Works* (Parker Soc.), ii. 247 ; see above, p. 227.

[4] No churchman held any of these great offices, lord chancellor, lord treasurer, lord privy seal, or president of the council for the rest of Henry's reign.

[5] *L.P.* v. 1069. Richard Rich, who was speaker in the parliament of 1536, also became lord chancellor ; but this particular symptom of co-operation between the crown and the house of commons disappeared in Mary's reign and has not been revived.

commended, him no less than his political training, as an antidote to Wolsey: the man who, as a 'beardless youth' is said to have thwarted Henry VII in the house of commons in 1504,[1] and had risen to be its speaker, was not likely to ignore its importance in the body politic, or to imitate his predecessor's pontifical aloofness. He had neither the inclination nor the means to perpetuate the dictatorial character with which Wolsey had invested the chancellorship. The cardinal's bending of the chancellor's bow had, indeed, strained it till it nearly broke; and his excessive use of its powers was as fatal to the mediæval chancellorship in England as it was to papal legacy. No successor on the woolsack, with the possible exceptions of Gardiner during the Marian reaction, and Clarendon at the Stuart restoration, approached to Wolsey's ministerial pre-eminence; and the revulsion against chancery threatened for a time to destroy the chancellor's peculiar position as the recorder of parliament. From Wolsey's fall 'to this daye' [5 Oct. 1556], runs an order in chancery, acts of parliament 'for the moste parte . . . have not been as yet certified [into chancery] but kept backe contrary to the old ancient order and custome tyme out of minde used';[2] and it would almost seem that parliament itself, or some other department of government, temporarily set up a parliament-office independent of chancery.[3] More himself had a voice but 'no vote or interest' among the 'lords of parliament' who were being reduced to a house of peers; and Audley was for a time keeper of the great seal, but 'no chancellor.'[4]

Outside parliament a good deal of the jurisdiction Wolsey had brought into chancery was quietly conveyed to other quarters. The council, indeed, asserted in 1533 that the civil law had no authority in England; and the

[1] This is one of Roper's stories which is inaccurate in detail and generally lacks corroboration.

[2] Sanders, *Orders in Chancery*, 2 vols. 1845-6, i. 14.

[3] Cromwell may have retained a good many parliamentary records in his own hands; and there is a curious note (*L.P.* iv. 6043 [3]) of 'the names of the parliament papers remaining in our counting house.'

[4] *L.P.* v. 1069. In Elizabeth's reign lord-keepers were the rule and lord-chancellors the exception.

pilgrims of grace, who made no request for a papal restoration, demanded a return to the common law.[1] Darcy had complained of the predominance of 'civilians indigne,' and there was a growing prejudice against them as 'citizens of a foreign state and strangers in their own.'[2] By the act of 1535 jurisdiction in uses and trusts was conveyed to common law; a few years later we find references to the privy council dealing with slander and to its general equitable jurisdiction;[3] and the jurisdiction in equity, which Wolsey and his predecessors had concentrated in chancery, reverted to the council and overflowed into the common law-courts. More, though a common lawyer, was not adverse to the liberalising of the common law by an infusion of equity; but he had to warn the judges that, if they refused to take cognisance of certain misdemeanours, he would be compelled to follow Wolsey's example and deal with them in chancery.[4] That struggle between the common law and equity lasted for centuries of legal history after Wolsey's time; but his fall frustrated the most likely opportunity for the reception of Roman law in England. Reaction also made itself felt against his work in the star chamber, and Sir Thomas Elyot complained in a letter to Cromwell on 8 December 1532 of 'all sharpnesse and diligence in justice nowadayes being everywhere odiouse.'[5] But the diminution in its business[6] was only the prelude to a revival which gave the star chamber a greater notoriety without an equal justification for its activity or as good a reputation for its impartiality.

The restoration of episcopal jurisdiction was still more chequered than that of the common law. For it revived a

---

[1] *L.P.* vi. 1501; cf. *ibid.* 1538 i. 1533; Maitland, *English Law and the Renaissance*, p. 18.

[2] *L.P.* iv. p. 2550; Holdsworth, *Hist. Eng. Law*, v. 25 (quoting Arthur Duck, 1648).

[3] *L.P.* 1542 i. 823; 1544 i. 1140; 1545 i. 273; Holdsworth, i. 454.

[4] Roper, *Life of More*, ed. Singer, 1832, p. 43.

[5] Ellis, *Original Letters*, I, ii. 118.

[6] It has even been said that after Wolsey's fall ' we seldom hear of the star chamber ' in Henry VIII's reign (John Bruce in *Archæologia*, xxv. 377-8); but this is an exaggeration (see *Eng. Hist. Rev.* Oct. 1922, pp. 532-9).

liberty which was not judiciously used, and showed that, if Wolsey was *primus inter pares* in his tenacity of ecclesiastical power, he was superior in the discretion with which he used it to deal with heresy. The reform of the ecclesiastical courts effected in 1531 was no doubt provoked by Wolsey's abuse of his legatine jurisdiction;[1] but it left them with a sufficient opportunity to prejudice what remained and provoke more drastic measures. One of the charges made against the cardinal in parliament was that by his legatine authority he had prevented bishops from dealing firmly enough with heretics; and the bishops rejoiced in the recovery of their liberty to discharge this duty. But they were bent on pushing their advantage in other directions. The legate *a latere* had disappeared, but the *legatus natus* still remained and with him the metropolitan's jurisdiction over his suffragans. Maitland has remarked that 'the statutory Reformation began, not with an act directed against Rome but against Canterbury';[2] and just as the bishops had reacted against Wolsey without repudiating Roman jurisdiction, so they now attacked the *legatus natus* without perhaps seeing whither their action tended. They were supported, possibly with some cynical amusement, by Henry VIII; for the act was one to prohibit the citation of persons outside their dioceses, and Henry had been cited to Rome. Warham protested, logically but in vain, that his was a papal-legatine jurisdiction; and he implied that its repudiation meant a breach with Rome.[3]

The bishops, however, bent on their independence protested against the 'primate'; and when Warham was succeeded by Cranmer they proceeded with even greater zest to repudiate the archbishop's right of metropolitical visitation. Gardiner, now bishop of Winchester,[4] was their ringleader; and he, perhaps, saw where he was going, for soon he was almost, in his 'De vera Obedientia,' to outvie Tyndale in his zeal for the royal supremacy. He was followed by Longland and Stokesley who denounced Cranmer's visitatorial authority as usurped and his primacy as

[1] Creighton, *Wolsey*, p. 147.   [2] *Roman Canon Law*, p. 120.
[3] *L.P.* v. 818, 1247.   [4] Since Nov. 1531.

a slur on the royal supremacy.[1] But, while independence of legatine and archiepiscopal jurisdiction might mean episcopal liberty, it threatened ecclesiastical disruption unless a score of free and independent bishops could achieve a greater degree of theological unanimity than seemed possible —in that age at least. Even in mediæval times 'the choice lay between anarchy and the *plenitudo potestatis*';[2] and the repudiation of other jurisdictions led by logical necessity straight to royal supremacy and to uniformity imposed by act of parliament. Indeed, within three months of Wolsey's death, convocation had admitted that the king was supreme head of the church in England, qualifying it with the phrase 'so far as the law of Christ allows.' Chapuys derided that as an empty form of words;[3] it did nothing, at any rate, to define the relation of suffragans to their archiepiscopal sovereigns.

But this was a submission by English clergy which had no legal force in the law of either the catholic church or the realm of England; and, pending parliamentary legislation, there was an interim in which the ecclesiastical courts, relieved of legatine incubus, recovered their statutory powers under the Lollard acts of Henry IV and Henry V. These they proceeded to exercise with a vigour unknown since the agitation over the case of Richard Hunne had induced some caution into the minds of either the legate or the episcopate. There were arrears to overtake, and no doubt the serious growth of heretical opinion and heretical literature afforded a plausible justification for severity. Wolsey himself appears to have been impressed; and in March 1529 a stringent proclamation against heretical books had been issued in general terms, which episcopal registrars kept up to date by adding specific works as they appeared or were brought to episcopal notice.[4] The new lay government professed to be more

---

[1] *L.P.* vii. 1683; viii. 312, 704-5.

[2] Maitland, *Roman Canon Law*, p. 122.

[3] *L.P.* v. 105; *Spanish Cal.* 1531-3, p. 63.

[4] Steele, *Proclamations*, i. 13; *L.P.* iv. 6402 Foxe, *Acts and Mon.* iv. 679, seems to be the only writer to get this clear in the words 'the books, which in this proclamation generally are restrained and forbidden,

orthodox than the old ; even bishop Nix despaired of the successful suppression of heresy ' by any spiritual man ' ;[1] and a solemn assembly of peers and prelates in the star chamber in Henry's presence on 25 May 1530 renewed and reinforced the prohibitions of the previous year. More's catholicism had been proved by his attacks on Tyndale. Norfolk's was none the less pronounced for being more illiterate : ' he had never read the scriptures,' he declared ten years later, ' nor never would, and it was a merry England before this new learning came up.'[2]

The attitude of the king himself, however, was beginning to be suspicious. A 'Lutheran' book, circulating at court in April 1529, had advocated the suppression of heresy by the simplification of the faith and the reduction, by Henry VIII and Francis I, of the ecclesiastical state to the form of the primitive church by taking away its temporalities.[3] Campeggio warned Henry that this was the devil in angel's clothing. Henry professed to be convinced : at least he promised to remain always, as he was then, a good christian ; and at his parting with Campeggio in September he had given assurances on the subject which the legate thought eminently satisfactory. But in the same month he desired the release of the prior of Reading, who had been imprisoned by Wolsey for Lutheranism, 'unless the matter were very heinous.'[4] Apparently it was, and the prior remained in prison for another year or more : Cromwell was still, in 1530, wishing that Luther had never been born.[5] But in December 1529 Henry was in touch with other

be afterwards in the register more especially named by the bishops ' of London, i.e. Tunstal and Stokesley (cf. *ibid*. pp. 667-71, 765). Steele, giving the right date for the proclamation as ' before 6 March 1528-29,' makes it prohibit books not published until 1530, e.g. Tyndale's *Practice of Prelates*, by representing the bishops' subsequent specification of books appear as part of the general proclamation under which they acted. A good deal of bibliographical confusion has resulted from the assumption that entries in registers were made at the date under which they appear.

[1] *L.P.* iv. 6367, 6377, 6385, 6487.   [2] *Ibid*. xvi. 101.

[3] ' Di ridurre il stato ecclesiastico al modo de la primitiva chiesa levandoli tutto il temporale ' (Campeggio to Salviati, Ehses, pp. 76-8, 105).

[4] Above, p. 201 ; *L.P.* iv. 4004, 5925 ; v. 854.   [5] *Ibid*. iv. 6391.

German envoys than those who were sent by the archbishop of Mainz to intercede for Wolsey, and was discoursing to Chapuys on abuses in the church and the
redeeming features of German Lutheran princes.[1] He was
beginning to investigate the charges on which Wycliffe had
been condemned, to repent of his book against Luther, and
to taste the political doctrines of Tyndale.[2]

Still, as he remarked a little later,[3] he could not unmake
laws by his own authority ; and his chancellor was supporting the church in the exercise of its statutory powers.
Norfolk was also willing that heretics should go to the
stake, though Anne Boleyn and her father protested.[4] So
Bilney was burnt by the bishop of Norwich on 16 August
1531 ; Bayfield, Tewkesbury, Bainham, and Frith (all by
Stokesley, bishop of London) on 4 and 20 December 1531,
30 April 1532, and 4 July 1533 respectively ; an Exeter
martyr* by its bishop, Veysey, on 10 January 1532 ; and
three or four more in eighteen months. Latimer barely
escaped, and Crome was constrained to recant.[5] As a final
exercise in ecclesiastical liberty, convocation repeated its
experiment on Hunne and ordered the exhumation, trial,
and condemnation of the body of William Tracy two years
after his death, on evidence of heresy detected in Tracy's
will which had come before the ecclesiastical court for
probate.[6] 'The inquisition which they have here,' wrote
Chapuys on 2 May 1532, 'is said to be more severe than
that in Spain.'[7]

The church had misread the signs of the times and
mistaken its English vocation. It thought that Wolsey
had fallen because he monopolised its jurisdiction and

---

[1] *Spanish Cal.* 1529-30, p. 349.

[2] *L.P.* vi. 296, 1501, 1510.   [3] *Ibid.* vi. 1479.

[4] *Ibid.* v. 1013. Chapuys says ' prevented,' and possibly their influence turned the scale in favour of some of the accused.

[5] Wriothesley's *Chron.* i. 16-17 ; Foxe, *Acts and Monuments*, iv
680-706 ; v. 1-43 ; *L.P.* v. 129, 148, 522, 589, 704, 1013, 1458, App. 30 ;
vi. 276, 1249 ; vii. 171, 270 ; * *E.H.R.* 1921, pp. 422-3.

[6] *Ibid.* v. 928 (p. 438), 1013 ; Wilkins, iii. 724 ; *D.N.B.* lvii. 149-1
and authorities there cited. See also Cromwell's notes, *L.P.* vi. p. 352.

[7] *Ibid.* v. 989.

suppressed episcopal liberties ; and it failed to realise that popular, as distinct from clerical, anger was excited not so much by the monopoly as by the jurisdiction. Controlled by the papal legate, it was tyranny to churchmen ; restricted to ecclesiastics, it was tyranny to laymen. The grievance was not personal but secular ; and the feeling aroused by the use the ecclesiastical courts made of their recovered jurisdiction provoked the parliamentary legislation of 1533-34 which imposed a secular curb on ecclesiastical independence. At its meeting on 26 March 1533 convocation besought Henry to protect the 'liberties' of the church ; but a year earlier he had promised to help the commons 'to mitigate the rigours of the inquisition.'[1] The crown resumed its control of its own officials : no sheriff was to burn a heretic on an ecclesiastical injunction ; and no one was to be condemned as such except in 'open court in an open place ' and on the testimony of two lawful witnesses to his crime.[2] The church must not damn men's souls on its *ipsa dixit* nor burn their bodies without a royal writ.[3]

Except in the matter of probate Wolsey had not greatly vexed the laity by his ecclesiastical jurisdiction ; and even in that respect his novel fees were chiefly extorted from the novel rich. But if the clergy felt the oppression of his legatine authority, the business world, represented especially by London, hated most his re-valuations for taxation and his demands for benevolences and loans. The fact that their wealth was already becoming the envy of the world did not make them any more ready to pay forced loans and subsidies ; for the richer a man, the more he is taxed and the more he objects to taxation. There was no enthusiasm in the city for any of Wolsey's wars. Englishmen had been willing enough to fight for trade with Flanders and the control of the narrow seas. But no commercial compensation promised from Wolsey's Italian intrigues ; and, while they were Burgundian rather than French in their sym-

---

[1] Chapuys to Charles V, 2 May 1532, *L.P.* v. 989 ; cf. vi. 276.

[2] *Ibid.* vii. 399 ; *Statutes of the Realm*, iii. 454-5.

[3] The latter prohibition was good mediæval law : ' vita et membra sunt in potestate regis ' (Bracton, quoted by Holdsworth, ii 272).

pathies, they did not believe in the conquest or the dismemberment of France. By 1523 they were heartily sick
of war, and, when Wolsey sought to renew it in 1528 against
their traditional allies, their opposition made itself felt for
other than sentimental reasons.[1] Within a few weeks Wolsey
had to patch up a truce, and no actual hostilities took place.
But the disturbance of trade and sudden increase of unemployment added fuel to the discontent with Wolsey's
policy and lack of commercial understanding. There was
a general refusal to pay his demands ; and he in turn
threatened that their opposition ' might fortune to cost some
of them their heads,' and told Henry that ' all London
were traitors to his grace.' ' He hated sore the citie of
London,' writes Hall, ' and feared it.'[2] Nowhere was
his fall greeted with greater satisfaction and no section of
his people did Henry afterwards cultivate with greater
assiduity. Indeed, from the economic, ecclesiastical, and
perhaps some other points of view, the later Tudor despotism
consisted to no small extent in the subordination of other
parts of England and sections of society to the interests and
opinions of the capital and what it represented.[3]

The fall of Wolsey had thus been brought about by
a heterogeneous concourse of interests, united only by a
common hostility to a despotic papal legate ; and the succeeding administration was a mosaic of diverse elements which
exhibited no other unity of design. The nearest approach
to harmony in the coalition—apart from its enmity to
Wolsey and its concurrence in the policy indicated by
Hall's statement that Henry ' leaving the glory of war,
took mercy on his subjects '[4]—was with regard to the
necessity for consulting parliament. During the first three
years of the reign stress had been laid on the need for
frequent sessions ;[5] but since Wolsey's advent to power
in 1511-12 there had been a growing estrangement which
led to an almost complete cessation of summons. By the

---

[1] See above, p. 159.   [2] *L.P.* iii. 3076 (2) ; Hall, pp. 696, 774.
[3] Cf. N. S. B. Gras, *Evolution of the English Corn Market*, 1915, p.
223-7, 242.
[4] *Chron.* p. 747.   [5] *L.P.* i. (new ed.) 1046, (1st ed.) 2082.

spring of 1529, however, it was realised that a meeting was inevitable. But, while there might be agreement on the necessity of calling a parliament, there was none about what that parliament should do ; and if the great council, which Hall says met on 1 October 'to devise divers actes' for parliament,[1] devised the bills against mortuaries, probate fees, and pluralities, its clerical members must have been less successful in council than they were in the house of lords. There is, however, no more reason to suppose that the government drafted these bills in 1529 than that it drafted the similar bills which Wolsey defeated in 1515. It was rather the bills of the commons, the temper exhibited in debate, and Fisher's vehement protest, which revealed the rifts in the coalition, indicated its future disruption, and gave Henry the lead which he followed. He had no reason to revert to the middle ages ; but he had every inducement to go back to 1515 and pick up the parliamentary thread which Wolsey had broken.

He probably took a hint from the reception of the one bill which certainly was devised by the council. It was to release him from the obligation to repay the loans which Wolsey had extorted in 1522 and the following years. It was only carried, says Hall, by the votes of members who were the king's servants ; and outside the house men 'spake ill of the hole parliament.'[2] Henry placated the commons by helping them against the spiritualty. After the rejection of their attempts to deal with ecclesiastical abuses, he caused two new bills to be drawn to limit probate dues and mortuary fees, and these were passed. He also invited Fisher to explain his attack on the catholic rectitude of the commons, but accepted what Hall calls the bishop's 'blind excuse.' The pluralities bill was also passed, but only through its submission to the joint vote of a conference between the two houses, in which the temporal lords voted with the commons against their episcopal colleagues.[3] The lesson which Henry learnt was

---

[1] *Chron.* p. 760.   [2] *Ibid.* p. 767.

[3] The conference, which was held in the star chamber, consisted of four spiritual and four temporal lords, and eight members of the house of commons (Stubbs, *Seventeen Lectures*, p. 317).

that, if he wanted his way in what he most desired, he must let the commons have theirs over what Norfolk called their 'infinite clamours against the misuse of spiritual jurisdiction.' He became 'very watchful,' as Chapuys says, 'of the countenance of the people,' and 'always fortified himself by the consent of parliament' : he even flattered Francis I by telling him he was following his advice that 'no way was so firm as by parliament.' [1]

But these parliamentary practices led to a parting of the ways for the coalition.   It managed to hold together over the sessions of November-December 1529 and January-March 1531, though More's refusal to sign the letter to Clement VII in favour of the divorce was a symptom of disagreement on one important question.   But More stood alone in the government on that matter ; [2] and we know from his own testimony that, when he accepted office as chancellor, the king had agreed to let him take his own line about the divorce.[3]   Nor, although Clement VII said that 'furies were at work ' in the session of January-March 1531,[4] did they succeed in driving More from office ; and apparently he acquiesced in the act depriving the pope of annates which was passed in March 1532.[5]   The cause in which he fell was not the revenues, but the liberties of the church ; his resignation was a protest not against the acts forbidding the payment of annates and appeals to the pope, but against the restraint by the secular arm of spiritual inquisition.   He retired at the prorogation of parliament

---

[1] *L.P.* v. 831 ; vi. 351, 720, 954.

[2] See the list of signatories in Herbert, p. 334.

[3] More's letter to Cromwell in his *English Works*, p. 1424 ; Strype' *Eccl. Mem.* i, ii. 48 ; and *L.P.* vii. 289 ; and cf. Roper's *More*, p. 64.

[4] *L.P.* v. 108 ; cf. *ibid.* 831.

[5] *Ibid.* v 722.   More's acceptance is not quite certain ; for the act, as passed while he was chancellor, simply enabled Henry to terminate their payment in case Clement VII proved unyielding, and it did not become law until after More's resignation.   For the purpose of the act cf. Tyndale, *Obedience*, p. 335, quoted above (p. 228), and stat. 23 Henry VIII, c. 7, ' for the maintenance of the navy.'   More was certainly opposed to the act of appeals, and encouraged Sir George Throckmorton's opposition to it in the house of commons (*L.P.* 1537 ii. 952).

on 14 May[1] and Audley moved up from the chair in the house of commons to the woolsack in the lords. Gardiner weathered the storm and remained nominal secretary until April 1534, but Cromwell had temporarily supplanted him in Henry's political affections.[2] On that same 14 May Henry gave the royal assent to the act for the submission of the clergy.

In one of the moments of inspiration, in which Lord Acton occasionally summed up the learning of a life-time, he described this development as 'the advent of a new polity.'[3] The modern state in England could not, indeed, have been born without an act for the submission of the clergy ; and under the guise of a reformation of the church parliament was effecting a revolution in the state.[*] The dying Warham, rising above his timorous counsel that *ira principis mors est*, followed up More's resignation with a protest in which he compared Henry VIII with Henry II and likened the new legislation to the constitutions of Clarendon ; he complained, in words he had used in opening parliament in February 1515, that temporal men were urging their temporal laws to the detriment of the church.[4] Tyndale had been before him with his Angevin precedents, but with a different moral ;[5] and Henry VIII took up the tale by telling Chapuys that he meant to repair the errors of Henry II and John who, by deceit and being in difficulties, had made this realm and Ireland tributary to the pope. He was also determined, he said, to re-unite to the crown the lands which the church held of it and his predecessors had had no right to alienate ; and declared he was bound so to do by his coronation oath.[6]

---

[1] See above, p. 213.

[2] In Nov. 1533 Chapuys remarks that 'Cromwell rules everything' (*L.P.* vi. 1445).

[3] *Lectures on Mod. Hist.* p. 142.

[4] 'Nostra respublica languet, nam moderni sola privata commoda curant' (*Lords' Journals*, i. 18 ; cf. *L.P.* v. 287 (p. 137), 818, 1247).

[5] *Works*, i. 249, 338 ; see above, pp. 228-9. It was Henry II's defeat which led to the enforcement of practically the whole body of Roman canon law in England (see Z. N. Brooke in *Cambridge Hist. Journal*, ii. 213-28, Oct. 1928).

[6] *L.P.* vi. 235, 1077 ; cf. Tyndale, *Works*, i. 240.

This was one of the rare occasions on which Henry's bark was worse than his bite. Eight months later he was only proposing to take half the temporalities of the church if the pope made war upon England. Lord Hussey, who was almost as catholic as Darcy, thought that many would be glad and few bemoan if the clergy lost them altogether; and Chapuys reports a proposal made, 'to please the people,' that they should be deprived of their revenues from letting houses. But Henry, he remarks in November 1534, was content to leave churchmen their property for the present on certain conditions: 'this morning,' he writes on the 17th, 'the king has been declared by act of parliament supreme head of the English church.'[1] The church, in short, might retain its property in so far as, unlike the monasteries, it could be brought within the sphere of national government.

'If a lion knew his own strength,' More is said to have told Cromwell on entering Henry's service, 'hard were it for any man to rule him';[2] and he proceeded to warn him against putting that knowledge into the head of Henry VIII. The warning came too late, addressed to Cromwell: for Wolsey had already displayed before the eyes of the king, the court, and the country a vision of power such as no man had yet seen wielded in England; and that exhibition profoundly affected the reformation and determines Wolsey's place in English history. It clearly does not depend upon his exiguous reform of ecclesiastical abuses, of which he was himself the most glaring incarnation. For Norfolk's objurgation in Shakespeare 'thou scarlet sin' has more to justify it than most political abuse; and Wolsey's importance consists not so much in his re-formation of the church as in his influence on the formation of the state. It is one of the ironies of history that, while the former was left to a king and parliament, his share in the latter was a cardinal's main achievement. But the anomaly falls into its place in natural development when it appears that the work of the king and parliament

---

[1] *L.P.* vii. 24, 114, 158, 871, 1141, 1206, 1355-6, 1381 (3), 1437, 1482.
[2] Roper's *More*, p. 55.

was to anglicise the Roman church, and that of the cardinal
was to romanise the remnants of the feudal, and the
rudiments of the modern, state. The reformation did not
come from Rome; but the ghost of the Roman empire,
in the guise of its learning and its law, was re-born and
received into the marrow and bones of the modern state.
Hobbes's 'Leviathan' was a steed produced from the contract and positive law of Roman stables to challenge the
mediæval offspring of divine right and teutonic custom;
and Wolsey's 'legacy of Rome' survived his mediæval
attainder in the king's bench.

'They intend,' wrote du Bellay in August 1529, 'to
hold a parliament and then act by their own absolute
power';[1] and the 'new polity' was framed and fashioned
by parliamentary statute. Its parents—there were many—
are said to have been primarily Luther and Machiavelli.
The imputation does Luther some injustice; he held varying views of the proper relations of church and state, but
was too insubordinate a churchman to believe in subordination to the secular arm.[2] For him, as for Calvin, Knox,
and other modern exponents of mediæval ideas, the duty
of the state was to hear and obey the voice of the church,
i.e. their church. In England its parents were rather
Tyndale, the protestant who was burnt, and Wolsey, the
legate who was attainted—Tyndale, of course, as a prophet
and Wolsey as a statesman. Tyndale visualised God as
being nothing but 'his word, his law, and his promises';
'and to imagine any other thing of God than that is
damnable idolatry.' Personality was an image : God consisted of the scriptures, a sort of written constitution of the
universe. This left ample scope for the impersonation of
the king : 'the king is in the room of God, and his law is

---

[1] *L.P.* iv. 5862 ; Le Grand, iii. 342.

[2] See J. W. Allen in *Social and Political Ideas of the Renaissance and
Reformation*, ed. Hearnshaw, 1925, pp. 171-91. Mr. Allen roundly
asserts that Luther ' never thought in terms of the State at all ' (p. 174).
This is probably true, and it is equally true of Wolsey. But parentage is
commonly due to action rather than to speculation ; and, if Machiavelli,
as Lord Acton says, ' released government from the restraint of law,'
Luther, by his action, released it from any effective restraint by the church.

God's law ' ; and '' one king, one law ' is God's ordin-
ance in every realm.'   Thus there was no room for 'the
priests' several kingdom ' ; and if the king executed those
' whom he judgeth not by his own laws,' he did so 'unto
his own damnation.'   Tyndale believed in passive obedience and complained that 'now, as ever, the most part
seek liberty'.[1]   Henry VIII was captivated by the book,[2]
and its inspiration may be traced in every act of parliament
that led up to the royal supremacy.   ' Whereas,' wrote
Brynklow in 1545 of Tyndale and other protestants, 'the
king was before but a shadow of a king, or at the most but
half a king, now he doth wholly reign through their preaching, writing, and suffering.'[3]   Simon Fish's 'Supplication of
Beggars' was a vulgarised epitome of Tyndale's 'Obedience
of a Christian Man' : men noted its popularity early in 1534,
and in 1535 Gardiner converted it, in his 'De vera
Obedientia,' to the uses of Anglo-catholic supporters of 'the
new papacy made here' of the king and parliament.[4]   By
such men, complained Brynklow, came nothing but a *translatio imperii* ; and the doctrine that 'parliament cannot err'
was erected into the 'thirteenth article of our creed, added
of late,' to which even royalist judges under Charles I were
found to subscribe.[5]

Parliament, however, was Henry's interpolation.   Wolsey had no use for it, and Tyndale little more.   His
'Obedience' is not a plea for liberty, but for power in the
hands of princes to suppress false doctrine and the church
of Rome.   But he had the root of the royal supremacy in
him.   Sovereignty was to be national in every realm ; 'in
England,' said Dr. Nicholas Wotton to Charles V, 'there
is but one king, and the king hath but one law to rule all
his subjects by.'[6]   The 'several kingdom' was to disappear,

[1] Tyndale, *Works*, i. 160, 165-7, 171, 240, 250, 336.

[2] See above, p. 229.

[3] *Complaynt of Roderick Mors* (Early Eng. Text Soc. extra series),
xxii. 23 ; cf. *L.P.* xx. p. 342 *n.*

[4] *Ibid.* vii. 112, 158.

[5] *Roderick Mors*, p. 14 ; *L.P.* 1545 ii. p. 345 ; S. R. Gardiner, *Documents of the Puritan Revolution*, ed. 1889, p. 54.

[6] *Cal. State Papers*, Foreign, 1547-53, p. 137.

and the goods of the church were to provide for the 'defence of the realm.' All coercive jurisdiction was to be vested in the crown : 'a spiritual officer ought to punish no sin, but and if any such break out, the king is ordained to punish it, and they not.' Nor should his ministers punish heresy merely at the priests' commandment, 'but let them look on God's word . . . and see whether it be right or no.' Sanctuary, the 'neck verse,' and other impediments to the course of the common law should be removed. 'The king hath in his hand a sword, not peacocks' feathers,' like Cardinal Wolsey's. The powers that be were ordained of God, and 'hath he not made the English tongue' as a vehicle for God's truth to the English people?[1]

Wolsey's contribution to the royal supremacy was practical and undesigned rather than theoretical and deliberate. But, as its official keeper, he gave the king's conscience as wide a sweep as Tyndale. Heresy was in principle excluded from Wolsey's conception of its scope ; but the appearance of cases of heresy among the chancery proceedings shows that Wolsey did not in practice draw a clear line between the king's royal, and his own legatine, conscience ; and in not a few fundamental respects he paved the way for the sovereignty of the modern state. Primarily that is based on the victory of positive law over mediæval conceptions of the immutable laws of God and nature, the binding force of custom and prescription, and the indestructibility of rights and liberties deduced therefrom. The crucial question, which accounts for Henry's ruthlessness, still distracts the modern state. Spiritual men, noted Saint-German, were saying, 'it bindeth not in conscience' ; and he wished that 'spiritual men and temporal men would charitably lay their heads together and fully determine what the parliament may do.'[2] Wolsey took no part in the vast expansion of the statute-book during the latter part of Henry's reign ;[3] but he

---

[1] Tyndale's *Works* (Parker Soc) i. 161, 166-7, 171, 180, 194, 240-1, 243, 250, 335-6. On Wolsey's peacocks' feathers see above, p. 225 *n*. 1 ; Skelton, *Works*, i. 365 ; Tottel, *Year-Books*, 18 Henry VIII, Michaelmas, f. ii.; and *L.P.* iv. 5746.

[2] *Doctor and Student*, ed. 1886, ' Additions,' p. 328.

[3] See above, p. 218 *n*.

stood none the less, almost as completely as Henry VIII, for the prevalence of specific decrees and enactments over the common and customary law of church and state. His abnormal legatine position was based entirely on papal bulls and plenitude of power ; and the 'intruding imperialism of Rome,' as Lord Acton has called it, had made havoc of the *jus commune* of the church before the king appropriated to himself and parliament the fruits of papal usurpation. The absorption of the mediæval 'estates of holy church'[1] into the single state of papal monarchy preceded the fusion of the three and more estates of mediæval England into the modern English state.

Hence Wolsey represented in England an absolutist papal curia and not a constitutional catholic church or an œcumenical council. He was commissioned by a despot to exercise despotic authority and by its means to legislate for, to govern, to judge, and to reform the church. His whole armament of bulls and briefs, licences and dispensations, suspensions, provisions, and faculties constituted a vast invasion of mediæval rights and liberties, custom and common law ; and it was significant that the English breach with Rome was occasioned by a papal claim to dispense, by positive papal enactment, with what men thought was the law of God.[2] Wolsey was the very embodiment of the idea that the work of God and nature could be improved by man and that unchangeable laws could be interpreted, suspended, dispensed with, and defied by statutes and decrees devised by mortal wit and imposed by human will.

This plenitude of ecclesiastical power was superimposed by Wolsey upon a corresponding secular authority ; though to one, who had taken particular care to secure a cardinal's hat before he sat himself in the chancellor's seat, chancery

----

[1] Nicolas, *Proc. P.C.* v. 88, 148. For some hints on the debt which the modern state owes to the papacy, see Acton, *Lectures on Mod. Hist.* pp. 44-9, 91.

[2] Cf. *L.P.* v. 468, on the claim that the pope's power to dispense with impediments to marriage was unlimited, extending even to marriage between brothers and sisters. Tyndale, it should be added, agreed with this view of dispensation, but denied it to the pope (*Practice of Prelates*, pp. 323-34).

can never have seemed a purely secular place. At any rate, he was convinced that it had, or ought to have, a conscience; and his noblest ambition was to invest the crown with a moral character. Conscience was to correct the common law and supplement the barbarous nature of feudal custom by a civil code. There was no divinity about the common law; and the presumption of its reformer was less pronounced than that of the dispenser with the law of God. When Henry VIII assumed the latter function, he was forced into the protestant position that the law he was reforming was not the law of God but papal usurpation; and, so far as the catholic faith was concerned, he put forth his hand, like Uzza, to hold the ark of the covenant only to save it from destruction; 'for the oxen stumbled' and the priests had proved unequal to their yoke.[1] Wolsey's reforms were never achieved; and the practical effect of his energy was limited to creating the means of reform, providing the opportunity, and revealing to Henry VIII a vision of sovereign power.

The essence of that sovereignty was its monopoly. The checks which the crown had imposed on ecclesiastical jurisdiction by means of prohibitions and outlawries, and the church on the king's courts by means of injunctions and excommunications, disappeared when the chancellor was legate *a latere* of the pope and the legate controlled the writs and the legal conscience of the king: the limited jurisdictions of the twain became the absolute power of the united pair. Wolsey disestablished what Maitland has called[2] 'the standing denial of sovereignty, the rivalry of the *regnum* and *sacerdotium*.' He put an end to the 'several kingdoms' by absorbing both; and the fact that he was a priest and Henry a king was less important than their common absorption. If a priest who was subject to a king could wield both the swords and keep the keys of the realm as well as those of heaven, could not a king who claimed to be subject to no one on earth keep at

---

[1] Cf. bishop Nix' complaint, cited above, p. 350.
[2] *Lectures on Constitutional History*, p. 507.

least the keys of the visible church in his realm? By the time of Wolsey's fall the

> two-handed engine at the door
> Stood ready to smite once and smite no more.[1]

Besides embodying the principle of positive law, and uniting in one man's hands its potential capacities in church and state, Wolsey provided Henry with a precedent for its schismatic national operation. He had extorted from successive popes authority to outrun the constable of the catholic church in the reform of the church in England; and the national scope and limitations of his legacy portended alike the unification of the two English provinces under the royal supremacy and their separation from Rome. The price, which the papal curia had to pay for its intruding but ghostly imperialism after the failure of the conciliar movement, was the tribute it was compelled to render by excessive delegations to the fissiparous impulse of insurgent nationality. The Roman empire had by its provincial organisation waylaid the national tendencies within it: Wolsey's legacy was only the most exorbitant of the exactions which the national spirit of the early sixteenth century levied upon the autocracy of the papal court. Even so, it was almost *ex hypothesi* inadequate to meet the vociferous demand for self-determination on the part of youthful and lusty English nationality. It needed a peculiar, political, and compromising abnegation of the twentieth century for imperialism to resolve itself into self-government by practically independent nations; and the genius of theology does not easily lend itself to the accommodation of many doctrinal or ritualistic mansions in a single house. Wolsey by his legatine authority could override provincial convocations, usurp episcopal jurisdiction, and suppress conventual elections within his English sphere. But, if the national scope and limitations of his authority implied a national reformation, the fact that his was a revocable delegation inhibited its effect: he

---

[1] W. Roy, *Rede me*, p. 114 (cf. *ibid.* p. 38):

> Yt is not for nought they fayne
> That the two sweardes to theyme pertayne.

valued it less for any independence it conferred on him than for the dependence on him to which it reduced the English church. He could rivet, but he could not break, the bonds of Rome.

The instruments he used to fashion his authority could, however, be converted to the uses of royal supremacy; and his servants for the most part entered the king's service. Henry's secretaries had generally been Wolsey's secretaries first and the agents of the reformation learnt their methods in his school. Harsh things are often said of Cromwell, Gardiner, Allen, Bonner, Legh, and other ministers of the royal supremacy and of the dissolution of the monasteries: but 'things incredible' were said of the same men when they were engaged on Wolsey's work.[1] The papal legate had cowed the English clergy before they submitted to Henry VIII; he had bent the universities to the legatine yoke before they bowed to reformation under the royal supremacy; and monks were convinced that the end of their world was at hand before Wolsey had finished his monastic dissolutions.[2] He had done his best to eradicate their freedom of election; and Henry had learned from him how to pack the house of lords with abbots far more effectively than he packed the house of commons with his nominees.[3] If he converted, Wolsey had planned to convert, monastic wealth to new episcopal foundations; by his legacy he had blocked recourse to the Roman throne of grace,[4] and thus he had provided a personal precedent for the permanent act of appeals. He had invoked the penalties of præmunire on others before they were turned against himself; and with his 'civilians indigne' he had given a powerful impulse towards that Romanism or Byzantinism, as Maitland preferred to call it, of English law, with its sum-

---

[1] See above, p. 203 n. 3.　　　　[2] Above, p. 183.

[3] For instances of Cromwell's use of methods he had learnt under Wolsey, see *L.P.* v. 300; vi. 716, 816, 1007, 1304, 1408, 1513; vii. 108, 147, 257, 297, 344, 376, 868, 1654

[4] Appeal to Rome for heresy has been denied (*Eccles. Courts Comm. Rep.* ii. 125-6); but there is a case in Booth's register (ed. Canterbury and York Soc. ii. 100), and Norfolk in 1531 denied that Rome had any jurisdiction in England except in cases of heresy (*L.P.* v. 45, p. 20).

mary procedure by inquisition, torture, *ex officio*, and *sine strepitu et figura judicii*, which became so prominent a feature of Tudor government.[1]

It has been shown that a good deal of Henry VIII's legislation, notably the act creating 'treason by words,' merely gave statutory sanction to what had long been a common-law practice ;[2] but it has not been realised that this was simply a conveyance to the use of the state of a principle long enforced by the church. For 'heresy by words' had always been the commonest form of the offence, though the ecclesiastical courts compelled the heretic, as far as they could, to commit his words to writing by signing or putting his mark to a confession ; and examination upon oath which was the essence of their procedure was, as parliament had complained in 1415, 'solonc la fourme de ley cyvyle et ley de Seinte Eglise, en subvercion de vostre commune ley.'[3] Conveyance from one jurisdiction to the other was rendered easy by Wolsey's control of both. The government of the Roman church had for centuries been the greatest government on earth, and its trend towards bureaucratic centralisation was reflected in the newer monarchies of Europe. The new men they employed were commonly churchmen, not only because they were better educated than other folk, but because their legal education was in the civil and canon law of Rome, and not like that of common lawyers—*hommes de la ley*—in the common and feudal customs of their respective countries.[4] They naturally made their influence felt in an absolutist and monarchical direction and from the mediæval papacy took the framework for their modern states.

[1] Cf. Holdsworth, *Hist. of Eng. Law*, v. 81-2, 106, 153, 171-3, 190-4.

[2] Isobel D. Thornley, *The Treason Legislation of Henry VIII* (Trans. Roy. Hist. Soc.), 1917, pp. 87-124. A not very convincing answer to this appeared in the *American Historical Review* for April 1928 ; but cf. *L.P.* viii. 326, 'it was never heard of before that words should be high treason.'

[3] *Rot. Parl.* iv. 84*a*. 'Bare words,' says Coke (*Third Inst.* f. 14) 'may make a heretic, but not a traitor without overt act '—except, of course, during the brief existence of Henry VIII's ' act of words.'

[4] Education in civil and canon law was the province of the universities, in common law that of the inns of court.

Its essence was despotic and Wolsey's was a purely personal authority. The papal legates who ministered to new monarchs were indifferent parliamentarians; mediæval estates withered under their romanising touch, and Wolsey's shadow fell darkly over the life of the mother of modern parliaments. The fatal defect in his edifice of power was that it contained no act of succession and provided his despot with no association. He believed in monarchy with all the emphasis on the first of its syllables, and was quite unable to share any authority he possessed with any one else. He was not so much prime minister as sole councillor to the crown; and the chancellor had some conception of conscience but none of a constitution. Had it been possible for others to continue his work on Wolsey's lines, the result could only have been yet another *ancien régime* to be overthrown in time by another revolution.

From that fate England was saved by the greatest parliamentarian who ever sat on the English throne. Henry VIII perceived that parliament could exalt a crown in ways that righteousness could not; he proclaimed, on a famous case of privilege, that at no time did he stand so high as when he as head and his subjects as members met as one body politic in parliament.[1] He sought support from below, and his foundations were of earth, earthy; but a king with his feet in the clay would be more securely fixed in his people's affections than a pope with his head in the clouds. Henry's contribution to the making of the English state was to retrieve monarchy from Wolsey's isolation, and to weave sovereignty into and out of parliament. He had no faith in the crown as a 'corporation sole.'[2] All his powers were made to look like gifts from his subjects, until lawyers under the Stuarts came to believe that parliament had created the monarchy and that what it had given it could take away. The charge that he merged parliament

[1] Ferrers' case in 1542. See *L.P.* 1542 pp. iv, 107; Nicolas, *Proc. P.C.* vii. 332; Holinshed, *Chron.* iii. 956; Hatsell, *Precedents*, 1786, i. 53-9.

[2] On the far-reaching implications of this 'strange conceit,' see Maitland's essays on 'The Corporation Sole' and 'The Crown as Corporation' (*Collected Papers*, iii. 210-43, 244-70).

in the crown is made plausible by the extent to which he merged the crown in the parliament : it gave him his royal supremacy, forgave him his debts without asking him to forgive his debtors, endowed him with papal annates, and provided for his succession.   This parliamentary association supplied the permanent basis which Wolsey's edifice lacked. Whatever was given to Henry was given to him, his heirs, and successors ; and in English law and the constitution the place of papal bulls and personal edicts was taken by statutes of the realm.

This man-made law, the *lex positiva*, became the bulk of English law, the organ of the English state, and the voice its sovereign power ; and in time no other law and no other right could hold except with its positive sanction or silent accord.   While crown and parliament long continued to check without checkmating one another, and monarchy withered as parliament grew more and more, combined they exercised a sovereignty which was absolute, absolved from the old immutable laws through the power of parliament to change them by its statutes.   In Tudor times the change looked like a realisation of Machiavelli's theoretical release of government from the restraint of law.   But it was also the release of a new-found confidence in the national community.   There was a new-found will and a new-found law before there was much of a new-found land ; and England felt at last that it was the captain of its soul and the master of its fate.

The 'ship of state,' as it was called in the year of the act of royal supremacy,[1] cast off from its mediæval moorings to the fundamentalism of immutable law and immemorial custom and started on its piratical cruise, at the cost of the catholic church and rival states, into the uncharted seas of self-determination.   The voyage led it into strange and troubled waters in other than theological spheres.   Catholicism yielded to a patriotism which found vent in the 'sea-divinity' of Elizabethan sea-dogs, the land hunger of adventurers in Ireland and abroad, and the 'spheres of

[1] *L.P.* vii. 1318.   For the user of the phrase, Sir Richard Morison, see *D.N.B.*

legitimate aspiration' of more refined and recent times ; and the statutes of the sovereign state condoned a multitude of modern sins. 'This,' writes Lord Acton,[1] 'was no survival of the dark ages. Both the oppression of Ireland and the oppression of America was the work of the modern school, of men who executed one king and expelled another. It was the work of parliament. . . . The real enemy was the house of commons.' The nation had reached the age of consent ; and *pactum legem vincit*.

Wolsey's crime was that he did not ask it. His whole position was a violation of the principle alleged in Standish's case in 1515, that the positive laws of the church only bind those who receive them.[2] He may have had a notion that the well-staged reception of his cardinal's hat in 1515, and his repeated receptions as legate *a latere* by the king, implied a public 'reception' of his jurisdiction and legatine enactments ; but the idea that the personal reception of a legate was a binding acceptance of whatever he might do could only have entered an egotistical mind steeped in the intruding imperialism of Rome. There was no formal reception by convocation, though Henry after Wolsey's fall fined the clergy heavily enough for their tacit acquiescence. He became himself more expert in the use of positive law than the papal legate. But his legislation was based on the consent of convocation as well as of the estates ; and his royal supremacy was not merely received, but enacted, in parliament. Parliament and convocation together, indeed, gave but a national and not a catholic sanction ; and Chapuys notes as a novelty in 1530 that Henry spoke of the ' English church.' Its English character was emphasised by the deprivation of its foreign bishops and the reservation of its benefices for English people ;[3] and it was made quite clear who were to be the recipients whose consent was essential to the reception of Roman law.

Beyond this Henry did not personally want to go : he

---

[1] *Lectures on Modern History*, p. 309.   [2] See above, pp. 46-8.

[3] *L.P.* vi. 951, 1069, 1510; vii. 54, 634. A cardinal consoled the pope with the reflection that England was but ' an unprofitable island ' (*ibid.* vi. 997).

was bent on rejecting what he considered the usurpations of papal positive law upon the *jus commune* of the catholic church ; and he regarded his royal supremacy mainly as a protection from papal imports. But the defence of the realm involved a great deal of governmental activity and positive legislation from which the *jus commune* of the church was not immune ; and its nationality could only be safeguarded by giving the ' church ' a national instead of a vocational content, by extending the meaning of ' church-men ' to lay members of the community, and by teaching them that they entered it by being baptized and not by being ordained. This was no novelty, though it meant an entirely different conception of the *ecclesia Anglicana* from that of Magna Carta. Marsiglio of Padua had in the early fourteenth century contended that the *ecclesia* consisted not of ecclesiastics alone, but of the community of the faithful, and that all authority emanated from that popular source.[1] His ' Defensor Pacis ' became part of the propaganda of the new polity, which Cromwell paid translators and publishers to produce[2] ; and Gardiner's ' De Vera Obedientia ' rejected the distinction between *regnum* and *sacerdotium*, and maintained that the *ecclesia* consisted of the same people as the realm. ' That part of the said body politic called the spirituality, now being usually called the English church ' —as the act of appeals phrased it in 1533—became in the act of six articles in 1539 ' this whole church and congregation of England.'[3]

The essential difference between Wolsey and Henry VIII was that the cardinal was the protagonist of the *sacerdotium* and the king of the *regnum* ; and that, rather than any question of theology, distinguished the Roman from the Anglican church. The one was a priest-, the other a king-ridden body. In the one the principles and

---

[1] See Gierke's summary in Maitland's *Political Theories of the Middle Ages*, pp. 191-2, and my *Evolution of Parliament*, pp. 222-3.

[2] See *D.N.B.* s.v. ' Marshall, William ' (*fl.* 1535), and authorities there cited.

[3] Tanner, *Tudor Constitutional Documents*, pp. 41, 95. Bishop Fisher's friends demurred in 1535 to the crucial argument that ' the king was head of his people, and the people was the church ' (*L.P.* viii. p. 326).

ideas of representative government were dead or dying :
in the other they were taking root and bearing fruit ; and
the parliamentary invasion of the liberties of the church
which Henry led was facilitated by the fact that Wolsey
had reduced it to a despotism, whose liberties consisted in
its jurisdiction over the laity and not in its government of
itself. By Henry's conquest and annexation the *ecclesia
Anglicana* was saved from sinking into a church of Wolsey's
conception, purely papal and autocratic, and incompatible
with the spirit of self-determination which was informing
and transforming the nation as a whole ; and into the
sphere of church government were thereby injected the
discords and debates which are the representative signs
of popular interest and intellectual life. The disputation
whether the church should be in principle, or was in fact,
Roman, Anglican, Lutheran, Zwinglian, Calvinistic, Presby-
terian, Erastian, Independent, or Unitarian, has often been
distressing enough ; but it was not inimical to the growth of
liberty, to the reluctant concession of toleration, to the age
of enlightenment, or to the idea of progress. Parliamentary
theology has not done much for the edification of any
particular church, but it was not without its value in the
political education of a people.

This was anathema to Wolsey's mind. He denied the
whole basis of government by consent, and relied exclusively upon the two autocratic authorities whose servant
and creature he was. His maxim was that of Boniface VIII,
in eo sufficit pro ratione voluntas.[1] He had as little regard
for the convocations of the church as for the parliaments of
the realm ; and his mixed autocracy held out no conceiv-
able prospects for the future. His fall, so far from being
due to an irrational and arbitrary impulse on the part of
Henry VIII and his personal entourage, was essential to the
preservation of the domestic institutions of the English
church and state and to their further development. The
inhibition of their activity by his personal government was
removed ; they sprang in 1529 into a new life, and by

---

[1] Lyndwood, *Provinciale*, p. 28 *b.n.q.* ; cf. Maitland, *Roman Canon
Law*, p. 17 (see above, p. 97).

their legislative labours completed the framework of what began to be called in the following century the English constitution.[1] That was an organisation based upon 'one body politic'; uniting its various 'estates' in a single state subject to the legal sovereignty of the crown in council and in parliament; and responding and responsible more and more fully to a growing constituency of the people.

England, said Henry VIII in words echoed by Shakespeare in 'King John,' could never be conquered so long as it remained united.[2] But the union was essential; and the tentacles of royal supremacy penetrated into the inmost recesses of every franchise in the realm and every self-conscious class in the community. The appeal for popular unity was somewhat overlaid by royal insistence; but the crucial acts of the reformation parliament were not only printed, published, and proclaimed, but posted in every parish church;[3] and its members were urged to take counsel with their constituents over what they saw and heard and did in its sessions, which were themselves unprecedented for their continuance, activity, and length. The king, no doubt, was a convinced believer in the maxim, which Hobbes evolved,[4] that 'in the well-governing of opinions consisteth the well-governing of men's actions'; but the poisoned sting of that despotic counsel was drawn by its own refreshing implication that opinion was the thing that mattered.

Independence of public opinion and bondage to selfish affections marred the potentialities of Wolsey's superb ability and force; but the absence of positive achieve-

---

[1] See the *N.E.D.* s.v. 'constitution,' and supplementary notes on the word in the *Bulletin* of the Institute of Historical Research, iv. 186; v. 60-1.

[2] *L.P.* vi. 324 (p. 150); *Spanish Cal.* iv, ii. pp. 629-30.

[3] E.g. *L.P.* vi. 1487. '9. Proclamations containing the whole act of appeals are to be made throughout the realm, and the act to be printed and set up on every church door. 10. The king's provocation and appellations from the bishop of Rome to a general council must also be set up on the church doors.'

[4] *Leviathan*, chap. xviii.

ment, which differentiates him from other English claimants to apostolic statesmanship, was also due to the dilemma in which he was placed. It may be that his work in chancery, the star chamber, and the court of requests was even greater than has been suggested in these pages; and that, when the mass of their records has been reduced to a form in which it can be sifted, digested, and explained by a legal historian specialising on that task, Wolsey's achievement as a legal reformer may redeem him from the reproach of sterility. But in the development of England's external policy and internal constitution Wolsey suffered from a fundamental inhibition. The last of England's ecclesiastical prime ministers, he was precluded by his peculiar legatine position and autocratic mentality, firstly, from associating the English clergy, and still more the English laity, with him in the government of the church, which was the only kind of reformation that England really wanted; and, secondly, from giving rein and expression to that flamboyant and insular patriotism which fused in the furnace of the English state the English fragments of a broken feudal and catholic world.

He helped to construct that furnace with no idea of what it would burn; and as minister to the king he fomented the force which blasted his papal foundations. His action in one capacity was implemented by the reaction against what he did in the other; and revulsion against his pontifical sway strengthened the secular arm and released the crown from the competition of papal supremacy. But this harmony of effect was not the result of design; and Wolsey's rank among English statesmen is due less to what he chose to do than to what he did in his own despite. In fact, though not in form, he was the first who wielded sovereignty in England because he ruled both church and state. But the monopoly he created could only accrue to the crown; and the greatest Roman of them all unwittingly conveyed the plenitude of papal power to an English king in an English parliament. Human design plays little part in human achievement: 'he goes farthest,' said Oliver Cromwell, 'who knows not whither he goes'; and the fame, as well as the infamy and perhaps the forgiveness, of men depends not seldom on the fact that they know not what they do. Wolsey moved about in realms not realised, and raised his altar to a 'mortal god' not yet revealed by Thomas Hobbes. But, while service to an England, that was growing young as well as old, redeemed both him and others from baser servitudes to meaner things, he never rose to service which is perfect freedom. The world was too much with him: getting and spending, he laid waste his powers, and craved, not for a heart of grace but for the husks of glory. 'Glorious,' says Sir Thomas More, 'was hee very farre above all measure, and that was great pitie; for it dyd harme and made him abuse many great gyftes that God hadde geven him.'

ADDITIONS AND CORRECTIONS

Page vii, after 'new year's day' add : (e.g. *Letters and Papers of Henry VIII*, X. 14).

Page 12, add : (cf. *L.P.* 967 [8] [21]) and *Star Chamber Proc.* (P.R.O. List, p. 84).

Page 13, add : Paulet was excepted from the King's general pardon on 30 April 1509 (*L.P.* i. 11 [10]).

Page 14, add : Earliest except for the mutilated drafts in *Letters and Papers of Richard III and Henry VII* (Rolls Ser.) i. 424-48.

Page 28, add : Except for 28 Nov.-11 Dec. 1461 (see W. H. Dunham, *The Fane Fragment of the 1461 Lords' Journal*, 1935).

Page 32, add : Cases in 1501 and 1502 in C. H. Williams, *Early Tudors*, pp. 176-7.

Page 35, add : His successor Pakyngton was appointed on 23 July. More's annuity dates from 21 June 1518 (*L.P.* ii. 4247).

Page 38, add : It is, however, badly printed, and has an absurd name 'Buzard' between 'Richard' and 'bishop of Lincoln'. (Williams, *Early Tudors*, p. 197.)

Page 38, add : (My *Henry VII*, iii. 284 'laici . . . semper clericis infesti ', and *Tudor Studies*, p. 36).

Page 52, add : *Lancs and Cheshire Star Chamber Proc.* (1916), p. 22.

Page 60, add : Hakewill has it (*Modus Tenendi Parliamentum*, 1659, p. 115).

Page 61, add : Palgrave had said it forty years before Stubbs : see *Merchant and Friar* (1837), p. 66.

Page 71, add : There was a prison on the walls at Calais. Cf. *L.P.* viii, 368 ; ix. 802.

Page 85, add : Also Kingsford, *Chronicle*, p. 257.

Page 108, add : Henry VIII himself wrote that he took the chancellorship from Warham (*L.P.* v. p. 154).

Page 125, add : He had crossed from Calais to Dover on 22 November (*L.P.* iv. p. 3107).

Page 138, add : *L.P.* XII. ii. 866.

Page 168, add : (Nicolas, *Privy Council*, iv. 104).

Page 178, add : *L.P.* iv. p. 1228 : apparently connected with the Coventry insurrection.

Page 184, add : (See Ellis, . . . III. ii. 387 ; *L.P.* ix. 622.)

Page 211, add : (Hall, *Chronicle*, p. 784).

Page 211, *add*: On the other hand, sheriffs and especially perhaps town-bailiffs were reluctant to burn heretics solely on ecclesiastical authority (although reinforced by statute) without a specific royal writ; and there is a Colchester case of their seeking one (Benham, *Colchester Red Paper Book*, pp. 52-3) in 1428. In the same year the abbot of St. John's, Colchester, was accusing the same bailiffs of heresy (*ib.* pp. 54-5) and of threatening to burn the abbot himself; and he was begging the town council that none of the sect of Lollards within them be sustained nor supported.

Page 212, *add*: (see below, p. 351).

Page 226, *add*: The anagram is explained in Cat. Harleian MSS. no. 2252 (30), which is the manuscript which Furnivall was printing.

Page 245, *add*: See also *L.P. Addenda*, No. 657.

Page 252, *add*: The mastership of Burton Lazars was apparently hereditary in the family of Sir Richard Sutton, co-founder of Brasenose College, who died in 1524 (see *D.N.B.*).

Page 253, *add*: The surrender of York House was confirmed by the dean and chapter of York (Hall, *Chronicle*, p. 774).

Page 254, *add*: See my article in *Bulletin I.H.R.* vii.

Page 273, *add*: (cf. *Trevelyan Papers*, i. 165).

Page 276, *add*: In 1519 there were 29 (*L.P.* iii. p. 1535), and in 1520, 30 (*ib.* p. 1539) and 31 in 1521 (*ib.* p. 1544); and at Edward VI's first Maundy, when he was not yet ten years old, there were twelve beneficiaries (*Literary Remains of Edward VI*, pp. xcvii-xcviii; *Trevelyan Papers*, i. 191).

Page 276, *add*: (Cf. *L.P.* iii. 1952, and Fiddes, *Collections*, p. 211).

Page 283, *add*: See *L.P.* XIV. i. 186;

Page 287, *add*: The letter was conveyed to Rome by Guron Bertano (*Trevelyan Papers*, i. 169), who was in 1546 active in the proposed reconciliation (*L.P.* vol. xxi).

Page 296, *add*: Agostini was appointed physician in ordinary to the king in 1539 (*L.P.* xv. p. 539; xvii. 220-9); but was living in Venice in 1546 (*Venetian Cal.* 1534-54, p. 182).

Page 298, *add*: Cavendish says the Blackfriars; but there never was a Dominican house at Doncaster.

Page 299, *add*: *Trevelyan Papers*, i. 177:

Page 301, *add*: Cf. *L.P.* vii. 1639. It took the officials of Jewel House three days to weigh the plate that came from Cawood (*Trevelyan Papers*, i. 175).

Page 306, *add*: H.M.C. *Var. Coll.* ii. 47; 'George Lygh of Adlington, esq.' (*Lancs and Cheshire Star Chamber Proc.* p. 73) in 1527-28; son of Thomas Lee, *dec.* by 1530 (*Visit. Lancs.* (1533), Chetham Soc. pt. ii. p. 209).

Page 307, *add*: He was dean of Chichester between Geoffrey Symeon and John Yonge.

Page 307, *add* to last line of text: She received a pension of £4 13s. 4d. on its dissolution in 1539.

Page 307, footnote 1, after '6534' *add*: H.M.C. *Var. Coll.* i. 195.

Page 307, footnote 5, after '228' *add*: XIV. i. 586 (2), XV. p. 543;

Page 308, *add*: and Prebendary of Faynol from 1538-64.

Page 325, *add*: *L.P. Addenda*, 467.

Page 327, *add*: Cf. 6 oxen at a single breakfast for the Kingmaker, and 104 oxen at George Neville's enthronement (Scofield, i. 399).

Page 329, *add*: While the mighty were put down from their seats, the poor in spirit received a share in the Kingdom of the Tudors.

Page 351, *add*: (Thomas Benet).

Page 351, footnote 5, *add*: H.M.C. *Var. Coll.* iv. 29; Exeter MSS. (H.M.C.) 362; *E.H.R.* 1921, pp. 422-3.

Page 356, footnote to the word 'state': The first words of the roll of parliament in 1529 are '*Ad laudem Dei . . . et Reformationem totius regni, reipublicae, et dotis Anglicanae.*' (*Rot. Parl.*, Suppl. p. cli.)

INDEX

U

Uniformity, ecclesiastical, 219, 349.
— legal, 219, 359.
Uses, 63-4, 88, 326, 347.
— ecclesiastical, 219.
Utrecht, the provost of, 315-16 *n*. 1.

V

'Valor Ecclesiasticus,' the, 322, 323 *n*.
Vannes, Peter, 70 *n*., 223, 280.
Vaughan, Stephen, 211.
Vaux, Sieur de. See Passano, Giovanni Giovacchino di.
— Sir Nicholas, 49 and *n*. 2.
Venice, 10, 15 *n*., 104, 107 *n*., 114, 115, 119 *n*., 160, 174, 296 *n*., 307, 316.
Vere, John de, 13th earl of Oxford (*d.* 1513), 76, 89 *n*. 4.
— — — 14th earl (*d.* 1526), 66 *n*.
— — — 15th earl (*d.* 1540), 157 *n*. 1.
Vergil, Polydore, historian, 5, 11 *n*., 14, 22, 25, 26 *n*., 39, 39 *n*., 53 *n*., 71 *n*., 83 *n*., 99 *n*., 107 *n*., 108 *n*., 109 *n*., 113 *n*., 116, 180 *n*., 189 *n*., 190, 193 *n*., 197 *n*., 198 *n*., 205 *n*., 226.
Veysey, John, bishop of Exeter, 48, 84 *n*., 188 *n*., 214, 225, 351.
Vice-chancellor of England, the, 70 *n*. 3. See also Master of the Rolls.
Vienna, siege of (1529), 73 *n*., 118, 224, 226 *n*., 284.
Villeinage, 329.
Vincent, David, 299, 300, 301.
Vives, Juan Luis, humanist, 142 *n*., 315 *n*.
Volusenus (or Wilson), Florence, 310.

W

Wales and its Marches, council of, 74, 89-90, 92 *n*. 2, 105-6.
Walsh, Walter, 294, 295, 298.
Walsingham, Sir Francis, 6 *n*., 105.
Waltham, 236.
Wanley, Humphrey, Bodley's librarian, 6.
Wardrobe, the great, 61, 73 *n*. 1, 128.
Warham, William, archbishop of Canterbury and chancellor, association with Foxe on council, 11, 162, 169 : pacific policy, 11, 17, 113, 162 : chancellor of Oxford, 11, 326 : custody of Horsey, 38-9 : his convocations, 47 *n*., 189 : in Standish's case, 47 *n*., 48, 49 : humbled by Wolsey, 57, 186 : surrenders great seal, 58 : as chancellor, 66, 89 *n*., 221 : conflicts with Wolsey, 108, 109, 173 : difficulty in raising loan for Wolsey, 141-3 : *legatus natus*, 167-8, 179, 193 : longevity, 174, 222 : threatened with præmunire, 172,

177, 196, 249 : testamentary jurisdiction, 182 *n*., 193-8 : is prevented from reform by Wolsey, 187 : returns to court, 254 : succeeds Wolsey as trier of petitions, 258 : retires from secular office to spiritual duties, 279 : signs appeal for divorce, 287 *n*. : stiffness, 304 : would have welcomed concordat with Rome, 335 : protests against attacks on his papal-legatine jurisdiction, 348 : defends church against state, 356 : other references, 55, 56, 74, 148 *n*., 205, 225, 226, 243, 252, 338.
Waynflete, William of, bishop of Winchester 199 *n*.
Wells, 41 *n*., 51 *n*., 190 *n*., 309.
— dean of. See Wynter, Thomas.
Wentworth, Thomas, earl of Strafford, 219.
West, council of the, 105 *n*.
— Nicholas, bishop of Ely, 75, 115, 132 *n*., 144, 188 *n*., 196, 204 *n*.
Westby, Bartholomew, surveyor-general, 130 *n*.
Westminster abbey, 37 and *n*., 53 *n*., 56-7, 172, 188, 189, 191, 196, 199 *n*., 245 *n*., 306 *n*. 4.
— abbot. See Islip, John.
— 'court at.' See Star Chamber.
— hall, 72, 80 *n*., 85 *n*., 92, 111, 156, 242-3 *n*., 256.
— palace, 152, 194 *n*., 241.
— Whitehall, 253, 325.
— York Place, 188 *n*., 199 *n*., 201, 253-4, 265, 277, 325.
Weston, Sir Richard, prior of St. John's, 184, 325 *n*.
Wetwang (York), prebend of, 296 *n*.
Whittington, Richard, 303.
Wigmore, the abbot of, 236.
Wilkins, David, his ' Concilia,' 34 *n*., 186, *et passim*.
Willesden, 308.
William I, 7.
— III, 7.
— of Newburgh, 46 *n*.
Williams, John, archbishop of York, lord-keeper, 5.
Wills, 65, 93-4, 193-8, 324-5, 338.
Wilson, Florence. See Volusenus.
— Richard, bishop of Meath, Wolsey's suffragan in York, 186 *n*.
Wilton, abbess of, 201-3.
Wiltshire, sedition in, 159.
— earl of. See Boleyn, Thomas.
Winchcombe, abbot of. See Kidderminster, Richard.
Winchester, 174, 186 *n*., 190, 198, 238, 253, 271, 277, 310.
— bishops of. See Foxe, Richard (1501-28) : Wolsey (1528-30) : Gardiner, Stephen (1531-56).

hARpER TORChBOOKS

HUMANITIES AND SOCIAL SCIENCES

American Studies: General

American Studies: Colonial

American Studies: From the Revolution to 1860

---

† The New American Nation Series, edited by Henry Steele Commager and Richard B. Morris.
‡ American Perspectives series, edited by Bernard Wishy and William E. Leuchtenburg.
* The Rise of Modern Europe series, edited by William L. Langer.
¶ Researches in the Social, Cultural, and Behavioral Sciences, edited by Benjamin Nelson.
§ The Library of Religion and Culture, edited by Benjamin Nelson.
Σ Harper Modern Science Series, edited by James R. Newman.
° Not for sale in Canada.
△ Not for sale in the U. K.

JAMES MADISON: The Forging of American Federalism: *Selected Writings of James Madison. Edited by Saul K. Padover* TB/1226

BERNARD MAYO: Myths and Men: *Patrick Henry, George Washington, Thomas Jefferson* TB/1108

JOHN C. MILLER: Alexander Hamilton and the Growth of the New Nation TB/3057

RICHARD B. MORRIS, Ed.: The Era of the American Revolution TB/1180

R. B. NYE: The Cultural Life of the New Nation: 1776-1801. † *Illus.* TB/3026

FRANCIS S. PHILBRICK: The Rise of the West, 1754-1830. † *Illus.* TB/3067

TIMOTHY L. SMITH: Revivalism and Social Reform: *American Protestantism on the Eve of the Civil War* TB/1229

FRANK THISTLETHWAITE: America and the Atlantic Community: *Anglo-American Aspects, 1790-1850* TB/1107

A. F. TYLER: Freedom's Ferment: *Phases of American Social History from the Revolution to the Outbreak of the Civil War. 31 illus.* TB/1074

GLYNDON G. VAN DEUSEN: The Jacksonian Era: 1828-1848. † *Illus.* TB/3028

LOUIS B. WRIGHT: Culture on the Moving Frontier TB/1053

American Studies: The Civil War to 1900

THOMAS C. COCHRAN & WILLIAM MILLER: The Age of Enterprise: *A Social History of Industrial America* TB/1054

W. A. DUNNING: Essays on the Civil War and Reconstruction. *Introduction by David Donald* TB/1181

W. A. DUNNING: Reconstruction, Political and Economic: 1865-1877 TB/1073

HAROLD U. FAULKNER: Politics, Reform and Expansion: 1890-1900. † *Illus.* TB/3020

HELEN HUNT JACKSON: A Century of Dishonor: *The Early Crusade for Indian Reform. ‡ Edited by Andrew F. Rolle* TB/3063

ALBERT D. KIRWAN: Revolt of the Rednecks: *Mississippi Politics, 1876-1925* TB/1199

ROBERT GREEN MC CLOSKEY: American Conservatism in the Age of Enterprise: 1865-1910 TB/1137

ARTHUR MANN: Yankee Reformers in the Urban Age: *Social Reform in Boston, 1880-1900* TB/1247

WHITELAW REID: After the War: *A Tour of the Southern States, 1865-1866. ‡ Edited by C. Vann Woodward* TB/3066

CHARLES H. SHINN: Mining Camps: *A Study in American Frontier Government. ‡ Edited by Rodman W. Paul* TB/3062

VERNON LANE WHARTON: The Negro in Mississippi: 1865-1890 TB/1178

American Studies: 1900 to the Present

RAY STANNARD BAKER: Following the Color Line: *American Negro Citizenship in Progressive Era. ‡ Illus. Edited by Dewey W. Grantham, Jr.* TB/3053

RANDOLPH S. BOURNE: War and the Intellectuals: *Collected Essays, 1915-1919. ‡ Edited by Carl Resek* TB/3043

A. RUSSELL BUCHANAN: The United States and World War II. † *Illus.*   Vol. I TB/3044; Vol. II TB/3045

ABRAHAM CAHAN: The Rise of David Levinsky: *a documentary novel of social mobility in early twentieth century America. Intro. by John Higham* TB/1028

THOMAS C. COCHRAN: The American Business System: *A Historical Perspective, 1900-1955* TB/1080

FOSTER RHEA DULLES: America's Rise to World Power: 1898-1954. † *Illus.* TB/3021

JOHN D. HICKS: Republican Ascendancy: 1921-1933. † *Illus.* TB/3041

SIDNEY HOOK: Reason, Social Myths, and Democracy TB/1237

ROBERT HUNTER: Poverty: *Social Conscience in the Progressive Era. ‡ Edited by Peter d'A. Jones* TB/3065

WILLIAM L. LANGER & S. EVERETT GLEASON: The Challenge to Isolation: *The World Crisis of 1937-1940 and American Foreign Policy*
Vol. I TB/3054; Vol. II TB/3055

WILLIAM E. LEUCHTENBURG: Franklin D. Roosevelt and the New Deal: 1932-1940. † *Illus.* TB/3025

ARTHUR S. LINK: Woodrow Wilson and the Progressive Era: 1910-1917. † *Illus.* TB/3023

GEORGE E. MOWRY: The Era of Theodore Roosevelt and the Birth of Modern America: 1900-1912. † *Illus.* TB/3022

RUSSEL B. NYE: Midwestern Progressive Politics: *A Historical Study of Its Origins and Development, 1870-1958* TB/1202

WALTER RAUSCHENBUSCH: Christianity and the Social Crisis. ‡ *Edited by Robert D. Cross* TB/3059

JACOB RIIS: The Making of an American. ‡ *Edited by Roy Lubove* TB/3070

PHILIP SELZNICK: TVA and the Grass Roots: *A Study in the Sociology of Formal Organization* TB/1230

IDA M. TARBELL: The History of the Standard Oil Company: *Briefer Version. ‡ Edited by David M. Chalmers* TB/3071

GEORGE B. TINDALL, Ed.: A Populist Reader ‡ TB/3069

TWELVE SOUTHERNERS: I'll Take My Stand: *The South and the Agrarian Tradition. Edited by Louis D. Rubin, Jr., Biographical Essays by Virginia Rock* TB/1072

WALTER E. WEYL: The New Democracy: *An Essay on Certain Political Tendencies in the United States. ‡ Edited by Charles B. Forcey* TB/3042

Anthropology

JACQUES BARZUN: Race: *A Study in Superstition. Revised Edition* TB/1172

JOSEPH B. CASAGRANDE, Ed.: In the Company of Man: *Twenty Portraits of Anthropological Informants. Illus.* TB/3047

W. E. LE GROS CLARK: The Antecedents of Man: *Intro. to Evolution of the Primates.* ○ △ *Illus.* TB/559

CORA DU BOIS: The People of Alor. *New Preface by the author. Illus.*   Vol. I TB/1042; Vol. II TB/1043

RAYMOND FIRTH, Ed.: Man and Culture: *An Evaluation of the Work of Bronislaw Malinowski* ¶ ○ △ TB/1133

DAVID LANDY: Tropical Childhood: *Cultural Transmission and Learning in a Puerto Rican Village* ¶ TB/1235

L. S. B. LEAKEY: Adam's Ancestors: *The Evolution of Man and His Culture.* △ *Illus.* TB/1019

ROBERT H. LOWIE: Primitive Society. *Introduction by Fred Eggan* TB/1056

EDWARD BURNETT TYLOR: The Origins of Culture. *Part I of "Primitive Culture."* § *Intro. by Paul Radin* TB/33

EDWARD BURNETT TYLOR: Religion in Primitive Culture. *Part II of "Primitive Culture."* § *Intro. by Paul Radin* TB/34

W. LLOYD WARNER: A Black Civilization: *A Study of an Australian Tribe.* ¶ *Illus.* TB/3056

Art and Art History

WALTER LOWRIE: Art in the Early Church. *Revised Edition. 452 illus.* TB/124

EMILE MÂLE: The Gothic Image: *Religious Art in France of the Thirteenth Century.* § △ *190 illus.* TB/44

MILLARD MEISS: Painting in Florence and Siena after the Black Death: *The Arts, Religion and Society in the Mid-Fourteenth Century. 169 illus.* TB/1148

ERICH NEUMANN: The Archetypal World of Henry Moore. △ *107 illus.* TB/2020

DORA & ERWIN PANOFSKY: Pandora's Box: *The Changing Aspects of a Mythical Symbol. Revised Edition. Illus.* TB/2021

ERWIN PANOFSKY: Studies in Iconology: *Humanistic Themes in the Art of the Renaissance.* △ *180 illustrations* TB/1077

ALEXANDRE PIANKOFF: The Shrines of Tut-Ankh-Amon. Edited by N. Rambova. *117 illus.* TB/2011

JEAN SEZNEC: The Survival of the Pagan Gods: *The Mythological Tradition and Its Place in Renaissance Humanism and Art. 108 illustrations* TB/2004

OTTO VON SIMSON: The Gothic Cathedral: *Origins of Gothic Architecture and the Medieval Concept of Order. △ 58 illus.* TB/2018

HEINRICH ZIMMER: Myth and Symbols in Indian Art and Civilization. *70 illustrations* TB/2005

Business, Economics & Economic History

REINHARD BENDIX: Work and Authority in Industry: *Ideologies of Management in the Course of Industrialization* TB/3035

GILBERT BURCK & EDITORS OF FORTUNE: The Computer Age: *And Its Potential for Management* TB/1179

THOMAS C. COCHRAN: The American Business System: *A Historical Perspective, 1900-1955* TB/1080

THOMAS C. COCHRAN: The Inner Revolution: *Essays on the Social Sciences in History* TB/1140

THOMAS C. COCHRAN & WILLIAM MILLER: The Age of Enterprise: *A Social History of Industrial America* TB/1054

ROBERT DAHL & CHARLES E. LINDBLOM: Politics, Economics, and Welfare: *Planning and Politico-Economic Systems Resolved into Basic Social Processes* TB/3037

PETER F. DRUCKER: The New Society: *The Anatomy of Industrial Order △* TB/1082

EDITORS OF FORTUNE: America in the Sixties: *The Economy and the Society* TB/1015

ROBERT L. HEILBRONER: The Great Ascent: *The Struggle for Economic Development in Our Time* TB/3030

FRANK H. KNIGHT: The Economic Organization TB/1214

FRANK H. KNIGHT: Risk, Uncertainty and Profit TB/1215

ABBA P. LERNER: Everybody's Business: *Current Assumptions in Economics and Public Policy* TB/3051

ROBERT GREEN MC CLOSKEY: American Conservatism in the Age of Enterprise, 1865-1910 △ TB/1137

PAUL MANTOUX: The Industrial Revolution in the Eighteenth Century: *The Beginnings of the Modern Factory System in England* ○ △ TB/1079

WILLIAM MILLER, Ed.: Men in Business: *Essays on the Historical Role of the Entrepreneur* TB/1081

RICHARD B. MORRIS: Government and Labor in Early America △ TB/1244

HERBERT SIMON: The Shape of Automation: *For Men and Management* TB/1245

PERRIN STRYKER: The Character of the Executive: *Eleven Studies in Managerial Qualities* TB/1041

PIERRE URI: Partnership for Progress: *A Program for Transatlantic Action* TB/3036

Contemporary Culture

JACQUES BARZUN: The House of Intellect △ TB/1051

CLARK KERR: The Uses of the University TB/1264

JOHN U. NEF: Cultural Foundations of Industrial Civilization △ TB/1024

NATHAN M. PUSEY: The Age of the Scholar: *Observations on Education in a Troubled Decade* TB/1157

PAUL VALÉRY: The Outlook for Intelligence △ TB/2016

RAYMOND WILLIAMS: Culture and Society, 1780-1950 ○ △ TB/1252

RAYMOND WILLIAMS: The Long Revolution.○ △ *Revised Edition* TB/1253

Historiography & Philosophy of History

JACOB BURCKHARDT: On History and Historians. △ *Introduction by H. R. Trevor-Roper* TB/1216

WILHELM DILTHEY: Pattern and Meaning in History: *Thoughts on History and Society.* ○ △ *Edited with an Introduction by H. P. Rickman* TB/1075

J. H. HEXTER: Reappraisals in History: *New Views on History & Society in Early Modern Europe △* TB/1100

H. STUART HUGHES: History as Art and as Science: *Twin Vistas on the Past* TB/1207

RAYMOND KLIBANSKY & H. J. PATON, Eds.: Philosophy and History: *The Ernst Cassirer Festschrift. Illus.* TB/1115

GEORGE H. NADEL, Ed.: Studies in the Philosophy of History: *Selected Essays from* History and Theory TB/1208

JOSE ORTEGA Y GASSET: The Modern Theme. *Introduction by Jose Ferrater Mora* TB/1038

KARL R. POPPER: The Open Society and Its Enemies △
Vol. I: *The Spell of Plato* TB/1101
Vol. II: *The High Tide of Prophecy: Hegel, Marx and the Aftermath* TB/1102

KARL R. POPPER: The Poverty of Historicism ○ △ TB/1126

G. J. RENIER: History: Its Purpose and Method △ TB/1209

W. H. WALSH: Philosophy of History: *An Introduction △* TB/1020

History: General

L. CARRINGTON GOODRICH: A Short History of the Chinese People. △ *Illus.* TB/3015

DAN N. JACOBS & HANS H. BAERWALD: Chinese Communism: *Selected Documents* TB/3031

BERNARD LEWIS: The Arabs in History △ TB/1029

History: Ancient and Medieval

A. ANDREWES: The Greek Tyrants △ TB/1103

ADOLF ERMAN, Ed.: The Ancient Egyptians: *A Sourcebook of Their Writings. New material and Introduction by William Kelly Simpson* TB/1233

MICHAEL GRANT: Ancient History ○ △ TB/1190

SAMUEL NOAH KRAMER: Sumerian Mythology TB/1055

NAPHTALI LEWIS & MEYER REINHOLD, Eds.: Roman Civilization. Sourcebook I: *The Republic* TB/1231

NAPHTALI LEWIS & MEYER REINHOLD, Eds.: Roman Civilization. Sourcebook II: *The Empire* TB/1232

History: Medieval

P. BOISSONNADE: Life and Work in Medieval Europe: *The Evolution of the Medieval Economy, the 5th to the 15th Century.* ○ △ *Preface by Lynn White, Jr.* TB/1141

HELEN CAM: England before Elizabeth △ TB/1026

NORMAN COHN: The Pursuit of the Millennium: *Revolutionary Messianism in Medieval and Reformation Europe △* TB/1037

G. G. COULTON: Medieval Village, Manor, and Monastery TB/1022

CHRISTOPHER DAWSON, Ed.: Mission to Asia: *Narratives and Letters of the Franciscan Missionaries in Mongolia and China in the 13th and 14 Centuries △* TB/315

HEINRICH FICHTENAU: The Carolingian Empire: *The Age of Charlemagne △* TB/1142

F. L. GANSHOF: Feudalism △ TB/1058

DENO GEANAKOPLOS: Byzantine East and Latin West: *Two Worlds of Christendom in the Middle Ages and Renaissance △* TB/1265

EDWARD GIBBON: The Triumph of Christendom in the Roman Empire *(Chaps. XV-XX of "Decline and Fall," J. B. Bury edition).* § *Illus.* TB/46

W. O. HASSALL, Ed.: Medieval England: *As Viewed by Contemporaries △* TB/1205

DENYS HAY: The Medieval Centuries ○ △ TB/1192

J. M. HUSSEY: The Byzantine World △ TB/1057

FERDINAND LOT: The End of the Ancient World and the Beginnings of the Middle Ages. *Introduction by Glanville Downey* TB/1044

G. MOLLAT: The Popes at Avignon: 1305-1378 △ TB/308

CHARLES PETIT-DUTAILLIS: The Feudal Monarchy in France and England: *From the Tenth to the Thirteenth Century* ○ △ TB/1165

HENRI PIRENNE: Early Democracies in the Low Countries: *Urban Society and Political Conflict in the Middle Ages and the Renaissance. Introduction by John H. Mundy* TB/1110

Intellectual History & History of Ideas

Literature, Poetry, The Novel & Criticism

Myth, Symbol & Folklore

Philosophy

RELIGION

Ancient & Classical

Biblical Thought & Literature

The Judaic Tradition

Christianity: General

Christianity: Origins & Early Development

Christianity: The Middle Ages and The Reformation

Christianity: The Protestant Tradition

Christianity: The Roman and Eastern Traditions

Oriental Religions: Far Eastern, Near Eastern

NATURAL SCIENCES
AND MATHEMATICS

Mathematics

E. W. BETH: The Foundations of Mathematics: *A Study in the Philosophy of Science* △ TB/581
H. DAVENPORT: The Higher Arithmetic: *An Introduction to the Theory of Numbers* △ TB/526
H. G. FORDER: Geometry: *An Introduction* △ TB/548
S. KÖRNER: The Philosophy of Mathematics: *An Introduction* △ TB/547
D. E. LITTLEWOOD: Skeleton Key of Mathematics: *A Simple Account of Complex Algebraic Problems* △ TB/525
GEORGE E. OWEN: Fundamentals of Scientific Mathematics TB/569
WILLARD VAN ORMAN QUINE: Mathematical Logic TB/558
O. G. SUTTON: Mathematics in Action. ○ △ *Foreword by James R. Newman. Illus.* TB/518
FREDERICK WAISMANN: Introduction to Mathematical Thinking. *Foreword by Karl Menger* TB/511

Philosophy of Science

R. B. BRAITHWAITE: Scientific Explanation TB/515
J. BRONOWSKI: Science and Human Values. △ *Revised and Enlarged Edition* TB/505
ALBERT EINSTEIN et al.: Albert Einstein: Philosopher-Scientist. *Edited by Paul A. Schilpp* Vol. I TB/502 Vol. II TB/503
WERNER HEISENBERG: Physics and Philosophy: *The Revolution in Modern Science* △ TB/549
JOHN MAYNARD KEYNES: A Treatise on Probability. ○ △ *Introduction by N. R. Hanson* TB/557
KARL R. POPPER: Logic of Scientific Discovery △ TB/576

STEPHEN TOULMIN: Foresight and Understanding: *An Enquiry into the Aims of Science.* △ *Foreword by Jacques Barzun* TB/564
STEPHEN TOULMIN: The Philosophy of Science: *An Introduction* △ TB/513
G. J. WHITROW: The Natural Philosophy of Time ○ △ TB/563

Physics and Cosmology

JOHN E. ALLEN: Aerodynamics: *A Space Age Survey* △ TB/582
STEPHEN TOULMIN & JUNE GOODFIELD: The Fabric of the Heavens: *The Development of Astronomy and Dynamics.* △ *Illus.* TB/579
DAVID BOHM: Causality and Chance in Modern Physics. △ *Foreword by Louis de Broglie* TB/536
P. W. BRIDGMAN: Nature of Thermodynamics TB/537
P. W. BRIDGMAN: A Sophisticate's Primer of Relativity △ TB/575
A. C. CROMBIE, Ed.: Turning Point in Physics TB/535
C. V. DURELL: Readable Relativity. △ *Foreword by Freeman J. Dyson* TB/530
ARTHUR EDDINGTON: Space, Time and Gravitation: *An Outline of the General Relativity Theory* TB/510
GEORGE GAMOW: Biography of Physics Σ △ TB/567
MAX JAMMER: Concepts of Force: *A Study in the Foundation of Dynamics* TB/550
MAX JAMMER: Concepts of Mass *in Classical and Modern Physics.* TB/571
MAX JAMMER: Concepts of Space: *The History of Theories of Space in Physics. Foreword by Albert Einstein* TB/533
G. J. WHITROW: The Structure and Evolution of the Universe: *An Introduction to Cosmology.* △ *Illus.* TB/504

Code to Torchbook Libraries:
TB/1+ : The Cloister Library
TB/301+ : The Cathedral Library
TB/501+ : The Science Library
TB/801+ : The Temple Library
TB/1001+ : The Academy Library
TB/2001+ : The Bollingen Library
TB/3001+ : The University Library
JP/1+ : The Jewish Publication Society Series